Approaches for Community Decision Making and Collective Reasoning:

Knowledge Technology Support

John Yearwood
University of Ballarat, Australia

Andrew Stranieri
University of Ballarat, Australia

Information Science
REFERENCE

Managing Director:	Lindsay Johnston
Senior Editorial Director:	Heather A. Probst
Book Production Manager:	Sean Woznicki
Development Manager:	Joel Gamon
Development Editor:	Hannah Abelbeck
Acquisitions Editor:	Erika Gallagher
Typesetter:	Jennifer Romanchak
Cover Design:	Nick Newcomer, Lisandro Gonzalez

Published in the United States of America by
Information Science Reference (an imprint of IGI Global)
701 E. Chocolate Avenue
Hershey PA 17033
Tel: 717-533-8845
Fax: 717-533-8661
E-mail: cust@igi-global.com
Web site: http://www.igi-global.com

Library of Congress Cataloging-in-Publication Data

Yearwood, John, 1954-
  Approaches for community decision making and collective reasoning: knowledge technology support / by John Yearwood and Andrew Stranieri.
       p. cm.
  Includes bibliographical references and index.
  Summary: "This book focuses on how groups can structure their activities toward making better decisions or in developing technologies for the support of decision-making in groups"--Provided by publisher.
  ISBN 978-1-4666-1818-3 (hardcover) -- ISBN 978-1-4666-1819-0 (ebook) -- ISBN 978-1-4666-1820-6 (print & perpetual access) 1. Communities. 2. Group decision making. 3. Reasoning. 4. Information technology--Social aspects. I. Stranieri, Andrew. II. Title.
  HM711.Y43 2012
  658.4'036--dc23
                            2012002874

British Cataloguing in Publication Data
A Cataloguing in Publication record for this book is available from the British Library.

All work contributed to this book is new, previously-unpublished material. The views expressed in this book are those of the authors, but not necessarily of the publisher.

Table of Contents

Detailed Table of Contents

Chapter 1

The aim of the book, to facilitate the design of technologies to support group reasoning, is presented. The concept of a reasoning community is introduced toward this aim.

Chapter 2

The nature of collective reasoning and existing approaches to supporting the collective reasoning that reasoning communities undertake is presented. The ways in which collective reasoning is indeed cognitive cooperation are described.

Chapter 3

The nature of the process that each participant engages in individually in order to contribute to collective reasoning is discussed. This iteratively includes phases of engagement, individual reasoning, group coalescing, until decision-making. Representations of reasoning, including the classical syllogism, first order logic, default reasoning, deontic reasoning, and argumentation schemes, are surveyed to illustrate their strengths and limitations to represent individual reasoning.

Chapter 4

The Generic/Actual Argument Model is presented as a model to support reasoning and decision-making by individuals within a reasoning community. It can be used by individuals without inference support, by individuals with varying degrees of inference support, or as a fully computational system.

Chapter 5

The role that communication of reasoning plays in contributing to the actions of reasoning communities is discussed.

Chapter 6

Reasoning that is conveyed and represented in stories and how it relates to other forms of representing and communicating reasoning is presented. The role of narrative in coalescing or confusing reasoning is discussed

Chapter 7

The way in which a set of concepts are necessary for communication and reasoning in the domain of discourse is discussed in this chapter.

Chapter 8

Approaches for supporting reasoning communities, including the identification of types of problems, techniques for organising text, and approaches for facilitating the sharing of information, are presented in this chapter.

Chapter 9

Technological innovations that support reasoning communities, including decision support systems, online dispute resolution systems, and tools for the representation of argumentation, are presented.

Chapter 10

Types of reasoning communities are identified and described. Technological tools appropriate for each type are discussed. Limitations of reasoning community ideas are described, and future developments are suggested.

Preface

Information and communication technologies enable the capture and storage of vast quantities of data for decision-makers to use. The same technologies also bring together groups of geographically dispersed individuals, either synchronously or asynchronously; therefore, it is not surprising to find decisions increasingly being made by groups rather than by individuals. Examples abound. Medical decisions are often made by multi-disciplinary teams of experts rather than single practitioners. Citizens in democratic communities expect a greater level of opportunities for participation in decisions that impact them and greater transparency of the decision-making that affects them.

Having groups operate effectively as reasoning and decision-making entities is not an easy task, and there have been spectacular disasters that have occurred from pathologies such as 'groupthink.' Clearly, information and communication technologies provide the tools to capture and store data and to facilitate communication between group members. However, these technologies do not readily help in the task of reasoning by groups. A fundamental aim of this book is to explore how technologies can be applied to enhance group reasoning for decision-making. In order to achieve this, a new perspective is adopted on the nature of group reasoning, the interplay between individual and collective views, tacit and explicit knowledge, narrative and structured reasoning, and diverse approaches to decision-making.

The notion of a *reasoning community* as a device for structuring the reasoning that groups use towards making judgments is advanced. Central to the notion is the idea of *coalescing* reasoning from the individuals in the group into a *co-operative product* that does two key things: it acts to provide each individual in the group with the broad structural wealth of reasoning from the group to support their reasoning, and it also acts as an explicit structure that technological devices for supporting reasoning within a group can hook onto.

The book presents the ideas in an accessible form for a broad audience of people ranging from community decision-makers, decision-makers and leaders within organizations, as well as reasoners and decision-makers in technical areas. There are some technical sections in later chapters that are more interesting for those who might be interested in implementing technologies to support dialogue and reasoning activities in groups. These sections are not necessary for the reader who is interested in following the broad set of ideas put forward here.

John Yearwood
University of Ballarat, Australia

Andrew Stranieri
University of Ballarat, Australia

Chapter 1
The Elements of Collective Decision Making

ABSTRACT

In this chapter, the concept of a reasoning community is introduced. The overarching motivation is to understand reasoning within groups in real world settings so that technologies can be designed to better support the process. Four phases of the process of reasoning by a community are discerned: engagement of participants, individual reasoning, group coalescing, and, ultimately, group decision making. A reasoning community is contrasted with communities of practice and juxtaposed against concepts in related endeavours including computer supported collaborative work, decision science, and artificial intelligence.

INTRODUCTION

In practice, the reasoning that underpins all problem solving and decision-making is rarely performed by an individual in isolation from others. Reasoning inherently involves a communicative exchange of facts, beliefs, and assertions within participants in a community. The community can range in size from two to many thousands. However, despite the prevalence of reasoning communities, most philosophical schemes for representing reasoning and technological tools that support reasoning focus on processes within an individual. This makes the case for a formulation of communal reasoning strong. Impetus for this derives fundamentally from the revolution of information and communication technologies in recent decades that bring forth increasingly intelligent support systems and enable an unprecedented frenzy of dialogue amongst individuals. Impetus for a new approach also comes from the social and political arena where public expectations for just

DOI: 10.4018/978-1-4666-1818-3.ch001

and transparent reasoning at all levels of public and private life continue to increase.

The central notion of the new approach is a community we identify and label a *reasoning community*. A reasoning community is a group of individuals connected by their desire to apply reasoning to solve a problem or reach a decision. Members of a reasoning community may or may not belong to the same organization, hold the same values, aim for the same outcomes or share much else in common except the need to reason toward the resolution of a problem. Examples of reasoning communities include a workplace committee examining overtime policies, a court interpreting law, academic researchers investigating a phenomenon and a convention drafting a national constitution.

In times when we have almost every conceivable community and group, if not existing as a physically located group then as a virtual community, it is surprising not to find the term reasoning community. We have Communities of Commitment (Lave & Wenger, 1991), which are formed to achieve specific external objectives and are accountable to the larger organization and that organization's stake holders. The staff, clients, and suppliers of a firm comprise a community bound together by the firm's objectives. Members of these communities share a commitment to the organization's objectives. Communities of Practice are formed around individuals' needs to improve competencies or families of competencies and are accountable to the individuals that comprise the community of practice (Lave & Wenger, 1991). They tend to transcend normal organizational boundaries. Associations of industry bodies that aim to self-regulate an industry exemplify Communities of Practice. Members of these communities share standards of practice. Teams are smaller communities of people who share a common purpose. Team members have complementary skills and performance goals for which they hold themselves mutually accountable.

The term *reasoning community* is broader and more encompassing than communities of commitment, practice, or purpose. A *reasoning community* is a group of participants that reason individually, communicate with each other, and attempt to coalesce their reasoning in order to reason collectively to perform an action or solve a problem.

The four key processes inherent in a reasoning community as formulated here include (see Figure 1):

- **Engagement:** This phase involves the engagement of participants, defining a protocol for communication and another protocol for decision-making. Participants in a reasoning community are the people that agree on the issue and directly engage in reasoning to solve the problem or perform an action. A protocol for communication is the set of rules that govern exchanges between participants. A decision protocol specifies how the community will ultimately reach a decision; by voting, consensus or other mechanisms.

- **Individual reasoning:** Each participant ascertains facts, makes inferences from facts to draw conclusions, and, by so doing, contributes reasons to a pool of reasons for the community. A key part of individual reasoning involves an individual's coalescing of reasoning. This is the process of juxtaposing background knowledge with reasons advanced by other participants in order to understand the issue and position his or her claims amidst the others. A participant's coalescing of reasoning involves making sense of reasons in order to assert their own claims or to understand the claims of others.

- **Group coalescing of reasoning:** The coalescing of reasoning for the entire community involves organizing the terms, concepts and reasoning advanced by par-

Figure 1. Reasoning community phases

INDIVIDUAL REASONING
Colaesce reasons,
Determine preference,
Communicate reference

ENGAGEMENT
Select participants,
Agree on how to decide,
Agree on how to communicate,
Agree on the issue

GROUP COALESCING
Colaesce individual reasoning,
Generate explicit representation;
cooperative product

DECISION MAKING
Reach group decision

ticipants to the community into an explicit, coherent representation. This is important for shared and democratic decision-making where decisions are made on the basis of reasoned debate. Further, group coalescing enables communities in the future to adopt coalesced reasoning as a starting point for their own deliberations. Most current reasoning communities perform individual coalescing but do not systematically perform group coalescing.

- **Decision-making:** Making a decision requires making a choice between alternatives, actions or solutions considered. In a practical sense, it involves the performance of an action or solution of a problem. The resolution of the problem requires the implementation of the decision-making protocols in order to reach a final decision.

Whenever a group of individuals gather to contribute to the resolution of a problem they form a reasoning community. A workplace subcommittee charged with the selection of a venue, a parliament, participants to a legal dispute and researchers dedicated to a specific question are examples of reasoning communities. Ultimately, the claim advanced in this work is that viewing fora for collective problem solving as reasoning communities enables the clearer specification of technological tools that can be used to support the work of a reasoning community.

The focus of this book will be on supporting the inherent desire of communities to engage in reasoning towards their decisions. The perspective adopted is that support has been adopted in the form of information technology tools such as Web search engines, expert systems, decision support systems and in the form of schemes for the representation of knowledge and reasoning such as ontologies. These include schemes designed to infer new knowledge such as syllogisms, first order logics and non-monotonic logics and also schemes for structuring knowledge such as argument maps and concept maps. Table 1 illustrates knowledge schemes and tools currently available for supporting each phase of the work of a reasoning community. It is clear from the table that most knowledge schemes developed to date can be seen to support an individual's coalescing of knowledge and separately, the drawing of inferences leading to assertions. Other schemes support the making of assertions. Few tools or knowledge schemes support the engagement phase, the group coalescing phase or the collective decision-making phase. The selection of participants, agreements on communication protocols and agreements on the decision-making approach best adopted by the community in the *Engagement* phase are tasks for which there are few tools. Weblogs and Web search engines can help to some extent identify appropriate participants for a community but these tools have not been designed for this purpose. The knowledge that facilitates *Engagement* tasks typically derives from social norms that are rarely represented explicitly.

The coalescing of relevant knowledge by each participant is supported by tools such as search engines, Weblogs, and wikis in the *Individual reasoning* phase. The task of drawing assertions by participants in the same phase is supported by expert systems and decision support system tools as well as knowledge schemes such as logic, decision trees, and belief networks. However, few existing tools combine the coalescing of reasoning and the drawing of assertions into an integrated tool. So individual reasoning, in totality, is currently not well supported.

In *Group coalescing* the common ground in each participant's individually coalesced knowledge is organized and made explicit as are the various assertions and beliefs held by the group. Most argument maps portray contrasting claims and can be adopted for this purpose. Although many group decision support systems have been advanced, the majority of these support communication between individuals. Voting algorithms, multi-criteria weighting schemes and argument preference heuristics are devices that can support the decision-making phase of a reasoning community.

The concept of a reasoning community is not advanced as a new utopian way for groups to co-operate rationally. The central claim is that humans often reason collectively and that a recognition of this enables the extrication of phases within the collective reasoning process that can better inform the technologies developed to support the

Table 1. Tools and knowledge schemes for reasoning community phases

PHASE sub phase	KNOWLEDGE SCHEMES	TOOLS
ENGAGEMENT Selecting Participants Communication protocol Decision protocol	Social norms	Search engine Blogs
INDIVIDUAL REASONING Individual coalescing Individual judgement	Domain ontologies Narrative Concept maps Argument maps Semantic Web Clustering Inference rule Decision trees Bayesian networks	Search engines Wiki Decision support systems Blogs Data and text mining Expert systems Logic formalisms
GROUP COALESCING	Group mind maps Argument maps Community narrative	Compendium gIBIS DialogMapper Zeno, Carneades
DECISION MAKING	Voting schemes Consensus schemes Argument Systems	Group Decision Support Negotiation Support

reasoning. Further, as the reasoning is exalted, demonstrably sub-optimal decision making on the basis of power plays and information hiding is diminished. The end product is to enable groups of people to reach decisions by supporting and elevating reasoning. A sample reasoning community in the field of urban planning is presented to illustrate the process of collective reasoning in a typical setting.

A SAMPLE REASONING COMMUNITY

Imagine a panel of stakeholders and consultants assembled by the planning division of a local government authority in a regional city to make recommendations regarding the relocation of cattle saleyards from the city fringe to an outlying township. Panel participants have been selected by the authority and include representatives from local government, property developers, businesses, farmers, resident groups, and town planners.

The selection of participants in the *Engagement* phase has been performed in a relatively ad hoc way by the authority because tools that automate or support this are not readily available. For instance, the panel may well have benefited from the insight of an environmental scientist. The communication protocol between participants is implicitly agreed upon according to implicit social norms. Participants expect to meet face to face on a regular basis and exchange phone calls and emails between meetings. Communications are expected to be courteous, non-inflammatory, and brief. The panel members expect the product of their deliberations to be communicated to the authority in the form of a written and confidential report. The decision-making protocol has not been made explicit but all panel members draw on social and professional norms and expect decisions about the report to be reached by consensus following deliberation.

One participant is a town planner with the local government authority. She has never previously dealt with sale yards so commences her *individual reasoning* by attempting to coalesce available knowledge about this issue with her knowledge of planning legislation, local government objectives, and the views of others. She uses a Web search engine in an attempt to locate a similar issue or relevant background knowledge. After some trawling, she discovers a controversial relocation of livestock sale yards in the city of Ballarat in regional Australia.

A detailed summary of the controversy was available on the City of Ballarat website. Consultants' reports, residents' objections, and council minutes provided insights into the types of issues that were pertinent. However, the volume of documentation was onerous and a succinct representation of the group's reasoning was not available as it would have been, had a *Group coalescing* process been explicated. After a great deal of effort, the town planner has identified odour, traffic, wastewater, noise, archaeological significance, economic benefits, and aesthetics as clearly relevant factors for the Ballarat reasoning community. Her summaries of salient issues are informal and represent her own individual coalescing of reasoning. If asked, she will describe her coalesced knowledge using verbal narrative expression. The effort to generate concept maps, argument maps, semantic networks, first order predicate logic clauses or domain ontologies is excessive so these schemes are not deployed.

In order to determine her own position on the issue, she makes assertions to herself based on her coalesced knowledge. At this stage, prior to input from other participants, she feels that the Saleyards relocation is acceptable provided a report on the impact of wastewater at the new site is performed. She asserts the result of her individual reasoning at the first meeting. Another participant raises strong concerns against the relocation on the basis of the impact on an endangered local bird, the Blue Jay.

Following the meeting, the town planner engages a Web search engine and, after some reflection and further reading about the Blue Jay, coalesces this new factor into her previously coalesced knowledge. She revises her earlier assertions and now believes the relocation should not occur without a consultant's report on the Blue Jay and another on the impact of wastewater. After an exchange of emails between participants, it is apparent that not all agree on the significance of the Blue Jay and counter the claim with assertions that the bird is not as local to the area as claimed.

During the next face-to-face meeting, the group is close to a stalemate on this issue and, although they had agreed to reach a decision by consensus, they are now close to changing the decision-making protocol in favour of a vote. A *Group coalescing* exercise is performed by our town planner to stimulate deliberation and remove the impasse. The group coalescing takes the form of an argument map where the main arguments to date are depicted diagrammatically. The group coalescing document does not represent agreement on the issues or recommendations but depicts explicitly the shared understanding within the

group. The Blue Jay factor is included in the map because it is a relevant consideration for some of the participants. The reasons for its relevance are depicted explicitly and it is accepted as valid for consideration. This factor is included in the community-accepted template though agreement on its impact or import has not been reached. This is illustrated in Figure 2.

Each participant uses the coalesced template to assert their own views to others for the decision-making, collective judgment phase. Seeing the group reasoning laid out succinctly facilitates understanding between participants and deliberation on the issues. Participants opposed to the Blue Jay argument do not accept the local Blue Jay is a distinct variety but given the consequences on the variety if they are incorrect, agree consensually to recommend refusal of the permit. This is illustrated in Figure 3. The group coalesced argument map is presented to the local government authority as a succinct summary of deliberations. This is uploaded to the Web along with the full report and will serve as the starting point for a community required to deliberate on a similar issue in the future. Figure 3 illustrates the par-

Figure 2. Coalesced reasoning for the saleyards community

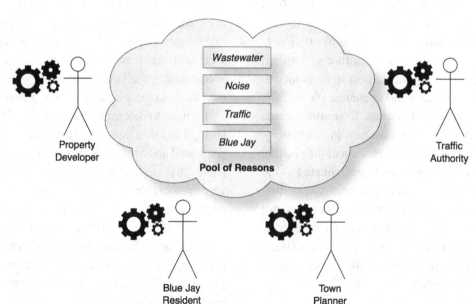

ticipants, pool of reasons, and the decision made by that community.

Many reasoning communities are not as large as the Saleyards example. A doctor and a patient can be seen to perform the *Engagement, Individual Reasoning,* and *Decision-Making* phases in minutes. Arguments are not always numerous or complex and a group coalescing process that results in an explicit representation of reasoning is not warranted. Further, the issues relate more immediately to the participants' lives than a discussion on policy options. Consequently, the individual coalescing more naturally occurs in narrative form. The patient tells his story about symptoms, and times and places and other phenomena. The doctor records the discussion in case notes that are invariably narrative in form (Kay & Purvis, 1996). In Chapter 6, the view is expressed that, as the reasoning community becomes larger and issues become more distanced from the immediate life experience of participants, the need for more structured representations of reasoning such as argument maps becomes more pressing. From a historical perspective, the need for a focus

on reasoning in groups has now become pertinent largely because information and communication technologies enable phenomena such as instant global news and electronic democracy. A historical perspective on the emergence of this need is presented in the next section.

PRECURSORS TO REASONING COMMUNITIES

From a historical perspective, the need for a focus on group reasoning and more sophisticated devices to support reasoning have emerged as a response to the increasingly complex thought processes that characterise modern information societies. Individuals had been reasoning to create new knowledge and draw new associations for thousands of years without any representation or embodiment outside the thinker. New knowledge was expressed verbally and a permanent representation only emerged relatively recently with the advent of writing. Verbal or oral reasoning can be performed in an explanatory cause-effect,

Figure 3. A saleyards community decision

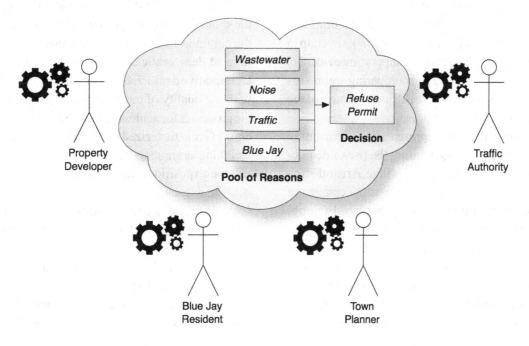

quasi-logical form or with the use of a narrative, story-telling form. However, regardless of the form, verbal reasoning soon reaches its limit as the concentration and memory of the listener are exhausted. Further, a complex verbal argument can easily involve circular reasoning or fallacies, which may be difficult to detect.

Schmandt-Besserat (1996) argues that writing was invented in Mesopotamia in the fourth millennium BC to create records that enabled traders and taxation officers to deal with arguments from traders that were too complex for verbal recollections. Literature, history, and philosophy came later. As an external representation of reasoning, writing was a significant advance over verbal processing because it brought reliable memory and permitted greater examination and rigour to be applied to a piece of reasoning. However, a written argument is linear and abstract and this generates a considerable cognitive load in terms of understanding, structuring and reproducing what the piece of prose says. For instance, in a community involved in discussing the benefits of nuclear power generation, written submissions from each participant represents arguments related to aspects of nuclear power generation perhaps including the disposal of waste, the risk of radioactive pollution and the costs of production. The submissions would contain considerable overlap in concepts and draw on similar supporting evidence. The task of contrasting and comparing arguments against each other is made difficult because of the unstructured nature of prose.

A more structured representation of reasoning than narrative emerged during the rise of democracy in Ancient Greece. At this time, Aristotle first developed the concept of logic as the essence of human rationality. Interestingly, he placed it alongside other modes of persuasion within a system of rhetoric. In rhetoric there are three modes of persuasion: logos, pathos and ethos. Logos refers to logical appeal. Pathos refers to appeals to the audience's emotion and ethos refers to appeals based on the qualifications of the speaker. Until

the resurrection of rhetoric in recent years by Perelman and Olbrechts-Tyteca (1971) and also by Toulmin (1958), reasoning had largely been equated with logic, and appeals to emotion or to the speaker's authority were frowned upon as unscientific.

More recently, in discussing co-operative ways individuals can reason together, McMahon (2001) suggests individuals assert claims to form a *pool of reasons* and then elect to embark on collective judgment to deem some reasons stronger than others and ultimately determine an outcome. In the community of reasoning as advanced here, the assembly of a pool of reasons occurs as formulated by McMahon but includes an additional step called group coalescing of reasoning that involves agreement that all reasons advanced are acceptable and plausible, even though some participants will not come to value them highly, if at all, during a collective judgment exercise. A detailed discussion on McMahon's concepts of collective reasoning (McMahon, 2001) is included in Chapter 2.

The notion of deliberative democracy is an idea that emerged in the 1990s as a way of deepening public engagement and involvement in decision-making (Dryzek, 1990). It arose as a response to the shortcomings of representative democracy as the common form of democracy that is practised in most democratic countries and organizations. Deliberative democracy is particularly concerned with the quality of outcomes of deliberation and the processes for achieving these outcomes. Deliberation is characterized by a process of reflection, weighing arguments and providing reasons for reaching a position on an issue. In particular, it values listening and understanding other perspectives so that the reasoned formulation of a position is an informed one. Dryzek and Niemeyer (2006) and Niemeyer (2011) argue that the goal of deliberation should generally be a 'meta-consensus' on the acceptable range and structure of beliefs, values and preferences, as opposed to a simple agreement on a course of action, or upon the ranking of decision options, or on the content of values. The notion of a 'meta-consensus' in the case of deliberation fits with our notion of coalescing reasoning into a collaborative product that can be used to support reasoning. The notion of a reasoning community put forward here is more general and has a stronger focus on reasoning than supporting deliberative rational outcomes.

Research in the recently emerging field of knowledge ecology operated in a similar vein to the philosophical discussions on co-operative reasoning. Knowledge ecology is an interdisciplinary field of management theory and practice, which is focused on the relational and social aspects of knowledge creation and utilization. Its primary study and domain of action is the design and support of self-organizing knowledge ecosystems, providing the infrastructure in which information, ideas, and inspiration can travel freely to cross-fertilize and feed on each other. The concept of communities of practice reflects the idea that a group of participants unified by their practice, engage in a process that is essentially social to advance knowledge. However, a reasoning community differs from a community of practice in a number of ways as illustrated by looking at indicators of communities of practice described by Wenger (1998):

1. Sustained mutual relationships—harmonious or conflictual. In a reasoning community, the relationships between participants are focused solely on their reasoning. Relationships are not necessarily sustained or mutual. The degree of internal harmony or combat is incidental to the purpose of participation; to reason.

2. Shared ways of engaging in doing things together. In a reasoning community, the principal thing a community does together is reason. Any other joint activities are incidental.

3. Rapid flow of information and propagation of innovation. In a reasoning community,

information typically though not necessarily flows rapidly. Similarly, innovation is typically though not necessarily propagated.

4. Absence of introductory preambles. In the engagement phase, participants determine a protocol for communication and decision-making. These introductory preambles are critical for the effectiveness of the community.

5. Quick set up of a problem to be discussed. A reasoning community is typically established to deal only with one specific problem though its processes can be used by other reasoning communities.

6. Substantial overlap in participants' description of who belongs. We would expect this to be the case in a reasoning community.

7. Knowing what others know, what they can do and how they can contribute to an enterprise. The enterprise in a reasoning community is the performance of reasoning usually in order to reach a decision. Knowing what others' know is central to the notion of group coalescing. Outside reasoning, what participants can do is not particularly relevant.

8. Ability to assess the appropriateness of actions and products. In a reasoning community, the communication and decision-making protocols agreed to describe agreement on appropriate ways to communicate and to reach a decision. Other assessments are not relevant in a reasoning community.

9. Specific tools, representations, and other artifacts. This is very important for a reasoning community so that the group reasoning can be transparent, inform all participants and other interested parties.

10. Local lore, shared stories, inside jokes, knowing laughter. In general, these are far less important for a reasoning community than communities of practice however shared stories are important for defining a sense of community

11. Jargon and shortcuts to communication as well as the ease of producing new ones. The communication protocol a reasoning community agrees upon may include shortcuts but they are not, in themselves, central to reasoning.
12. Certain styles recognised as displaying membership. Membership of a reasoning community is not contingent on style but on the capacity to reason in the field of question.
13. A shared discourse reflecting a certain perspective on the world. Participants may bring diverse perspectives of the world into a reasoning community. The group coalescing process is aimed at abstracting out shared understandings but this does not necessarily entail shared discourse.

Themes related to the nature of reasoning and reasoning in groups emerged in a variety of research endeavors including artificial intelligence, Computer-Supported Collaborative Work (CSCW), social psychology, and the knowledge ecology and the semantic Web emerged in recent decades. Insights from each of these fields inform the reasoning community and an overview is presented.

The Artificial Intelligence Movement

The emergence of artificial intelligence in recent decades includes three sub-fields of direct relevance to reasoning communities: knowledge based systems, logic, and multi-agent systems. Knowledge based systems is a generic term that encompasses technologies that model knowledge in some way and embed the knowledge into computer based systems that facilitate tasks. Logic based approaches model knowledge and reasoning using a logic based formalism. In contrast, multi-agent systems solve problems using a population of autonomous artificial agents, possibly accessing different knowledge bases, in communication with each other. Expert systems perhaps exemplify the

knowledge based system approaches best for this discussion.

Expert systems are programs that capture a model of reasoning that an expert in a field would use so that non-experts can make high quality decisions. Despite early excitement associated with the development of the first expert systems by Shortliffe and colleagues (Shortliffe, 1976) over thirty years ago, these systems remain far from prevalent. Lenat, Prakash, and Shephard (1986) has attributed this in part to the enormous resources required to model expert knowledge as rules. Although the knowledge acquisition bottleneck is well known to be resource intensive, the relative paucity of commercially viable expert systems cannot be explained by this alone. Rather, the lack of prevalence can more readily be explained from the perspective of a reasoning community in that expert systems do not support the *Engagement, Individual Reasoning, Group Coalescing,* or *Decision Making* phases very well.

A non-expert end user of an expert system does not coalesce reasoning related to a decision because this coalescing has been performed by knowledge engineers in consultation with experts when creating the knowledge base. However, the knowledge base is typically not directly accessible or sufficiently understandable for the end user to peruse. Furthermore, the individual reasoning that involves forming one's own claims is deferred to the system because most expert systems are configured to draw all inferences from user input. The decision-making or collective judgment phase of a reasoning community is similarly unsupported by expert systems in that, typically, the decision-making inferences are performed by the system.

The advent of artificial intelligence realized perfect implementations of forms of logic such as first order predicate calculus in computer languages like Prolog. Rather than lead to perfect automated reasoners, the new implementations only served to illustrate shortcomings in representing reasoning using first order logic. In legal reasoning, Sergot, Sadri, Kowalski, Kriwaczek,

Hammond, and Cory (1986) claimed success in modeling a citizenship Act with Prolog but issues related to the interpretation of legal terms rose to the fore. The concept of open texture, introduced by Waismann (1951) that no empirical term can be completely defined prior to its use added uncertainty to the precision of logic. The importance of the argument in law led to interest in non-monotonic logics exemplified by Dung (1995), Hage (1997), Bench-Capon and Sartor (2001), Prakken (1997), and Gordon and Karacapilidis (1997). These non-monotonic logics permitted differing interpretations of concepts and modeled the inference of different assertions from the same facts but do not attempt to place the reasoning in the context of a broader framework of a community of reasoners.

Argument mapping schemes emerged as diagrammatic devices to represent different interpretations and assertions. The majority of argument mapping schemes represent contrasting arguments but do not automate or support the generation of assertions. Diagrams advanced by Wigmore (1937) provide an early attempt last century to record the way evidence is combined in legal arguments. In the 1970s, Rittel and Webber (1973) developed the Issue Based Information System (IBIS) as a diagrammatic representation of arguments. More recently, Topic Maps (Park & Hunting, 2002) and ArguMaps (Rinner, 2001) present other diagrammatic ways of structuring the reasoning involved in argumentation. Yearwood and Stranieri (2006) advanced the Generic Actual Argumentation Model to represent the arguments a group of thinkers share and procedures participants deploy for performing inferences. Gurkan et al. (2010) report on the way a worldwide community developed and engaged with the largest argument map assembled to date. Chapter 3 describes argumentation schemes in some detail.

Multi-agent system research in artificial intelligence is concerned with the establishment of communities of communicating artificial agents that co-operate to solve problems. An agent is a computer system that is situated in some environment, and that is capable of autonomous action in this environment in order to meet its design objectives (Wooldridge & Jennings, 1995). Research into agent-based systems focuses on three main groups:

- **Agent theories:** This involves the theoretical specification of the nature of agents, the nature of self-knowledge, free will, the self and other, and the nature of a society of agents.
- **Agent Architectures:** Agent architectures provide the structural framework for developing Agent systems. The two prominent architectures are known as the Belief Desire Intention (BDI) framework advanced by Wooldridge (2002) where each agent has a set of beliefs about itself, the world and others, a set of goals or desires and the ability to make plans or intentions in order to initiate actions to realize goals. In contrast, the subsumption architecture first advanced by Brooks (1991) describes a community of agents that each follows simple rules. Complex and sophisticated behaviour is not built into each agent as it is in the BDI architecture but emerges as a property of the entire community when it is observed by outsiders.
- **Agent languages and tools:** These are tools that facilitate the implementation of agent based systems and include formally specified agent languages such as Jack (Shoham, 1993).

Although, the concept of agency is central to a reasoning community because such a community is a collection of autonomously motivated reasoners, the majority of multi-agent systems research, in focusing on agent theories, architectures, and languages does not directly contribute to discussions on reasoning communities.

The field of computer-supported collaborative work, discussed next, is directly focused on supporting groups of people working cooperatively.

Computer-Supported Collaborative Work

Computer-Supported Collaborative Work (CSCW) is a multi-disciplinary research field that focuses on tools and techniques to support multiple people working on related tasks. CSCW provides individuals and organizations with support for group cooperation and task orientation in distributed or networked settings. CSCW has been interpreted and understood in a number of different ways. It can be used to express the idea of collaboration among a group of people using computers (Howard, 1988; Kling, 1991). CSCW is also known as software for groups of people or groupware. Others, especially Scandinavian system developers, emphasize participatory design (Clement & van den Besselaar, 1993).

Bannon and Schmidt (1989) define CSCW as:

an endeavor to understand the nature and characteristics of cooperative work with the objective of designing adequate computer-based technologies (pp. 3–5).

This combines an understanding of how people work in groups and how computer networking technologies can be designed to support activities. CSCW systems are collaborative environments that support dispersed working groups so as to improve quality and productivity. Supporting community reasoning, in this context, is taken as different from supporting a decision formulated under a mixture of experts model; it is more akin to a model of connection of reasoners.

A community, such as a single judge court of law, that has agreed to vest authority for the ultimate decision in one participant, supports the work of that individual by merging the reasoning templates containing disparate views of participants into one document. Steps toward tools that can perform this have been developed by Yearwood and Stranieri (2000). A community that has agreed to reach a decision by deliberation could benefit from the anonymity and asynchronicity of Afshar, Yearwood, and Stranieri (2006). A community that has quantified the importance of a collection of criteria can deploy multi-objective decision-making tools as described by Szidarovszky, Gershon, and Duckstein (1986). A community that has agreed to reach a decision by negotiation will benefit from the use of negotiation support tools such as those advanced by Bellucci and Zeleznikow (2001).

When groups have the responsibility for decision-making, there is usually an agreed process for interaction and for reaching a group decision. Probably the most usual is for the group to use a fairly standard meeting style where papers or positions on the issue are presented and considered, these are discussed through the chair of the meeting. At some point when there has been enough discussion, one particular decision or motion is articulated and tested with a seconder. This motion is discussed and then the chair may select to put the motion to the vote. In most cases, the vote is a simple majority vote. Alternatives to a majority vote are often used: decision by authority, decision by expert, decision by minority, and decision by consensus.

The shortcomings of this approach are clear. Dialogue in such group discussions may be quite constrained and in its strict application is almost a series of monologues to the chair. In most group discussions, dialogue is a key element to the progression of the decision-making process. In many familiar circumstances, such as the discussion processes of governing bodies, dialogue can be adversarial from the outset and degenerate into eristic dialogue. Therefore, meeting style, dialogue, voting, and negotiation can be important aspects of a group decision-making process.

Research conducted by Wheelen, Murphy, Tsumura, and Kline (1998) demonstrates a clear correlation between positive group dynamics and team productivity. Knowing how to draw together a team and how to provide them with the skills and tools necessary for teamwork may be among the most crucial roles of the project manager.

It is particularly noteworthy that, while social psychologists have produced an extensive body of research in the area of group processes, group dynamics, communication and decision-making within groups, there is hardly any research (yet) into the specifics of multi-stakeholder processes. Janis originally defined groupthink as a mode of thinking that people engage in when they are deeply involved in a cohesive in-group, when the members' strivings for unanimity override their motivation to realistically appraise alternative courses of action (Janis, 1972, 1983). According to his definition, groupthink occurs only when cohesiveness is high. When group participants operate in a groupthink mode, they automatically try to preserve group harmony. Janis was convinced that a concurrence-seeking tendency of highly cohesive groups can cause them to make inferior decisions. He originally studied the Pearl Harbor bombing, the Vietnam War, and the Bay of Pigs Invasion. Similarly, the US Senate Intelligence Committee's Report (2004) on the U.S. Intelligence Community's Pre-War Intelligence Assessments on Iraq blamed groupthink for failures to correctly interpret intelligence relating to Iraq's weapons of mass destruction capabilities.

In the next section, each phase of the work of a reasoning community is described in more detail in order to illustrate the point that current technological tools or knowledge schemes do not adequately support participants engaged in reasoning within a community.

PHASES OF REASONING WITHIN COMMUNITIES

As outlined above, a reasoning community engages in four main processes: *Engagement*, *Individual Reasoning*, *Group Coalescing*, and *Decision-Making*. Each participant in a reasoning community actively engages at each phase of a community's activities. During the *Engagement* phase a participant reasons to determine the suitability of other participants, the breadth of the audience intended and an appropriate protocol for the decision-making phase. In the *Decision-Making* phase a protocol such as an election by secret ballot voting is performed in order to reach a decision. Some comments about each process will be made in describing tools that could be used to support the reasoning.

Engagement

This phase involves the engagement of participants, defining a protocol for communication, another protocol for decision-making, the determination of the future audience intended to use the community's reasoning and agreement on the issue to be reasoned about.

Social and legal norms within reasoning communities assist in the admission of participants. In some reasoning communities, norms strictly prescribe membership and in others, membership is quite open. The reasoning community in an appeal court is well defined and includes the deliberating judges and the barristers acting for the defendant and plaintiff. These participants agree by a decision-making protocol that deems that the judge alone decides the case. A reasoning community concerned with personality disorders at a psychiatric workshop is ostensibly open to any researcher interested in the topic though tacit barriers may exist to preclude participants from espousing views that are considered unacceptable.

Protocols for communication between participants are also determined during the engagement phase yet they are often implicitly specified. In the case of a divorce, a lawyer representing the husband will rarely contact the lawyer representing the wife face to face in the first instance, but may occasionally do so by telephone. More typically, early exchanges between lawyers occur in writing delivered by post. All communications are implicitly expected to be brief, to the point and devoid of personal judgements on the parties. In a reasoning community comprised of residents and town planners, the communication protocols may be quite different; the community only meets face to face, and discussions are free flowing, often drift from the issue at hand and can be quite passionate. A workplace meeting implicitly adopts a variation of meeting rules such as those articulated by Robert (2000). On the other hand, a commercial consortium develops complex documents as communication plans to precisely specify timelines, methods, and confidentiality for communication between consortium members.

Protocols for decision-making are also determined during the engagement phase yet these are more often explicit. A community assembled to assess the performance of a student is bound by the University constitution to reach a decision by consensus. Another community may form with the understanding that a decision is ultimately made by secret ballot vote using a preferential vote counting system. Yet another understands that the ultimate decision will be made solely by a manager and all discussion is intended to thrash out issues so that the manager can be more comprehensively informed.

An aspect of the decision-making protocol involves the specification of actions to be taken if the reasoning community breaks down and fails to reach a decision. In a family law custody dispute in Australia, for instance, if the reasoning community fails to reach a negotiated settlement, the parties are obliged by law to take the issue to a reasoning community that involves a first instance judge of the Family Court. Law prescribes clear grounds of appeal in the event that the reasoning community fails to reach a decision acceptable to all parties. Reasoning communities involving law differ from communities in other fields primarily because participants have a prescribed appeal process.

During the engagement phase, participants envisage future communities that may re-use the reasoning. Participants in a reasoning community often do not identify the communities that are intended to benefit from, or use, their reasoning. The *intended audience* of a reasoning community is the future community that will adopt or use the reasoning used by the current community. The intended audience in some communities extends to all communities dealing with similar problems in the future, whereas in others no future community is expected to use the reasoning. Further, as with membership, views on the intended audience are currently often left implicit. Most academic reasoning communities expect their reasoning to be used, and built upon, by any and all future researchers solving related problems. For example, reasoning first advancing the germ theory of illness occurred hundreds of years ago but is still implicit in any modern day research on bacterial pathogenesis. A task force in a workplace charged with determining equal opportunity policy exemplifies a reasoning community that may assume that the current staff will be the intended audience. However, if the organization is perceived to be a corporate leader, the community may well expect that their reasoning will be deployed by others.

Participants in a reasoning community have expectations regarding the likelihood that future reasoning communities will use the reasoning of the current community. The re-use of a community's reasoning involves more than an interest in the outcome. Most family law disputes do not involve controversial issues so, although parties in a typical dispute may expect immediate family and friends to be interested in outcomes, they do not expect their reasoning to be adopted as a template by a future reasoning community. A reasoning community centred around the highest court in family law will expect that most reasoning communities formed to resolve issues in family law within the jurisdiction will adopt their reasoning. We label the future communities who are expected to adopt a community's reasoning as the *intended audience*.

The group coalescing process outlined below results in a representation of the entire community's reasoning in a succinct form. In this way, a future community may readily re-use earlier reasoning. This is made difficult currently because many reasoning communities do not systematically record their reasoning at all while others record their reasoning solely in narrative form. Minutes of meetings record decisions and outcomes but rarely represent the deliberations that occurred within the meeting. Judges in lower courts in most jurisdictions provide a verbal account in court of the reasons for a decision but only the outcome is recorded. In higher courts, judges are often compelled to provide reasons for their judgements. These are expressed in narrative form in that a judge weaves the background of the case, the parties' circumstances, the finding of fact and final outcome into story-like prose that explains the decision.

In addition to the engagement of participants, the determination of a communication protocol and the identification of the intended audience, a reasoning community must also determine whether the issue as formulated is the right issue. For example, a management community formed to rank organisational research projects may feel that the more pressing issue involves whether or not to maintain a research program at all. As with other elements of the engagement phase, agreement that the issue is the right issue for discussion is typically performed implicitly. Further, this agreement is by no means straightforward. It involves trust that the stated issue is the real issue and not subterfuge while the real issue is determined elsewhere. The real issue may sometimes emerge once deliberation has commenced and sufficient background knowledge has been processed individually for a re-assessment of the issue. In a workplace setting, the initial issue may have involved actions toward the reduction of workloads but is reformulated as

the creation of policies that enhance organisational justice once deliberations commenced.

Currently, many reasoning communities perform key activities in the *Engagement* phase implicitly and therefore do not draw on support from tools despite the technological advances in recent decades. In the *Individual Reasoning* phase, outlined next, technological tools are utilised to a greater extent.

Individual Reasoning

The *Individual Reasoning* component represents the work done by a participant to understand the issue at hand and other participants' claims. The reasoning that an individual performs can be represented using models of reasoning or theoretical perspectives on reasoning that abound. However, although the primitive elements of reasoning differ from one reasoning model or theoretical perspective to another, the differences, as important as they are, are not central to the discussion here and taking a broader view allows for the identification of processes apparent when individuals reason in a community. For instance, the basic elements of reasoning for the argument theorist Toulmin (1958) include the *claim, datum, warrant, rebuttal,* and *backing*. In the statement, Peterson will be acquitted is a claim drawn from datum, Peterson has a strong defence, and the police case is weak. The warrant is that rule or observation that anyone with a strong defence against a weak case will normally be acquitted. The elements in first order logic are different.

In the first order logic, the basic elements of reasoning are clauses that represent facts and clauses that represent rules. Facts are statements declared to be true and rules are statements, also declared to be true, but permit the derivation of new knowledge. Peterson has a strong defence, if true is a fact and, anyone with a strong defence will be acquitted, if true is a rule. In other forms of logic, the basic elements vary according to the aims of the model. In the Reason-based logic of Hage (1997), clauses are extended with reasons that provide a justification for rules and permit the derivation of more abstract new knowledge. For McMahon (2001), reasons are assertions made in support of other assertions. In the non-monotonic logic known as default reasoning, statements that provide a preference for one rule over another can be said to be *meta-rules*.

Some argument mapping techniques such as the Issue Based Information System (IBIS) of Rittel and Webber (1973) cannot be used to derive new knowledge yet provide a powerful device for the organization of reasoning. Base elements in IBIS are *issues, positions, pro-arguments,* and *con-arguments.*

Although the basic elements of reasoning differ across theoretical perspectives and model the process of individual reasoning within a reasoning community context can be described independently of the approach adopted to model reasoning. In this vein, we can say that *Individual reasoning* involves two main elements:

- **An individual's coalescing of reasoning that has been asserted by others:** Participants rarely reason from a blank starting point but invariably draw on knowledge that has emerged in the past. Each participant coalesces past reasoning such as background knowledge, facts, claims, and reasons from other participants to yield an understanding of the arguments. During the individual's coalescing, a husband in a family law dispute reads widely and discovers that *health* is a relevant consideration because this factor was central to deliberations in a past appeal court reasoning community.
- **The individual's determination and communication to others of the element statements to be adopted as true, desirable, or preferred:** Once *health* is adopted as relevant, fact-finding occurs by assem-

bling evidence to support the claim that his own health is poor. Inference is deployed to derive the conclusion that he should receive a greater share of assets given the fact that his health is poor. This is communicated to other participants and their feedback is again coalesced for the assertion of new or revised facts, claims, and reasons.

Individual reasoning is intimately concerned with gaining an understanding of issues. In general, many of our attempts to understand aspects of the world has taken the form of stories and narrative myths. These myths and stories have often passed on, in a compressed form, reasoning that has been important practically as well as in a literary sense. McCloskey (1990) describes stories and metaphors as the two ways of understanding things and suggests that they can work together to provide answers. Narrative reasoning addresses situations that find difficulty in being addressed with the sequential form of verbal reasoning. The situations often involve multiple causes and multiple effects. Many social phenomena are like this and it would be fair to say that the great body of our accumulated social wisdom is expressed as narrative. Denning (2001) reminds us of some of the features of stories that make them useful in assimilating complex situations:

Storytelling is natural and easy and entertaining and energizing. Stories help us to understand complexity. Stories can enhance or change perceptions. Stories are easy to remember. Stories are inherently non-adversarial and non-hierarchical. They bypass normal defence mechanisms and engage our feelings.

In both logical reasoning and narrative reasoning, cause and effect relations are established between factors and used in sequential patterns. Both aim to organize and make sense of human experience in a way that can guide problem solving and decision-making. Whilst we recognize the product of logical or analytical reasoning as laws or rules that are largely context free and testable, the product of narrative reasoning is a story that is highly contextual and testable mainly through personal and interpersonal experience.

A contention in this work is that participants engaged in individual reasoning tend to deploy narrative when the community is small and the issues relate directly to individuals. For instance, both participants in a small reasoning community comprised of a doctor and a patient tend to use narrative. A patient depicts their symptoms, concerns, and thoughts on a diagnosis in a story form. The doctor explains a diagnosis and prognosis in narrative form and typically records the interaction in narrative form as case notes (Kay & Purvis, 1996). In contrast, communities that discuss issues such as new policies that relate less directly to an individual's experience tend to deploy more structured forms of reasoning. Perhaps argument mapping schemes provide the most structured form of representation of reasoning.

A participant in a reasoning community draws on reasoning recorded verbally, narratively or in more structured forms from previous communities to perform individual coalescing of reasoning. However, a participant performing *Individual Reasoning* may deploy narrative or logical reasoning, perhaps with the use of argument structuring devices, but must also communicate with other members. Insights from dialogue theorists provide a useful framework for the depiction of communications that occur within a reasoning community. Walton and Krabbe (1995) classify human dialogues into six basic types based on the objectives of the dialogue, the objectives of the participants and the information available to participants at the start of the dialogue:

- Information-seeking,
- Inquiry,
- Persuasion,
- Negotiation,
- Deliberation, and

- Eristic dialogues.

Information-seeking dialogues describe those interactions where an individual engages with another to seek information. Inquiry dialogues describe interactions where individuals interact to clarify an issue or deepen their understanding. In persuasion dialogues, an individual attempts to persuade another to adopt a particular view. Negotiation describes interactions where individuals bargain and resolve an issue. Deliberative dialogues are characterized by a desire to understand all views and reach outcomes that are rationally identified as optimal for the problem even though they may be detrimental to some participants.

Deliberative discourse has been advanced as an ideal for modern democratic states with advanced Internet technologies (Wilhelm, 2000). However, the extent to which this form of dialogue spontaneously occurs within groups is unclear. Workshop methods such as the *Search Conference* advanced by Emery and Purser (1996), exalt deliberation because this form of dialogue leads to more commitment and better decisions than other forms of communication and decision-making.

The reasoning an individual in a community engages in covers a broad spectrum of activities including fact-finding, evaluating, and setting claims, communicating with other participants and working toward a problem resolution. A key element in a reasoning community concerns communal agreement on the framework and bounds of the reasoning. This is beyond the realm of a single participant and occurs at the group level in a phase we call *Group coalescing*. This is described in overview in the next section and more fully in Chapter 3.

Group Coalescing of Reasoning

The group coalescing process involves a representation of the participants' reasoning organized to make explicit shared understanding about relevant factors and issues in contention. This is akin to making explicit the *pool of reasons* that, according to McMahon (2001), individuals should assemble before invoking some collective judgement process to evaluate the claims and ultimately determine an outcome. Although a group coalescing process is not common in many reasoning communities, there are a number of communities in which it is highly regarded. In academic circles, a survey article represents group coalescing in that it coalesces known research and claims related to a line of inquiry. The well-written survey article typically does not advocate for one theory while attacking another but instead compares and contrasts competing evidence and theories. In reasoning communities surrounding a legal issue, a case review article portrays a group coalescing process in a similar fashion.

The coalescing of group reasoning involves the construction of an explicit representation of the reasoning illustrated by all participants. The explicit representation is an organization of claims and reasons into a structure that serves four purposes:

- *Group coalescing* enhances deliberation,
- *Group coalescing* improves individual reasoning,
- *Group coalescing* serves to make reasoning, democratically transparent to all,
- *Group coalescing* enables a permanent record of the community's reasoning to be re-used for future reasoning communities.

Further, technological tools designed specifically to enhance group coalescing can make a profound impact on collective reasoning.

The group coalescing process does not necessarily result in agreement or dispute facilitation. The main benefit of a group coalescing process is the scope for understanding other perspectives and beliefs, enhancement of the clarity in communication and the potential for re-use of the reasoning. A new divorce dispute may take as a starting point, the group coalesced reasoning from a similar community in the past. The positions of the husband and wife may not be the same, however the hierarchy of concepts will be relevant. In common law countries, the group coalesced reasoning of the highest court is typically used as the starting point for deliberations by a new community.

van Gelder (2003) illustrates a debate centred on a decision to re-organise a Sydney based workplace from a one-person, one-job, single-tasking practice to a multi-tasking based practice. He described the role of a facilitator called in to help staff initially deliberate to define the main issue: *The workplace should return to a one-person one-job policy*. Following the definition of the issue, an argument mapping visualization method advanced by van Gelder (2003) that represents arguments as trees was used to elicit all reasons relevant for the issue from staff. This was done in a systematic, top-down manner, commencing with reasons for and against the issue. The map was later produced as a large poster so that the reasoning could be easily referred to in the future. Finally, once all arguments were canvassed, a consensus was achieved and a solution that the workplace should not return to a single-person, single-job policy was adopted.

The reasoning community in that study included a sample of workers and managers. Each participant engaged in some individual reasoning on the issue in the time prior to the facilitated sessions and advanced those reasons during the sessions. Being careful to solely record the reasons in a systematic way and not to engage in premature resolution, the facilitator created a map of all arguments. Agreement on the map constituted a group coalescing of reasoning though this occurred prior to a resolution of the issue. van Gelder (2003) noted that the use of an argument map facilitated an understanding and appreciation of all points of view by participants. The phase involving the resolution of the problem was deliberative and occurred without fuss because of the argument map.

The coalescing of group reasoning involves the construction of an explicit representation of the reasoning illustrated by all participants. The explicit representation is an organization of claims and reasons into a structure that facilitates individual understanding, serves to make reasoning democratically transparent to all and remains as a permanent record of the community's reasoning. Further, technological tools designed specifically to enhance group coalescing can make a profound impact on collective reasoning. The use of an argument mapping method by van Gelder (2003) can be seen to be at the heart of a group coalescing process.

The decision-making phase described next, illustrates processes used by the community to reach an outcome.

Decision-Making

The decision-making phase involves the determination of an outcome or solution to the problem at hand. Strategies for the final judgement include voting, referring to a sole arbiter, bargaining, or deliberation. The field of decision sciences has focused in depth on the discovery of models of decision-making.

Reasoning communities involving law are typically obliged to accept that the final decision will be made by one participant, the judge. In a conventional patient-doctor reasoning community comprising a doctor and a patient, the assumption made by both participants is that the doctor will ultimately determine a diagnosis and treatment plan. In many committee meetings, consensus loosely defined as agreement from all, is the norm whereas in more formal meetings, decisions are made by a majority vote.

Larger reasoning communities such as those involved in e-democracy settings cannot practically have a decision-making process by consensus and must resort to a voting algorithm. Smaller com-munities may still adopt voting as the preferred decision-making approach in order to ensure a decision will always be reached. Communities that value consensus very highly may prefer decisions to be reached in this way so much so that no other mechanism is permitted and decisions are often not reached at all.

Technological decision-making models based on utility theory have been advanced in recent years (Fishburn, 1970). Taking the reasoning community into account, it is apparent that the decision-making can be out-sourced to an algorithm only in those communities that have agreed to do so. However, in the vast majority of reasoning communities, the decision-making is deferred to a subset of participants or made by consensus. Other communities are so large that a voting protocol is required. A model-driven, decision-making protocol could conceivably be deployed in the remaining types of communities but all participants would typically need to be in agreement. In practice though, it is difficult to reach agreement on a decision-making model during the *Engagement* phase because participants need to cede authority to the model before knowing that the model will not unfairly decide against them.

Decision-making models are not emphasised in this text. Once a reasoning community perspective is adopted to describe the way in which individuals typically reason collectively, it becomes apparent that the decision-making protocol, while important to final outcomes, is overshadowed by less obvious processes of selecting participants, determining a communication protocol, individual coalescing, inference and group coalescing,

In this section, we provided an overview of the four processes in which a reasoning community engages: *Engagement, Individual Reasoning, Group Coalescing,* and *Decision-Making.* In the next section, we use three cases from the domain of Family Law to demonstrate these processes in a succession of reasoning communities.

REASONING COMMUNITIES SURROUNDING A FAILED MARRIAGE

Disputes following divorce typically concern responsibilities for children and distribution of assets. The husband and wife commence reasoning typically by consulting their respective lawyers regarding claims that may reasonably be upheld at law. The reasoning community that emerges for a specific marriage initially includes the husband and wife and their respective legal advisors. In providing advice, lawyers for the husband and the wife independently draw on knowledge about family law and judicial practices gleaned from their experiences in past family law reasoning communities. This includes knowledge of arguments successfully and unsuccessfully advanced in reasoning communities outside family law. The reasoning community that most lawyers in common law countries implicitly use as a starting point in a current dispute is one involving the latest decision from the highest court. Common law countries exemplified by the United States, Australia, and Britain are those countries that have legal systems where decisions made by courts stand as precedents and must be followed by future courts

Three examples of deliberations following marriage breakdown will be used to illustrate the way in which reasoning communities operate. In the first example, Marriage A, the parties commence reasoning by consulting their respective lawyers. The small community in Marriage A has succeeded in individual coalescing of reasoning, though no attempt was made to perform group coalescing. In Marriage B, the reasoning is not coalesced and an appeal is made to a reasoning community involving a trial judge. In this case, the reasoning is not coalesced individually by all participants and an appeal is made to the highest court. In the third example, Marriage C, the husband and wife consult an online dispute resolution system that facilitates their resolution but

also leaves an explicit record of their respective claims, reasons advanced, points of agreements and disagreements.

Marriage A

The wife and husband in the reasoning community of Marriage A initially learn about family law from their respective lawyers. Despite the discretionary nature of family law, the lawyers quickly and independently predict a likely court outcome and also identify arguments that could be used to bolster outcomes for their respective clients. In so doing, the lawyers have engaged in individual reasoning. The basis for the individual reasoning is the latest reasoning in the field. In the Australian context, this derives from the community surrounding the latest High Court of Australia case.

Discussions between lawyer and client are aimed at jointly agreeing on a list of claims and desired outcomes to be presented to the opposing lawyer. The negotiation dialogue that ensues relates to facts about the marriage such as ascertaining the marital assets and predicting judicial findings. Will the judge find that the husband contributed far more than the wife as a homemaker? Although agreement on outcomes may not be reached before many iterations, each participant understands the reasons advanced by the other party to support claims and accepts that the reasons are legitimate, even if they are exaggerated or untrue. If each individual coalesces their reasoning, they implicitly reach agreement on relevant factors and on relevant prior family law knowledge. The reasons advanced by both parties are accepted as valid in the context of the dispute, though the truth of the claims is not necessarily agreed upon. At this point, we say that the reasoning has coalesced primarily because the parties have a shared understanding of the reasoning deployed by higher court communities and have, typically implicitly, agreed to accept the reasoning as a template for their own community.

Figure 4. Reasoning community for marriage B

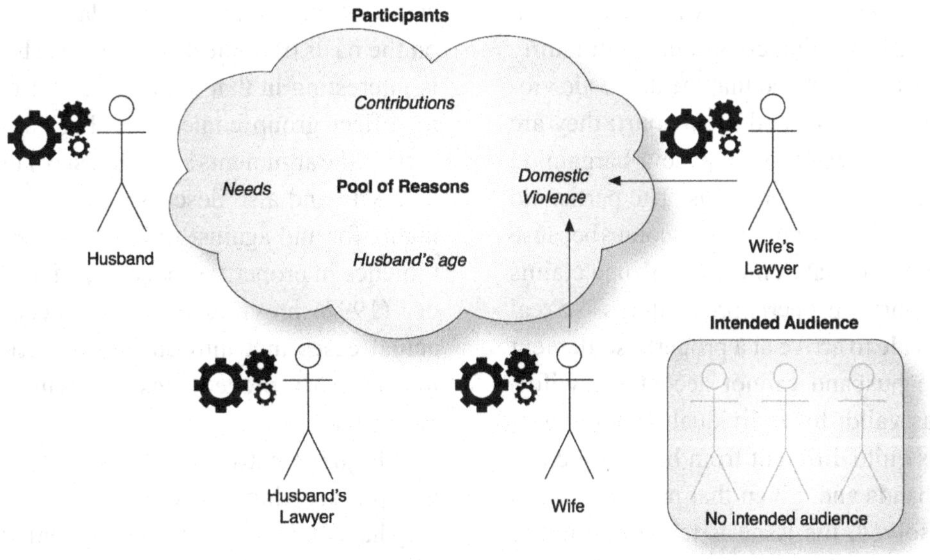

Once the reasoning is coalesced by each participant, efforts can be directed to the resolution of the problem and determination of a course of action. In some reasoning communities, this involves deliberation, whereas other communities may deploy negotiation, arbitration or voting. As Walton and Krabbe (1995) note, deliberative dialogues are those where participants attempt to listen intently to others, to reflect and to offer solutions that are the best solutions for the problem at hand without regard to self gain. Marital disputes are typically characterized by a great deal of emotion and anger so deliberation is difficult. In these communities, negotiation is more common. Chapter 4 discusses issues related to the problem resolution strategy deployed by a community.

In Marriage B the resolution of the issue is delayed because each participant in the initial community does not satisfactorily coalesce reasoning.

Marriage B

In Marriage B, the wife introduces claims for property based on domestic violence. The community is depicted in Figure 4. The wife, in Marriage B

cannot understand why years of emotional and physical violence perpetrated against her by the husband, does not entitle her to a greater share of the assets. She shocks her lawyer by weaving a twenty-year narrative characterized by fear and abuse. Her lawyer, drawing on the experience with many family law reasoning communities, explains that domestic violence has never been considered relevant by any judge in property proceedings. However, the lawyer has noticed that in reasoning communities related to occupational health and safety in the workplace, violent practices once accepted as pranks have recently resulted in financial penalties for perpetrators. This may signal a change in community attitudes and warrant the advancement of domestic violence grounds in property proceedings. According to Berman and Hafner (1995) lawyers keenly sense when a change in judicial practice is imminent; they actively seek *red flags*.

The wife's lawyer shares his reasoning with his client who decides to support the advancement of claims based on domestic violence in correspondence to the husband and his representative. The husband engages in individual reasoning in denying the veracity of her claims that he perpetrated violence. His lawyer, drawing on reasoning from previous reasoning communities in family law, reassures the husband that the domestic violence claims will not stand up in court; they are ambit claims designed to advance a bargaining position in pre-trial negotiations. The parties do not reach agreement on property outcomes because they do not agree that domestic violence claims have any import in property proceedings. No real attempt is made to arrive at a property settlement because the husband cannot accept the wife's reasoning as valid; his individual coalescing of reasoning is quite different from hers. The community disbands and, given that property issues must be resolved, the issue is taken to another reasoning community, namely the first instance or trial court. There is no attempt to perform group coalescing. Active participants in the trial court reasoning community include the parties, their lawyers and, now, a single presiding judge. Further, in the *Engagement* phase both parties also accept the authority of the court, the use of the latest High Court cases as a starting point in the reasoning, the rules of evidence for presenting facts, the empowerment to advance claims that depart from existing doctrine and the acceptance that the judge is the final arbiter. This community accepts that the individual coalescing of reasoning that the judge performs will be the outcome. At court, the trial judge accepts the wife's claims that the violence against her justifies a greater share of the property and awards property to her accordingly.

The husband and his lawyers are indignant that the trial judge has erred in the way he has coalesced all reasoning, particularly the reasoning related to domestic violence, and initiates an appeal to a higher court. The matter is referred to a third reasoning community, the High Court community illustrated in Figure 5. The active participants in the High Court reasoning community include all the parties in the original community, those in the trial court community and the panel of judges on the bench of the higher court.

The High Court judges hand down their decision that clearly legitimises claims for property on the basis of domestic violence. The judgment is interesting in that a major part of it is drafted to reflect group coalescing. The judgment describes the arguments and interests of the husband and wife and also describes more general arguments for and against the inclusion of domestic violence in property proceedings for all. Alexander (1992) provides a detailed account of the actual cases that introduced domestic violence into property proceedings following divorce in Australia.

The judgment document does not purely reflect group coalescing. A dissenting view that a judge may have is included in the judgment, though this represents his or her individual reasoning rather than group coalescing. In addition, the judgment is drafted in a narrative form, weaving facts, legal principles and points of view into a story whose primary purpose is to justify the bench's decision.

As we shall discuss at length throughout this work, a more effective group coalescing process serves to collect all arguments surrounding an issue into an organized whole. The purpose of group coalescing is so that a succinct generalisation of the community's reasoning remains for use by another, similarly constituted reasoning community. Although narrative has been central to human expression throughout time, it is unstructured and makes the reuse of reasoning difficult. Representations of reasoning such as the first order predicate logic are, at best, useful for capturing individual reasoning and are not designed to coalesce reasoning by a group of individuals. Schemes suitable for group coalescing are described at length in Chapter 6.

Marriage C is the subject of a law school case study in progress. The law school professor summarizes and contextualises comments and arguments made by both sides for her students. Independently and without bias, she constantly relates evidence to statutes or precedents. She performs the group coalescing role.

Figure 5. Reasoning community for family law

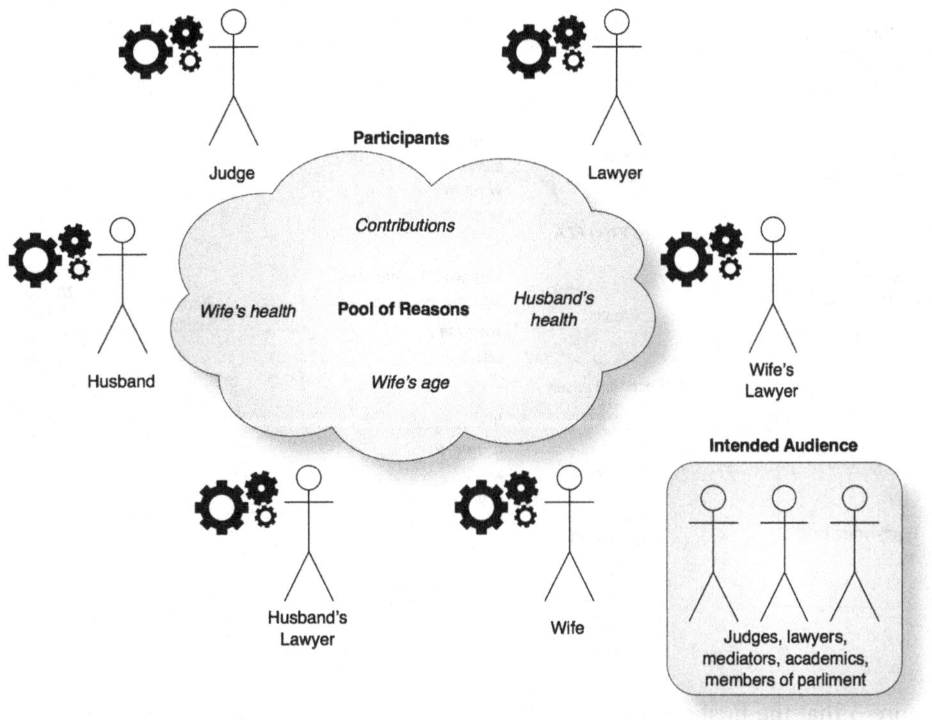

Marriage C

At many points during the dispute in Marriage C, individual participants attempt to coalesce the reasoning of the community. The husband's attempts to understand family law, his legal advice and the arguments advanced by his wife constitute his individual effort to coalesce reasoning specific to his case. In consultation with his legal advisor, he deploys the Issue Based Information System (IBIS) argument mapping scheme advanced by Rittel and Webber (1973) to depict on one simple diagram his positions, and those of his wife, including the pro and con arguments. The wife also coalesces the reasoning though she uses an argument map based on the layout of arguments advanced by Toulmin (1958). The pair exchange maps with each other and by so doing, succinctly identify points of departure. In this marriage, the maps are also forwarded to the law school profes-

sor who deploys an argument structure advanced by Yearwood and Stranieri (2006) to merge the two individual views of coalescing into a group one. The merging does not weigh the strength of one party's arguments over those of the other to determine the strongest arguments, rather it integrates the disparate points of view into one structure. Part of the generic argument structure is illustrated in Figure 6.

The structure in Figure 6 depicts the main issue as the root of a hierarchy of concepts; percentage split of assets. The possible values range from a split of 100%:0% to 0%:100% to the wife and husband, respectively. Prior experience with the statutes and precedents informs the law professor that a percentage split value is determined by three factors: past contributions to the marriage, future needs of both parties and the level of wealth of the marriage. The H in Figure 6 depicts the husband's position and the W depicts the wife's. We

Figure 6. Generic argument structure for group coalescing in family law

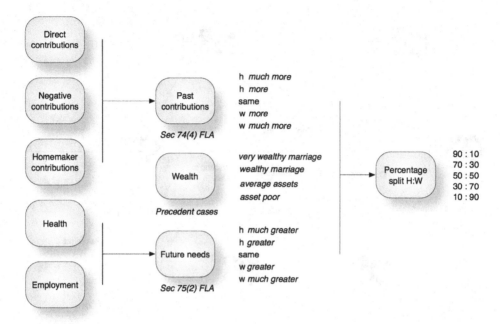

see from Figure 6 that the husband claims 30% of the assets because he has contributed as much as the wife to the marriage, there are few assets and they both have substantial needs for resources in the future. The wife believes she has made much greater contributions resulting in a claim for 90% of the property.

The three examples presented briefly here, Marriage A, B, and C, illustrate the four features of a reasoning community: identification of participants, individual reasoning and coalescing, group coalescing of reasoning and problem resolution.

In the next section, we step back from processes within a reasoning community to explore the nature of a community. The use of the term community to describe a group that can be as small as two, may at first glance, appear counter-intuitive. We see in the next section that this is in keeping with the evolution of the concept of community in recent years. Following that, reasoning community ideas are juxtaposed with the concept of crowd sourcing and wisdom of the crowds. A note on

the relationship between reasoning and intuition follows before concluding remarks.

THE CONCEPT OF COMMUNITY

Throughout this work, the claim is made that conceptualising a reasoning community as a type of community enables us to more appropriately identify the relationship between individuals in groups reasoning toward problem resolutions and consequently, to design technologies to best support the process. In this section, the notion of a reasoning community is placed within the context of change in concepts of community throughout sociological thought.

Delanty (2010) traces the history of the concept of community to identify a major transition in the concept in recent years. For Aristotle, a community was largely synonymous with the polis or the state so issues like membership of a community and individual experience of belonging to communities were not dealt with. Later, others commentators on community discussed these aspects but there always remain a tension between locality, membership based concept of community and univerlistic—polis of the state concept of community.

However, in recent decades the idea of community as communication attributed mainly to Habermas (1984) has emerged in contrast to the earlier concepts of community. This essentially means that social relations within communities are organised more around communicative acts than by authority, status or rituals. For instance, science and the institution of modern universities represents a community characterised by communicative exchanges dedicated to the discovery of truth. This transcends a sense of community based on locality, membership, culture, or ritual.

Another recent departure from the classical conception of community is illustrated by Lichterman (1996) who argues that grass-roots political movements, self-help groups illustrate new kinds of communities characterised by a confluence of individualism and a collective solidarity. This leads to more open and democratic communities. This view emphasises the relationship between the individual and the collective and as Taylor (1990) indicates the self must be seen to be rooted in the collective self; the individual is shaped in a community.

Delanty (2010) argues that the recent reconcptualisations of the concept of community lead to a concept he calls the postmodern community. Group membership is more fluid in modern society, membership of communities based on class, race, nationality or gender is replaced with multiple belongings. Everyday life presents examples of small groups embodying community. Commuters on a train, regulars at a café, friend networks and backpacker travellers are modern examples of postmodern communities. Far from being tied to a single community, individuals have multiple and often overlapping belongings to groups that may be small and often quite transitory. As Delanty states, postmodern communities are nomadic,

highly mobile, emotional and communicative. The postmodern community is a new kind of grouping that is understood beyond unity and identity.

A concept of a reasoning community advanced here is viewed as a postmodern community where the group's activities are focused on the resolution of a problem. The communicative exchanges define the community to a large extent and the communities may be as small and as transitory as a patient-doctor community.

CROWD SOURCING

Surowiecki (2004) introduced crowd sourcing, the notion that, under certain conditions, the aggregation of information and views from many individuals often results in better decisions than those made by a single individual regardless of expertise. Anecdotal examples abound and include one made famous by Surowiecki involving a competition at an agricultural fair that required participants to guess the weight of an ox. Perhaps counter-intuitively, taking the average of participants guesses of the ox's weight resulted in more accurate estimates than those of expert butchers and farmers; an example of the wisdom of crowds.

The conditions that Surowiecki advanced for the wisdom of the crowds to function include the need for opinions to be diverse, for participants to arrive at their own views independently and for individuals to draw from different and local knowledge. In addition, an effective mechanism for the aggregation of opinions must exist. Without these conditions, the wisdom of the crowds fails and decisions are made sub-optimally based on incomplete information or unduly based on the views of dominant individuals.

The Delphi method described by Linstone and Murray (1975) is an approach for structured communication between group members that realises conditions for the wisdom of the crowds. In this approach individuals avoid contact with each other to ensure anonymity and therefore, independence.

In the first round of a Delphi procedure, a facilitator gathers and collates the opinion of participants and feeds back the summarised opinions to each participant who has an opportunity to revise their views for submission to subsequent rounds.

Rowe and Wright (1999) describe the Delphi approach for forecasting tasks and identify issues including the propensity for participants to ascribe a degree of confidence to their forecast that is often, for novices, overly high. In forecasting tasks, the aggregation of participants' forecasts typically takes the form of feedback of frequency counts for each alternative forecast made by members of the Delphi group. For example, in a football tipping study by Bolger et al. (2011), some participants were provided with feedback that involved the number of participants that tipped each team and their average confidence. Other participants were provided with richer feedback that also included reasons for their tip.

Relating reasoning community processes with conditions for realising the wisdom of crowds, we see that the individual reasoning phase of a reasoning community involves the independent judgement critical for the wisdom of the crowds. The aggregation of views takes the form of a coalescing of reasoning that involves the generation of a cooperative product that is fed back to participants to inform their reasoning for subsequent rounds. A decision is ultimately reached by a decision making process that was agreed to by participants in the first, engagement phase.

The notion of reasoning community assumes participants are working as a group to a greater extent than that assumed in wisdom of the crowd ideas. Under the reasoning community formulation, the process of selecting individuals is not assumed to be a random process designed to realise as wide a diversity of views as possible, but instead is assumed to be a process that is a key component of group reasoning. As illustrated with examples earlier in this chapter, participants may be assigned to a reasoning community by virtue of their role in society such as judges in a court-based community. In other communities, participants are selected specifically because they represent diverse views, have diverse skill sets, or satisfy regulatory or political requirements, as exemplified in the Blue Jay example above.

The engagement phase of a reasoning community also includes the requirement for a decision making protocol to be agreed upon by participants. This elevates the ultimate group decision-making to a process the community makes explicit and participants agree with. In wisdom of the crowd implementations exemplified by the Delphi, the methods to ultimately collate views to reach a final decision is typically not made explicit or elevated in importance to group reasoning.

Perhaps the greatest point of difference between reasoning communities and wisdom of the crowd ideas is the position of individual reasoning. In the wisdom of crowds, the reasoning process an individual deploys to arrive at a view is not particularly important to share with others. Aggregation is typically performed with views, and not with reasoning that led to each participant's view. In the reasoning community, the coalescing of reasoning involves a merging of the reasoning used by each participant in reaching their respective views. This is considered important because the coalescing of reasons plausibly enhances each individual's reasoning in that others' views can more completely be understood. In this way, the reasoning of others can influence participants to modify their own reasoning.

In diminishing the importance of individual reasoning that leads to a judgement, wisdom of the crowds accommodates an intuitive basis for judgements. Guesses of the ox's weight are intuitive judgements not readily reducible to reasoning steps. In that example, the power of the crowds arises from the aggregation of intuitive judgements. This calls into question the relationship between intuition and reasoning which is discussed in the next section, prior to concluding this chapter.

THE ROLE OF INTUITION
IN DECISION MAKING

In posing the question, why do humans reason, Mercier and Sperber (2011) make the case that reasoning can best be regarded as a phenomena that arises from persuasive exchanges with others aimed at advancing or defending claims held. Further, views held by an individual seem to arise as a result of an intuitive judgment and not from a careful application of reasoning. The follow-on question we might pose is why do humans reason in groups? According to a narrow interpretation of the Mercier and Sperber's argument, humans do not actually reason in groups but instead enter a dialectical battlefield where each participant is intent on persuading others or defending their own arguments with very little incentive to modify their beliefs based on the views of others.

The Mercier and Sperber (2011) argument is not dissimilar to the positions advanced in jurisprudence by adherents of the movement known as legal realism. Llewellyn (1962) advocated that what judges actually do in deciding a case, is intuitively reach a decision rather than doing so using a deductive process involving legal principles or statutes. The written judgment is more aptly seen as a document written to justify the intuition and to reduce the risk of appeal. A debate has raged in jurisprudence regarding sentencing decisions for some years between adherents of the so called intuitive or instinctive synthesis exemplified by Tata (1997) and the more analytic schools. Interestingly, neurological evidence from brain mapping studies reported by Bennett and Broe (2007) suggest the emotional areas of the brain associated with intuitive judgment play a central role in judges decision-making.

The reasoning community ideas advanced here assume that individual's in a community may well intuitively arrive at their own views intuitively. The process of coalescing the reasoning displayed by all participants in an explicit representation provides each individual with a tool to improve their own reasoning. Some individuals will no doubt use the coalesced product in order to refine their own arguments to better combat those of others along the lines Mercier and Sperber (2011) describe. However, other individuals can be expected to use the coalesced product to deliberate and refine or retract their previous views in a more deliberate show of co-operative effort. Either way, the coalesced product can be regarded as useful for individual reasoning.

The coalesced product can be regarded as useful for an entire reasoning community charged with collectively making a specific decision and for other communities charged with making similar decisions in the future. In advancing this claim, we assume that reasoning does not necessarily arise solely in the context of combative exchanges. With the emergence of new technologies to facilitate the coalescing of community reasoning and making more of the process explicit and available for future reference, a more deliberative form of group interaction can plausibly emerge.

SUMMARY

The main contention of this chapter is that most situations in which reasoning is performed in practice involve a group of people ranging in size from two to many thousands deliberating toward a decision regarding practical action. Identifying a group as a community bound together by the need to reason entices the use of the label *reasoning community*. Doing so permits us to identify four main phases of the process that participants in a group engage in when reasoning: *engagement*, *individual reasoning*, *group coalescing*, and *decision-making*. In the *engagement* phase the problem or issue that requires practical action, as initially perceived is agreed upon, participants are selected, agreements about how communication will occur are reached, and the method used to ultimately reach a group decision is specified. Typically, these elements of the *engagement* phase are performed implictly with little discussion or explicit annotation. In the *individual reasoning* phase, participants first draw on their own resources to make sense of the issue. This is labelled individual coalescing. Individual coalescing involves a bringing together of the reasons underpinning the decision and leads to sufficient understanding of the issue for the participant to form an opinion of a preliminary, preferred decision outcome. This need not be the final preference the participant holds. Indeed, for groups engaging in discussions deliberatively, participants bring their views to the discussion with a preparedness to modify their own view after hearing the views of others. The preferred decision outcomes and reasons are communicated to others during the individual reasoning phase. In the *group coalescing* phase the group takes stock of reasons supplied by all participants. Group coalescing results in an explicit representation of the group's reasoning that is called a cooperative product. Argument mapping methods are well suited to the explicit representation of the cooperative product. Group coalescing that involves the explicit generation of a representation of all reasons advanced by participants is not often performed in reasoning communities. However, group coalescing becomes important with larger communities such as deliberative democracies and when issues become complex. Further, group coalescing enables a community to more readily reuse the reasoning performed by other reasoning communities. The *decision-making* phase involves the invocation of a procedure to convert the reasoning into a final group decision. This can be achieved by a simple majority vote, more complex voting schemes, consensus, or by nominating a single entity to reach the ultimate decision.

A reasoning community is quite different from a community of practice. The latter term describes a community bound together by parties that share many attributes in common including a relatively long-term interest in the practice area. A reasoning community requires that participants

have little in common. The community may not last longer than minutes and it may be as small as two participants.

The next chapter discusses issues to do with collective reasoning and the coalescing of reasoning. Argument mapping methods are introduced. In Chapter 3, individual reasoning is discussed. Representations of individual reasoning including the classical syllogism, first order logic and non-monotonic logic are described from a reasoning community perspective. Following that, a chapter is presented that expands an argument model called the Generic Actual Argument Model to illustrate features that make this structure particularly suitable for group coalescing. In Chapter 5, a model for dialogue moves based on the argument structure is presented. A closer examination of coalescing is included in the chapter following that. Chapter 7 is devoted to describing the importance of narrative and the role of stories for a reasoning community. Chapter 8 relates work on the semantic Web and ontologies to reasoning community ideas. The final chapters relate insights from a reasoning community perspective to technologies that can support reasoning in groups.

REFERENCES

Afshar, F., Yearwood, J., & Stranieri, A. (2006). A tool for assisting group decision-making for consensus outcomes in organizations. In Voges, K. E., & Pope, N. K. L. (Eds.), *Business Applications and Computational Intelligence* (pp. 316–343). Hershey, PA: IGI Global. doi:10.4018/978-1-59140-702-7.ch016

Alexander, R. (1992). Mediation, violence and the family. *Alternative Law Journal, 17*(6), 276–299.

Bannon, L. J., & Schmidt, K. (1989). CSCW: Four characters in search of a context. In *Proceedings of the First European Conference on Computer Supported Cooperative Work*, (pp. 358-372). London, UK: CSCW.

Bellucci, E., & Zeleznikow, J. (2006). Developing negotiation decision support systems that support mediators: A case study of the family-winner system. *Artificial Intelligence and Law*, *13*(2), 233–271. doi:10.1007/s10506-006-9013-1

Bench-Capon, T., & Sartor, G. (2001). Theory based explanation of case law domains. In *Proceedings of the Eighth International Conference on Artificial Intelligence and Law*, (pp. 12–21). ACM Press.

Bennett, H., & Broe, G. A. (2007). Judicial neurobiology, Markarian synthesis and emotion: How can the human brain make sentencing decisions? *Criminal Law Journal*, *31*, 75.

Berman, D. H., & Hafner, C. D. (1995). Understanding precedents in a temporal context of evolving legal doctrine. In *Proceedings of the Fifth International Conference on Artificial Intelligence and Law*, (pp. 42-51). New York NY: ACM Press.

Bolger, F., Stranieri, A., Wright, G., & Yearwood, J. (1999). Does the delphi process lead to increased accuracy in group-based judgmental forecasts or does it simply induce Consensus Amongst Judgement Forecasters. *Technological Forecasting and Social Change*, *78*(9), 1671–1680. doi:10.1016/j.techfore.2011.06.002

Brooks, R. (1991). Intelligence without representation. *Artificial Intelligence Journal*, *47*, 139–159. doi:10.1016/0004-3702(91)90053-M

Clement, A., & van den Besselaar, P. (1993). A retrospective look at pd projects. *Communications of the ACM*, *36*(6), 29–37. doi:10.1145/153571.163264

Delanty, G. (2010). *Community* (2nd ed.). London, UK: Routledge.

Denning, S. (2001). *The springboard: How storytelling ignites action in knowledge-era organizations*. Boston, MA: Butterworth Heinemann.

Dryzek, J. (1990). *Discursive democracy: Politics, policy and political science*. Cambridge, UK: Cambridge University Press.

Dryzek, J., & Niemeyer, S. (2006). Reconciling pluralism and consensus as political ideals. *American Journal of Political Science*, *50*(3), 634–649. doi:10.1111/j.1540-5907.2006.00206.x

Dung, P. M. (1995). On the acceptability of arguments and its fundamental role in non-monotonic reasoning, logic programming and n-person games. *Artificial Intelligence*, *77*(2), 321–357. doi:10.1016/0004-3702(94)00041-X

Emery, M., & Purser, R. E. (1996). *The search conference: A powerful method for planning organisational change and community action*. San Francisco, CA: Jossey Bass.

Fishburn, P. C. (1970). *Utility theory for decision making*. New York, NY: Operations Research Society of America.

Gordon, T., & Karacapilidis, N. (1997). The zeno argumentation framework. In *Proceedings of the Sixth International Conference on Artificial Intelligence and Law*, (pp. 10-18). Melbourne, Australia: ACM Press.

Gürkan, A., Iandoli, L., Klein, M., & Zollo, G. (2010). Mediating debate through on-line large-scale argumentation: Evidence from the field. *Information Sciences*, *180*(19), 3686–3702. doi:10.1016/j.ins.2010.06.011

Habermas, J. (1984). *The theory of communicative action. Thomas McCarthy (Trans.)*. Cambridge, UK: Polity.

Hage, J. C. (1997). *Reasoning with rules: An essay on legal reasoning and its underlying logic. VDordrecht*. The Netherlands: Kluwer.

Howard, R. (1988). Panel remarks: CSCW: What does it mean? In *Proceedings of the Conference on Computer-Supported Cooperative Work*. New York, NY: ACM Press.

Janis, I. (1972). *Victims of groupthink: A psychological study of foreign-policy decisions and fiascoes* (2nd ed.). Boston, MA: Houghton Mifflin.

Janis, I. (1983). *Groupthink: Psychological studies of policy decisions and fiascoes*. Boston, MA: Houghton Mifflin.

Kay, S., & Purvis, I. (1996). Medical records and other stories: A narratological framework. *Methods of Information in Medicine, 35*, 72–87.

Kling, R. (1991). Cooperation, coordination and control in computer-supported work. *Communications of the ACM, 34*(12), 83–88. doi:10.1145/125319.125396

Lave, J., & Wenger, E. (1991). *Situated learning: Legitimate peripheral participation*. Cambridge, UK: Cambridge University Press.

Lenat, D., Prakash, M., & Shephard, M. (1986). Cyc: Using commone sense knowledge to overcome brittleness and knowledge acquisition bottlenecks. *AI Magazine, 6*(4), 65–85.

Lichterman, P. (1996). *The search for political community: American activists reinventing commitment*. Cambridge, UK: Cambridge University Press. doi:10.1017/CBO9780511628146

Linstone, H. A., & Turoff, M. (1975). *The delphi method: Techniques and applications*. Reading, MA: Addison-Wesley.

Llewellyn, K. N. (1962). *Jurisprudence: Realism in theory and practice*. Chicago, IL: The University of Chicago Press.

McCloskey, D. N. (1990). Storytelling in economics. In Nash, C. (Ed.), *Narrative in Culture: The Uses of Storytelling in the Sciences, Philosophy and Literature* (pp. 5–22). London, UK: Routledge.

McMahon, C. (2001). *Collective rationality and collective reasoning*. Cambridge, UK: Cambridge University Press.

Mercier, H., & Sperber, D. (2011). Why do humans reason? Arguments for an argumentative theory philosophy, politics and economics program, University of Pennsylvania. *The Behavioral and Brain Sciences, 34*, 57–111. doi:10.1017/S0140525X10000968

Niemeyer, S. J. (2011). Intersubjective reasoning and the formation of metaconsensus. In Yearwood, J., & Stranieri, A. (Eds.), *Technologies for Supporting Reasoning Communities and Collaborative Decision Making: Cooperative Approaches*. Hershey, PA: IGI Global. doi:10.4018/978-1-60960-091-4.ch002

Park, J., & Hunting, S. (2002). *XML topic maps: Creating and using topic maps for the web*. Boston, MA: Addison-Wesley.

Perelman, C., & Olbrechts-Tyteca, L. (1971). *The new rhetoric: A treatise on argumentation* (Wilkinson, J., & Weaver, P., Trans.). London, UK: University of Notre Dame Press.

Prakken, H. (1997). *Logical tools for modelling legal argument*. Dordrecht, The Netherlands: Kluwer. doi:10.1007/978-94-011-5668-4

Rinner, C. (2001). Argumentation maps: GIS-based discussion support for on-line planning. *Environment and Planning. B, Planning & Design, 28*, 847–863. doi:10.1068/b2748t

Rittel, H. J., & Webber, M. M. (1973). Dilemmas in a general theory of planning. *Policy Sciences, 4*, 155–169. doi:10.1007/BF01405730

Robert, H. M. I. (2000). *Robert's rules of order* (10th ed.). Cambridge, MA: Perseus Publishing.

Rowe, G., & Wright, G. (1999). The delphi technique as a forecasting tool: Issues and analysis. *International Journal of Forecasting, 15*, 353–375. doi:10.1016/S0169-2070(99)00018-7

Schmandt-Besserat, D. (1996). *How writing came about*. Austin, TX: University of Texas Press.

Sergot, M. J., Sadri, F., Kowalski, R. A., Kriwaczek, F., Hammond, P., & Cory, H. T. (1986). The British nationality act as a logic program. *Communications of the ACM, 29*(5), 370–386. doi:10.1145/5689.5920

Shoham, Y. (1993). Agent-oriented programming. *Artificial Intelligence, 60*(1), 51–92. doi:10.1016/0004-3702(93)90034-9

Shortliffe, E. H. (1976). *Computer based medical consultations: MYCIN.* New York, NY: Elsevier.

Surowiecki, J. (2004). *The wisdom of crowds: Why the many are smarter than the few and how collective wisdom shapes business, economies, societies and nations.* New York, NY: Doubleday.

Szidarovszky, F., Gershon, M., & Duckstein, L. (1986). *Techniques for multiobjective decision making in systems management.* London, UK: Elsevier.

Tata, C. (1997). Conceptions and representations of the sentencing decision process. *Journal of Law and Society, 24,* 395. doi:10.1111/j.1467-6478.1997.tb00004.x

Taylor, C. (1990). *Sources of the self.* Cambridge, MA: Harvard University Press.

Toulmin, S. (1958). *The uses of argument.* Cambridge, UK: Cambridge University Press.

US Senate Intelligence Committee. (2004). *Report of the select committee on intelligence on the US intelligence community's prewar intelligence assessments on Iraq.* Washington, DC: US Senate Intelligence Committee.

van Gelder, T. (2003). Enhancing deliberation through computer supported argument mapping. In Kirschner, P. A., Shum, S. J. B., & Carr, C. S. (Eds.), *Visualizing argumentation: Software tools for collaborative and educational sense-making.* London, UK: Springer Verlag.

Waismann, F. (1951). Verifiability. In Flew, A. (Ed.), *Logic and language.* Oxford, UK: Blackwell.

Walton, D., & Krabbe, E. (1995). *Commitment in dialogue: Basic concepts of interpersonal reasoning.* Albany, NY: State University of New York Press.

Wenger, E. (1998). *Communities of practice: Learning, meaning and identity.* Cambridge, UK: Cambridge University Press.

Wheelen, S. A., Murphy, D., Tsumura, E., & Kline, S. F. (1998). Member perceptions of internal group dynamics and productivity. *Small Group Research, 29*(3), 371–393. doi:10.1177/1046496498293005

Wigmore, J. H. (1937). *The science of judicial proof as given by logic, psychology and general experience.* New York, NY: Little, Brown and Company.

Wilhelm, A. G. (2000). *Democracy in the digital age: Challenges to political life in the digital age.* New York, NY: Routledge.

Wooldridge, M. (2002). *An introduction to MultiAgent systems.* Hoboken, NJ: Wiley.

Wooldridge, M., & Jennings, N. (1995). Intelligent agents: Theory and practice. *The Knowledge Engineering Review, 10,* 115–152. doi:10.1017/S0269888900008122

Yearwood, J., & Stranieri, A. (2000). An argumentation shell for knowledge based systems. In *Proceedings of IASTED International Conference on Law and Technology,* (pp. 105–111). IASTED.

Yearwood, J., & Stranieri, A. (2006). The generic actual argument model of practical reasoning. *Decision Support Systems, 41*(2), 358–379. doi:10.1016/j.dss.2004.07.004

Chapter 2
Collective Reasoning and Coalescing Reasoning

ABSTRACT

In this chapter, we consider in some detail the nature of collective reasoning and the existing approaches to supporting the collective reasoning that reasoning communities undertake. In approaching the development of technologies to support the functioning of reasoning communities, it is important to be clear on the nature of the tasks involved in collective reasoning. In Chapter 1, we have outlined the main tasks of collective reasoning as: individual reasoning, reasoning communication, and the coalescing of reasoning. However, it is important to identify the ways in which collective reasoning is indeed cognitive cooperation and to what extent there is a case that it is mutually beneficial cooperation as well as being beneficial in its outcomes.

People who are not prepared to allow fairness to bend, soften, or demote their moral concerns command our respect. We often call them, with approval, "principled." But people who are prepared to relax their principles to some extent in order to achieve cooperation on a basis all can accept also command our respect. We call them, with approval, "reasonable."

Christopher McMahon

DOI: 10.4018/978-1-4666-1818-3.ch002

COLLECTIVE REASONING

Collective reasoning is one way in which we might expect a reasoning community to operate. It is not the only way, because different communities operate in different ways and the product of their operation can be different in form. For example, the Australian Refugee Review Tribunal (RRT) determinations are decisions made by individuals but yet the decision makers collectively form a reasoning community.

What is meant by collective reasoning? Does an ordinary meeting in most organizations where decisions are made involve what we might think collective reasoning to be? Does the democratic election of a political party to office involve collective reasoning? Does the decision of a jury in a criminal trial involve collective reasoning? Does the decision of a group of physicians considering treatment of a patient involve collective reasoning?

These questions provoke the realization that there are many different contexts for collective decision-making and the possibility of collective reasoning. It is well understood that if commitment to a decision by the group is important - so that there can be agreeable and supportive participation in the actions, then participation in the decision-making and acceptance of the decision is a key element (O'Brien, 2002). If the parties can deliberate to a consensus on a course of action, they would be able to understand the outcome as guided by reason and the group cooperation as a whole to be guided by reason. This process of community or group deliberation is worthy of some consideration. Firstly, the group nature implies a shared nature in the deliberation. So what are people or agents doing when they deliberate together? McMahon (2001) calls "cooperation to achieve epistemic goals," *cognitive cooperation*. One aspect of this cooperation is the gathering of facts or fact finding. This fact finding is an important stage that works to provide evidence relevant to the issue being considered. The other aspect that we might more clearly identify as *collective reasoning* is the cooperative construction and understanding of the rational force behind a decision. This process aspect of the activity would entail the development of the reasoning to decisions in some mutual way as well as a mutual understanding of the strength of this reasoning. Therefore, the process would involve the identification of evidence, grounds and facts as well as the reasoning that connects these to the conclusion and provides the force of the justification for a decision based on the facts and reasons. However, this still does not seem to make clear what collective reasoning is. We need to ask what the product of collective reasoning

would be. That is, what it is that those engaged in collective reasoning produce and how is it of benefit?

As we have introduced it in Chapter 1, collective reasoning as undertaken by a reasoning community involves individual reasoning, communication of reasoning and a cooperative effort in coalescing reasoning to better support individual reasoning and reach a decision or answer a question on some particular issue that is a concern for the reasoning group. For reasoning communities or groups, each participant in the group is interested in obtaining a decision or solution that could not be obtained, or obtained with the same level of quality, by reasoning alone as a sole reasoning agent. It is in this sense that collective reasoning can be regarded as being mutually beneficial. The benefit that each individual agent seeks is a well *justified* or well reasoned decision. There can be a dual benefit here as the individual may adopt modifications and improvements to their own individual reasoning, but of course, the overall improvement in group reasoning and decision-making is also a reason for participation. By well justified, in this context we mean a decision that is well supported by relevant reasons that are structured as a cogent and forceful argument. This avoids the issue of whether this is the correct or 'true' decision as it sets its evaluative framework and priorities with those that we attribute to a reasoning community, namely that the decision is the one that is most strongly justified by the strength of the reasons that the group accepts support it. The approach of viewing justification as being connected with or being a route to truth has some backing (see Bonjour (1985) pp. 7-8). However, in our notion of collective reasoning within a reasoning community each participant expects to obtain a justified decision. This decision should also be one that has undergone a broad consideration of the relevant factors from many different perspectives as well as reasons and selected as the decision that is most forcefully and convincingly supported by the relevant reasons.

The goal of collective reasoning is in fact the same as the goal of individual reasoning, which will be discussed in more detail in Chapter 3. However, in the case of collective reasoning, the reason to contribute is provided by the prospect of obtaining a decision that is better justified than the best justified decision that could have been obtained by reasoning independently. This is an example of McMahon's Principle of Collective Rationality, which he puts forward as a more acceptable reason to contribute in collaborative schemes where the most common explanation for contributing is some moral reason such as fairness.

Disagreement within a group may often indicate that a group could benefit from collective reasoning because the existence of opposing views suggests that one's own views may be able to be improved. However, even in the case of agreement a group may choose to reason collectively with an expectation that collective reasoning may lead to a better justified decision. There are two ways of interpreting disagreement within a group. Disagreement could imply that some members are mistaken in what the reasons support or justify. McMahon refers to this as *cognitive malfunction*. Cognitive malfunctioning by an individual can be characterised by misunderstanding or misuse of concepts or a lack of the relevant concepts, flawed construction of reasoning or fallacious argument. Collective reasoning offers an opportunity to work towards eliminating malfunction by ensuring that all participants have the same concepts and that these concepts are used in the same way. As a result there is more likely to be agreement. However, the goal of collective reasoning is not agreement, the goal of each participant is a well justified decision. Agreement may be a by-product of the attainment of the goal of having a well justified decision by each individual. Whilst a unanimously considered, justified decision will provide agreement, agreement alone does not ensure that the decision is justified. So what does agreement signify? At most, it indicates that the group has exhausted its resources in considering compelling alternatives and their justificatory force.

When disagreement is not taken to imply cognitive malfunction in the group, then either of two situations may be occurring. There is a set of concepts that relates to the issue being considered by the group and is used in formulating reasons and justification for the problem. However, because there can be human variability in the application of these concepts and in the construction of reasoning, it is possible that different conclusions may be reached. This is what Rawls (1993) tries to capture with his notion of 'burdens of judgment' in public reasoning. The burdens are various features of the human condition/situation that explain the inevitability of reasoners who employ the same concepts disagreeing about what conclusions the facts support. The other possibility is that there is not a single set of concepts that can be employed in the reasoning and disagreement stems from individuals using different concept sets and therefore different reasons. This will be explored further in Chapter 7, where ontologies are discussed.

COLLECTIVE REASONING AS A FORM OF COOPERATION

Whether or not disagreement is due to malfunctioning within the group, there is a place for collective reasoning. To make clear what we mean by this, it may be best to describe elements of reasoning. Figure 1 shows the elements that we have mentioned to date in our informal discussion of reasoning. It shows that facts are important and that the relevant facts can be taken as reasons. As well, there are reasons that may be rules, norms, or principles. A set of concepts underpins the facts and knowledge of the relevant area. From these reasons, judgments or decisions are made to determine an outcome on the issue or problem under consideration.

Reasoning by an individual results in a decision by the individual made on the basis of the outcome that the relevant reasons most strongly support. So individual reasoning is followed by an individual decision or judgment. Note that this is consistent with Pettit (1993) who distinguishes between an agent coming to believe something intentionally after checking the evidence and the agent coming unthinkingly to believe. He says that in the former case the agent makes a judgment. In the case of collective reasoning, we can consider cooperation as possibly occurring at the reasoning stage or at the judgment stage. So collective reasoning may occur by individuals cooperating in the reasoning that they do—the gathering of facts, assessing their rational significance (and their force towards intermediate reasoning steps and outcomes) as well as the possibility of cooperation in making a collective decision about which outcome the reasons most strongly support. Therefore, there are four possible sequences and two of these correspond to types of collective reasoning:

- **Individual reasoning:** individual reasoning followed by individual judgment
- **Individual reasoning followed by collective judgment:** not possible
- **Collective reasoning:** collective reasoning followed by individual judgment
- **Collective reasoning and judgment:** collective reasoning followed by collective judgment

In the second case, it does not make sense to have a collective judgment unless we consider some cooperative way of using the individual reasoning in a collective judgment. The most common way in which individual reasoning is followed by judgment is through the use of a voting scheme but we are reluctant to call this a collective judgment. In the second case of collective judgment, each individual would suspend their decision about what the collection of reasons supports until a conclusion that all can accept is found. The distinguishing feature of the fourth option is the movement to have the determination of the best justified course made collectively whereas the third option allows each individual to make their own judgment.

McMahon (2001) advances the view that the cooperation involved in collective reasoning is essentially the *pooling* of reasons. Each individual contributes to the group, the set of "presumptive facts" thought to be potentially relevant to the issue. Additionally, each individual offers arguments for these presumptive facts as well as arguments relating to the significance that they have in the problem being considered. So his idea of the *pool* includes facts, reasons and reasons that may be organised into arguments or criticised arguments.

Figure 1. Aspects of reasoning

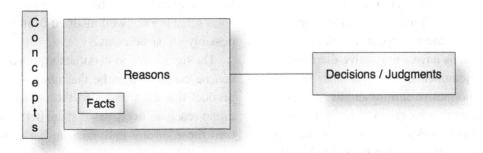

The two key ideas are *relevance* and *arguments for significance*. The creation of this pool benefits each individual in the group because it may be drawn on by an individual in making their own decision. He argues that this pool of reasons is a public good in that it cannot be provided to any in the group without being provided to all and any individual drawing on it to make a (better) justified decision does not diminish the opportunities of the others to do the same.

THE COOPERATIVE PRODUCT

According to McMahon, the product of collective reasoning is a pool of reasons and criticised arguments whilst the product of collective reasoning and judgment would be the pool of reasons and criticised arguments as well as a collective judgment. The pool is a public good and it can be used by individuals to make better justified decisions.

McMahon argues that there is no advantage in collective judgment over forming individual judgments based on the pooled reasons. In examining whether in fact collective reasoning followed by collective judgment (so that each person suspends judgment concerning what the pool supports until there is some conclusion that all participants accept), he identifies two distinct forms of consensus. *Piecemeal consensus* is a de facto concurrence of individual judgments, whilst *integral consensus* is one where accepting a position is conditional on all the other judgments. Saying that the product of collective reasoning should ideally be a collective judgment, then, is envisaging an integral consensus. To test the claim or presupposition that independent judgment is necessarily inferior to collective judgment he considers the nature of reasons. Reasons have a normative dimension - they justify judgments. This idea that 'reasons are abstract normative entities and that relations in an abstract normative realm underlie the status of certain facts as reasons' has led to attempts to find a place for normativity in the natural world.

One way is to invoke the psychological elements of desire and aversion, but this does not seem to provide what is needed and it may even be that the notion of desire presupposes taking something to be a reason. Therefore, this view provides no support for the case that the ideal outcome of collective reasoning should be a collective judgment. Another way of trying to fit normativity in is to invoke practices. 'A fact is constituted as a reason by a rule that warrants the drawing of a certain conclusion from facts of that kind, and these reason-constituting rules are grounded in practices.' Therefore, to make a judgment capturing the force of the relevant reasons is to participate in such a practice. McMahon also argues that this view does not distinguish collective judgment sufficiently as superior to individual judgment. This leaves us with an important position for decision-making in groups - integral consensus is not necessarily the best approach but a key stepping stone is to provide each individual with a platform for making an individual, well justified decision.

Without piecemeal consensus, the next stage may be to understand the imperatives for the community to reach agreement and so consider integral consensus—what the community would accept in the light of all judgments. If such an integral consensus cannot be found and there is an imperative to reach agreement then participants within the community may decide to negotiate with each other towards an agreed and acceptable decision. This approach is against the principles and endeavours of a reasoning community in that negotiation can be seen as a break down in reasoning to an outcome. Negotiation involves bargaining and trade-offs and so can lead to outcomes that are not well justified from many and possibly all participants.

The significant point is that the pool of reasons can be considered to be the major cooperative product that contributes to the possibility of a group reaching decisions that are better justified than those of any individual in the group. The cooperative product also allows each individual a means of achieving their individual best justified reasoning. Our aim is to focus on the best ways that reasoning can be supported in a reasoning community, so attention needs to be focused on supporting collective reasoning by considering ways of assisting the creation of something like a pool of reasons and also on how access to this pool can be provided to best develop individual decisions. This will be done in Chapter 4 where a framework based on separating reasoning structure from the internal ways of combining reasons to a conclusion, which we call inference, is described.

THE PROCESS OF COLLECTIVE REASONING

We have discussed the product of collective reasoning but not yet considered the process by which reasoning should proceed. Chapter 3 discusses individual reasoning in detail but McMahon takes the view that practical reasoning is 'the process that produces judgments regarding what the applicable reasons for action require.' Goldman (1999) has formulated rules of argumentation that guide the process by actions like anticipating objections and retracting claims previously made.

We could allow the cooperative product, the pool of reasons, to be constructed simply by the flow of discussion where an individual offers an argument and this is added to or rebutted with a record being kept as the basis of the pool of reasons and criticised arguments. The discussion ends when no one has anything more to say. However, it is important to recognize the importance of everyone having the opportunity to contribute to the discussion and contribute all that they think needs to be said. These requirements are often not met by the normal flow of discussion. The process of responding to contributions of others can be either more collaborative or more adversarial. When this point is considered in detail, it is precisely because the adversarial approach may discourage individuals from contributing that makes the

collaborative approach more likely to provide a richer cooperative product, or a more complete pool of reasons. Anyone who would contribute to the adversarial scheme would also contribute to the collaborative scheme.

Aiming to provide support for the process of collective reasoning within reasoning communities may take some different forms. In the first instance, simply making participants aware of the benefits of collective reasoning may have the effect of enhancing individuals' participation, their individual contribution as well as outcomes. Providing human facilitation for the processes involved in collective reasoning would be another way of supporting reasoning communities in collective reasoning. To some extent, these require an understanding of the process of collective reasoning to be able to impart this understanding and enable the practices that are of benefit in collective reasoning. In considering technological support there are various levels that need to be tackled. The understanding or conceptualization of collective reasoning has to be at least partially modelled and then the models used to develop systems that may either interface with human or other agents directly or indirectly. The latter aspect involves human factors and human-machine interface considerations. We now describe some models of human reasoning.

TOULMIN ARGUMENT STRUCTURES

Toulmin (1958) concluded that most arguments, regardless of the domain, have a structure that consists of six basic invariants: claim, data, modality, rebuttal, warrant, and backing. Every argument makes a claim based on some data. The argument in Figure 2 is drawn from reasoning regarding refugee status according to the 1951 United Nations Convention relating to the Status of Refugees (as amended by the 1967 United Nations Protocol relating to the Status of Refugees), and relevant High Court of Australia rulings. The claim of the argument in Figure 2 is the statement that Reff, an applicant for refugee status, has a well founded fear of persecution. This claim is made on the basis of two data items, that Reff has a real chance of persecution and that relocation within Reff's country of origin is not appropriate. A mechanism is required to act as a justification for why the claim follows from data. This justification is known as the warrant, which is, in Figure 2, the statement that 'The test for well founded fear is real chance of persecution unless relocation affords protection.' The backing provides authority for the warrant and in a legal argument is typically a reference to a statute or a precedent case. The rebuttal component specifies an exception or condition that obviates the claim. Reff may well have a real chance of persecution and relocation is unlikely; however, the claim that his fear is well founded does not hold if Reff's persecution is due to criminal activities.

Toulmin structures can provide a representation of reasoning, either individual or collective, as arguments with the components mentioned above. The representation enables identification of the components of a particular argument that are common and those that are different. The Toulmin structure only weakly represents the strength of an argument through the modality. A more useful approach for considering the weight of an argument is provided by Wigmore.

Wigmore Diagrams

Wigmore (1937) introduced a method of portraying legal arguments in diagrammatic form that have come to be known as Wigmore diagrams. They are similar to standard diagrams, using a box and arrow structure. A statement is supported by one or more other statements, and in turn can form part of the support of another statement. Wigmore, however, constrains the types of support allowed to the types of statement and inference used in a court case. The diagrams can be intricate and complex, Each statement in a Wigmore diagram is referred to as a type of evidence. Evidence can be affirmatory (supporting a statement) or negatory (arguing against a statement). Support arrows in the diagram are referred to as forces, and can have varying degrees, ranging from no effect to very strong positive or negative force. There are

Figure 2. Toulmin argument structure for well founded fear

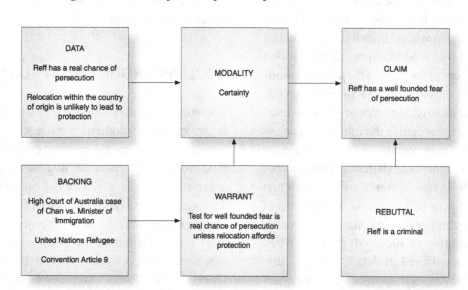

various types of evidence and forces used. Evidence falls into several broad categories. First, evidence can be classified by the party that offers it, typically either the prosecution or the defence. Then, evidence can be testimonial, circumstantial, explanatory, or corroborative. This Wigmore approach helps with the weighing of evidence that is important in making legal decisions.

IBIS

IBIS (Issues Based Information System) can be viewed as a model of the main elements of concern when groups address problems. It can be viewed as a grammar for making explicit representation of important elements in capturing and representing individual and group views and reasons on an issue. There are just three basic elements: questions or issues, ideas, and arguments (very simply represented as pros and cons) (Rittel & Webber, 1973). The ideas respond to the questions, offering possible solutions; the arguments argue for and against the various ideas. Questions can expand on or challenge other questions, ideas, or arguments. Figure 3 shows an IBIS representation of an issue concerned with how the Australian government should deal with unauthorised entry by 'boat people.' The basic elements of the IBIS model may be linked together in many ways to produce finite argumentation graphs. Using hypertext techniques, graphical user interfaces have been built for browsing IBIS graphs. The nodes of the graphs can contain arbitrary natural language expressions and other forms of media. Such systems can be quite useful for structuring and organizing information, despite their lack of formal semantics. Almost any creative conversation -brainstorming, design, planning, analysis, problem solving can be captured in terms of IBIS questions, ideas, and arguments. Dialogue Mapping is a problem-structuring method developed by Conklin based on the IBIS model (Conklin & Begeman, 1988). It uses IBIS as a grammar to provide an explicit on-screen representation of

the contributions of a reasoning (problem-solving) group. Contributions to the explicit, on-screen representation are usually facilitated by an external facilitator. This approach is one of many problem-structuring methods that try to elicit the different interpretations of a problem and reflect them back as a whole to the problem owners so that the richness of the problem can be tackled by all. The richness and complexity of the problem is a function of the number of individuals in the group. They usually involve a facilitator in the process of elicitation and reflection.

The Zeno argumentation framework uses a formal variant of the IBIS grammar to build (dialectical) argumentation graphs. The dialectical graphs show the state of an argument at a particular point in time and emphasize the role of speech acts rather than their history. Participants make positions (rather than propositions), which are records of a speech act. Whilst propositions are declarative statements (true or false), a position is a statement whose veracity is context dependent. Each chosen position of an issue is labelled either in or out to indicate whether or not it meets the proof standard selected for the issue. Zeno extends IBIS by including a means for expressing preferences and computing position labels. Given a set of preference expressions, it becomes possible to make inferences about the relative quality of alternative proposed solutions of an issue. A set of burden of proof standards was defined for this purpose. It is possible that more than one position may satisfy the proof standard for a particular issue. This enables interested parties to see whether their position is winning or losing at any point in time (Gordon & Karacapilidis, 1997).

Delphi

Delphi was originally established by Olaf Helmer and Norman Dalkey in the 1950s and developed in the 1960s by Turoff and Hiltz (Turoff, Hiltz, Bieber, Fjermestad, & Rana, 1999) as a tech-

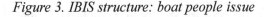

Figure 3. IBIS structure: boat people issue

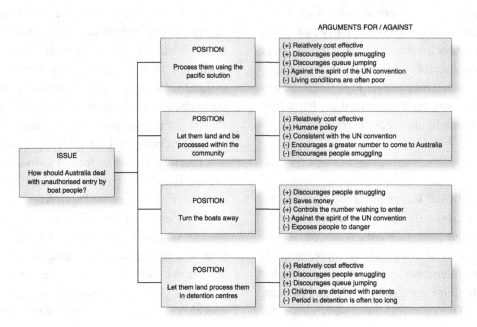

nique for technological forecasting and corporate planning. Since then its area of application has expanded to include many other contexts. Essentially, Delphi can be seen as a method for structuring group communication so that the process is effective in allowing a group to deal with a complex problem. Delphi is essentially a paper and pencil technique that uses a facilitator and has a heavy emphasis on obtaining agreement within the group.

The Delphi method is a structured process for acquiring and capturing knowledge from a group of individuals by utilization of a paper and pencil or (asynchronous/synchronous) computer communication process, in which repeated rounds of questionnaires, together with controlled feedback, are sent to the participants. The technique requires facilitators to collect, interpret and summarise the content of the discussion to help its participants to systematically explore and present their solutions to complex problems. These questionnaires are designed to help experts develop their responses to a problem by refining their views according to

the responses of the group. The heart of a Delphi is the structure that relates all the contributions made by the individuals in the group and which produces a group view or perspective. In a computer-based Delphi, the structure is one that reflects continuous operation and contributions. This is somewhat different from the paper and pencil mode where the structure must be divided into discrete rounds. The members should reach a consensus on the solution that is most acceptable to the group as a whole. This process may be conducted several times before the facilitator feels a sense of agreement and a certain degree of consensus is reached (Ziglio, 1996).

Key to the improvement of the quality of the results in a paper and pencil Delphi study is the analysis that the facilitators or design and coordination team can perform on the results of each round. This analysis has a number of specific objectives (Turoff, et al., 1999):

- Improve the understanding of the participants through analysis of subjective judgments to produce a clear presentation of the range of views and considerations

- Detect hidden disagreements and judgmental biases that should be exposed for further clarification
- Detect missing information or cases of ambiguity in interpretation by different participants
- Allow the examination of very complex situations that can only be summarized by analysis procedures.
- Detect patterns of information and of subgroup positions.
- Detect critical items that need to be focused upon.

Interpreting this in the vein of collective reasoning within a reasoning community, the facilitators or the design and coordination team analyse the contributions from each round and attempt to communicate to all participants the nature of the results. These results are akin to the pool of reasons but what is being done here in the analysis is a summarization, an identification of critical items that require focus, some exposure of biases and missing information so that each participant has communicated to them an overview of the group contributions. This can be described as a critical organization and communication back to the group.

ConSULT

The ConSULT approach (Afshar, et al., 2006) is based on a foundation, structure, and collection of various techniques that attempt to provide an environment for efficient and productive group discussions. The foundation is based on the value of diversity and different viewpoints, on cooperation and democratic principles of free and respectful deliberation of all the participants to resolve disagreements and conflicts through consensual decision-making. Although the structure is based on existing theories and techniques, it will

be flexible enough to be customised according to the needs of different situations. ConSULTs argumentation process has elements from both Toulmin and IBIS argumentation structures. Its procedural features resemble some of Delphis, and its outputs resemble a variation of the Toulmin argumentation framework.

Hitchcock, McBurney, and Parsons (2001) present a formal, high-level, five-stage model for deliberation dialogues which consists of:

1. Opening of the dialogue
2. Sharing of the information
3. Making proposals or counter-proposals
4. Confirming the accepted proposals
5. Closing the dialogue.

ConSULT follows an informal but similar structure for deliberations to the one presented by Hitchcock et al. (2001). As is illustrated in Figure 4, in searching for a consensus based on a shared understanding of a situation or a collective agreement to undertake certain actions, ConSULT adopts:

1. A deliberative, dialectical argumentation, in which the suggestions under discussion are provided by participants in an approach based on arguments, not opinions. ConSULT utilises characteristics of two argumentation structures:
   ○ C-TAS (ConSULT-Toulmin Argument Structure): to capture the data (suggestions) and reasons supporting it. (Opening of the dialogue)
   ○ C-IBIS (ConSULT-IBIS): to allow discussion by providing reasons for and against each suggestion (Making proposals or counter-proposals).
2. C-Delphi (ConSULT-Delphi): to provide a collection of all options for evaluation and voting by an approach similar to that used by the Delphi method (Sharing of the information)

Figure 4. Process of ConSULT

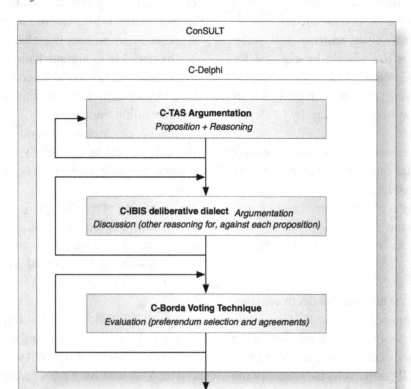

3. C-Borda (ConSULT-Borda): a variation of the Borda voting technique and a scaling method to enable the participants to reach a consensus based on their shared understanding (Confirming the accepted proposals; Closing the dialogue). For a Borda Count, each alternative gets 1 point for each last place vote received, 2 points for each second-last place, and so on.

4. C-TAS: The outcome represents the ConSULT version of all the elements of the Toulmin Argumentation Structure.

Although the ConSULT approach suggests a formal process for its participants to follow, the roles, techniques, and skills necessary for the smooth operation of this approach need to be upheld by all participants. In this approach individual reasoning is contributed and captured as arguments (Toulmin style), these arguments are discussed (IBIS style) and then the pool of reasoning is used with a Borda voting technique to move participants to a consensus based on their shared understanding.

In this approach, there is a focus on structuring the individual reasoning of participants so that the pool of reasons and reasoning is clear. The subsequent discussion focuses on coalescing the reasoning, not through the use of facilitators, but through the use of a voting technique that also includes the reasons. This may be best envisaged as a form of automated collective judgment.

The Generic/Actual Argument Model (GAAM)

The framework called the Generic Actual Argument Model (GAAM) (Yearwood & Stranieri, 2006) is a variant of the layout of arguments advanced by Toulmin. Reasoning is represented at two levels of abstraction: the generic and the actual level. The generic level is sufficiently general so as to represent claims made by all members of a reasoning community. All participants use the same generic arguments to construct, by instantiation, their own actual arguments. The generic arguments represent a detailed layout of arguments that are acceptable to all participants, whereas the actual arguments capture a participant's position with respect to each argument. The actual arguments that one participant advances are more easily compared with those advanced by another in a dialectical exercise because, in both cases, the actual arguments have been derived from a generic template that all participants share.

Figure 5 represents the basic template for the knowledge representation we call a *generic argument*. A generic argument is an instantiation of the template that models a group of arguments. The idea is that the generic argument sets up a template for arguments that allows the representation of the claim and the grounds for the claim. The claim of a generic argument is a predicate with an unspecified value (which can be chosen from a set when an actual argument is being made). Each data item is also a predicate with an unspecified value, which can be taken from a specified set of values.

One of the features of the generic argument structure is that it does not explicitly promote adversarial positions but insists that the structure be established so that arguments and counter-arguments can both arise from within the generic template. This is different from IBIS where the polarities in the argument slots appear explicitly.

The GAAM is essentially an approach that focuses first on the construction of the *generic arguments*. These capture, in a general form, the reasons that are relevant to the top-level claim or issue being discussed. This *Generic Argument Structure* (GAS) is the equivalent of the pool of reasons and criticized arguments. This structure is an explicit representation that can then be used by individuals to develop and represent their reasoning.

Figure 5. GAAM structure: what should Australia do about boat people?

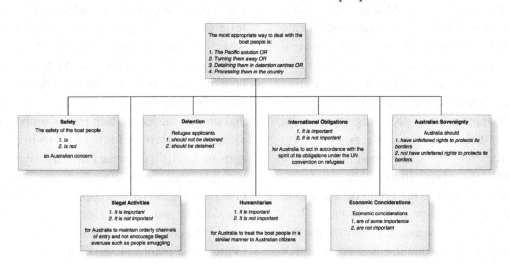

RECONSIDERING THE PRODUCT OF COLLECTIVE REASONING FOR SUPPORT

In its general form the product of collective reasoning is the pool of relevant reasons and criticized arguments. However, we have noticed that in the models discussed above, this can take different forms. In IBIS, a particular representation in terms of pro-and con arguments is used and various support tools exploit the IBIS grammar to reflect these arguments back to participants. Delphi uses facilitators to analyse the pool of contributions and re-challenge the group participants with the results in a cycle of rounds. ConSULT is a complex approach that represents the pool as arguments within a TAS structure and uses IBIS-based discussion and a Borda voting technique to assist in the reaching of a collective consensual decision. The GAAM collects the pool of reasoning in a slightly more abstract form as argument templates and provides the structure for participants to use in constructing individual reasoning and judgments.

The examples described could all be viewed as models that provide an approach for collecting, representing, and making explicit the cooperative product—the pool of reasons. In fact, in some cases, there is a mixture of model and system. Therefore, for example, in Delphi we glimpse more of the approach to producing the cooperative product as well as the final outcome and are less clear about the model. ConSULT uses several models arranged in a process that is used to lead the group through greater shared understanding to a consensual outcome. It is important to note that these approaches to providing groups with support for their decision making, problem solving and reasoning all identify and make use of the product of cooperation by either structuring it, communicating it to the group or structuring group and individual processes around it. It is evident that the approaches attempt to make this cooperative product explicit, either as a model or

schema or as a refined and restructured digest that is communicated back to the group.

Coalescing

It is clear that the Delphi technique takes the individual reasoning of group participants and performs analysis of these reasonings to provide some overall picture of the reasoning to date as well as conflicts and omissions which can be communicated back to the group. Therefore, in each round of a Delphi process there is:

- Individual reasoning
- A summarization of reasoning
- Communication of this to the group

The summarization of the individual reasoning of participants at the end of a round is, in effect, an attempt to coalesce the reasoning of the individuals into a single summary that can be communicated back to the group. The explicit representation is the summary and this is developed in a way that enables communication to all group participants. It has some focus on the main conflicts that are occurring and also on things that may have been omitted and may deserve consideration in the next round. This type of coalescing employs the intelligence and experience of facilitators to produce the explicit representation, which can be in the form of natural language, free text or, at most, what we might call semi-structured text.

Techniques based on IBIS try to capture the pool of reasons as ideas relating to the issue or as ways of solving the problem and then as arguments that support the ideas. Each reason supporting an idea/claim is classified either as a pro-or a con-argument. The IBIS grammar can be used recursively with questions further expanding questions, ideas, or arguments. So IBIS is used as a framework or template for gathering the ideas and reasoning of a group around an issue. The structure is also used to provide a graphical and visual representation of the collection of ideas and arguments that the individuals in the group perceive to be relevant. One tool that uses a visual display to present this to the group is Quest Map and this has been used in the approach called Dialogue Mapping to enable a group to contribute reasoning on an issue, create a visual map and have a sense of ownership and understanding in the group contributions to the map (Conklin, 2006).

Dialogue Mapping is a form of structural augmentation of group communication. As discussion within a group proceeds and the map grows, each person can see a summary of the discussion to date. The map serves as a "group memory," eliminating the need for participants to repeat themselves to get their points made.

Claimed benefits of Dialogue Mapping include:

- Each participant's contribution is recognized and included in the map.
- Each participant can see how their comments relate to others.
- The group sees from the map where they are, and the progression of the discussion.
- Using a shared display of the map helps the group to act collaboratively.
- The map increases the group's shared understanding of the problem at hand, possible solutions, issues, roles, and responsibilities.

Collaboratively constructing the map gives participants a sense of ownership in the map as an explicit representation of their thinking. In this approach, the map is the collaborative product and representation of the coalesced reasoning. Figure 6 (from http://www.cognexus.org/id41.htm) shows an example map generated by QuestMap which is a proprietary implementation of Dialog Mapping.

The ConSULT approach encourages participants to contribute their individual reasoning on the issue in a form that is based on TAS. Discussion of individual reasoning can occur between participants with support or disagreement captured in an IBIS-style representation. There are many stages here and participants can see all reasoning of all individuals before the Borda system of voting is used to move to a group consensus. Although various structuring methods are used, there is not a single explicit representation that captures the collective product.

The GAAM as a model concentrates on two levels of representing reasoning or argument: the generic level and the actual level. The underlying structure of each of these is the Toulmin argument structure. At the generic level, claims are abstracted to predicates that can be instantiated with a prescribed set of values. Any instantiation with one of the values obtains a claim. For a given issue, these abstract claims are gathered as the reasons that are relevant to the issue under consideration and the structured collection is called a *Generic Argument Structure* (GAS). A GAS captures in a graph the reasons that support the top-level generic claim on the issue as well as the reasons that support each of these individual generic claims. In essence, the structure is a diagram that is an explicit representation of the generic form of reasons that all participants contribute and agree are relevant in the way that the structure indicates. Therefore, the GAS is an explicit representation of the pool of reasons in an abstract form that captures the structure of reasoning on the issue. In this form, it does not represent any single individual's reasoning but should allow for an individual's reasoning to be made explicit by instantiation of the generic claims with values. The coalescing of reasoning and the product of collective reasoning at this point is the GAS. It is a cooperative product that explicitly captures the collective view of the relevant reasons, facts, and the way in which they interrelate.

In a broad sense, the notion of coalescing tries to capture natural ways to bring individual reasoning processes together in some common form but also to identify natural groups of agreement between individuals in a community as well as to identify the basis of differences in reasoning

Figure 6. A QuestMap screen: screen shot from dialog mapping website

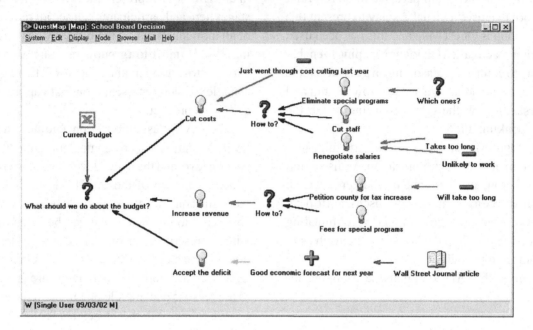

within the community. It is important to say that the notion of coalescing reasoning does not carry with it an expectation that the group reaches a consensus in its final judgment or indeed in their reasoning. Makau and Marty (2001) contend that 'Deliberative communities rely on diversity and disagreement to arrive at the fullest understanding of particular issues and to make the best decision possible under the circumstances.' It is important to be able to be involved broadly and critically with information and reasons surrounding an issue. If this can be achieved, then it is valuable to be able to crystallize individual reasoning to judgments on the issue that are understanding of alternative perceptions, views, reasons and values that underpin reasons and decisions.

APPROACHES TO COLLECTIVE REASONING

A number of examples of reasoning communities are described in Chapter 1 and illustrate the fact that in some reasoning communities' individuals have

to make judgments, whilst in others the decisions are seen to be made by a collection of decision makers. We contend that the best decisions are made by being informed of the collective set of reasons available in the community. In reasoning communities involved in collective reasoning, the community faces a question that is of concern to the individual members of the community to varying degrees. We assume that individuals in the community are interested in the answer to the question to the extent that they derive benefit from the solution, not in the sense of self-interest in the outcome or consequences of the outcome but in the sense of a well justified piece of reasoning. There are two defining characteristics of a reasoning community:

1. Individual members participate because each expects to achieve a better justified judgment or solution than they would be able to achieve alone;

2. The community exists to support both individual and collective reasoning without a

prior requirement of reaching agreement or consensus.

So individuals within a reasoning community expect to be able to reach an individual decision based on reasoning where the force of the reasons actually relevant to the question being considered has been explored in depth by the community. Four approaches to the way reasoning communities may operate was outlined above as:

- Individual reasoning, followed by collective pooling of reasons followed by individual judgment;
- Individual reasoning followed by collective pooling of reasons followed by collective judgment;
- Collective reasoning followed by collective pooling of reasons followed by individual judgment; and
- Collective reasoning followed by collective pooling of reasons followed by collective judgment.

We can now reconsider these four approaches incorporating explicitly the communication and pooling phase. The first case above corresponds to collectively supported reasoning to individual judgment or decision whilst the second is collectively supported reasoning to a collective decision. However, in the approaches that we have discussed, Delphi and ConsSULT collect individual reasoning at the beginning, whilst IBIS based approaches and the GAAM start by encouraging a different form of individual reasoning. This individual reasoning is abductive in the sense that the individual is looking to identify the factors that contribute to explanations of possible outcomes (or claim values) on the issue. The distinction here is that with IBIS and the GAAM the initial individual reasoning that is encouraged is more clearly directed towards an intermediate collaborative product rather than (at least) a first

pass at a formulation of individual reasoning towards individual judgment.

It is important to point out that in the case where there is disagreement within the community, there are situations where there may be a rational case for reaching agreement. That is, there is a significant overall benefit to the community in being able to reach agreement or provide consensus on an issue. If the disagreement in the group is not due to individual cognitive malfunction, then it would be useful if collective consideration of the issue could identify this and along with a clear rational force for agreement, come to a reasoned way of assimilating the added requirement for agreement. Given this, it is useful to consider whether there are ways of reasoning to agreement and again consider ways in which this process could be supported.

In Chapter 3, individual coalescing is discussed. Some of the ways of structuring individual reasoning can also be useful for structuring reasoning in general and so have application in the group context.

A View of How Coalescing Currently Works

The examples in Chapter 1 describe the way in which individual reasoning is underpinned by reasoning that has been coalesced through the human and group processes that have been developed in each of the areas. In law, the statutes summarise the current core of coalesced reasoning, sometimes in quite specific rules but often only as guidelines to decision makers. The process of coalescing comes through the accepted route of testing individual reasoning in a court. The potential to alter the current version of coalesced reasoning derives from reasoning that challenges the accepted rules, guidelines and principles. If this reasoning is accepted by the courts, then it changes the current version of the coalescent reasoning. Figure 7 illustrates an individual reasoner and/or their lawyer preparing their reasoning from the

Figure 7. Coalescing in a legal community

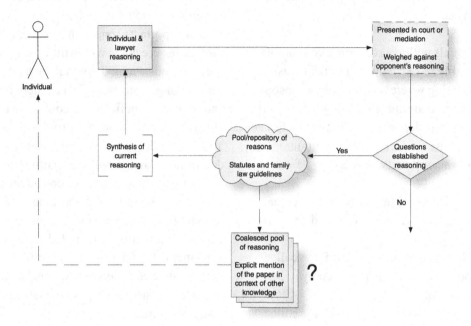

accepted law. This reasoning is put to the court or mediator community and usually a decision is made based on the law. If the findings of the court are not in line with the established law, there is the potential for this decision to become part of the case law that contributes to reasoning in the future or becomes enshrined in the law through a higher court decision.

In a scientific or academic community, the process of coalescing reasoning is one of testing individual reasoning through a process of independent peer review and publication. The process of publication adds to the pool or repository of reasoning but arguably is not coalesced until others within the community begin to use this reasoning to underpin further reasoning. Figure 8 shows the overall process, indicating that the individual is involved in the synthesis of the current reasoning in the repository. To this synthesis, they contribute their own reasoning to the relevant academic community. Their reasoning, through a process of peer review, is either admitted to the repository or not. That is, their contribution is

either published or not. At this point, their contribution is synthesized with the repository of reasoning, in this case publications, through the identity of the journal within that academic area. The figure also suggests that a more explicit representation of an individual's reasoning contribution in the repository, one that immediately updates the representation of reasoning in the area, may allow a more direct use of the coalesced reasoning by individuals for their reasoning.

In all of these communities, practice needs to be underpinned by knowledge of the current best reasoning in the area. The path from the most recent reasoning in the repository to its impact on practice and providing evidence for practice is critical for the most effective operation of the reasoning community. Medicine is just one example where there is a significant need for the evidence that is provided by the vast amount of medical research carried out and published in medical journals to be understood, accepted, and incorporated into practice. If the rate at which this happens could be increased, arguably the practice

Figure 8. Coalescing in an academic community

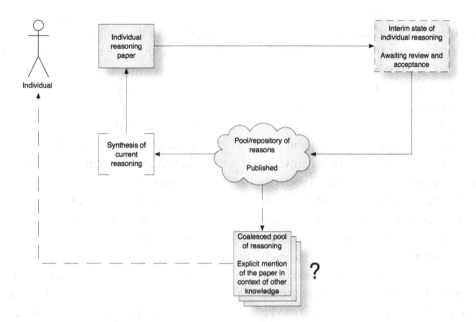

of medicine would be improved. There are of course different levels of latency involved in the process of coalescing and incorporating into practice in different reasoning communities. For example, the community of reasoning surrounding climate change might be a community that could be described as one where there is a large degree of latency whilst the degree of latency in a reasoning community surrounding market research into some product might be seen as having a much shorter latency. This latency is attributable to a number of factors:

• The delay in the process of designing the reasoning and this of course has to address issues and insights that come from having to resort to indirect measurements;

• The delay in gathering data and making indirect measurements; and

• The delay in coalescing the reasoning from its current state.

There is a need to identify approaches and technologies that are useful in addressing the last two points, but in particular the delay in coalescing the reasoning from its current state. At any point in time, there is a certain degree of coalescence of the reasoning of a reasoning community. In an academic community, there may be books or significant review articles that capture the reasoning to date but simultaneously there will be some reasoning that is new and has not been captured in this way. It is largely true to say that, currently, the pool of reasoning within a community would consist of natural-language documents, some of which would be consolidations of the knowledge and reasoning, individual pieces of reasoning as documents and of course there may also be implicit knowledge and reasoning that is not even in a written form. It may also be useful at this stage to point out that very often books and review articles have sole authors. Some of these have undergone the peer review process that is common in academic communities but they are rarely the collective work of the whole community. Therefore, the coalescing process is carried out by a few members of the community for the public good. It can only be viewed as collective pooling in the sense that the scholarly activity is the activity of positioning the reasoning of individuals contributed to the pool (in the form of articles), so that their reasoning and contribution forms a coherent representation of the total reasoning within the community. Without the consolidation that these review articles provide, each individual in the community has to perform a detailed and extensive review of the literature and perform their own synthesis of this. To some extent, the process of coalescing is a manual process of discovering and pointing out where each contribution to reasoning fits. What is also clear is that each new contribution (although it may do so internally) does not have the capacity to be synthesised into the current coalesced representation (review article) in an efficient way.

Currently, community repositories range from public and private libraries containing paper-based articles but more often now augmented with electronic documents, digital libraries, bibliographic and document databases, to some extent knowledge bases and of course the World Wide Web. Even in specialised reasoning communities, for example communities of reason in family law, access to the reasoning is through the usual search and information retrieval processes to which we have become accustomed. Parliamentary legislation goes through a process where periodic consolidations of the acts and their amendments are published. This represents a reasonably highly structured form of reasoning and consolidations are issued to provide ready access to the current state of the legislation so that individual reasoning in this area or reasoning that needs to be based on the legislation can be more readily and clearly undertaken. These consolidations act to reduce the latency in the process of reasoning but also achieve increased visibility, accessibility and usage of the community accepted version of reasoning on an issue. These are examples of current approaches to coalescing reasoning and it is reasonable to argue that this coalescing is done for the benefits it provides to the overall functioning of reasoning communities. We can make the following observations from the examples mentioned in Chapter 1 and above:

- Coalescing of reasoning within reasoning communities currently happens
- Coalescing is currently still a manual process
- Coalescing is a process of positioning the reasoning of individuals, revised reasoning or new reasoning relative to a body of reasoning
- A distinct form of coalescing that we shall call *individual coalescing* involves an individual integrating their new reasoning with the already known reasoning of the community
- A distinct form of coalescing that we shall call *community coalescing* involves the community in integrating the reasoning of individuals into the community reasoning pool or reasoning structure
- *Community coalescing* enables individual reasoning
- *Individual coalescing* enables collective reasoning
- The more explicit the representation of the coalesced reasoning the greater the efficiency with which it can be used, the smaller the delay in developing individual reasoning and the greater the prospects for reuse.

Simply having reasoning existing in unstructured repositories or even databases does not address the need for individuals to draw on the broader reasoning within a community. Arguably, a repository or simple collection of the reasoning of individuals or groups of individuals within the community is not a coalesced form of the reasoning in the same way that a synthesised literature review or a consolidation of legislation would be. Another form of coalesced reasoning is required that provides a synthesis and positions the key elements that appear across the repository (of reasons) relative to each other and relative to their influence on the outcome of the issue. Figure 9 shows the way in which we may currently think of the reasoning pool and the process of coalescing. Key aspects of tools that support the coalescing of reasoning will be structures, processes, and techniques for representing, presenting, and communicating coalesced reasoning.

WHAT DO CURRENT TOOLS DO?

The tools that are commonly used to assist groups in deliberation, problem solving, and decision making can be examined on the basis of the extent to which they support the coalescing of reasoning within the group. We examine the models behind three tools: Delphi, ConSULT and the GAAM. Further consideration of tools is given in Chapter 10.

Delphi

In Delphi, individual reasoning on an issue is used by facilitators to collect, interpret and summarise the content of the discussion to help its participants systematically explore and present their solutions to complex problems. Therefore, in its live synchronous form, a Delphi approach records and collects the discussion, interprets and summarises this so that the individual participants have a coalesced version of the current round. The questionnaires are designed by the facilitators to help experts develop their responses to a problem by refining their views according to the responses of the group. The heart of a Delphi is the structure that relates all the contributions made by the individuals in the group and which produces a group view or perspective. This structure, al-

though not explicit, is a key aspect in providing individual reasoners with a frame of reference. In this case the frame of reference is the group. The process is essentially the positioning process of the individual reasoning within the coalesced reasoning of the group. Again, we can notice that this coalescing is undertaken in Delphi and that it is essentially a summarisation process but also a process of communicating back to the participants how their reasoning sits relative to the group. In particular, points of contention within the group may be highlighted for careful consideration by the group.

The process of coalescing in Delphi is a manual one that focuses on problem solution rather than having a reusable representation of the reasoning within a community. The focus is also on having the group reach agreement or consensus on the solution to the problem or on the issue. The Delphi method focuses on moving the group towards a consensus on an issue and each iteration of the process works towards clarifying the issues and points of conflict within the group. A record of each iteration provides an audit trail in textual form of the trajectory of the group position and the disagreements that have to be tackled at the next stage.

It is clear that, within the Delphi context, agreement is an explicit goal. To the extent that agreement is valued by the group, Delphi produces a solution that delivers a consensual outcome. From the point of view of a reasoning community, it may not explicitly support mechanisms that allow either group or individual realisation (identification) of the extent to which their reasoning on the issue or problem has been compromised, mitigated, or perturbed. It is not clear that there is sufficient structure within the Delphi representation of reasoning to allow the explicit identification of the extent to which individuals or groups have relaxed commitments to various points or sub-issues in the overall reasoning process.

Figure 9. A view of the reasoning pool for a current reasoning community

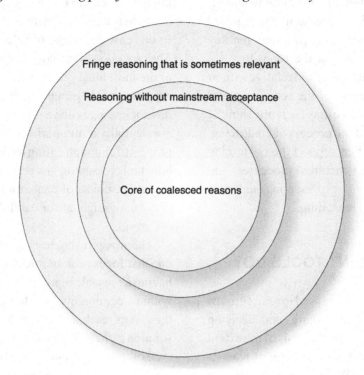

A reasoning community using a Delphi approach should have accepted consensus as the decision-making protocol. It is important that this is clear and reasoned as acceptable by all participants.

ConSULT

There is very little coalescing in ConSULT. It is very much a repository of individual reasons and individual responses to the reasoning of others with a view of bringing about a consensus through an automated voting process. In fact, in collecting reasons from each individual ConSULT explicitly captures and represents the pool of reasons. Furthermore, it is likely that individuals will use this repository to further coalesce their individual reasoning. However, there is no group coalescing, that is the coalescing of all of the individual reasons into a (reusable) form that each individual may use to make individual judgment.

IBIS

The IBIS grammar can be used to encode and represent individual positions on an issue. The grammar can be used to represent some of the structure in reasoning by graphs and argument maps that record and represent community and individual reasoning at the instance level. The structure itself is a useful form of coalescing reasoning on an issue. It is not clear that it has been used beyond this and therefore suffers from a reusability problem. This could be rectified, and the grammar could be more generally used as a coalescing structure

The GAAM

The GAAM focuses on having an explicit structure that captures and represents the pool of reasoning in the community. An individual reasoner can accept and make use of the generic argument structure on an issue or not accept it. In the case that they accept the existing structure, then they can use it to help develop their own reasoning in a way that is transparent to other reasoning participants who accept the structure. If the structure is not accepted by them, then they can embark on communication with others in the group on modifying the GAS to a mutually acceptable structure for reasoning.

A GAS is the heart of collective reasoning using the GAAM in that it is a structure for reasoning on an issue that is collectively agreed to by the participants of the reasoning community. It supports both individual reasoning and collective reasoning through the communication processes already described earlier. A GAS can act as an explicit coalesced representation of the community accepted structure or template for reasoning on an issue.

REPRESENTING COALESCED REASONING

Earlier, the way in which the reasoning is pooled and coalesced was discussed. The opportunity to reduce the latency in the ability of individuals to access the pool and obtain an overview of the resources became apparent. An effective, coalesced product of reasoning would reduce the individual effort required to synthesize a view and understanding of the pool for the purposes of constructing their individual reasoning. This would provide each individual with a springboard, the group coalesced structure, on which to initialize or contextualize their own reasoning.

Structuring Reasoning

One way in which coalesced reasoning might be represented is through the use of a structure. There are many structures that have been used for organising knowledge and are based

on the characteristics that need to be captured and represented. If we are trying to capture the main characteristics of reasoning then it makes sense that the notions of premise inference and conclusion are captured. Given the large range of reasoning instances, any ability to generalize these notions would also be useful. The GAAM is a model for structuring reasoning on an issue that has associated levels of detail that allow individuals, as well as groups, to represent and structure their reasoning. The GAAM model of using a generic argument structure to represent reasoning on an issue has already been described in Chapter 4. Each generic argument structure can act as an explicit representation of the structure of reasoning upon which a reasoning community has agreed. Individual reasoning can then be developed and individuals have the ability to identify points in common and points of difference within the structure.

A Community Normative Structure for Reasoning

It is arguable that a generic argument structure provides the norm for the representation and communication of reasoning and in doing so directly influences the individual reasoning process of each member of the community. In providing such an explicit structure for reasoning, there can be an acceleration of understanding and assimilation of the reasoning within a domain on an issue as well as an encouragement for the reasoning individual to subscribe to the structure and use it as a template for their own reasoning. Whilst there may be a fear that this is a strong encouragement to not move outside this structure, any reasoning community subscribing to the GAAM model would understand that the structure is owned by them and can be questioned at any time if individuals think that there are discrepancies or shortcomings in it.

A PROCESS FOR COALESCING

The process of coalescing reasoning on an issue can be carried out both by an individual and by a community. In the case of an individual we can consider the way in which this might happen as part of a reasoning community or as a sole agent albeit immersed in a greater social context.

Individual Coalescing

If we consider an individual in their broad social context as a part of a particular reasoning community then the task of coalescing reasoning can be challenging and may be undertaken to the extent that the individual's resources permit. The task of coalescing is one primarily of becoming aware and piecing together the existing reasoning of others on the issue at hand. In most cases, this activity would involve collecting what others have expressed or communicated on the issue and assimilating these in a way that gives a mental picture or model of the overall reasoning surrounding the issue. Some individuals may see this as understanding the main arguments surrounding the issue and formulating their own position against this background.

An individual within a reasoning community can either use the already coalesced reasoning or they can contribute to the community process of coalescing.

Community Coalescing

A community has at its disposal the resources of all of the individuals and this can be a great asset in collating and pooling reasons surrounding an issue. The additional concern that the community has to address is the agreement amongst its members on the inclusion of what is potentially a larger range of reasons and their assimilation and endorsement. This is often not an easy process and one that has to be carefully executed in a way that respects, values and avoids the suppression of diversity. If the benefits of diversity in reasoning are to be realized then it is important that coalescing allows places for these diverse reasons to be represented rather than to be summarised out of the picture. Therefore, the process should be one that permits the inclusion of a broad range of concepts and ways of reasoning.

Ongoing Change

The process of coalescing has to be seen as an ongoing activity, not merely because a reasoning community may be involved in reasoning concurrently with developing its reasoning pool and resources, but in order to recognise the fact that reasoning changes as society changes and underlying concepts drift in their meaning. For example, the concept of mail has changed over the last three decades to include e-mail.

COALESCING FOR AGREEMENT

We have considered an individual's motivation for participating in a reasoning community as the desire to achieve a better justified judgment or solution than they would be able to achieve alone. The community exists to support both individual and collective reasoning without a prior requirement of reaching agreement or consensus. Let us again consider the situation where there is disagreement in the community. Either the disagreement can be attributed to cognitive malfunctioning on the part of individual members or the disagreement has occurred without malfunctioning. In the case where the disagreement is attributable to malfunction, the recognition of the disagreement, within the context of the reasoning community, naturally promotes a tendency to have members critically review their reasoning and possibly identify the malfunction. The extent to which this process is supported by tools will be dealt with in Chapter 10. When the disagreement is not attributable to malfunction, then it is fair to say that a range of reasonable views on the issue exist within the community. There are, however, instances where the community itself understands that there is a rational case, or indeed some other accepted requirement for a single agreed outcome. That is, each individual accepts that cooperation towards an agreement will produce an outcome that would be regarded as preferable to the non-cooperative outcome from that individual's point of view and values.

The two most common approaches to resolving disagreement in the case of disagreement without malfunction are to agree, in the engagement phase, on a voting process and resort to a vote or to resort to negotiation between the differing individuals or factions within the community. From the point of view of a reasoning community, it is important to deliberate and support actions that are based on reasoning, to support the process of reasoning at all levels and to endorse actions, decisions and recommendations that are underpinned by the best reasoning. So, both of these alternatives, voting and negotiation, can be seen as the community abrogating its commitment to the value of reasoning at this point.

In the case of voting, most voting schemes have an underlying rationale. For example in straight majority voting, a community subscription to this would mean that there is agreement that the way forward from different positions that have been reached by groups within the community would be decided on the basis of the position that has greatest support in a simple numerical sense. Other schemes consider ways of enabling groups that have reached different positions to express a level of support for the alternative positions and try to account for this added information in some way. The result of any voting process means that there is a single position on the issue for the whole reasoning community. However, it is important to realise that this position is not one that has been reasoned towards by all in the community. Therefore, many individuals in the community support some alternative position by their reasoning and

collectively there may be alignment in reasoning support for these alternatives.

Negotiation may be agreed as the process that is used to reach agreement within the community. Each of the parties holding a different position would then attempt to reach a single agreed position. In doing so, each individual faces the question of relaxing their commitment to their reasoned position. There are many factors that influence the negotiation process and more importantly the outcomes from negotiation. It is also clear that the negotiation process can again motivate an examination of an individual's reasoning again as well as their commitment to each step of the reasoning. However, the outcome of negotiation can be strongly influenced by power, game strategies and intimidation. Over the last few years, a number of Web-based tools have been developed to support on-line dispute resolution and these take a range of approaches to negotiation (Bellucci & Zeleznikow, 2006). In negotiation theory, the best alternative to a negotiated agreement or BATNA (Fisher, Ury, & Patton, 1992) is the course of action that will be taken by a party if the current negotiations fail and an agreement cannot be reached. Generally, a party would not accept a position that they rated below their BATNA. From the perspective of a reasoning community where the stated aim is to support the position that is most strongly supported by reasoning, we have to consider the BATNA differently and distinguish between the BATNA with an emphasis on the best alternative reasoning to the negotiated alternative reasoning. Even if the bargaining is deemed to be rational in the sense of rational behaviour (there are theories of bargaining that elaborate on what constitutes a rational bargain), it still appears to be outside the realm of *reasoning* as we understand it in the reasoning community context. In the reasoning community, we are concerned with identifying the force of the reasons that are the ones agreed to be relevant to the issue. Acquiescing or conceding on the conclusion that is best supported by the relevant reasons would seem to be failure to uphold the value of reason to which individuals in the community presumably subscribe.

Consider an individual who is strongly wedded to a set of values that she regards as highly valuable features of the world rather than as a set of preferences. In many instances, reasons for action generate a ranking of possible outcomes and it is arguable that she can reason to the choice of the highest ranked outcome that is attainable. Therefore, it is quite reasonable to acquiesce to an outcome that is suboptimal in the case that the ideal is, in fact, not attainable. In a similar sense, if we accept that there is a certain distribution of bargaining power within the community, then in the case of working towards a solution through bargaining we may admit that no other result is attainable given this distribution. We can regard each individual as acting rationally with regard to their values by accepting the resulting outcome.

Let us examine more carefully how the community might deliberate to agreement in the situation of agreement that is not due to cognitive error. We mentioned above that one way of achieving agreement is for an individual to acquiesce by conceding from the values that she holds that underlie the initial disagreement. Therefore, either there is a reasoning process that can avoid these concessions on values or there is a reasoning process that can transform these values so that they are no longer in conflict. In the first case, it is important to recognise that there is a large set of values that is accessible to all, but that no individual can maintain commitment to all values simultaneously. This is because values provide reasons for action and acting on one value or in ways that promote one value will, often preclude action to promote another. The notion of a *perspective* is the set of values that provide an individual with reasons for action. Whilst it is often the case that an individual will choose not to alter or enlarge the set of values to which they are committed, it may be possible for each individual to recognise and accept a need for the group to subscribe to a broader range of values in a way that respects the perspective of each individual. This combining of perspectives based on combining sets of values may then open the way for reasoning from the group as a whole based on this more comprehensive set of values that each individual will accept in the context of the group but preserve the ability of each individual to remain committed to their individual perspective based on their individual values. Of course this does not necessarily provide a solution, in the decision phase, as it may happen that the combined set of values across the disagreeing parties is again too broad for the group as a whole to subscribe to and organise itself around in any practical way. In this case the problem of disagreement re-emerges. It is an important aspect of deliberation for individuals to become aware and accepting at certain levels of multiple perspectives.

Let us consider an informal but practical everyday example of a group of individuals that have just met up and are deciding to go to a cafe. We call this informal because there is most likely no agreement, either within the group or from an external point of view, that this group has set itself up as a reasoning community. A few of the individuals suggest a few different cafes and some discussion towards a decision ensues. Some of the individuals provide reasons to support their choice of cafe and on that basis each individual comments on which cafe they would prefer. The predominant view is that they should go to the new cafe that is two blocks away; however, Jane would prefer to go to a quieter cafe that is closer and where they would have a better opportunity to talk to each other. Jane's reasoning is based on the value that she places on communication in the cafe setting, but she is aware as a member of the group that they have always valued doing things together. The others' choice is based on their desire to try something new. Jane is prepared to modify her reasoning by relaxing her commitment to the value of communication and strengthening her commitment to the value of 'doing things together.' When she adjusts her commitment to her values and values held within the group in this way, she agrees with the others and agreement on which cafe to visit is made.

An alternative to the enlargement of the set of values to a group or community perspective is to recognise that in most instances reasoning is not seen as the rigid application of rules. In complex reasoning and decision-making, judgment plays an important role. For instance when a new case is encountered by a reasoning community, it is not always clear how the existing reasoning should be applied to this case. Determining the best decision for the new case can be quite complex. Cases where the rules are straightforwardly applied are known as 'easy cases.' The application of the rules and existing reasoning to the new case involves a process that might be similar to 'bending the rules' and in some instances this aligns with the notions of non-monotonic logic. The question is, in the context of a reasoning community, to what extent is the process of bending the rules a reasoning process and what are the characteristics of this process?

Let us focus for a moment on the difference between judgment and following the rules. Easy cases allow for the straightforward application of the rules that the community has endorsed. In a complex case, the first reasoning step involves identifying that there is difficulty in applying the rules. As a consequence, individuals come to a disagreement and this disagreement is not identifiable as malfunction on anyone's part. Rawls' (1993) "burdens of judgment" capture the experience that various features of the human situation lead reasoners who even employ the same concepts in reasoning on an issue can disagree about their judgments. With an easy case, the way in which the case is assimilated to the community's concepts stands out, but with a complex case it is less clear how the concepts and the case fit. The second step then is to try to see what the new case is saying about the past practice of the community, or at least their rules and most importantly the concepts underlying or

being part of these rules. In finding a way to apply a concept to a new case, the content of the concept may be altered. The concept itself is altered in a way that is determined by what the community interprets as the necessary impact from this case. The modified or 'evolved' concept then becomes the one that will be applied to future cases. This is usually seen as an alteration or extension based on the new case and as an extension or transformation of the old rule. It is the necessity to respond to the new case in a reasoned way that has led to this transformation. To this extent, the process of rule bending or rule modification to provide the best justified judgment in a complex new case has led to a reasoned approach that has overcome the disagreement.

SUPPORTING REACHING AGREEMENT

In the last section we discussed, in detail, ways in which a reasoning community could try to reason to agreement where there was disagreement within the community and this disagreement was not based on a cognitive malfunction of the individual reasoners. We argued that for a reasoning community the goal should be to reason to agreement rather than resort to a voting process or to negotiation and bargaining which can be seen as a move away from continuing to reason to agreement. We are now interested in revisiting some knowledge technologies and consider how they offer support for reasoning to agreement in the case where there is disagreement in the community.

In the GAAM (as discussed in Chapter 4), a generic argument structure is used to represent the coalesced reasoning of the community. Individuals make their individual actual arguments as instantiations of the generic arguments in the GAS and within each generic argument, there is a choice of inference procedures. Reasons or data items for claims are underpinned by reasons for relevance and have backings in the form of statutes, verifiable results, or evidence of some form. Each inference procedure has associated with it a reason and this reason is based on a certain approach to making an inference from data to claim. The reason for an inference procedure is usually associated with a certain value or set of values or principles -perspective. We have already described the dialogue that can be used to explore agreements and disagreements in Chapter 5. In situations where the community accepts that there is a desire to move to agreement, the GAAM approach allows a range of ways that reasoning participants can identify difference and understand the basis of the difference by virtue of the role that the point of difference plays in the structure. The two main ways of moving to agreement that we discussed in the previous section were to reexamine values and an individual's commitment to values and the bending of reasons. The fact that an inference that is represented in the GAAM has associated with it an explicit set of values means that the model readily supports individuals in an examination of not only their inferences in terms of the associated values but also the values associated with alternative inferences which are also explicit. This allows transparency to the individual and the group on the ways in which moves to agreement are made with respect to values. Of course, the GAAM also permits the inclusion of new inference procedures that might be coalesced from the new sets of values that are required to reach agreement. The 'bending' or modification of reasons translates into looking again at the relevant factors, how they are expressed, and the values that they can take and this is also supported in the GAAM and can be tracked through revisions to the structure.

In IBIS, the grammar of questions, ideas, and arguments is useful in capturing and representing the community structure of reasoning as well as individuals' reasoning. When there is disagreement, the sources of disagreement within this structure can be identified. The structure itself does not lead us to considerations of values although we think that this could be developed on top of IBIS. The

more formal systems, such as the Zeno argumentation framework (Gordon & Karacapilidis, 1997), that use the IBIS grammar do not focus on ways of reasoning to agreement. Because reasons in IBIS tend to be only represented at the instance level, the 'bending' of reasons would most likely appear as a rewriting of reasons.

ConSULT acts more as a pool of reasons without much structure, other than identifying reasons for and reasons against and support or rebuttal of each of these. Therefore, it does not explicitly offer support for linking reasons to underlying values or to 'reason bending.' Despite this, it is certainly flexible enough to have participants express these transformations in their communications. However, ConSULT (Afshar, et al., 2006) has an in-built voting process and, although this tries to factor in reasons, it is still achieves a judgment (and not necessarily an agreement) by resorting to voting.

At the outset, the Delphi process is concerned with reaching agreement and so it is a process that, at each iteration, identifies disagreements and tries to highlight these against the summary of the discourse so far so that the differences can be resolved. It is very possible that, if used in a reasoning community with the appropriate value placed on being able to present the best community justified case, then it could work to identify values and 'reason bending.' It is fair to say that it does not offer any explicit coalesced structure that supports either of these.

COLLECTIVE INTELLIGENCE

Complex systems evolve more organised brains to control the functions that they require. For example the neural networks in mice are very spaghetti like, but the brains of human beings have a highly organised laminar structure. The structure has evolved to best enable the requirements of the human brain. In the same way, we can appreciate the evolution of a reasoning framework that enables the knowledge surrounding an issue to be used to reason on this issue. The evolution of such structures arises from, or is driven by, the need to deal with increasingly complex issues.

The global brain is the idea of an intelligent network formed by human agents with access to a vast knowledge base or encyclopedia and communication technologies that interconnect them. Gershenson and Heylighen (2005) distinguished three main aspects of the global brain: organicism, encyclopedism, and emergentism.

These complex systems all seem to rely on a significant knowledge base with good communication capabilities. A reasoning community with a highly structured coalesced collaborative product is a form an actionable form for this notion of collective intelligence. This particular form with a highly organized structure could potentially perform even more complex tasks.

SUMMARY

In this chapter, we have focused on the nature of collective reasoning and have argued that, regardless of whether or not there is final agreement within the group, the quality of reasoning benefits from collective contribution to a product loosely called the pool of reasons. The quality of reasoning does not necessarily improve if collective judgment is then subsequently used.

As we are interested in the most appropriate ways of providing support to reasoning communities, we have examined the ways in which some approaches have been effective in supporting group decision-making and problem solving. It can be seen that these approaches support:

- The gathering of reasons,
- The use of a model or grammar, to gather and represent the reasons,
- The use of summarization,
- The use of abstraction,

- The use of graphical or hypertext models to make an explicit representation of reasoning.

It will be seen later that the models that are more formal and abstract (such as IBIS and the GAAM) often have higher-level support tools, whilst other approaches that have weaker models underlying the representation of reasoning tend to be associated with greater use of human facilitators in making the pool useful to the group.

In this chapter, we have examined in detail what coalescing reasoning means and how it can be supported. Coalescing of reasoning is done at the individual level and explicit examples, such as scholarly research papers are produced. Group coalescing of reasoning is not well advanced and neither are technologies to support it. In later chapters, we consider how knowledge structures, such as ontologies are used to collectively support reasoning; however, these are not coalesced reasoning. In Chapter 7, a very common form of reasoning is discussed, narrative, and ways of transforming from explicit reasoning to narrative are developed. Coalescing individual narratives is an important activity within a reasoning community and we have not discussed this in detail in this chapter. Nevertheless, the notion of group coalescing and of a coalesced product should be an important on that governs the process with narrative as with other forms of reasoning.

We have considered the case of it being acknowledged by the reasoning community that there is a benefit in reaching agreement on an issue where there is disagreement without malfunction of individuals in the group. In this case, the reasoning community moves to elevate the community reaching a decision that is its collectively best justified decision above the case of each individual reaching their own best justified decision. This preserves the focus of the reasoning community on reaching reasoned decisions and we have explored the ways in which this might still be achieved and the emphasis on reasoning preserved.

The next chapter takes us back to consider in some detail the processes around *individual reasoning*, but in the context of a reasoning community.

REFERENCES

Afshar, F., Yearwood, J., & Stranieri, A. (2006). A tool for assisting group decision-making for consensus outcomes in organizations. In Voges, K. E., & Pope, N. K. L. (Eds.), *Business Applications and Computational Intelligence* (pp. 316–343). Hershey, PA: IGI Global. doi:10.4018/978-1-59140-702-7.ch016

Bellucci, E., & Zeleznikow, J. (2006). Developing negotiation decision support systems that support mediators: A case study of the family-winner system. *Artificial Intelligence and Law*, *13*(2), 233–271. doi:10.1007/s10506-006-9013-1

Bonjour, L. (1985). *The structure of empirical knowledge*. Boston, MA: Harvard University Press.

Fisher, R., Ury, W. L., & Patton, B. (1992). *Getting to yes: Negotiating agreement without giving in* (2nd ed.). Boston, MA: Houghton Mifflin.

Fisher, W. (1985). The narrative paradigm: An elaboration. *Communication Monographs*, *52*, 347–367. doi:10.1080/03637758509376117

Gershenson, C., & Heylighen, F. (2005). How can we think the complex? In Richardson, K. (Ed.), *Managing the Complex: Philosophy, Theory and Application* (*Vol. 1*, pp. 47–62). Charlotte, NC: Information Age Publishing.

Goldman, A. (1999). *Knowledge in a social world*. Oxford, UK: Clarendon Press. doi:10.1093/0198238207.001.0001

Gordon, T., & Karacapilidis, N. (1997). The zeno argumentation framework. In *Proceedings of the Sixth International Conference on Artificial Intelligence and Law*, (pp. 10-18). Melbourne, Australia: ACM Press.

Makau, J. M., & Marty, D. L. (2001). *Cooperative argumentation: A model for deliberative community*. Long Grove, IL: Waveland Press Inc.

McMahon, C. (2001). *Collective rationality and collective reasoning*. Cambridge, UK: Cambridge University Press.

O'Brien, G. (2002). Participation as the key to successful change: A public sector case. *Leadership and Organization Development Journal*, *23*(8), 442–455. doi:10.1108/01437730210449339

Pettit, P. (1993). *The common mind: An essay on psychology, society and politics*. Oxford, UK: Oxford University Press.

Rawls, J. (1993). *Political liberalism*. New York, NY: Columbia University Press.

Toulmin, S. (1958). *The uses of argument*. Cambridge, UK: Cambridge University Press.

van de Ven, A. H., & Delbecq, A. L. (1971). Nominal versus interacting group processes for committee decision making effectiveness. *Academy of Management Journal*, *14*, 203–212. doi:10.2307/255307

Chapter 3
Individual Reasoning within a Reasoning Community

ABSTRACT

In this chapter, the nature of the process that each participant engages in individually in order to contribute to collective reasoning is discussed. The design of technological systems that will best support reasoning in its communal context requires the specification of schemes for representing knowledge and for the inference of new knowledge. Further, it is also necessary to articulate a model for the process that individuals engage in when reasoning in groups. The assertion we make is that the process iteratively includes phases of engagement, individual reasoning, group coalescing, until decision making. Representations, including the classical syllogism, first order logic, default reasoning, deontic reasoning, and argumentation schemes, are surveyed to illustrate their strengths and limitations to represent individual reasoning.

It is not really difficult to construct a series of inferences, each dependent upon its predecessor and each simple in itself. If, after doing so, one simply knocks out all the central inferences and presents one's audience with the starting-point and the conclusion, one may produce a startling, though perhaps a meretricious, effect.

Sir Arthur Conan Doyle (1859 - 1930), Sherlock Holmes in "The Dancing Men"

INTRODUCTION

A participant in a community of reasoning is involved in reasoning individually and independently from others though constantly communicates with others to exchange knowledge and insights. A reasoning community iterates through the phases of *engagement, individual reasoning,* and *group coalescing* until the issue and all views are sufficiently well canvassed that the group moves to the *decision* phase to reach an ultimate decision.

DOI: 10.4018/978-1-4666-1818-3.ch003

Within the *individual reasoning* phase an individual performs two main tasks:

- **Individual coalescing:** The coalescing, by an individual participant, of relevant background knowledge, facts, claims and reasons asserted by others.
- **Individual judgment:** The determination of assertions that an individual holds as their own.

Before launching into ways that reasoning has been represented, it is useful to step back and identify the kind of reasoning that is the focus of our attention. Broadly, reasoning types can be discerned based on the tasks to be achieved:

- **Spatial Reasoning**: High speed reasoning used in movement and balance.
- **Social Reasoning:** The type of reasoning which allows an agent to reason about other agents. In particular it involves the calculation of dependence relations and dependence situations.
- **Verbal Reasoning:** Being able to reason about future events and actions that might cause these is an important abstraction from the social reasoning mentioned above. Verbal reasoning can be the process of forming ideas by assembling symbols into meaningful sequences. Verbal reasoning can then be built into quite complex chains. Such chains can go on indefinitely, provided each link makes a valid argument by using the conclusion of the previously developed link as the antecedent of its conditional premise. It allows the expansion of sentences such as, If A then B into reasoning chains which are explaining, convincing or simply the sequence of steps that need to be executed to get to the destination.
- **Narrative Reasoning:** Narrative reasoning addresses situations that find difficulty in being addressed with the sequential form of verbal reasoning. The situations often involve multiple causes and multiple effects. Many social phenomena are like this and it would be fair to say that the great body of our accumulated social wisdom is expressed as narrative. Narrative reasoning could be viewed as an efficient way of dealing with complexity. Whereas verbal reasoning relies on long chains of logical steps, each small enough to be considered proven, narrative reasoning addresses situations that cannot be addressed in this way.

Other terms advanced as types of reasoning include practical reasoning, theoretical reasoning, diagrammatic reasoning cut across these areas of reasoning. Reasoning might be associated with thought in the abstract or thought without any representation or embodiment outside the thinker. More complex thought is built upon the communication of ideas with others and against the backdrop of an accumulated mass of recorded knowledge and ideas. This at least requires verbal reasoning but verbal reasoning soon reaches its limit. Very often, a complex verbal argument is found to involve circular reasoning or the fallacy of *begging the question, petitio principii, arguing in a circle* or *circulus probandi*. As depicted in Chapter 1, Schmandt-Besserat (1996) argues that writing was invented starting in Mesopotamia in the fourth millennium BC to create records that enabled traders and taxation officers to deal with complex arguments. Literature, history, and philosophy came later. Writing is a significant advance over unaided verbal processing because it brings reliable memory and permits greater examination and rigor to be applied to a piece of reasoning. However, as a representation of reasoning it suffers from certain disadvantages in terms of clarity as arguments become more complex.

Processes involved in individual reasoning are described in the next section prior to a discussion on ways that reasoning has been represented in the past.

INDIVIDUAL REASONING AS COALESCING AND ASSERTING

An individual in a community of reasoning must accept that the issue under discussion is the issue that should be discussed and is formulated appropriately. Workplace discussions concerning policies for public holidays may uncover that the pressing issue to be resolved actually concerns production targets. In addition to clarity that the issue under discussion is the appropriate issue, participants must share something of the purpose of deliberations. Although each participant may have their own individual and varied purposes for attending deliberations, they must share, to some extent, an understanding of the common purpose underpinning deliberations. Individual coalescing becomes difficult without a sense of this shared purpose. For instance, staff members engaged in deliberations about organizational processes may implicitly understand that the purpose underpinning deliberations is an increase in quality, efficiency, or morale around the workplace. Participants in an on-line debate about the introduction of nuclear power generation appreciate that the discussion is intended to impact directly or indirectly on government policy.

An individual in a community of reasoning involved in deliberations about custody proceedings will source relevant claims directly from other participants, from historical case or databases, law, scientific theories or from the broader community. Claims relevant to nuclear power generation reasoning include concerns about safety, efficiency, reliability, and environmental damage. These may be sourced from power generation stakeholders such as nuclear power groups, environmental groups, government departments, energy corporations and the wider community. Only claims relevant to the deliberation at hand will be of use to the reasoning community. For example, the introduction of claims regarding global warming are unlikely to be well received in custody discussions.

Participants engaged in individual coalescing within a reasoning community may not initially have sufficient background knowledge to understand claims advanced. A participant in a nuclear power generation discussion for instance, may not understand atomic physics sufficiently to fully appreciate the concerns others have of the dangers inherent in the storage of nuclear waste. A community of reasoning in Australian family law requires a substantial level of knowledge of family law and the legal system. Newcomers to the community will need to source and process background knowledge in order to fully appreciate claims made by others and, ultimately, to assert their own claims.

Individual coalescing differs from group coalescing because it is performed by and for a participant, from the perspective of that participant. Group coalescing refers to the process of organizing claims and background knowledge for the purposes of producing a structured account of group reasoning. Group coalescing is performed to facilitate clarity and deliberation within a community and to ensure a permanent record of the entire reasoning is maintained for use by future reasoning communities. Group coalescing could be performed by an independent purveyor of a community or it could be performed by participants themselves collectively.

A wide variety of schemes for the representation of knowledge and reasoning have been advanced throughout history. Structures based on narrative, logic, networks, ontologies, and arguments can all be regarded to be devices that facilitate the individual coalescing of reasoning. However, many schemes are closely associated with the mechanisms used to infer new claims. For example, the inference rules called modus ponens in propositional logic, provides a mechanism for inferring a new proposition given other propositions. In the argument scheme advanced by Toulmin (1958) claims and background knowledge are depicted as data, backing, warrant, modality, claim, and rebuttal.

Structures for representing reasoning based on narrative hold a special place in individual reasoning. The individual coalescing a participant engages in to initially understand an issue and then to form beliefs prior to their assertion can sometimes be modelled using a narrative framework as opposed to a more structured representation such as a first order logic, or a semantic network. Individuals do not initially articulate their thought processes as clauses in a logic or other forms of abstract notations; rather they tell a story that weaves together the facts and reasons underpinning an issue.

Aristotle is attributed with at least one of the earliest written accounts of the study of thought which he felt to be the basis of all knowledge (Aristotle, 2006). The advancement of the classical syllogism by him was an early attempt to describe the inference of new knowledge in a systematic way. The syllogism led to more formal systems of logic including the propositional and predicate calculus much later in history. Following the development of logic programming languages in recent decades, a spate of non-monotonic logics that extend predicate logics by enabling uncertainty and open texture to be represented have been advanced. In somewhat of a recent tangent, informal schemes proposed by Toulmin (1958) and also by Rittel and Webber (1984) represent reasoning using schemes that are intuitively appealing, though not formally specified. The classical syllogism, predicate logic, the non-monotonic logic called default reasoning, deontic logic, and Toulmin layout of arguments and the Issue Based Information System (IBIS) will be described in this section.

Narrative

Aristotle, in the Poetics was one of the earliest to analyze narratives and identify their elements and structure. He focused on tragedy, and identified six main components: Action, Character, Thought, Language, Pattern, and Enactment. In enactment,

Muthos (plot) and Mimesis are the two main concepts. Mimesis is the representation of action and behaviours. Muthos is the arrangement of the events that form the overall plot. The structure of the plot was central in constructing narratives.

In drama, the author constructs a plot that is supposed to explicate a theme. The formal cause is the authorial view of the play. The characters are determined by the plot and so plot is the formal cause of the characters. The characters' thought processes are determined by their nature; the language spoken by them is determined by their thought, and the spectacle presented to the audience is determined by the enactment of the characters. Consider a narrative that depicts a dramatic scenario of a small reasoning community of two pilots faced with a mid-flight crisis:

The plot begins with the aircraft shuddering violently and smoke entering the cockpit. The chief pilot imagines the passengers are in a panic. He expresses frustration at not being able to see the engines and hears from his colleague that smoke can only enter the cockpit through the air conditioning system which is driven by the right hand engine. He believes this engine to be at fault and infers that it must be shut down. His co-pilot agrees and the engine is shutdown. Immediately, the shuddering ceases to the immense relief of passengers and pilots. Although some of the passengers can still see flames from an engine, they assume and hope that all is well and do not inform the crew of the continued flames. In the relative calm of smooth flight, the pilots re-examine their coalescing and assertions and modify their flight plan to land at the nearest airport.

An alternative story is now immediately considered.

The plot begins with the aircraft shuddering violently and smoke entering the cockpit. The chief pilot imagines the passengers are in a panic. He expresses frustration at not being able to see the

engines and hears from his colleague that smoke can only enter the cockpit through the air conditioning system which is driven by the right hand engine. He checks the vibration monitor and is puzzled by the indication that the left engine is shaking, not the right. He asks his chief steward for a visual inspection of both sides of the plane. The steward phones in some alarm that flames can be seen from the left engine. Perhaps the assumption that the air-conditioning is solely derived from the right engine is incorrect. The co-pilot agrees and, in this story, the left engine is shut down. Immediately, the shuddering ceases to the immense relief of passengers and pilots. In the relative calm of smooth flight, the pilots re-examine their coalescing and assertions and modify their flight plan to land at the nearest airport.

Both narratives are plausible and indeed are derived loosely from an actual and tragic incident that resulted in many deaths. The main contention advanced here is that this kind of reasoning, performed by an individual is often narrative in nature. The reasoning is full of context, has characters and a plot. Events that occur follow on from previous events in a plausible manner. The reasoning is not particularly well structured or abstracted. However, the reasoning in narrative form is natural and as Pennington and Hastie (1992) note at least jury members seem to reason in this way.

During individual coalescing, a participant may abstract from the narrative to other structures in order to more clearly identify reasons. The contention here is that the process of deploying narrative for individual coalescing occurs in all reasoning communities. Participants in communities that involve many participants or complex issues transform their narrative reasoning into more structured representations for specific purposes. The transformation is always an abstraction and as such, loses some information. However, rather than viewing narrative reasoning as an inadequate representation of reason, we view narrative rea-

soning as the first, most natural and most rich form of reasoning when reasoning is performed in a community. Further, in some situations, the transformation of narrative reasoning to more structured representations advances some tangible benefit for individual coalescing. However, the transformation of narrative to more structured representations is indispensable for group coalescing, particularly for larger, more complex reasoning communities.

Individual judgment involves the inferences made by story characters that underpin their actions. This is woven naturally into a narrative as events unfold causally from other events. In the classical syllogism discussed next, inference is explicitly separated from the coalescing of knowledge.

Individually coalesced narratives and ensuing judgments are communicated naturally to others as stories. In Chapter 6, the importance of narrative in the human experience and reasoning is analyzed. However, the features of narrative that enable other participants to identify, empathize and understand a personal story are the same features that thwart the coalescing of knowledge and the re-use of reasoning. Claims, facts, and beliefs are typically expressed implicitly and indirectly in a story through the setting, characters, and actions. In Chapter 9, we illustrate how smaller reasoning communities such as those involving a single patient and doctor do not expect their reasoning to be re-used and are more likely to rely on narrative based coalescing and communication of reasoning. Larger communities, such as deliberative democracy forums discussed in Chapter 8 that do not structure reasoning in more explicit ways than narrative can provide, run the risk of being too long winded, inefficient and prone to misunderstandings.

As alluded to above, Aristotle is attributed with one of the first analytic studies of narrative and also one of the earliest written accounts of the study of thought that resulted in the classical syllogism as a way to describe the inference of new knowledge in a systematic way. The classical syllogism and how it relates to the reasoning a community of participants engage in, is discussed next.

Classical Syllogism

Aristotle, in his Prior Analytics (Aristotle, 2006) investigated whether certain sentences can be said to be true because they are related to other things; the now well known syllogisms. He defines syllogism as:

a discourse in which, certain things having been supposed, something different from the things supposed results of necessity because these things are so.

Prior and Posterior Analytics Book 1 (Aristotle, 2006)

Having defined a syllogism broadly Aristotle then describes the syllogism as having a rigid structure comprising a major premise sentence, a minor premise sentence and an inference rule that enables a third sentence to be inferred as new knowledge. For example:

> **Major premise:** All men are mortal
> **Minor premise:** Socrates is a man
> *Therefore*
> Socrates is mortal

The syllogistic layout of reasoning helps to make explicit, in a systematic fashion, the way in which the new knowledge that Socrates is mortal is inferred. Background knowledge, facts and claims; indeed everything in a narrative representation are compressed into a minor premise and major premise in the classical syllogism. The syllogism is a device for individual coalescing of reasoning. However, the syllogism abstracts away a great deal of the context and emotion present in most narratives so background knowledge, facts, and claims are modelled in a very rudimentary way.

The syllogism does not include a representation of the purpose of the reasoning. For example, the syllogism above could conceivably be used to counter claims by adoring students of Socrates who claim that he remains forever immortal in their hearts. Such context adds quite a different flavour to the interpretation of the syllogism. The source of the major premise or the minor premise is not questioned in the classical syllogism because that schema solely draws attention to the idea that if the major and minor premises are true the conclusion can be inferred. In practice, premises are almost never universally true or universally false. Further, the minor premise is assumed to be relevant to the major premise. However, the concept of relevance is far from straightforward.

In human practical thinking, the conditional between two propositions depends not only on the truth of the two propositions but also on some causal relationship between them (Cheng 1996). The propositions: All fish are mortal, Socrates is a man are considered *true* however the conclusion that Socrates is mortal would be rejected by human practical reasoning on grounds that the propositions are not relevant; a fish is not a man. *Relevance logic* was brought to the attention of mathematical logicians by Ackermann (1956) and tries to provide a mathematically satisfactory way of grasping the idea of relevance in implication. It makes sense that in practical reasoning the search for the premises be constrained to those that are the relevant grounds.

Another limitation of the syllogism for representing the individual reasoning within a community of reasoning concerns a deep knowledge of the meaning of premises. For example, the sample syllogism about Socrates presumes an understanding of the concept of mortality. Without this, background knowledge defining mortality is required in order to appreciate new claims inferred. The classical syllogism presumes all background knowledge required to understand the major and minor premises have been sought.

The syllogism organizes claims into a general rule and a statement of fact. A representation about the strength of claims is not required because both are assumed to be true for the syllogism to hold. Numerous fallacies such as the fallacy of drawing claims by appeals to emotion or to force can be seen to be methods that derive from claims that appear to be organized as a single general rule and statement of fact but are actually not.

The use of the syllogism is limited for describing real world arguments because few premises can be found with universal appeal. Even the premise, 'All men are mortal' may seem universally true; however, its veracity depends on precisely how terms, *man* and *mortal* are defined.

Individual judgment is represented in the classical syllogism with inference rules. Formalization of reasoning occurred two thousand years after Aristotle's syllogism by Frege (1884), Whitehead and Russell (1913), and others. The formal development of logics could be seen as one of the main efforts in studying reasoning. From this point of view, we might see logic as a representation as well as a formalization of reasoning. The scope of logic has changed immensely since Frege. It encompasses First Order Predicate Logic (FOPL), deontic logic and includes many non-monotonic logics such as default logic, defeasible logics, and para-consistent logics. The representation of reasoning as well formed formulas with a formal calculus of syntax and semantics has formed the basis of computational reasoning to date and is discussed next. Modern logics maintain the separation of individual coalescing and individual judgment, though, have more sophisticated representations for each process than the classical syllogism. The first order predicate logic is discussed next.

First Order Predicate Logic

First order logic extends the syllogism with the use of predicates, variables and quantifiers. Sentences in predicate logic comprise predicates, literals, and connectives. In the FOPL sentence man (Socrates), *man* is a predicate and *Socrates* is a literal. The rule, $\forall X \; man(X) \Rightarrow mortal(X)$, read as *For all X, if X is a man, X is mortal*, uses the *implies* connective, the variable X and the universal quantifier $\forall$ to capture the scope of the variable. A FOPL database includes all sentences that are known to be true. First order logic provides greater clarity about knowledge known or inferred to be true than does the syllogism.

Computer implementations of FOPL such as Prolog include an algorithm called unification that searches for, and attempts to match predicates, variables, and literals. Presented with a task to find all men that are mortal, the unification algorithm will return *Socrates* after matching the variable X with *Socrates* and the *m*an predicate with the clause $\forall X \; man(X) \Rightarrow mortal(X)$. The unification algorithm is however a small step toward the automation of individual coalescing.

Though the unification algorithm is not part of FOPL which defines inference for individual judgment, its association with the logic represents an advance over the syllogism because it is a mechanism for searching for plausible evidence to infer new claims. As all clauses in a FOPL database are assumed to be true the need to search for clauses involves searching systematically through the sentences for matches. As is the case with the classical syllogism, relevance is not taken into account so propositions are assumed to be relevant to each other and conclusions.

The FOPL is monotonic in that knowledge can be added to the database of true sentences without the need to remove existing sentences. This is because inferences are deductively valid so the addition of any new sentence will not alter inferences. Further, in computer implementations like Prolog, an assumption is made that if a sentence is not in the database then it is assumed false. This is known as the *closed world assumption*. Unless there is a fact in the database that indicates Socrates is a man then the assumption is made that he is not. Prolog implements the closed world assumption by defining the negation of a clause as the failure to prove its truth. Sergot et al. (1986) identify drawbacks inherent in this assumption when applied to legal reasoning.

The monotonicity of FOPL and the limitations of the closed world assumptions have triggered the development of a range of non-monotonic logics. A representative non-monotonic logic, default reasoning is discussed below. Claims are organized in a FOPL database as facts and rules though both can be made more general with the use of variables. An assessment of the strength of claims is not required in the FOPL because all claims inferred are presumed to be true. Categorising claims into those to be adopted as beliefs or goals is sidestepped because inferred claims are also assumed true.

First order predicate logic is not well suited as a model of individual coalescing for similar reasons that the classical syllogism is not well suited. First of all, there is no scope for the representation of the purpose of inference. Further, although FOPL, with its use of variables, allows for more abstract concepts than the classical syllogism, the insistence that propositions be universally true and thus non-contradictory, militates against the use of FOPL for practical reasoning.

FOPL has been applied to model reasoning in a wide variety of applications, particularly since the introduction of the Prolog language. However, FOPL proved to be limiting for many real world applications and is clearly too restrictive for widespread use in a community of reasoning. This is not to say that FOPL cannot be usefully applied within restricted domains.

The communication of knowledge that has been coalesced as FOPL clauses allows more scope than the syllogisms. A deductive database is a logic program that performs inferences by drawing on a database of facts and rules (Ceri, Gottlob, & Tanca, 1990). Deductive databases can conceivably present a rich depiction of the facts and beliefs held by an individual. Passed to others in the community, the database contains all the information required to ascertain the participant's

individual judgment. Although more expressive than the syllogism and more explicit than narrative, the FOPL still leaves little room for disagreement between community participants. Limitations of predicate logic were addressed with the introduction of non-monotonic logics. Default reasoning, a non-monotonic extension to predicate logic is discussed next.

Default Reasoning: A Non-Monotonic Logic

Default reasoning, advanced by Nute (1994) is a variation on the FOPL that can conceivably be applied for individual coalescing and judgment in a more sophisticated way than its precursor. Antoniou (1997) provides a description of default reasoning and illustrates numerous applications. Default reasoning has two types of rules: hard rules and defeasible rules. Hard rules are the same as FOPL rules. Defeasible rules differ in that rules can be defeated by other rules that have greater force. A preference relation ranks rules according to their force. An example from Governatori and Stranieri (2001) describes the regulation of airspace. When two aircraft are on converging headings at approximately the same height, the aircraft that has the other on its right shall give way, except that power-driven heavier-than-air aircraft shall give way to airships, gliders, and balloons. This norm can be represented in defeasible logic as follows:

1. $\neg$ rightOfWay(Y,X) $\Rightarrow$ rightOfWay(X,Y) Given two aircraft, if one has the right of way the other cannot also have it.
2. $\neg$ onTheRightOf(X,Y) $\Rightarrow$ rightOfWay(X,Y) If an aircraft is on the right of another it has the right of way
3. powerDriven(X), $\neg$ powerDriven(Y) $\Rightarrow$ $\neg$ rightOfWay(X,Y) Power-driven aircraft do not have right of way over non power-driven craft.

4.   balloon(X) ⇒¬ powerDriven(X) Balloon aircraft are not power-driven
5.   glider(X) ⇒¬ powerDriven(X) Gliders aircraft are not power-driven
6.   powerDriven(X) (assume power-driven) If it is not known if a craft is power-driven or not, assume it be power-driven
7.   fact: glider(myGlider)
8.   fact: powerDriven(myPlane)
9.   fact: onTherightOf(myGlider, myPlane)

Rule preference relations: rule 1 > rule 3; rule 3 > rule 2; rule 4 > rule 6; rule 5 > rule 6.

The default reasoning extends first order logic by providing a new way to organise claims. The rule preference relation orders those claims that are default rules according to their force or strength. The inference of new claims differs from first order logic because the force or strength expressed as a rule preference relation is taken into account. Therefore, if myPlane and myGlider were in the same airspace and myGlider was on the right of myPlane then by rule 5, the reasoner infers that myGlider is not power driven, and by rule, 2 could infer that myPlane has right of way because it is on the right. However, by rule 3 the opposite is inferred because myGlider is not power driven and myPlane is, so myGlider has the right of way. The rule preference relation is used to resolve this ambiguity in favor of myGlider because rule 3 is stronger than rule 2.

Default reasoning permits contradictions so can represent competing assertions collected during an individual coalescing exercise. The specification of a rule preference relation enables an individual judgment to be reached. This is more flexible than the syllogism and FOPL however the organization of knowledge is still quite restrictive. Approaches known as modal logics permit contradictions by introducing operators that specifically represent clauses that are not known to be universally true. Deontic logic is closely related to modal logics that have operators including *obligatory*, *permissible,* and *prohibited*. Deontic logic, discussed next, differs from default reasoning in that the latter permits contradictions and uses rule preference relations to select one inference over others. Deontic logic permits contradictory clauses with the use of special operators.

Deontic Logic

The modern deontic logic, introduced by von Wright (1951) and expanded upon by McNamara (1996), exists in numerous forms that differ from each by the modalities (operators) defined and axiomatic assumptions. All versions have three main modalities:

- **It is obligatory that**... (OB). For example. It is obligatory that vehicles travel faster than 60km per hour on the freeway
- **It is permissible that**... (PE). For example. It is permissible for vehicles to travel between 60km and 100km per hour on the freeway
- **It is prohibited that**... (IM). For example. It is prohibited for vehicles to travel faster than 100km per hour on the freeway

Deontic logic naturally represents norms. Norms are statements made to tell us something about the world or how we want the world to be. For instance, a prevalent kind of norm is one that prescribes the regulation of some action. The purpose of the three statements above is to regulate the action of driving down a freeway. A norm differs from other statements because it does not describe what is true in the world. On any day, on any freeway, it is true that vehicles travel at speeds that are not at all consistent with the norms. Norms prescribe what the freeway ought to be like so are not true or false in the same way that a fact that my vehicle is traveling 120 km per hour is true.

Jorgensen (1937) noted the deontic modalities including obligation, permission and prohibition cannot depict true sentences because they represent norms which are sentences that do not describe what is true about the world. The observation is known as Jorgensen's Paradox. However, the paradox is resolved if we assume that the norm itself describes something true about the world; that there is a statute that dictates that drivers of vehicles travelling faster than 100km per hour will be prosecuted. This involves interpreting the norm as a normative proposition

Deontic logic axioms have been defined that involve the modalities, obligation, permission and prohibition. Typically, the axioms give rise to paradoxes that serve to highlight logical problems with the axiomitazation. The paradox raised by Chisholm (1963) known as Chisholm's Paradox arises because some norms are conditional.

1. Jones has an obligation to go to the assistance of his neighbours. This is depicted as OB(go)
2. If Jones goes, then he has an obligation to tell them he is coming. OB (go ⇒tell).
3. If Jones doesn't go, then he ought not tell them he is coming. OB(¬go ⇒OB ¬ tell).
4. Jones doesn't go. ¬ go.

The standard deontic logic SDL axiomitazation will lead to contradictory inferences of *tell* from the first two statements and *not tell* from the second two. The problem arises because the second statement is a conditional obligation; an obligation to tell them he is coming that only holds if he is going. Chisholm's paradox can superficially be resolved by preferring the inference that derives from the observable fact *Jones doesn't go*, called Factual Detachment over the inference that derives from the obligation, called Deontic Detachment, or vice-versa. However, either approach has limitations.

Jones (1990) and Jones and Sergot (1992) have promoted the adoption of deontic logic for legal reasoning. Law is readily regarded as an entire system of norms so deontic logic seems naturally suitable. Prakken (1996) describes the integration of deontic operators with Reiter's non-monotonic logic to yield an approach that overcomes some

of the limitations of deontic logic alone that is particularly adept at modelling legal reasoning. By the late 1990s, according to Wieringa and Meyer (1998), a number of applications of deontic logic to law had been developed including systems that modelled company policies, normative integrity constraints, and scheduling under normative constraints. A common thread across the diverse applications was that the difference between actual and ideal behaviour was particularly pertinent.

In a similar vein to the classical syllogism, first order logic, and default reasoning, deontic logic does not model reasoning involving a group of participants. An emphasis is placed on the veracity of inferences and contradictions, whilst permitted, are constrained to those pre-defined by the modalities. Although deontic logic neatly represents norms, there is little scope to represent the context, purpose, and reasons underpinning assertions.

Verbal reasoning, written reasoning, and the formalization of reasoning with logic have brought us a long way in terms of being able to deal with complex reasoning tasks. However, they still require a considerable cognitive load for human understanding of the reasoning or a considerable computing power to carry out the search required to make appropriate inferences. Further, they are far from effective for representing the processes apparent within a reasoning community.

Toulmin's (1958) approach was to look at practical reasoning from the point of view of arguments. He observed that arguments lead not to things that are absolutely true but more to qualified assertions or defeasible conclusions. He relaxed concerns with the formalisms of arguments in terms of formal logic involving premises, connectives, operators, and conclusions and focused on arguments as claims supported with varying force, by data and warrants. The Toulmin structure of arguments is then discussed below. The next section outlines attempts to use diagramming represent aspects of reasoning.

Representing Reasoning as Diagrams

The field of diagrammatic reasoning (Anderson, Meyer, & Olivier, 2001) uses direct inspection and manipulation of a diagram as primary means of inference. For example, an old Chinese work dated at approximately 600 BC (Trufte, 1989) contains the visual proof of Pythagoras' Theorem. Geometers of ancient China and India extensively used the visual method rather than propositional argument. Later Euclid laid the foundation for the development of formal deductive systems by presenting the whole argument, based on different drawings, textually, in a formal step-by-step sequence of logically connected propositions. Euclid's proof of Pythagoras' theorem is intricate and non-intuitive.

Kulpa (1994) gives examples of diagrammatic reasoning, which compare a predicate calculus formulation of a simple mechanical problem to demonstrate that without the guidance of a mental model of the mechanical system described by the set of formulae there are significant search problems in trying to match candidate rules with appropriate facts to make inferences.

The conceptual graph notation was advanced by Sowa (1984) in order to facilitate the representation of knowledge in a form that was easily readable by humans while being able to be easily translated to a logic in a machine readable format. Figure 1 illustrates a graph from http://www.jfsowa.com/cg/. The corresponding predicate calculus representation, easily generated automatically, is as follows:

$$(\exists x:Go)(\exists y:Person)(\exists z:City)(\exists w:Bus)$$

$$(name\ (y,'John') \wedge name(z,'Boston') \wedge agnt(x,y) \wedge dest(x,z) \wedge inst(x,w))$$

Sowa (1984) based conceptual graphs on the existential logic advanced by C. S Pierce in the 1890's. Pierce saw the need for a diagrammatic representation of logic for a number of reasons including its utility in serving a community of inquiring scientists. Conceptual graphs have been used as a representation of knowledge in many database and expert system applications. Although more readable by humans, conceptual graphs, like the first order logic, default reasoning and deontic logic, do not readily permit contradictory assertions that will emerge from a group of reason-

Figure 1. Conceptual graph for John is going to Boston by bus

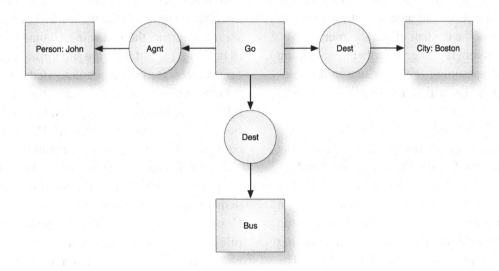

ing participants. Further, reasons for assertions are not immediately and obviously represented as reasons. An adherence to truth from a single perspective is still as prominent as it is in the underpinning logic.

The essential point to note here is that diagrammatic reasoning is a different approach where the knowledge is represented as diagrams and the reasoning is based on these diagrams. In extreme cases, the diagram may capture the reasoning but it usually assists the reasoning. It does not have the power to represent any reasoning as diagrams.

The argumentation approach of Toulmin (1958) relaxed the need for truth and permitted qualified assertions. He was less concerned with formalisms of arguments and presented an informal model of argumentation. The Toulmin Argument Structure, discussed next, has some features that can model and, hence, support individual reasoning in the context of a reasoning community.

Toulmin Argument Structure

Toulmin (1958) illustrated that scientific reasoning could be seen as a kind of generalised jurisprudence rather than as a system of logic. Jurisprudence focuses attention on procedures by which legal claims are advanced and attacked and, in a similar way, Toulmin sought to identify procedures by which any claim, in general is advanced. He identified a layout of arguments that was constant regardless of the content of the argument.

The Toulmin layout goes further in describing individual reasoning within a reasoning community than classical syllogism, FOPL or non-monotonic logics.

Figure 2 illustrates a Toulmin layout involving an Australian government policy for processing applicants for refugee status who arrived on Australian shores without travel documents. Rather than process claims while applicants were in detention centres in Australia, the Pacific Island solution transferred applicants to neighbouring nations and processed their claims there. The

claim illustrated in Figure 2 asserts that the Pacific Island solution is entirely appropriate.

The data items used for this claim include the accordance with United Nations conventions, the processing is quite orderly, cost effective and enhances safety of applicants. Knowing the data and the claim does not necessarily convince an audience that the claim follows from the data. A mechanism is required to act as a justification for the claim. This justification is known as the warrant. A warrant statement supports why each data item leads to the claim asserted. The backing provides evidentiary support for warrant elements.

As a structure for coalescing, the Toulmin layout is far richer than the syllogism or formal logics. Although, the information captured by the Toulmin layout is broader in scope than that represented by the classical syllogism, first order logic or default reasoning, the purpose for advancing the claims is still left implicit. Relevant claims in the Toulmin layout must be expressed as data items, claim items, warrants, rebuttal items, and backing items. With the introduction of the warrant, the Toulmin layout provides some guidance to an individual reasoner about how to assemble claims because data items are those claims that make sense, or can reasonably be regarded as relevant in the inference of a claim, given a warrant.

Although the assumption is made that an individual performing the reasoning has full understanding of all claims, the layout provides some insight into their meaning. Claims advanced as backing, for instance, are supporting evidence for warrants. The background knowledge required is made explicit and is, in the example above, the relevant sections of the United Nations Convention on the Status of Refugees. However, the background knowledge required to understand the warrant is not represented in the Toulmin layout.

The inference of the Toulmin claims from data items is made somewhat explicit in the warrant. However, the warrant is not a precise inference rule or procedure in the way that modus ponens is. The Toulmin structure was not advanced as a

Figure 2. Toulmin argument for Pacific island solution

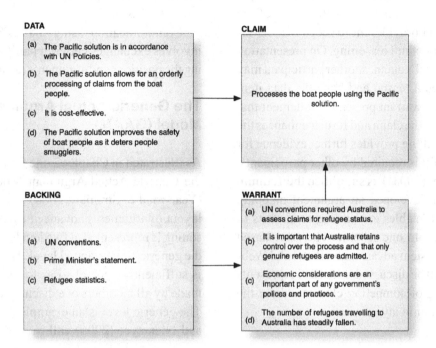

formal specification of how new claims can be inferred so an application of the warrant to data items to yield the claim advanced remains unclear. The individual judgment performed to infer the Pacific Island solution is appropriate given the data items is not specified.

Stranieri, Yearwood, and Zeleznikow (2001) survey adaptations of the Toulmin layout that have been advanced for the purpose of developing technological support for reasoning and found that the majority of applications vary the structure from the original formulation. Johnson, Zualkernan, and Tukey (1993) identified different types of expertise with the Toulmin structure and Bench-Capon, Lowes, and McEnery (1991) used the structure to explain logic programming conclusions. Branting (1994) expanded TAS warrants as a model of the legal concept of ratio decidendi. In the Split Up project, Stranieri, Zeleznikow, Gawler, and Lewis (1999) used the Toulmin layout to represent family law knowledge in a manner that facilitated rule/neural hybrid development.

Toulmin proposed his views on argumentation informally and never claimed to have advanced a theory of argumentation. He does not rigorously define key terms such as warrant and backing. He only loosely specifies how arguments relate to other arguments and provides no guidance as to how to evaluate the best argument or identify implausible ones. Nevertheless, the structure was found to be useful as a tool for organizing knowledge. Operators to question, attack, or qualify opposition assertions are not explicit. Nor is there the facility to represent a participant's beliefs as they differ from those of another. Many knowledge engineering applications of the Toulmin framework have not modelled discursive exchanges at all, but have applied the framework to structure knowledge.

The communication of reasoning amongst participants of a community with the use of the Toulmin layout provides more scope than narrative, FOPL or default reasoning. On presentation of one individual's claim, another participant may demand to see a reason and have the data item displayed. The warrant presents a statement that links the data to the claim and further enhances the claim. The backing provides further evidence for the warrant if it is required by other participants.

van Gelder (2003) has simplified the Toulmin structure and developed an argument mapping approach that enables contrasting arguments to be integrated into one scheme. The issue based information system advanced by Rittel and Webber (1973) will be discussed next. IBIS represents the coalescing of competing claims without the use of the Toulmin layout.

IBIS

IBIS (Issues Based Information System) introduced in Chapter 2 contains three basic elements: questions or issues, positions on an issue, and arguments that support or refute a position (Rittel and Webber, 1973). Figure 3 in Chapter 2 illustrated competing positions related to the Australian refugee policy. The IBIS structure represents a coalescing of reasoning that an individual may make in understanding an issue. However, there is no representation of the relative importance of each *pro* or *con* argument. Further, there is no specification of the evidence that could be drawn on to support each argument. The way a position is inferred as preferable to competing positions by an individual is not specified at all. Like the Toulmin structure and in contrast to the syllogism and logic, IBIS emphasises the structuring of knowledge and does not have inference mechanisms by which conclusions can be inferred. However, in some computer-based applications based on IBIS, a logic to implement the drawing of inferences is included. For example, the Zeno argumentation framework

(Gordon, 1995a) embeds a non-monotonic logic into the IBIS structure.

Communication using the IBIS framework involves exchanges between participants regarding the positions and arguments related to an issue.

The Generic/Actual Argument Model (GAAM)

As illustrated in Chapter 2, the framework called the Generic Actual Argument Model (GAAM) (Yearwood & Stranieri, 2006) is a variant of the layout of arguments advanced by Toulmin. Reasoning is represented at two levels of abstraction; the generic and the actual level. The generic level is sufficiently general so as to represent claims made by all members of a discursive community. The generic level is an example of what Dryzek and Niemeyer (2006) call meta-consensus. All participants in a reasoning community use the same generic arguments to construct, largely by instantiation, their own actual arguments. The generic arguments represent a detailed layout of arguments acceptable to all participants whereas the actual arguments capture a participant's position with respect to each argument. The actual arguments that one participant advances are more easily compared with those advanced by another because, in both cases, the actual arguments have been derived from a generic template that all participants share.

The Generic Actual Argument Model derives from the Toulmin layout but is tailored to represent the views of an entire community and facilitate the incorporation of technological systems.

Figure 3 represents the basic template for the knowledge representation we call a *generic argument*. A generic argument is an instantiation of the template that models a group of arguments. The generic argument differs from the Toulmin formulation and includes:

- **Claims:** a variable-value representation of the claim with a certainty slot in place of

Figure 3. The generic argument template

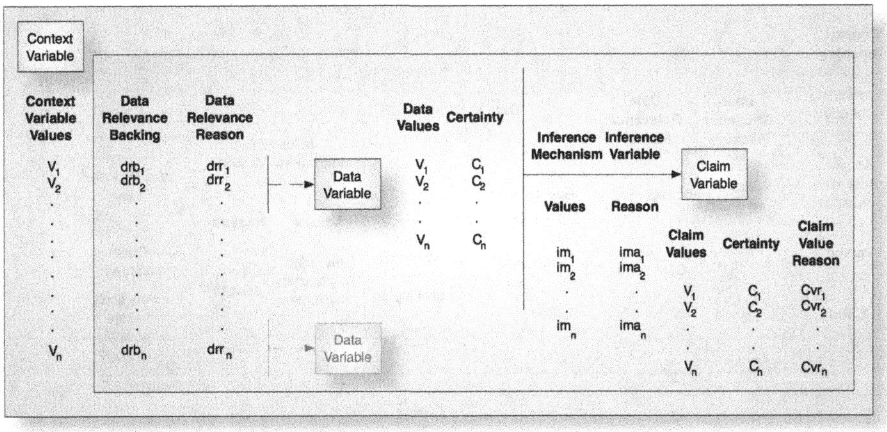

singlc statcmcnts in thc Toulmin formulation. This enables the incorporation of machine made inferences and ontologies.

- **Data:** a variable-value representation of the data items (with certainty slots) as the grounds on which such claims are made
- **Reasons for relevance of a data item:** This is in place of the Toulmin warrant and provides a placeholder for the specification of evidence for the inclusion of the data item.
- **A list of inference procedures that may be used to infer a claim value from data values in place of the warrant:** Modus ponens in First Order Predicate Logic is advanced as a universal inference procedure that applies under all interpretations. However, reasoning in practice often entails the use of different inference rules or procedures in different contexts. Each different inference procedure possibly in use in a reasoning community is labelled and listed in the inference procedure placeholder.
- **Reasons for the appropriateness of the inference procedure:** This is a statement that describes a reason for why an inference procedure is appropriate. Reasons for

inference procedures often reflect core values underpinning the use of an inference procedure.

- **Context variables:** This is a variable:value representation of a concept that provides context to an argument. For instance, the structure of claims, data, reasons for relevance and inference procedures for a refugee status argument are identical in the Australian context as they are in another United Nations signatory country. However, in one context, some reasons for relevance may not apply, some inference procedures are not acceptable. The context variable also specifies the scope of the reasoning.
- **The absence of the rebuttal component present in Toulmin's formulation:** The rebuttal component in Toulmin is subsumed as an alternate claim value in the GAAM.

There are two levels of instantiation made in applying the template to model arguments within a domain; the generic level and the actual level. A generic argument is an instantiation of the template where the following components are set:

Figure 4. Generic argument for well founded fear

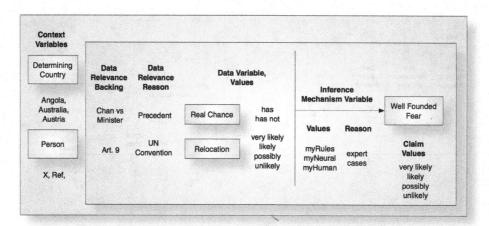

- Claim, data and context variables are specified but not assigned values,
- Relevance reason statements and backing statements are specified,
- Inference procedures are listed but a commitment to any one procedure is avoided,
- Inference procedure reasons are specified for each procedure,
- Claim and data variables are not assigned certainty values.

The generic argument is intended to be sufficiently general so as to capture the variety of perspectives displayed by members of a discursive community. It is a structure that meets the requirements of modelling a range of actual arguments and defined pre-suppositions found in a reasoning community. A generic argument now finds synergy with and implements the concept of meta-consensus deployed by advocates of deliberative democracy such as Niemeyer (2007).

Figure 4 illustrates the refugee argument above, as a generic argument. The claim variable has been labelled 'Well founded fear' and acceptable values specified. There are three inference procedures known to be appropriate in this example; the first is a rule set that derives from heuristics an immigration expert uses, the second is a neural network trained from past cases and the third is a human inference. This latter inference indicates that a human is empowered with sufficient discretion to infer a claim value from data item values in any way he or she likes.

Individual judgment involves a participant in the performance of an inference to reach a conclusion that represents his or her stance. This is modelled in the GAAM with the use of inference procedure an inference procedure which is an algorithm or method used to infer a claim value from data item values. Under this interpretation, an inference procedure is an operator on data variable values to deliver claim variable values. It is any procedure that will perform a mapping from data items to claim items. A mathematical function, an algorithm, a rule set, a neural network, or procedures yet to be discovered are examples of inference procedures. Many inference procedures can be implemented in software. Thus, they can be automated in computer-based systems. However, this need not be necessarily the case for a knowledge engineering framework. Claims can sometimes be inferred from data items by human agents without the explicit specification of an inference procedure. This occurs frequently in discretionary fields of law where decision makers weight and combine relevant factors in their own way without articulating precisely how claims were inferred. This situation can be accommodated within the Generic Actual Argument framework with the specification of an inference type labelled, simply, human.

Figure 5 in Chapter 2 represents the basic template for the knowledge representation we call a *generic argument* tree for the Australian government refugee policy issue. It illustrates a generic argument structure for competing policies regarding the processing of refugee applicants. The top-level issue is 'the most appropriate way to deal with the Boat People,' and the four alternatives shown represent the competing claims.

One of the features of the generic argument structure is that it does not explicitly promote adversarial positions but insists that the structure be established so that arguments and counter arguments can both arise from within the generic template. This is different from IBIS where the polarities in the argument slots appear explicitly.

The GAAM is essentially an approach that focuses first on the construction of the *generic arguments* as a group of agreed factors, organized in a group agreed way. These capture in a general form the relevant reasons to the top level claim or issue being discussed. This *Generic Argument Structure* (GAS) is the equivalent of the pool of reasons and criticized arguments. This structure is an explicit representation that can then be used by individuals to develop and represent their reasoning.

FURTHER REFLECTIONS ON REASONING

When we usually refer to reasoning we tend to concentrate on reasoning from knowledge, but from a computational viewpoint, we are required to first represent the knowledge. Complementing general questions of how to represent knowledge is the need to understand how knowledge can be used. Newell and Simon (1976) proposed that intelligent behaviour arises from the manipulation

of symbols, and that the process by which intelligence arises is heuristic search. However, realistic problems have enormous associated spaces of possible solutions, which must be searched to find an actual solution that meets the requirements of the problem. These spaces are much too large to be searched in their entirety, and ways must be found to focus or short-circuit the search for solutions if systems are to have any practical utility.

One of the main problems in considering reasoning is that for a long time reasoning was associated with *being logical* and reasoning was evaluated by the strict criteria of logical formalisms and proof. It was not until philosophers studied, in depth the character of human reasoning and looked towards alternative representations and logics to capture the nature of informal reasoning that progress has been made in aiding the representation and process of complex reasoning.

The notion of reasoning is closely connected with rationality and the notion of reasons with principles and goals. From the *normative* logical perspective it is required that reasoning systems be sound and complete but there are other possible views. In many instances, reasoning towards action simply requires *getting the job done* as distinct from having considered a range of possibilities or all possibilities and selected the best. The logicist approach could be summed up as *If it's sound, do it* (Doyle, 1992). With this approach, issues of the purpose of the reasoning and the value of beliefs and inferences to the reasoner are ignored. The heuristic problem solving approach can also downplay issues of making rational choices unless the heuristics are also used to compare reasoning methods. In his characterization of the knowledge level, Newell (1982) formulates his fundamental principle of rationality as:

If an agent has knowledge that one of its actions will lead to one of its goals, then the agent will select that action.

(Newell, 1982, p. 102).

Whilst this approach yields solutions it does not compare different methods for achieving goals.

The notion of reason is fundamental to reasoning and there has been much written on reasons by numerous authors including Raz (1990) and Hage (1997). Raz (1990) for example, argues that reasons are facts but also allows beliefs to be explanatory reasons in the case of reasons that function as causes and guiding reasons in the case of reasons to act.

Dictionary definitions of *reasoning* tend to define it as the process by which a judgment is deduced from other judgments or statements which are given. The Oxford English dictionary defines reasoning as:

A statement, narrative, or speech

but also

A connected series of statements or reasons intended to establish a position

and, hence, to refute the opposite.

Relevance, practical reasoning, rationality, and fallacies are all intimately associated with reasoning. Each of these are discussed next.

Relevance

The idea of relevance in logic which was central in classical philosophers from the time of Aristotle was abandoned by the more mathematical approach of Frege, Whitehead and Russell (Anderson & Belnap, 1975). "Relevance" is the idea that in "if then" propositions the antecedent must be in some way "relevant" to the consequent. In human practical thinking the conditional between two propositions depends not only on the truth of the two propositions but also on some causal relationship between them (Cheng, 2001). In the mathematical treatment of the "if... then" propositions the antecedent need not be relevant to the consequent. In fact, propositions such as

$(\neg X \wedge X) \rightarrow Y$ are considered "true," even though human practical reasoning would reject them. "Relevance logic" was brought to the attention of mathematical logicians by Ackermann (1956) and tries to provide a mathematically satisfactory way of grasping the idea of relevance in implication.

Entailment logics try to require that logical theorems should correspond to a valid form of human reasoning and reject the notion of material implication found in mathematical logic. One of the earliest mathematicians to argue that in order for the proposition $X \rightarrow Y$ to be true there needed to be some connection in meaning between X and Y was Nelson (1933). Later, many relevance logic systems were developed. Delgrande (1988) created a conditional logic based on the idea of irrelevance. Evidence is irrelevant in his logic if it contributes only to arguments that are defeated. His work found acceptance in the Artificial Intelligence (AI) community, because AI required a semantic understanding of the conditional.

It makes sense that in practical reasoning the search for the premises or data be constrained to those that are the relevant grounds. In much of the work presented on reasoning and argumentation, the analysis is of instances and the notion of relevance is not captured. Ensuring that all possible evidence has been accounted for is often limited by the rationality of individuals in making their reasoning. One of our contentions is that the notion of relevance is determined by the community of practitioners within the domain of reasoning.

Practical Reasoning

Practical reasoning is reasoning about what is to be done rather than reasoning about belief which might be called theoretical reasoning. So practical reasoning entails the requirements of doing: actions; series of actions; plans—intentions to initiate a sequence of actions; policies; organizational actions, plans, and policies.

Whereas simple actions such as the movement of a hand would be classified as practical reasoning that is spatial reasoning, the greatest part of practical reasoning would be captured as verbal reasoning. Philosophers have been interested in practical reasoning from two points of view: explanation and guidance. Raz (1990) makes the distinction between explanation and guidance but from the point of view of decision support systems to support practical reasoning, we are interested in the general issue of how individuals or groups rationally arrive at and implement decisions about what to do. It is sometimes difficult to tell whether a discourse would be classed as guidance or as explanation and Walton further makes the point that it is difficult to distinguish argument from explanation (Walton, 1996a).

Practical reasoning is by its nature domain-dependent and only in clearly defined and limited domains of decision-making would it make sense to use a single approach to practical reasoning. For example, such a domain is in the medical prescription of drugs. The factors relevant to such a decision are known and few in number. Fox and Das (2000) discuss such a decision making scheme and list the factors: efficacy, side effects, interaction with other drugs being taken, contra indications, patient's past experience with the drug, cost, recommendations by the authorities, local policy, and whether a drug is proprietary or generic. As only a small number of drugs are possible in any given situation, it is possible to list the points in favour and those against for each candidate drug with respect to each relevant factor, to arrange the candidate drugs in a hierarchy according to the decreasing number of supporting points and to present this information to the prescribing clinician. This is in contrast to decisions in domains where the number of relevant factors is not known and where the goals of the decision may be multiple or conflicting and where knowledge is incomplete or uncertain.

Practical reasoning is complex because of the possible scope of the decisions that may be addressed but also in the number of types of argumentation schemes that it may involve. Walton

(1996b) lists 25 argumentation schemes, which may act as the vehicle of practical reasoning to a conclusion about what is to be done. His list of schemes includes "argument from...": example, commitment, expert opinion, sign, position to know, verbal classification, and evidence to a hypothesis. Other such lists are given in Perelman and Olbrechts-Tyteca (1971) and Grennan (1997). One argumentation scheme involves weighing the points for and the points against a certain action. Indeed the application of these schemes represents a particular form of presumptive reasoning and only gives defeasible support to the courses of action. We say that they are normally only *presumptively* valid, in the sense that the schemes do not always lead to their conclusion when the premises apply. The presumption can be defeated in the case of there being exceptional circumstances. The 'critical questions' associated with each argumentation scheme serve to direct attention to the conditions that must be satisfied if the presumption is to stand up.

The idea of presumptive validity contrasts with classical logic where the inference rules, such as modus ponens, are considered to be unconditionally valid. The development of defeasible reasoning and defeasible logic formalisms to support this reasoning was initiated by (Reiter 1980) in his non-monotonic logic of default rules. Walton sums up presumptive reasoning as:

neither deductive nor inductive in nature, but represents a third distinct type of reasoning of the kind classified by Rescher (1976) as plausible reasoning, an inherently tentative kind of reasoning subject to defeat by the special circumstances (not defined inductively or statistically) of a particular case Walton (1996b).

It should also be noted that practical reasoning typically involves subordinate reasoning that would be classed as epistemic reasoning, directed at determining what to believe. In fact, Pollock (1995) claims that the epistemic reasoning required by practical reasoning is probably much more complicated than the structure of the practical reasoning itself.

Fallacies

Historically, the analysis of reasoning and arguments has also paid attention to reasoning that is faulty and concentrated on classifying common or typical errors. These errors or fallacies as they are often called are to be avoided, but finding fallacies in others' statements can make a rebuttal of their reasoning or argument easier. There are many fallacies that can be found in texts on critical thinking and many of them are explained in Walton (1996a). For example, the *ad hominem* fallacy occurs when an arguer moves a discussion to a personal level through character assassination or personal attacks.

Walton (1996b) showed how different forms of presumptive reasoning can be captured in argumentation schemes and how lists of critical questions can be attached to each scheme to identify the critical qualifications that must be met for the reasoning to be cogent. If the qualifications are ignored by the arguer then the argument will be fallacious. For example, Walton provides an argumentation scheme for argument from popular opinion (*argumentum ad populum*) as:

If a large majority accepts A as true, then there exists a presumption in favour of A. A large majority accept A as true. Therefore, there exists a presumption in favour of A.

If the reasoner reaches the conclusion that A holds, then she has committed the *argumentum ad populum* fallacy. There is a close connection between the argumentation schemes and fallacies. These fallacies highlight the fact that reasoning and argument are often used to both knowingly and unknowingly reach false conclusions. The detection of fallacious reasoning requires quite careful analysis of the reasoning used. A useful feature of a reasoning support or decision support system would be the ability to guide the user to reasoning that is transparent in its legitimate structure as well as being able to identify fallacious construction.

Economic Rationality

In contrast to the logical conception of rationality, there is the notion of economic rationality. In economic rationality, the fundamental issue is *choice among alternatives*. The theory requires the notions of strict preference as a partial order on the alternatives, indifference as an equivalence relation on the alternatives and any two alternatives are either indifferent or one is preferred over the other. These rationality constraints mean that the set of preferences may be represented by a utility function u which ranks the alternatives according to their degree of desirability, so that $u(A)<u(B)$ whenever $A<B$ and $u(A)=u(B)$ whenever $A~B$. Working with utility functions instead of sets of preferences moves rational choice to choosing to maximize utility. There is the common idea that expected-utility theory (see Luce & Raiffa, 1957) is a satisfactory rendition of practical reasoning; While different variants of the expected-utility theory model exist, the underlying idea is that the individual will choose the course of action that maximizes the expected utility for that individual (See Shoemaker, 1982).

PROBLEM STRUCTURING METHODS

Approaches that have been advanced to help individuals or groups reason without formalising or modelling the drawing of new inferences include Problem Structuring Methods (PSM) outlined by Rosenhead (1989). Mingers and Rosenhead (2004) review PSM methods in numerous practical applications that involve multiple actors with conflicting interests engaged to solve a problem that involves considerable uncertainty. The methods broadly aim to help a group develop a model of the conflicting perspectives so that the issues become clearer and solutions more readily apparent. For instance, with soft systems methodology described by Checkland (1981) and Checkland and Scholes (1990), participants build conceptual models, for each relevant world view before comparing them. Along a similar vein, the Strategic Options Development and Analysis (SODA) approach advanced by Eden (1990) requires that each stakeholder generate a cognitive map, a model that describes the causal connection between key factors inherent in a decision. The maps are then compared and contrasted in a group session for the generation of a collective map. This provides an effective framework for the facilitation of group decision making and guides participants towards commitment to a portfolio of actions. According to Mingers and Rosenhead (2004), the cognitive maps of the SODA approach often have many hundreds of nodes interconnected in complex ways.

As Ackerman et al. (1997) illustrate, the process requires a great deal of effort on the part of facilitators and participants. The generation of models or maps by participants requires deep knowledge, creativity, and considerable time, so does not readily scale up to widespread engagement of communities. Problem structuring methods are usually performed by small groups of participants in a decision-making context. The methods typically provide a useful framework for a facilitator to manage the endeavors of a disparate group and are not designed to scale up to very large groups that encompass many members of a community.

Other approaches under the problem structuring methods banner include scenario modelling used for water allocation decisions by Young et al. (2000), Wang et al. (2008), Cai (2008), Chung et al. (2008), Bravo and Gonzalez (2009), and Li et al. (2009). With this approach, decision makers identify possible future scenarios and formulate allocation policies accordingly. Scenario maps

can facilitate transparency, though the reasons for allocations under different scenarios are typically not made explicit in maps. The capacity for scenario modelling to scale up to facilitate active public participation has yet to be demonstrated.

SUMMARY

Many formalisms for the representation of reasoning have focused on reasoning primarily as an activity that emphasises the inference of new assertions from existing knowledge by a single reasoner. The early work by Aristotle (2006) on the classical syllogism set the scene for this by structuring knowledge in the form of general and specific propositions that were known or assumed to be true. Much later, work to formalise these notions by Frege (1884) and others led to the first order predicate logic. Inference rules such as modus ponens were clearly and formally defined. The existential and universal quantifiers for variables similarly well defined along with concepts of soundness and completeness. The increase in formal rigour led to confidence in the correctness of inferences drawn, and also led to the specification of computer language such as Prolog that were based purely on the logic. However, the emphasis on the inference of new assertions from existing, true assertions remained.

The advent of logic programming enabled first order logic as a representation of reasoning to be examined to an unprecedented extent; however, the reliance on true and non-contradictory deductive databases was soon identified as too onerous in practice. The observation of open texture by Waismann (1951) that no empirical concept could be precisely defined prior to its use, issues to do with defining negation as failure in logic programming languages and other pragmatic considerations led to the search for variants of logic that permitted contradiction.

The non-monotonic logic called default reasoning advanced by Nute (1988) models uncertainty and permits contradictory clauses by defining two types of implication; one that is hard and always holds and another that can be defeated. In order to manage rule conflicts a preference order for rules is pre-specified. Default reasoning models uncertainty and contradictions in a computationally feasible and elegant way. However, its reliance on a fixed, pre-specified ordering of rules is too restrictive for many large scale, real world applications.

Deontic logic model uncertainty and permits contradiction with the introduction of new operators rather than with the introduction of new implications. Operators include permitted, it is permitted to travel up to 60 kilometers per hour; necessary, it is necessary to travel faster than 10 kilometers per hour and; prohibited, it is prohibited to travel faster than 100 kilometers per hour. The operators enable the definition of specific context where contradictions are permitted, and also prescribe a mechanism for their resolution. Although deontic logic had some application in modelling legal reasoning, where legal norms are readily represented in the formalism, it too has proven to be too restrictive for many real world applications.

Toulmin (1958) did not seek to introduce a new logical formalism. His informal model, now called the Toulmin Argument Structure (TAS) sought to demonstrate that reasoning in most real world settings was modelled as a kind of generalised jurisprudence than an application of logical deduction. The structure consisted of components claim, data, warrant, backing, rebuttal, and modality. This informally specified structure captured more naturally the way in which arguments are advanced, upheld, and rebutted.

In recent years, a number of non-monotonic logics have been advanced that aim to model reasoning using argumentation concepts. Logics advanced by Gordon and Walton (2006), Prakken and Sartor (1996), Prakken (1997), and Bench-Capon and Sartor (2001) are some notable examples. Whilst these formalisms are useful

in clearly defined computational situations, to date, they provide limited support to agents in individual reasoning situations within reasoning communities.

The Issue Based Information System (IBIS) of Rittel and Webber (1973) sought to provide a structure to organise the views of a number of participants engaged in collective decision making. With IBIS, an issue can be argued for by advancing positions on the issue. Arguments in favour or against each position are then collected. The approach does not seek to model the strongest argument, or include any mechanism for inferring new knowledge. It is not a computational model although IBIS has been embedded in a dialectical game in the Zeno system advanced by Gordon (1995a).

The Generic Actual Argument Model (GAAM) by Yearwood and Stranieri (2006) adapted the Toulmin formulation into a two level model. At the generic level, claims and data items are restricted to specification of a claim variable and possible values. There is no warrant but instead, at the generic level, there is a specification of numerous inference procedures that could be used to infer a claim value from data values, at the actual argument level. There is a a reason articulated for the relevance of each data item and also for the appropriateness of each inference procedure. The generic level is intended to represent an organized, collective abstraction of arguments that participants in a collective decision make. The specification of inference procedures makes the model a computational model. At the actual argument level of the GAAM, an argument that a participant actually makes is declared as an instantiation of the generic level. There is no attempt in the GAAM to model a winning argument. This is presumed to involve deliberations among participants because it involves the identification of one inference procedure as superior to others, a feature that should not be pre-specified.

In this chapter, a survey of the ways in which reasoning has been modelled has been presented.

We have sought to illustrate that many approaches to systematically model reasoning focused on the inference of new knowledge by a single agent and ignored the practical reality that reasoning often occurs amongst a group of agents. Further, many approaches have focused on the representation of what is true in the world, and what can be inferred as true to the exclusion of representing what a group of agents are asserting, or how they are asserting their claims. We further advance the notion that the organization of assertions and reasons held by participants, into an explicit structure is beneficial for collective reasoning, and discussed the way in which the Generic Actual Argument Model is intended to do this. In the next chapter, the way in which dialectical discussion around an explicit structure such as the GAAM's generic arguments can be modelled is presented.

REFERENCES

Ackermann, W. (1956). Begrndung einer strengen implication. *Journal of Symbolic Logic, 21*, 113–128. doi:10.2307/2268750

Anderson, A. R., & Belnap, N. D. (1975). *Entailment -The logic of relevance and necessity*. Princeton, NJ: Princeton University Press.

Anderson, M., Meyer, B., & Olivier, P. (Eds.). (2001). *Diagrammatic representation and reasoning*. London, UK: Springer.

Antoniou, G. (1997). *Nonmonotonic reasoning with incomplete and changing information*. Cambridge, MA: MIT Press.

Aristotle. (2006). *Prior and posterior analytics*. A. J. Jenkinson & R. G. Mure (Trans.). Retrieved from http://www.digireads.com.

Bench-Capon, T., & Sartor, G. (2001). Theory based explanation of case law domains. In *Proceedings of the Eighth International Conference on Artificial Intelligence and Law*, (pp. 12–21). ACM Press.

Bench-Capon, T. J. M., Lowes, D., & McEnery, A. M. (1991). Argument-based explanation of logic programs. *Knowledge-Based Systems, 4*(3), 177–183. doi:10.1016/0950-7051(91)90007-O

Branting, K. (1994). A computational model of ratio decidendi. *Artificial Intelligence and Law: An International Journal, 2*, 1–31. doi:10.1007/BF00871744

Ceri, S., Gottlob, G., & Tanca, L. (1990). *Logic programming and databases*. New York, NY: Springer-Verlag.

Cheng, J. (1996). The fundamental role of entailment in knowledge representation and reasoning. *Journal of Computing and Information, 2*(1), 853–873.

Cheng, J. (2001). Strong relevance as a logical validity criterion for scientific reasoning. In Proceedings of the 2001 International Conference on Artificial Intelligence, (pp. 916-923). Las Vegas, NV: ACM Press.

Chisholm, R. M. (1963). Contrary-to-duty imperatives and deontic logic. *Analysis, 24*, 33–36. Retrieved from http://www.citeseer.nj.nec.com/carlos00logical.html doi:10.2307/3327064

Delgrande, J. (1988). An approach to default reasoning based on a first-order conditional logic: Revised report. *Artificial Intelligence, 36*(1), 63–90. doi:10.1016/0004-3702(88)90079-3

Doyle, J. (1992). Rationality and its roles in reasoning. *Computational Intelligence, 8*(2), 376–409. doi:10.1111/j.1467-8640.1992.tb00371.x

Dryzek, J., & Niemeyer, S. (2006). Reconciling pluralism and consensus as political ideals. *American Journal of Political Science, 50*(3), 634–649. doi:10.1111/j.1540-5907.2006.00206.x

Eden, C. (1990). Strategic thinking with computers. *Long Range Planning, 23*(6), 35–43. doi:10.1016/0024-6301(90)90100-I

Fox, J., & Das, S. (2000). *Safe and sound: Artificial intelligence in hazardous applications.* Menlo Park, CA: AAAI Press.

Frege, G. (1884). *The foundations of arithmetic: A logico-mathematical enquiry into the concept of number* (Austin, J. L., Trans.). Evanston, IL: Northwestern University Press.

Gordon, T. (1995a). The pleadings game: An exercise in computational dialectics. *Artificial Intelligence and Law, 2*(4), 239–292. doi:10.1007/BF00871972

Gordon, T., & Walton, D. (2006). The carneades argumentation framework: Using presumptions and exceptions to model critical questions. In *Proceedings of the First International Conference on Computational Models of Argument (COMMA 2006)*, (pp. 208-219). Liverpool, UK: IOS Press.

Governatori, G., & Stranieri, A. (2001). Towards the application of association rules for defeasible rule discovery. In *Proceedings of the Fourteenth Annual International Conference on Legal Knowledge and Information Systems Jurix 2001*, (pp. 63-75). Amsterdam, The Netherlands: IOS Press.

Grennan, W. (1997). *Informal logic: Issues and techniques.* Montreal, Canada: McGill-Queen's University Press.

Hage, J. C. (1997). *Reasoning with rules: An essay on legal reasoning and its underlying logic.* Dordrecht, The Netherlands: Kluwer.

Johnson, P., Zualkernan, I., & Tukey, D. (1993). Types of expertise: An invariant of problem solving. *International Journal of Man-Machine Studies, 39*, 641–652. doi:10.1006/imms.1993.1077

Jones, A. (1990). Deontic logic and legal knowledge representation. *Ratio Juris, 3*(2), 237–244. doi:10.1111/j.1467-9337.1990.tb00060.x

Jones, A., & Sergot, M. (1992). Deontic logic in the representation of law: Towards a methodology. *Artificial Intelligence and Law, 1*(1), 45–64. doi:10.1007/BF00118478

Jorgensen, J. (1937). Imperatives and logic. *Erkenntnis, 7*, 288–296.

Kulpa, Z. (1994). Diagrammatic representation and reasoning. *Machine Graphics and Vision, 3*(1/2), 77–103.

Luce, R. D., & Raiffa, H. (1957). *Games and decisions.* New York, NY: John Wiley and Sons.

McNamara, P. (1996). Making room for going beyond the call. *Mind, 105*(419), 415–450. doi:10.1093/mind/105.419.415

Nelson, E. J. (1933). On three logical principles in intension. *The Monist, 43*(2), 268–284.

Newell, A. (1982). The knowledge level. *Artificial Intelligence, 18*(1), 87–127. doi:10.1016/0004-3702(82)90012-1

Newell, A., & Simon, H. (1976). Computer science as empirical inquiry: Symbols and search. *Communications of the ACM, 19*(3), 113–126. doi:10.1145/360018.360022

Niemeyer, S. J. (2007). *Intersubjective rationality: Measuring deliberative quality.* Paper presented to Political Science Seminar, RSSS, ANU. Helsinki, Finland.

Nute, D. (1988). Defeasible reasoning. In Fetzer, J. H. (Ed.), *Aspects of Artificial Intelligence* (pp. 251–288). Norwell, MA: Kluwer Academic Publishers. doi:10.1007/978-94-009-2699-8_9

Nute, D. (1994). Defeasible logic. In Gabbay, D., & Hogger, M. (Eds.), *Handbook of Logic in Artificial Intelligence and Logic Programming* (pp. 353–394). London, UK: Clarendon Press.

Pennington, N., & Hastie, R. (1992). Explaining the evidence: Tests of the story model for juror decision making. *Journal of Personality and Social Psychology, 62*, 189–206. doi:10.1037/0022-3514.62.2.189

Perelman, C., & Olbrechts-Tyteca, L. (1971). *The new rhetoric: A treatise on argumentation* (Wilkinson, J., & Weaver, P., Trans.). London, UK: University of Notre Dame Press.

Pollock, J. L. (1995). *Cognitive carpentry: A blueprint for how to build a person*. Cambridge, MA: MIT Press.

Prakken, H. (1996). Two approaches to the formalisation of defeasible deontic reasoning. *Studia Logica, 57*(1), 73–90. doi:10.1007/BF00370670

Prakken, H. (1997). *Logical tools for modelling legal argument*. Dordrecht, The Netherlands: Kluwer. doi:10.1007/978-94-011-5668-4

Prakken, H., & Sartor, G. (1996). A dialectical model of assessing conflicting arguments in legal reasoning. *Artificial Intelligence and Law, 4*(3-4), 331–368. doi:10.1007/BF00118496

Raz, J. (1990). *Practical reason and norms* (2nd ed.). Oxford, UK: Oxford University Press.

Reiter, R. (1980). A logic for default reasoning. *Artificial Intelligence, 13*, 81–132. doi:10.1016/0004-3702(80)90014-4

Rescher, N. (1976). *Plausible reasoning*. Amsterdam, The Netherlands: Van Gorcum.

Rittel, H. J., & Webber, M. M. (1973). Dilemmas in a general theory of planning. *Policy Sciences, 4*, 155–169. doi:10.1007/BF01405730

Rittel, H. J., & Webber, M. M. (1984). Planning problems are wicked problems. In Cross, N. (Ed.), *Developments in Design Methodology* (pp. 135–144). New York, NY: John Wiley and Sons.

Schmandt-Besserat, D. (1996). *How writing came about*. Austin, TX: University of Texas Press.

Sergot, M. J., Sadri, F., Kowalski, R. A., Kriwaczek, F., Hammond, P., & Cory, H. T. (1986). The British nationality act as a logic program. *Communications of the ACM, 29*(5), 370–386. doi:10.1145/5689.5920

Shoemaker, P. (1982). The expected utility model: Its variants, purposes, evidence and limitations. *Journal of Economic Literature, 20*, 529–563.

Sowa, J. (1984). *Conceptual structures: Information processing in mind and machine*. Reading, MA: Addison-Wesley.

Stranieri, A., Yearwood, J., & Zeleznikow, J. (2001). Tools for placing legal decision support systems on the world wide web. In *Proceedings of the 8th International Conference on Artificial Intelligence and Law (ICAIL)*, (pp. 206-214). St. Louis, MO: ACM Press.

Stranieri, A., Zeleznikow, J., Gawler, M., & Lewis, B. (1999). A hybrid rule-neural approach for the automation of legal reasoning in the discretionary domain of family law in Australia. *Artificial Intelligence and Law, 7*(2-3), 153–183. doi:10.1023/A:1008325826599

Toulmin, S. (1958). *The uses of argument*. Cambridge, UK: Cambridge University Press.

Trufte, E. R. (1989). *Envisioning information*. Cheshire, CT: Graphics Press.

van Gelder, T. (2003). Enhancing deliberation through computer supported argument mapping. In Kirschner, P. A., Shum, S. J. B., & Carr, C. S. (Eds.), *Visualizing Argumentation: Software Tools for Collaborative and Educational Sense-Making*. London, UK: Springer Verlag.

von Wright, G. H. (1951). Deontic logic. *Mind, 60*, 1–15. doi:10.1093/mind/LX.237.1

Waismann, F. (1951). Verifiability. In Flew, A. (Ed.), *Logic and language*. Oxford, UK: Blackwell.

Walton, D. (1996a). *Argument structure: A pragmatic theory*. Toronto, Canada: University of Toronto Press.

Walton, D. (1996b). *Argumentation schemes for presumptive reasoning*. Mahwah, NJ: Lawrence Erlbaum Associates.

Whitehead, A. N., & Russell, B. (1913). *Principia mathematica*. Cambridge, UK: Cambridge University Press.

Wieringa, R., & Meyer, J. (1998). Applications of deontic logic in computer science: A concise overview. In *Proceedings of the ECAI-98 Workshop on Practical Reasoning and Rationality*. Brighton, UK: John Wiley and Sons.

Yearwood, J., & Stranieri, A. (2006). The generic actual argument model of practical reasoning. *Decision Support Systems, 41*(2), 358–379. doi:10.1016/j.dss.2004.07.004

Chapter 4
The Generic/Actual Argument Model

ABSTRACT

In this chapter, we present a formal description of the Generic/Actual Argument Model (GAAM) and develop from this some of its characteristics, practical advantages, and disadvantages. The GAAM is intended as a model to support reasoning and decision making by individuals within a reasoning community. It can be used by individuals without inference support, by individuals with varying degrees of inference support, or as a fully computational system.

INTRODUCTION

The GAAM has been used to model reasoning in copyright law by Stranieri and Zeleznikow (2000a), predict judicial decisions regarding a property split following divorce by Stranieri and Zeleznikow (1998b), support refugee status decision makers by Yearwood and Stranieri (1999), facilitate interactive e-commerce by Yearwood and Avery (Yearwood, Stranieri, & Avery, 2001), implement multi-agent negotiation by Avery and Yearwood (Avery, Yearwood, & Stranieri, 2001), and in determining eligibility for government funded legal aid by Stranieri (Stranieri & Zeleznikow, 2001). Two shell programs that implement GAAM ideas are described in Stranieri and Zeleznikow (2001) and Yearwood and Stanieri (2002).

The GAAM was developed as a framework for modelling discretionary reasoning and has been used to develop practical decision support systems over the last five years. The objective of this chapter is to provide a description of the GAAM in terms of:

- Identifying the basic set of propositions it supports and how they are combined
- Identifying the elements that formally control or represent the structure of reasoning
- Its inference mechanisms and how propositions are derived
- The extent to which derived propositions are valid and accepted.
- The way in which it supports discretionary decision making

DOI: 10.4018/978-1-4666-1818-3.ch004

- Setting out its capabilities as a non-dialectical model upon which a dialectical model can be built.

The remainder of this chapter is organised as follows: Section 2 sets out how the elements of the GAAM relate to Toulmin argument structures and discusses inferences and the separation of inference from the structure of reasoning. Section 3 presents the GAAM more formally and in detail. Section 4 discusses some of the characteristics of the model, exploring deducibility and possible notions of argument strength and validity. Section 5 compares the model with other approaches.

Argumentation has been used in knowledge engineering in two distinct ways; with a focus on the use of argumentation to structure reasoning (a non-dialectical emphasis) and with a focus on the use of argumentation to model discourse (a dialectical emphasis—See Chapter 5). In contrast, many uses of argumentation for knowledge engineering applications do not model discourse and this corresponds more closely to a non-dialectical perspective.

A non-dialectical representation facilitated the organisation of complex legal knowledge for information retrieval by Dick (1987) and Dick (1991). She illustrates how relevant cases for an information retrieval query can be retrieved despite sharing no surface features if the arguments used in case judgments are represented as Toulmin structures. Marshall (1989), Ball (1994), and Loui, Norman, Altepeter, Pinkard, Craven, Lindsay, and Foltz (1997) have built hypertext based computer implementations that draw on knowledge organised as Toulmin arguments. Hypertext links connect an argument's assertions with the warrants, backing, and data of the same argument and also link the data of one argument with the assertion of other arguments. In this way, complex reasoning can be represented succinctly enabling convenient search and retrieval of relevant information.

Clark (1991) represented the opinions of individual geologists as Toulmin structures so that his group decision support system could identify points of disagreement between experts. Matthijssen (1999) provides a further example of benefits that arise from the use of the original Toulmin structure. He represented user tasks as Toulmin arguments and associated a list of keywords to the structure. These keywords were used as information retrieval queries into a range of databases. Results indicate considerable advantages in precision and recall of documents as a result of this approach compared with approaches that require the user to invent queries. Johnson et al. (1993) identified different types of expertise using this structure and Bench-Capon et al. (1991) used TAS to explain logic programming conclusions. Branting (1994) expands TAS warrants as a model of the legal concept of ratio decidendi. In the Split Up project, Zeleznikow and Stranieri (1995) and Stranieri and Zeleznikow (1998b) used TAS to represent family law knowledge in a manner that facilitated rule/neural hybrid development.

Toulmin proposed his views on argumentation informally and never claimed to have advanced a theory of argumentation. He does not rigorously define key terms such as warrant and backing. He loosely specifies how arguments relate to other arguments and provides no guidance as to how to evaluate the best argument or identify implausible ones. Nevertheless, the structure was found to be useful as a tool for organising knowledge.

THE GENERIC/ACTUAL ARGUMENT MODEL

Often reasoning occurs in the context of a small group of stakeholders involved in dialogue who would like to reach agreement on some issue. Whilst there is much anecdotal evidence for this it is also true that most organizations like to see a team approach to the solution of problems but are keen to have frameworks that permit a range of views. In general, we can distil the following characteristics of small group reasoning:

- Membership of the discursive community is usually well defined
- Members have different beliefs about the base facts and also have different preferences for how to infer from base facts to claims
- The truth value of a claim or proposition, if it exists at all, is difficult to ascertain.

A key assumption underpinning the approach taken in the GAAM is the principle that reasoning within a community can be represented as a set of *generic arguments* which link together to form a tree or graph structure. Each generic argument represents a class of actual arguments that may be made and structurally embodies the components that go towards shaping well-considered decision making in uncertain domains. The framework called the Generic Actual Argument Model (GAAM) is an attempt to develop a model for non-adversarial, structured reasoning. It currently acts as a non-dialectical framework in which a decision maker can be supported in making decisions about an issue. The model will underpin a dialectical model that will be developed in Chapter 5.

Our approach is in contrast to other argument-based models such as IBIS (Rittel & Webber, 1973) and Gordon and Karacapilidis' Zeno argumentation framework (Gordon & Karacapilidis, 1997) which focus heavily on the way in which multiple agents combat and defeat each other. One of the important features of the GAAM is that it invites a discursive community to construct an agreed framework for reasoning that is flexible enough to permit a broad range of points of view. This framework is then used to make the reasoning of individuals clear to the group. The development of models that encourage deliberation and are helpful in moving groups towards agreement or at least understandings of the basis for disagreements is a social ideal. Such models not only have the potential to present a fresh approach to group and organizational decision-making but also have the potential to contribute to more effective and informed decision making generally. Furthermore, increasingly, participants to a discussion are software agents. As software agents currently are not as flexible as humans, their use can more easily be integrated into a highly structured model that is designed for non-combative structured reasoning rather than adversarial based approaches. Using a highly structured non-dialectical model helps agent communication as dialogue is more structured.

AN EXAMPLE FROM REFUGEE LAW

In order to demonstrate some of the ideas involved in the GAAM we shall consider the story of Anju who is an applicant for refugee status in Australia. Australia is a signatory to the United Nations Convention on the Status of Refugees and so there are laws and guidelines that set out to some degree the basis for determining refugee status.

Anju was a Sikh born in India in the 1970s. She had thirteen years of education there before she travelled to Australia in the 1990s and married a Muslim. Her culture does not approve of marriage into other religions. She feels that her relatives in India would have nothing to do with her if she returned because she has done something that is culturally unacceptable. If she were to return to India now, at the very least she would face taunting and social ridicule over her marriage. She has recently divorced her husband and is being supported by relatives. She feels that it would be difficult to live in India without the support of relatives.

A Structure for Reasoning in this Domain

The members of the Refugee Review Tribunal of Australia represent a community of decision makers. From consultations with members of this community, we have been able to represent the reasoning that they use in determinations on refugee status as a tree of *generic arguments*. This tree comprises approximately 300 nodes and it sets out the structure of reasoning for these determinations. In determining refugee status, one component of the reasoning is concerned with establishing whether the applicant has a well-founded fear of persecution. A well-founded fear of persecution depends on a number of relevant data: the incidents of harassment that have occurred in the past; the credibility of the applicant's story; practices and policies in the country or region that target the applicant; whether these practices and policies have changed recently and whether or not the applicant could be relocated within the country of origin. Each one of these in turn depends on other nodes in the tree. This approach simply sets out a tree structure for reasoning in this domain where each node has a label that indicates the issues or facts that are used to construct reasoning.

Generalizing the Structure

The Toulmin argument structure represents reasoning as arguments constructed from sentences which are claims and data. The reasoning that represents the position of the applicant (Anju) and the reasoning of the RRT member would be represented as two separate Toulmin diagrams. Figure 1 sets out the section of a more complete tree that represents reasoning towards a claim on 'well-founded fear.' Each claim and data item are generalised to a sentence with a variable-value component that can accommodate the claims of both the applicant (Anju) and the member. In fact, a range of claims can be accommodated.

The Case as an Actual Argument

Anju's actual argument is captured within this generic argument structure by the selection of values for each data and claim item as shown in Figure 1. The argument could be expressed as:

Anju has a well-founded fear of persecution because: the incidents of harassment that have occurred in the past certainly constitute persecution due to a convention reason; her story is completely credible; relocation within her country of origin is not feasible; practices/policies of harassment that target her are likely and recently there has not been any change to these.

Generic Arguments

The Generic Actual Argument Model (GAAM) uses a variant of the layout of arguments advanced by Toulmin (1958). Arguments are represented at two levels of abstraction; the generic and the actual level. The generic level is sufficiently general so as to represent claims made by all members of a discursive community. All participants use the same generic arguments to construct, by instantiation, their own actual arguments. The generic arguments represent a detailed layout of arguments acceptable to all participants whereas the actual arguments capture a participant's position with respect to each argument. The actual arguments that one participant advances are more easily compared with those advanced by another, in a dialectical exercise because, in both cases the actual arguments have been derived from a generic template that all participants share.

The idea is that the generic argument sets up a template for arguments that allows the representation of the claim and the grounds for the claim. The claim of a generic argument is a predicate with an unspecified value (which can be chosen from a set when an actual argument is being made). A claim takes the form

Figure 1. The well-founded fear argument for Anju

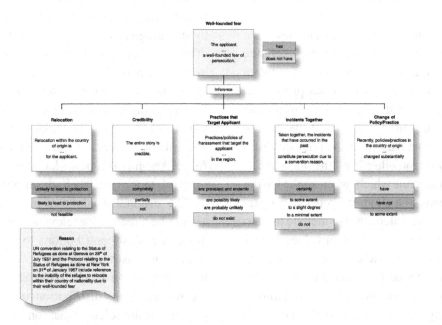

<PREFIX>{VALUES}<SUFFIX>as seen in Figure 1. For example, the "Well-founded fear" slot has the form "The applicant {has, does not have}a well-founded fear of persecution." Each data item is also a predicate with an unspecified value, which can be taken from a specified set of values. The connection between the data variables and the claim variable is called an inference procedure and maps the data space to the claim space.

The argument template (Figure 3, Chapter 3) represents knowledge at a very high level of abstraction. There are two levels of instantiation made in applying the template to model arguments within a domain; the generic level and the actual level. A generic argument is an instantiation of the template where the following components are set:

• Claim, data and context variables are specified but not assigned values,
• Relevance reason statements and backing statements are specified,

• Inference procedures are listed but a commitment to any one procedure is avoided,
• Inference procedure reasons are specified for each procedure,
• Claim and data variables are not assigned certainty values.

The generic argument is sufficiently general so as to capture the variety of perspectives displayed by members of a discursive community.

Figure 2 illustrates the refugee argument above as a generic argument. The claim variable has been labelled 'Well-founded fear' and acceptable values specified. There are three inference procedures known to be appropriate in this example; the first is a rule set that derives from heuristics an immigration expert uses, the second is a neural network trained from past cases and the third is a human inference. This latter inference indicates that a human is empowered with sufficient discretion to infer a claim value from data item values in any way he or she likes.

Inference Procedures

In the GAAM, the Toulmin warrant has been translated into three components: the inference procedure; the reasons for relevance of the data items and the reasons for the inference procedure. This relates to two different roles a warrant can play in an argument. As described above, the warrant indicates a reason for the relevance of a data item and on the other hand the warrant can be interpreted as a rule which, when applied to the data items, leads to a claim inference. An inference procedure is an algorithm or method used to infer a claim value from data item values. Under this interpretation, an inference procedure is an operator on data variable values to deliver claim variable values. It is any procedure that will perform a mapping from data items to claim items. A mathematical function, an algorithm, a rule set, a neural network, or procedures yet to be discovered are examples of inference procedures. Many inference procedures can be implemented in software. Thus, they can be automated in computer-based systems. However, this need not be necessarily

the case for a knowledge engineering framework. Claims can sometimes be inferred from data items by human agents without the explicit specification of an inference procedure. This occurs frequently in discretionary fields of law where, as Christie (1986) notes, decision makers weight and combine relevant factors in their own way without articulating precisely how claims were inferred. This situation is accommodated within the Generic Actual Argument framework with the specification of an inference type labelled, simply, myHuman.

The original Toulmin warrant can also be seen to be a reason for relevance or an inference procedure. Past contributions to a marriage are relevant in Australian family law. Past contributions appears as a data item in a generic argument regarding property distribution following divorce because a statute dictates that contributions are relevant. The wealth level of a marriage in Australia is made relevant by past cases and not by statute. The hair colour of the wife is considered irrelevant because there is no statutory or precedent basis for its relevance. Further, domain experts can think of no reason that would make this feature relevant.

Figure 2. Generic argument for claims about 'well-founded fear'

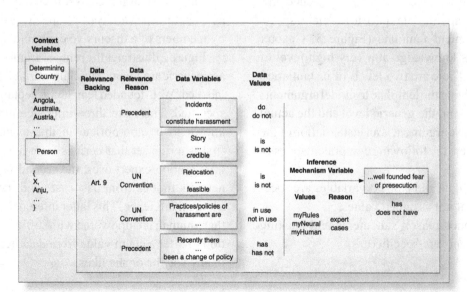

Separation of Inference from the Structure of Reasoning

Explicitly representing the inference method enables the use of a variety of inference procedures. For example, the method used to infer an assertion in the family law application, Split Up is a rule for some arguments and a neural network for others (Stranieri & Zeleznikow, 1998b). Branting (2000) provides a framework that captures legal reasoning using both rules and exemplars. In his framework, rules and exemplars differ primarily in that exemplars are much less abstract than rules and can be used to provide a bridge between the abstract rule descriptions and the specific case descriptions. A knowledge representation framework that separates the inference method from other components is very flexible. We argue that our argument-based approach captures the granularity of reasoning necessary in the most appropriate way by:

- Collectively deciding on a set of generic arguments;
- Collectively agreeing on the set of inference procedures;
- Allowing actual arguments to be built by instantiating generic arguments. In fact agreeing on the set of values that claims and data items may be drawn from;
- Allowing actual arguments to be built that extend the generic set.

The argumentation framework advanced here not only departs from the Toulmin formulation by distinguishing inference procedure from reason for relevance but it also represents context explicitly.

Context

Figure 2 illustrates two context variables: the Determining country and the Person about which the argument is being made. The respective values

Figure 3. Diagram of a formal generic argument

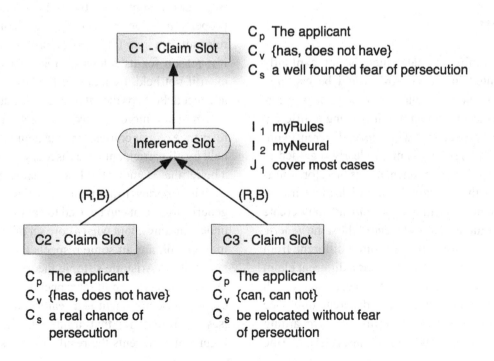

are a list of world nations for the Determining Country and Anju or the more universal X for the Person. Context variables represent something of the background knowledge that impacts on the generic argument. For example, the context variable Determining country in Figure 2 represents a scope constraint on the argument. This indicates that an actual argument can be made based on the generic argument; however, the determining country sets a context for the argument. The context variable is an articulation of the presuppositions that underpin the generic argument.

The context variable can also represent the scope of variables used in the generic argument. For example, the Person context variable will be assigned the value X for a discourse participant intent on making the more universal argument that relates to well-founded fear of anyone. The participant that restricts the argument to Anju does so be setting the context variable to Anju. In general, context is a difficult concept to define. In the framework defined here, context is defined as presupposition and variable scope. However, other definitions can also be accommodated as long as they can be captured as variable-value tuples.

Rebuttal

The Toulmin rebuttal which is not explicitly represented in the GAAM would be captured within a generic argument structure as a different instance argument possibly using a different inference procedure that produces different claim values. The rebuttal is more clearly regarded to be a dialectical component and is therefore omitted from this essentially non-dialectical frame. For instance, discursive participants may create actual arguments as instances of the same generic argument in ways that are quite different from others. Participant A may assert a different claim value than B, yet have perfect agreement on all data item values because a different inference procedure was selected. Any discussion regarding this difference, including exchanges that make the

point that the difference constitutes an attack, or exchanges that seek to defend A or B's assertion, or exchanges that seek to identify the stronger argument involve dialectical exchange and are omitted from the non-dialectical frame.

A generic argument has to capture the whole range of claims including the rebuttal claim. The model is therefore able to represent the rebuttal and reasoning towards it, however the fact that it is a rebuttal of some other proposition that the generic argument permits is not represented at this level. It will be a matter for a further dialectical model based on the GAAM.

Relevance

The concept of relevance is in itself difficult to define generally. van Dijk (1989) describes the concept of relevance as it applies to a class of modal logics broadly called 'relevance logics' as a concept grounded firmly in the pragmatics, and not the semantics or syntax of language. Within a discursive community, the data items in a generic argument must be relevant to the claim to the satisfaction of members of the community. A generic argument in the field of family law property division may include hair colour as a relevant data item for inferring property division if a reason for its relevance that is acceptable, even if not held, by many in the community, is advanced. Perhaps the utterance "Blonde women will remarry more readily" as a reason for the relevance of hair colour as a data item may not be held by all participants to a discourse but reflects a belief that is understood as plausible by many.

It is important to appreciate that the notion of a generic argument can be used to capture a shared understanding about what a core set of arguments in a domain are. In some respects there is some similarity to Aristotle's 'topic theory' (Aristotle, 1928), in that an important aspect in constructing each generic argument is a search for the premises or grounds for that argument. The generic argument represents the results of this search as the data items articulated and their reasons for relevance. These are considered to be 'nearly' complete knowledge about the possible grounds for that argument. As such, they would include general exclusionary reasons as described by Raz (1990) which are often the basis for rebuttals. Establishing the generic arguments in a domain provides considerable structure for developing arguments. Engisch (1960) observes that 'reaching a conclusion as such gives rise to a minimum of effort; the main difficulty lies in finding premises for it.' We argue that establishing the generic arguments in a domain is an effective part of acquiring, representing, reasoning and providing justification and transparency for decision making.

Figure 3 in Chapter 3 also includes *certainty* slots for each data item, claim and inference procedure. These recognize that there is uncertainty in the processes of developing actual arguments. The certainty values are assigned when values are assigned in the process of constructing an actual argument. A generic argument is an agreed approximation to a world but still may only be partial knowledge. We do not explicitly put a certainty or confidence value on a generic argument although we permit generic arguments to change over time. The structure of generic arguments that describe a domain will not be static. As knowledge within the domain evolves new versions of the generic argument structure will be required. New factors emerge as being relevant to some arguments and new inference procedures may be needed as new legal rules emerge or new cases become precedents. Most actual arguments in a domain are then underpinned by a particular version of the generic argument structure.

The knowledge in a domain of discourse can be represented as a tree of these generic arguments with a data item of an argument being the claim of another argument. Part of the tree for reasoning in refugee law appears in Figure 1 where the reason for relevance of the 'relocation' data item is shown (as being specified in the UN convention). The generic arguments within a domain can be established by engaging participants in a discussion in the development of the Generic Argument Structure (GAS) or through their contributions to a common view of the structure and each participants reasons for relevance (Afshar, Yearwood, & Stranieri, 2002). The intention is to have participants agree on a structure for reasoning developed from their shared understanding. The open textured nature of many areas of reasoning mitigates against the representation of all arguments in a domain as generic arguments but a large proportion of arguments in many domains can be represented in this way. It is also useful to know when particular actual arguments diverge from instantiations of generic arguments and to detect whether or not they are accepted.

Making Actual Arguments

Actual arguments made are instances of a generic argument where each data slot has a value, an inference procedure can be chosen and executed to deliver a value for the claim slot. Figure 1 illustrates an actual argument for the story of Anju described earlier with data values indicated as the dark shaded selections and the particular inference procedure selected is inferencing based on her own human reasoning, which may be captured by the myHuman inference procedure. The reasoning of the tribunal member is also indicated as the light-coloured selections and these may conform to an inference based on a ruleset myRules.

The claim value reason for this actual argument provides a reason for the specific claim value inferred rather than other claim values. The claim value reason in Figure 1 would express a reason for why well-founded fear is likely, given the data items and inference procedure selected. With human inferencing there is not necessarily a reason for the inference procedure given at the generic level and there is therefore a need to justify the claim value produced by the human inference. This is represented in an actual argument diagram as the *claim value reason* slot. In Anju's case, the reason for claiming well-founded fear is based on her personal perception of difficult circumstances if returned to India.

The member's justification for his claim would come from the reasons for the rules in this rule set and their appropriateness for reasoning with this data about this claim. This is what would be called *deductive justification* by MacCormick (1978). The claim value asserted in Figure 1 "*does not have*" needs to be justified and this justification is the claim value reason, which is provided at the stage of making an actual argument rather than at the generic argument stage. If the inference procedure is a mathematical function or has mechanisms that are not visible, such as a neural network, then the articulation of a reason for the inference procedure is not an adequate justification of the value. Conceptually, it is more correct to say it is a reason for a particular value that has arisen as a result of the application of an inference procedure.

Certainty values are assigned when a participant creates an actual argument. The certainty value represents the degree of certainty the participant has that the claim (or data) variable value selected is the true value. A certainty value may be set directly by the participant or calculated by the inference procedure. A certainty value of 80% associated with the data item value, 'does not have' for the well-founded fear variable in Figure 1, would be read as a high (80%) degree of certainty that well-founded fear of persecution is likely. This is calculated by the inference procedure selected, myRules. However, if the inference procedure selected does not calculate certainty values then the participant must set a certainty value. The way in which the data item certainty values are combined is a feature of the mapping performed by the particular inference procedure selected so is not made explicit in the GAAM.

Linguistic variables values such as very elderly, elderly, middle aged, young and very young seem to represent certainty in themselves so as to make the specification of a certainty value redundant.

However, the inclusion of a certainty value slot in the GAAM enables the specification of membership function values if fuzzy reasoning was selected as the inference procedure, conditional probability if a Bayesian inference (Robert, 2001) was selected or certainty factors if Mycin (Buchanan & Shortliffe, 1984) like rule inferences were used as the inference procedure.

Generic and actual argument structures correspond to a non-dialectical perspective. They do not directly model an exchange of views between discursive participants but rather describe assertions made from premises and the way in which multiple claims are organized. Claim variables are inferred using an inference procedure, which may not necessarily be automated, from data item values. The reasoning occurs within a context and the extent to which the data items correspond to true values, according to the proponent of the argument, is captured by certainty values.

The generic argument provides a level of abstraction that accommodates most points of view within a reasoning community and anticipates the creation of actual arguments, by participants, as instantiations of a generic argument. However, it is conceivable, given the open-textured nature of reasoning, that a participant will seek to advance an actual argument that is a departure from the generic argument. This is a manifestation of discretion and can be realized with the introduction of a new variable (data, claim, or context) value, with the use of a new inference procedure or, with a new claim value reason.

A non-dialectical argumentation model must model discretion and open texture. The concept of open texture was introduced by Waismann (1951) to assert that empirical concepts are necessarily indeterminate. A definition for open textured terms cannot be advanced with absolute certainty unless terms are defined axiomatically, as they are, for example in mathematics. Gold may be defined as that substance which has a certain set of spectral emission lines, and is coloured deep yellow. However, because there is the possibility of a substance with the same spectral emission as gold but without the colour of gold, the concept for gold is open textured.

The concept of open texture is significant in the legal domain because new uses for terms, and new situations constantly arise in legal cases. Prakken (1993b) discerns three sources of open texture; reasoning which involves defeasible rules; vague terms; or classification ambiguities. Judicial discretion is conceptualised by Christie (1986) and Bayles (1990) as the flexibility decision-makers have in weighing relevant factors when exercising discretion although articulating an assignment of weights is typically difficult. This view of discretion does not derive from defeasible rules, vague terms, or classification ambiguities; so it is regarded as a fourth type of situation that contributes to the open textured nature of law.

The link between the GAAM and discretion is described in detail by Stranieri, Yearwood, and Meikle (2000). Broadly, discretion manifests as the flexibility for a participant to construct an actual argument from a generic argument by:

- Adding data item factors into the actual argument that are not in the generic tree
- Removing a data item factors from the actual argument that is in the generic tree
- Selecting a data, claim, or context variable value from those specified in the generic tree
- Selecting a data, claim, or context variable value that has not been specified in the generic tree
- Selecting an inference procedure from the list specified in the generic tree
- Selecting an inference procedure not specified in the generic tree
- Leaving data items, reasons for relevance, inference procedure, and reasons for the appropriateness of inference procedures implicit
- Introducing a claim value reason statement
- Selecting certainty values.

This framework including the generic/actual distinction, the clear separation of inference procedure from other components and the inclusion of reasons for relevance and context introduces a structure that represents knowledge applicable to a reasoning community.

Situations will arise where an argument needs to be made for which no generic argument exists. In these cases, a new argument specific to that situation is created. Ultimately, the series of actual arguments made in a case is built and represents the full argument in that situation. Some of the arguments are instances of generic arguments, others are newly created.

DEFINING THE GAAM

In this section, the GAAM is described using formal notation in order to precisely define the model. The GAAM is a means of specifying *generic argument structures* to model reasoning within a domain.

A Generic Argument Structure

Definition: A Generic Argument Structure (GAS) is a pair (*CV, G*) where *CV* is a set of context variables and *G* is a connected directed bipartite graph that has two kinds of nodes called, *claim slots C* and *inference slots I*.

The term *bipartite* means that every arc links a claim slot with an inference slot. There are no arcs that link claim slots together or link inference slots together.

- Every arc *a* of *G* must link an inference slot *I* in *G* to a claim slot *C* in *G*. The arc a is said to *belong* to the inference slot *I*, it is said to be *attached* to the claim slot *C* but does not belong to *I*
- Every arc that belongs to an inference slot in *G* must be attached to exactly one claim slot in *G*.

The tree of Figure 1 is part of a GAS for reasoning in refugee law. Each of the nodes represents a claim slot. The inference slot would be located at the junction of the arcs labelled 'inference.'

Definition: Claim slot. Every claim slot *C* has a *prefix* C_p, *set of values* C_v and a *suffix* C_v. Each claim slot also has two variables. A variable *r* of type string and a variable *c* of type *num* $\in [-1,1]$.

The variable *r* is a placeholder for the claim value reason and the variable *c* a place holder for the certainty factor. These are not instantiated at the generic level but at the actual argument level.

For example, the claim slot in Anju's argument for well-founded fear is [The applicant *has, does not have* a well-founded fear of persecution]. The prefix is 'The applicant', the set of values is *has, does not have* and the suffix is 'a well-founded fear of persecution.'

Definition: Inference slot. Every inference slot *I* has an *arity* (*n*) and a set of pairs of operators and strings $(I_j, J_j):j=1\ldots k$.

The number of arcs that belong to *I* is one more than its arity. An inference slot of arity n is represented with n inward arcs and one outward arc. Such an inference slot is called an n-ary inference slot. The set of *n*+1 claim slots $<C_1,\ldots C_n,C_{n+1}>$ is called the signature of *I*. The set of operators is a set of *n*-ary operators. Each operator is of the form $I_j : C_{1_v} \times \ldots \times C_{n_v} \times CVV \to C_{n+1_v}$ and operates on the sets of values of the first *n* claim slots in its signature and the set of *context variable values*. The strings J_j are intended to store the justification for the jth operator.

For example, in making an inference about a claim of 'well-founded fear of persecution' the arity of the inference slot would be 5, and there may be three operators that map the sets of values of the 'Relocation,' 'Credibility,' 'Practices/Policies that target the applicant,' 'Incidents,' and the 'Change of Practice/Policy' claim slots (as well as a set of context variable values) to the values of the 'Well-founded fear' claim slot. The three operators shown in Figure 2 are myRules, myNeural, and myHuman.

Definition: Claim slot to Inference slot Arc. Every arc from a claim slot to an inference slot is a relevance relation pair (C_i, C_{n+1}) and has two string attributes, *RR* and *B*.

For the relevance relation pair (C_i, C_{n+1}), *RR* is of type string and is the reason that C_i is relevant to inferring C_{n+1}. *B* is also of type string and is the backing that provides authority for the *reason for relevance* and in a legal argument is typically a reference to a statute or a precedent case.

Definition: Inference slot to Claim slot Arc. There is a unique arc from an inference slot to a claim slot.

If *G* is connected with at most one arc from any claim slot, at most one arc into any claim slot and only one claim slot has no leaving arc then the GAS *G* is a tree. In this case, the claim with no leaving arcs is the root or top-level claim. A claim with no entering arcs is a leaf.

A reasoning tree is a structure in which there is a unique path from any claim slot C_i to another C_j. A *source* in a reasoning tree is a unique claim from which all other claims in the structure are accessible. A reasoning tree with a source may be called an 'out tree.' In a reasoning tree all reasoning towards a claim must pass through a single inference slot. So, semicircles are avoided. In the case of a single claim slot with no leaving arc then we have a structure that represents reasoning towards a single claim or decision node. In most cases of representing practical reasoning, the above conditions have been met and the GAS avoids circularity.

Defining Generic Arguments

A generic argument is a GAS that consists of a single inference slot and the claim slots that are attached to its arcs. A full GAS can be formed by connecting individual generic arguments one for each inference slot in *G*. Figure 3 illustrates in diagrammatic form a formal generic argument corresponding to that in Figure 1 although not all 5 claim slots that act as data are visible. The single inference slot with the choice of three inference procedures is the focus of the generic argument.

Defining Actual Arguments

An actual argument is an instantiation of a GAS with context variable values, a choice of inference operator (and reason pair) for the inference slot, the assignment of claim values, claim value reasons to the claim value reason variables and the assignment of certainty values to the certainty factor variables.

First note that a claim slot C_i defines a set of propositions and the choice of a particular value C_{vk} from the set of values C_v defines a proposition (claim): $C_p C_{vk} C_s$. The actual (atomic) argument for this proposition is then represented as being derived by the application of an inference procedure I_h from the inference slot I (leading to the claim slot C_i) to n values $(C_{1v_{i_1}}, ... C_{nv_{i_n}})$ and CCV.

So, $I_h(C_{1v_{i_1}}, ... C_{nv_{i_n}}, CVV) = C_p C_{vk} C_s$.

Linked and Convergent Reasoning

One of the significant features of a complete generic argument is that it captures all claims that are relevant to making an inference about the target claim of an inference slot. Therefore, for a complete generic argument the only path into a claim is through the inference slot of its generic argument. This requires the inference slot to be able to represent the different ways in which inferences to the target claim can be made. The operators of this inference slot then need to deliver reasoning that may be *linked* or *convergent*. Walton (1996a) discusses in detail the distinction between linked arguments (where the premises work cooperatively and both are needed, see Figure 4a) and convergent arguments (where the premises work independently, see Figure 4b) and strongly puts the case that there is a third option when it is not known whether the argument is linked or convergent. He considers it a serious

problem with the conventional method of argument diagramming that the third option cannot be represented. He suggests that the way out of this, in cases where the evidence is incomplete to judge an argument as linked or convergent, is through the use of digraphs and numbering the arrows leading to a common point. In Figure 4, the two arrows into Z having the same numbers would indicate that both steps are part of the same inference (linked). In contrast, in Figure 4c the two arrows have different numbers and would indicate two separate steps of inference making the reasoning convergent.

For example, in representing the top level of reasoning in refugee law, a determination has to be made on the basis of whether the tribunal has jurisdiction, whether or not the applicant is excluded from refugee status on the basis of the UN Convention and whether or not the applicant has a well-founded fear of persecution. The application of this reasoning proceeds by first considering if the tribunal has jurisdiction in the matter, then whether the applicant is excluded and then the case for well-founded fear is considered. This reasoning is most usually represented by the more procedural nature of a decision tree. The representation as a generic argument puts aside the considerations of procedural order and questions of whether the inferences are linked or convergent in its top-level structural representation. That is, the three considerations as claims are the input claim nodes to the single inference slot of this generic argument.

It is at the stage of constructing the operator/justification pairs that form the inference slot that the linked/convergent distinction may need to be resolved. If we consider the example of refugee determination above more carefully then we observe that if the value of the jurisdiction variable is 'has (jurisdiction)' and the value of the exclusion variable is 'not (excluded)' then the determination depends on the 'well-founded fear of persecution' variable. Therefore, the three factors with these values are linked in making an inference about

Figure 4. Argument diagrams

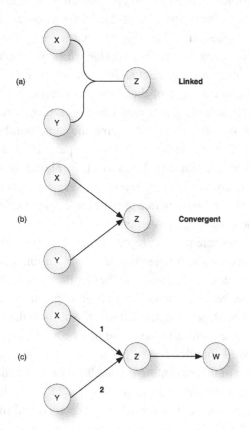

the 'determination' variable. However if either of the 'jurisdiction' or 'exclusion' variables has the value 'no,' then the values of the 'well-founded fear of persecution' variable are not linked into the consideration.

Returning to our example of Reff, the actual argument that Reff has a well-founded fear of persecution can be represented in the software Araucaria by Chris Reed and Glenn Rowe (Rowe, Reed, & Katzav, 2003) as a linked argument as shown in Figure 5. Indeed the actual argument for Anju would also be represented as a linked argument.

Arguments for 'well-founded fear of persecution', according to the UN convention may be made on grounds of persecution due to race, religion, nationality, political opinion, and social group. It is possible that severity values of inci-

dents of persecution due to race and the severity values of incidents of persecution due to political opinion combine to provide a linked inference about the 'yes' value of well-founded fear. However, each of the incidents independently may have been severe enough to provide independent arguments for a 'yes' value on 'well-founded fear of persecution.' In this case, the inference would be convergent.

Prior knowledge about the linked/convergent nature of an inference can be useful in the construction of an inference operator. In cases where the nature is not clear, it can be investigated after construction of the operator by consideration of the values and how they are assigned. However, it is worth noting that the GAAM allows the setting out of reasoning in a GAS and permits the linked/convergent distinction to be made later at the level of individual inference values.

In the case of an operator that is simply a support for human reasoning the justification variable can be used to provide information on the order of considering factors in a human inference process.

FORMAL CHARACTERISTICS OF THE GAAM

Syntax and Deducibility

The propositions of a GAS for a domain modelled by the GAAM are the claims that can be formed within claim slots. So, this is the finite set of expressions of the form $C_p C_{v_k} C_s$. All logical connectives, if needed, are encoded in the inference procedures of inference slots. Propositions can only be combined if they occur together attached to inward arcs of the same inference slot. Their combination then has to be with any other claim slots that occur in the domain of this inference slot.

There is also a set of meta-propositions that fill out the reasoning but are not involved at the

Figure 5. Araucaria representation of Reff actual argument as a linked argument

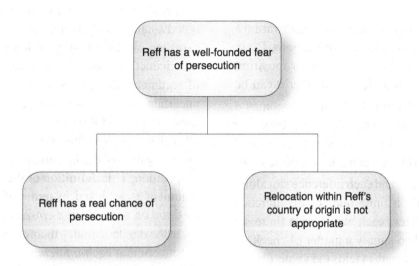

level of the calculus. These are reasons for relevance propositions, inference procedure justifications, and claim value reasons. Their function is to allow the synthesis of reasoning in the case of human reasoning or the automatic construction of verbal reasoning that is human understandable when computational reasoning has been used. It is possible that a relevance calculus be developed that would permit gauging the importance of claims based on properties of the reasons for relevance, however this is not considered here. A proposition $C_p C_{v_k} C_s$ is deducible if there is an instantiated subtree of the GAS with this claim as top level. By an instantiated subtree we mean a choice of inference procedure from each inference slot and a selection of claim values at the leaf node level so that the application and composition of the inference procedures to the leaf level claim values leads to the proposition. Because each inference procedure is an operator (function) it is not possible to get different claims from the same data values with a single set of inference procedures. However, allowing different choices of inference procedures may permit the same data

to derive different claims. In this sense, the model permits inconsistency and the inconsistencies can be identified and resolved. In Figure 1 different claims are made by the tribunal member and Anju. These different claims are made on the basis of different data and different inference procedures but it would have been possible for them to agree on the data and reach different conclusions by differences in the inference procedures used myRules and myHuman. It can also be seen that we can have more than a single derivation of a proposition C from a set of propositions Γ. For example, $I_j^1(I_k^2(\Gamma))$ may be one derivation and $I_l^1(I_m^2(\Gamma))$ another. Here we are assuming that the proposition can be obtained by the composition of just two inference procedures:

$$\Gamma : \xrightarrow{\ I_k^2\ } C_t \xrightarrow{\ I_m^1\ } C$$

where I_k^2 is an inference procedure from the slot I^2 and I_m^1 is an inference procedure from the slot I^1.

Deducibility

The methods for deducing (reasoning towards) a proposition C. from a set of propositions Γ are presented above. Now, given a proposition $C_p C_{v_k} C_s$ and asked to decide whether it can be proved (reasoned towards) from Γ becomes a search problem which is best done by proceeding forward from Γ to the claim slot C associated with $C_p C_{v_k} C_s$. This is reachable in a finite number of compositions and each inference slot along the way has only a finite number of inference procedures to check, each acting on a finite set of values. It is then simply a matter of checking whether any of the paths yields the value C_{v_k}. In fact, all distinct arguments that yield $C_p C_{v_k} C_s$ will be returned.

Argument Strength and Validity

So far, the focus has been on the syntactic aspects of the GAAM. It is clear what constitutes a proposition and how they can be acted on by inference procedures to produce new propositions. At the syntactic level each inference procedure is internally consistent but the use of different inference procedures may produce inconsistent results. The usual approach is now to consider the semantics of the model. One approach to semantics is to use truth tables, whereby any proposition in the system is assigned a truth-value. Another approach is to use *model theory* where meaning is attached to propositions in terms of possible *interpretations* of the propositions. Krause, Ambler, Elvang-Goransson, and Fox (1995) use a different approach from the Tarskian approach by ascribing a meaning to the proofs in their Logic of Argumentation (LA) and not to the propositions themselves. As arguments are what makes LA different from other logics, they, in fact ascribe meaning to the arguments in LA. They develop a proof theoretic semantics of LA, which is expressed using category theory. Ambler (1996) achieves this by using

the *Curry-Howard isomorphism*, which relates the proofs of minimal logic to terms of a simply typed λ-calculus and hence to the arrows of a free cartesian closed category which can be viewed as a deductive system. The notion of a category of arguments that can be viewed as a system of uncertain inference is developed by providing a general theory of the strength of an argument in all such categories. This allows the accumulation or aggregation of distinct arguments for the same proposition. This definition of the strength of an argument is achieved in terms of a *confidence measure* on an *evidential closed category*.

In the standard model, theoretic approach there is concern that each *inference rule* is *sound* and *complete*. These notions depend on the notion of C *logically following* from a set of propositions Γ. This simply means that C is true for every interpretation where Γ is true.

This requirement (logically following) is too strong for the generic argument structures developed by the GAAM. The derivation of inconsistent propositions from the same data Γ is permitted and so there will be some interpretations in which C is true and somewhere C' is true. The only cases for which we might expect that propositions logically follow in the GAAM is for inference slots where there is a unique inference operator. In this case, the reasoning community has decided that all arguments from Γ and context variable values CVV can be effectively reasoned about in a single way. Whilst this is an appeal to a single syntactic mechanism, it also means that the validity of the proposition must be strong.

We take an approach that is closer to that taken by Krause et al. (1995) with LA. They go to some length to establish a confidence measure on their evidential closed category of propositions and arguments between them. Considering a semantics for the GAAM is interesting. First we note that there may be a number of arguments that lead to a given proposition. So, one possible view of the validity of a proposition may take account of this by aggregating these arguments.

The rationale for this approach would be that the truth of a proposition should reflect something of the ways that it can be established. Given that the GAAM has associated with each GAS a reasoning community and the inference procedures reflect the agreed ways of reasoning within that community it makes some sense to give more credibility to a proposition that is supported by many arguments than one that is only supported by a few. 'Just because there are more roads leading to Rome, does not make Rome better to go to than Florence—but somehow it does.' The GAAM as a model, prescribes by agreement of the reasoning community, the structure of the reasoning in a domain as well as the variety of permissable inference procedures in each inference slot. The specification of a set of inference procedures in an inference slot permits a notion of strength to be defined which is based on an aggregation of similar arguments. This is similar to the approach taken by Krause et al. (1995).

Consider a single actual argument A which can be represented as a set of propositions, (actually each proposition in Γ specifies a value) Γ mapped to a claim value C_v by an inference procedure I_j. This actual argument is instantiated from a generic argument with inference slot I. Let I contain a set of inference procedures $\{I_i \mid i = 1...k\}$. We may define the strength of A as:

$$s_{\Gamma,C}(A) = \frac{|\{I_i \mid I_i(\Gamma) = I_j(\Gamma) \wedge i = 1...k\}|}{k} = \frac{number\_of\_agreements}{k}$$

where I_j is the inference procedure used in A.

Note that from this definition of strength we have the following. If there is a unique inference procedure in the inference slot ($k=1$) then the strength of any argument based on this slot is 1 and this corresponds to a situation of having no alternative ways of reasoning and total agreement on the values inferred from the reason values given. Furthermore, the strength of all arguments based on the generic argument corresponding to

this slot is the same. The formula defines the strength of an actual argument and not the strength of an inference procedure although the strength of an inference procedure may now be defined as a function on the various sets of propositions Γ in its domain using the above.

The above approach, simply counts the arguments in support. It could be called the *inference agreement approach*. It can be augmented by the certainty values for those inference operators that generates the claim of A. One way of doing this would be to weight the effect of each contributing inference operator by the certainty factor that it gives to the claim of A.

$$s_{\Gamma,C}(A) = \frac{\sum_{\{i \mid I_i(\Gamma) = I_j(\Gamma) \wedge i = 1...k\}} C_i}{\sum i = 1...k^{C_i}}$$

where C_i is the certainty associated with the inference operator I_i in slot I. The weighting means that arguments in which a minority of inference operators support the claim but do so with high certainty would count as much as having some support from many.

There are other possible approaches and we mention two others here. It is possible within the model to consult the extent to which a particular claim is supported by past actual arguments and then assign strength to an actual argument on the basis of support from these arguments. This approach might be called the *data agreement approach*. In the last approach, we recognize that each inference operator within an inference slot is supported by a reason. The weighted formula above could further be modified by a factor representing the strength of the reason for the inference procedure. For example, in law an inference procedure may derive from the latest most on point precedent yet not fully accepted by the community. In this case, the older inference procedures may not be yet deleted. The new inference procedure ought to be the strongest but it will not be on data agreement and probably not on number or weighted number agreement.

The approaches considered above all adopt a formulation of the strength of an argument from within the GAS. Another set of approaches could be categorized as taking evidence for the strength of an argument from within the reasoning community attached to the GAS. For example, the evidence of the strength of an argument from within the reasoning community could be based on the number of members of the community that advance the claim of argument A. Another approach would be to consider the authority of each member advancing that claim.

The approach to the formulation and view of strength of an argument is connected to the nature of the reasoning community. For example, in the scientific community an argument's strength would be based more on the number of methodologies that support it rather than the number of individuals (actual arguments) that support it. This would therefore correspond to the inference agreement approach. On the other hand, a group of medical experts may choose to deviate from the established ways of reasoning and act based on a number of them agreeing to the same line of action. This would be an approach based on a notion of strength outside the GAS and based more in the reasoning community.

Comparing Arguments: Classes of Arguments

In considering the validity and strength of arguments, we are able to give a measure of confidence to any atomic actual argument. In the case of actual arguments that are not atomic, we can specify the strength of the compound argument as the product of the atomic arguments, which compose it. Notice that different arguments can be obtained by using different inference procedures in each slot and the strengths of the resulting arguments to the same conclusion may be different. It would therefore be possible to computationally define the strength

of a non-atomic argument as the average of the strength of all arguments from the same data to the same claim and this could be based on any of the formulae considered above. In the case of not using certainty values then it may be appropriate to simply have a binary weighting of strength indicating classes as either "weak" or "strong" based on a cutoff value for the numerical value of strength.

In the case of the actual argument of Anju (Figure 1 on well-founded fear) and the conflicting argument of the tribunal member, it is easy to identify that they make a conclusion on 'well-founded fear' based on different data but also by using different inference procedures. For example, the different claim for whether 'the incidents taken together constitute persecution' highlight attention for the argument towards this claim slot and some focus on the strength of each of these arguments. The strength of the well-founded fear argument may also depend on the community acceptability of the inference procedure used.

The GAAM does not specify how the certainty values for each proposition are combined for any inference procedure in an inference slot. Therefore, the GAAM leaves open the way in which inferences are made within each inference slot and the way in which certainty values are obtained. This can be elaborated at the level of the inference procedures themselves.

In the next section, we return to an another example of the application of an argument trees within the GAAM in a reasoning context quite removed from health or law.

AN EXAMPLE FROM WATER MANAGEMENT

Decisions about the allocation of water, particularly when demand and supply fluctuate markedly, are notoriously difficult to make. Jeffrey and Gearey (2006) and Biswas (2004) note that the active engagement of the public in allocation decision leads to widespread confidence and compliance. Though desirable, public participation in water allocation decisions is difficult to achieve. Allocations in many catchment areas are currently the result of negotiations that involve 'making a deal' with concessions and compromises made out of sight of the public. As Walton and Krabbe (1995) note, dialogues that are based on negotiation are essentially power based so that the final outcomes derive more from a stakeholder's power position than pure reason. Decisions made on the basis of stakeholder power leave little room for active public participation.

Graymore et al. (2011) consulted water resource management experts with experience in making water allocation decisions to develop a *Generic Argument Structure (GAS)* for water allocation decision making. In that study, water allocation novices used a GAS to individually arrive at *Actual Arguments* that represent their preferred allocation then brought their *Actual arguments* to a group meeting to coalesce reasoning and arrive at a group allocation. In this way, the novices were able to can make and explain allocation decisions that were comparable in quality with those made by experts. Novices were restricted to making a hypothetical decision for the Wimmera-Mallee region of Australia to increase or decrease allocations for the following uses:

- **Towns connected to supply:** This is water for domestic, industrial and recreational use delivered to towns connected by main water pipelines
- **Towns not connected to supply:** This is water for domestic, industrial and recreational use that is not delivered through the main water pipelines but through secondary systems that are typically more costly and in which delivery losses are greater
- **Domestic and stock:** This is water for stock and non-potable domestic use on rural properties

- **Flora and Fauna:** This is water for rivers, wetlands and lakes in the basin, also called environmental flow
- **Glenelg compensation flow:** This water is a legal requirement following construction of a reservoir some years ago, that substantially depleted water available for the Glenelg River

Each novice was presented with a scenario that provided the allocations for each use and asked to indicate the strength of the case for an increase in allocation for one of the uses, towns connected to supply. In a real public participation exercise, participants would be asked for to reason toward the strength of the case for each water use. The possible responses are *"very strong, strong, not so strong, weak,* and *very weak."* Those responses are claim values for the root node of the *Argument Tree* as illustrated in Figure 6.

Relevant factors that, taken together, are considered sufficient for an inference of the strength of the case for an increase to towns connected to supply illustrated as subordinate nodes in Figure 6 are:

- **Current allocation:** The case for an increase to towns connected to supply depends in some way on the current level allocated. This is measured in terms of a percentage of the maximum possible. A measure based on a multiple of the minimum was rejected as a definitive minimum was considered by water experts as too difficult to identify.
- **Local wellbeing:** The case for an increase to towns connected to supply depends in some way on the extent to which an increase enhances the wellbeing of the town communities and immediate environment. Three factors were deemed relevant by water experts; the extent to which an increased allocation to towns connected to supply is important for the economic wellbeing of

Figure 6. Root node for the towns connected to supply water allocation argument tree

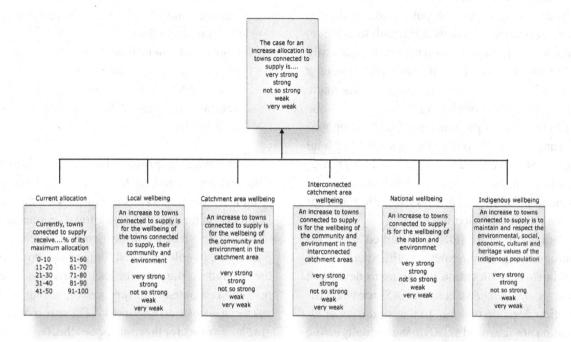

the local community, the social wellbeing and local environmental health as illustrated in Figure 7. Participants in a water allocation exercise who are unsure of how important an increased allocation for towns is to the local community are invited to drill down to the subordinate nodes where the issue is decomposed into the three relevant factors. If the decomposition is still not sufficiently fine-grained, participants were invited to drill down further. Figure 8 illustrates the subordinate factors for local economic wellbeing. One of those factors relates to the impact of low quality water on the local economy. Water storages that have blue-green algae, for instance, impact on local economies as tourism declines, and adverse publicity impacts more generally on the region. Other factors relate to the impact on local businesses and health services. These factors have no subordinate nodes because it was considered that

participants would be able to make a judgment at this level and/or identify relevant information to assist. For instance, a participant is expected to be able to determine his own view as to the impact of increasing water to local health services.

• **Catchment area wellbeing:** This factor relates to the extent to which an increase to towns connected to supply enhances the wellbeing of the broader catchment area. This is consistent with Melloul and Collin's (2003) observation that the needs of the regional area are also relevant. Subordinate factors for the catchment area wellbeing are not illustrated here as they follow a similar structure that includes economic, social and environmental impacts/benefits.

• **Inter-connected catchment area wellbeing:** This factor relates to a broader geographical area than the local or catchment area. Water supply systems often traverse catchment regions so the impact of an increased allocation to towns connected to supply in the Wimmera catchment on neighbouring catchment areas is a relevant consideration. Subordinate factors, used to infer this node, include the notion that reserves for firefighting endeavours typically serve more than a single catchment area.

- **National wellbeing:** This factor relates to the wellbeing of the nation. Subordinate nodes are not illustrated here for brevity but include a factor that represents the impact that an increase to towns connected to supply will have on a broader public discontent with the water distribution process.

- **Indigenous wellbeing:** The wellbeing of indigenous communities has been identified as a consideration relevant at the top level of an allocation decision. The factor is represented with the prompt; 'an increase to towns connected to supply to

maintain and respect the environmental, social, economic, cultural and heritage values of the indigenous population in the region is (*very important, important, slightly important, not important, not applicable*).'

The argument tree described by Graymore et al. (2011) was designed to facilitate public participation and transparency by providing a ready-built scaffold for participants to engage immediately in reasoning toward an allocation decision. There is no need to elicit and explicitly weight or rank criteria, a process that is often found to be a difficult and time-consuming exercise. Similarly, a participant is not overwhelmed by the abundance of information related to the issue.

- **The relevant factors are represented as variables with possible values.** Participants are invited to represent their

Figure 7. First level nodes in towns connected to supply water allocation argument tree

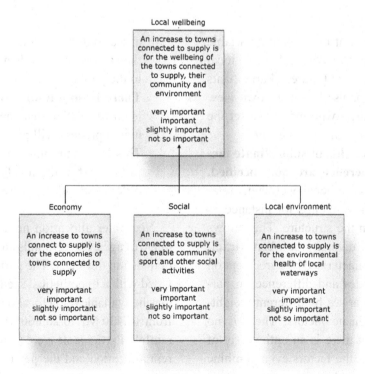

Figure 8. Economic well being in towns connected to supply water allocation argument tree

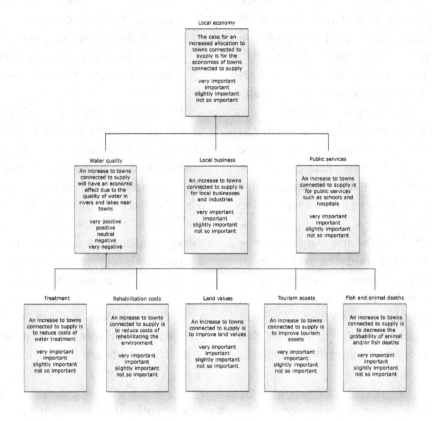

view by couching it in terms of a variable value such as '*important*', for the local wellbeing variable in Figure 7. Participants can readily recognise how their own view differs from others who may have set the same variable to '*not so important.*'

- **The relative weights of subordinate factors in an inference are not specified.** The importance of local wellbeing relative to national wellbeing, for instance, is not specified in the structure. This allows for the kind of diversity between participants that is characterised by agreement on subordinate nodes and difference on parent values that arises by different weightings on subordinate factors. There is no assumption that there is an optimal set of weights, or that the factors even combine linearly. Since the objective was to provide

a scaffold for public participation rather than a presentation of an optimal allocation to the public.

- **There is no automated inference.** There is no suggestion that an algorithm or automated process will perform any inference. This leaves the inferences from one level to the next in the hands of participants in order to stimulate greater engagement.

Six water allocation novices representing a range of ages, backgrounds and occupations participated in the study. The participants were provided with a hypothetical scenario that indicated that the available water for allocation had increased from 10,430 ML to 20,860 ML due to additional rainfall. Participants were provided with the current allocation and the percentage of maximum entitlements for each current use. For instance, the allocation to flora and fauna at 10,430ML was 0, and the maximum entitlement in the event of abundance was given as 32,240ML. Participants were also provided with links to relevant websites and the local government sustainability policy.

Each participant was provided with hardcopy diagrams of the entire argument tree and individually briefed on its use. They were asked to circle the value on each node on the diagram that best reflects their views and ultimately to assess the strength of the case for an increase for each allocation. They were asked to bring the diagrams to a group deliberation three to five days later where they would meet other participants and deliberate toward a single group view. The same scenario was presented to two water allocation experts who were asked to provide a water allocation decision based on their own experience, without recourse to the framework.

At the workshop, the six participants were first asked to fill in a short questionnaire about their experience with using the tree as individuals. The group then proceeded to deliberate over the decisions with minimal facilitation to ensure they kept to the task and time. The collaboration team were also in the room to make observations (notes) on the process. After the group had made their decisions, they were presented with the decisions made by the water allocation expert for comparison. The participants were then asked to fill in another short questionnaire about the group experience and then the workshop was drawn to a close.

The assessment of the results revealed that the water allocation novices were able to make water allocation decisions individually using the argument tree, with all bar one participant using the tree directly to make the water allocation decisions. That participant found the decomposition of factors into sub-factors unintuitive and instead exercised a 'gut feeling' assessment at most nodes in the tree.

How the participants used the tree to make their decision differed between each of the par-

ticipants. This appeared to be dependent on the past experience of the participant with a school-aged student (aged 18 years) appearing to use the tree by drilling down from the uppermost node to all subordinate nodes and, once leaf nodes were reached, making inferences up the hierarchy. However, one participant in the 65-74 age group who had some experience with water allocation decisions used the tree in a different way; making judgments on each of the subordinate nodes and then seemingly using his own intuition to make the first level decisions rather than some combination of sub-criteria judgments. This was evident because the first level decision did not always reflect the sub-criteria judgments recorded. Most of the participants reported that they felt the tree helped them make the decisions, but that some parts of the tree were hard to understand.

The results of the workshop demonstrated that a group of water allocation novices given the background information and the argument tree can make high level decisions about water allocation through group deliberation. The deliberation between the novices was strikingly non-combative with participants discussing their different opinions in an open way. Each person's opinion was heard and considered with a consensus arrived at for each decision though the discussion was more in-depth for some uses than others.

The group did not use the tree directly during the deliberation, but they were using it indirectly. For each use, the participants went around the table expressing their thoughts on how important it was to increase allocation to the use and why. Each participant referred to their tree to explain their reasoning and often used the same words as in the criteria and sub-criteria, demonstrating that they were indirectly using the tree as a tool to guide the deliberative process. Also the majority of the participants felt that the tree helped them make the group decision as it was able to clarify and focus the process, raised issues and produced discussion, and gave a common starting point for the discussion. The participants also identified strengths and weaknesses of the tree as a decision support tool. Ultimately, the water allocation decision arrived at by the novices was similar to allocations arrived at by water management experts given the same scenarios.

OTHER APPROACHES

Our work here has focused on the use of argumentation to structure reasoning (i.e. a non-dialectical emphasis) rather than on the use of argumentation to model discourse (i.e. a dialectical emphasis). Argumentation has usually been associated with defeasible reasoning and many have approached defeasible reasoning from the point of view of developing formal logics. For example, Nute (1988) describes defeasible reasoning as:

"When some new fact causes us to reject a prior conclusion, we will say that the conclusion together with the reasoning that gave rise to it are *defeated*. Any bit of reasoning that could in principle be defeated by further information we will call *defeasible reasoning*."

Two methods that have been most often used to capture defeasible reasoning are probabilistic reasoning and approaches that require the explicit listing of all exceptions as conditions for a rule. Nute argues that neither of these approaches provides a natural representation of many simple patterns of defeasible reasoning. He reviews other approaches by Glymour and Thomason (1984), which rejects conditionals as new evidence is discovered -order of antecedent dependent; Reiter's (1980) default logic also cannot handle the example of Nute (here order of antecedents is not important but the order in which the rules are applied makes a difference). McDermott and Doyle develop what they call nonmonotonic logic and do not allow a choice of the order of rule application they propose instead that only those conclusions that show up regardless of the order of rule application should be accepted (McDermott & Doyle, 1980). Nute develops the

defeasible logic system LDR with absolute rules, defeasible rules and defeaters. The usual way to explain meaning in formal semantics is by giving *truth conditions*. We understand a sentence when we know what circumstances would make it true and what circumstances would make it false. Nute uses another approach to thinking about the meaning of a defeasible rule. This approach suggests that we understand a rule when we know how to follow it or comply with it. Therefore, instead of truth conditions, we can explain what a rule means by specifying compliance conditions for it. So rules of LDR can be thought of as policies for belief revision.

In the GAAM defeasible reasoning is captured as actual arguments which differ in their claim values. Whilst operations such as attack and rebut are not modelled explicitly, it is easy to identify differences in the actual arguments for the purposes of comparison. Accepting that one argument defeats another could be based on strength as discussed. Sometimes, a new defeating argument will require a revision of the GAS by the introduction of a new data item and inference procedure.

Hua and Kimbrough describe the development of a Hypermedia-Based Argumentation Decision Support System (HADSS) based on logic graphs and sweeping presumptions (Hua & Kimbrough, 1988). Formal logic can be thought of as providing a computational and normative theory of argument. As might be expected of any effort in formalization, there are problems of limitations in scope. These limitations mean that formal logical languages still fall well short of the requirements of everyday practical deliberation. Formal logics have a second serious problem in that it is simply not reasonable to expect users to have a meaningful understanding of formalized expressions. These problems have led to the study of informal logics. Any HADSS would have two broad categories of hypermedia links: links between elements of the argumentation network (internal links), and links to the elements outside the network (external links). An external link might be used to display corroborating documents, videos, and so on for the assertion of that node. These systems should facilitate interactive ad hoc construction and modification of arguments and provide hypertext style access to documents relevant to particular arguments. An example of such a system is gIBIS (Conklin & Begeman, 1988). The most salient limitation of the gIBIS framework, is that it is not a logic and does not support logical inference. Hua and Kimbrough also carried out experiments, which indicate that the logic graph representation method is a useful tool for helping people in deductive reasoning. The graphical representation of conditional statements allows inductive reasoning processes to be simply represented as graph traversal. These experiments may provide some indirect support for using the GAAM to help participants in a discussion structure their reasoning.

Bart Verheij's ArguMed (Verheij, 1999) is an argument assistance system based on the defeasible logic DEFLOG. The ArguMed system uses the notion of a *warranted dialectical argument*. A dialectical argument is one in which counter-arguments (based on undercutting exceptions) are incorporated. The system allows warrants, both for argument steps (the reasons that support conclusions) and for undercutters (for the exceptions that block the connections between a reason and the conclusion). Step warrants express that a particular statement can be adduced as a reason for another statement. Undercutter warrants express that a particular statement provides an exception that breaks the connection between a reason and conclusion. Whether a dialectical argument justifies its conclusion depends on the structure of the argument that is on the reasons, conclusions, exceptions, and warrants that occur in it, and on the way they are related. The system automatically determines the justification status of an argument. The notions of reason, conclusion, step warrant, and reason for a step warrant are respectively similar to the GAAM's notions of data item, claim, inference and reason for infer-

ence procedure. The exceptions, like the Toulmin rebuttal make the argumentation defeasible. The undercutter warrants have no counterpart in Toulmin's scheme but would correspond to an inference to a contrary claim at the actual argument level in the GAAM. Toulmin does not give an explicit characterisation of the justification status of statements and the GAAM does not necessarily attempt to do this in an absolute sense but relative to the norm of the group's GAS. This approach is much more explicit for dialectic and is free in terms of adducing reasons (backwards) or inferring conclusions (forwards) but is not as explicit in structuring reasoning. In the GAAM, adduction takes place at the first stage when the group establishes the structure then individual inference to conclusions can proceed subsequently within the structure.

Dialectical approaches typically automate the construction of an argument and counter arguments normally with the use of a non-monotonic logic. Raghu, Ramesh, Chang, and Whinston (2001) have developed and analysed a connectionist framework for systems support for dialectical argumentative processes in collaborative decision making. This is a different approach from those mentioned earlier. Collaborative decisions in most organisations typically arise from either formal or informal deliberations in groups, where the group members consider and debate various possible decision options. These decision problems tend to be highly unstructured and are therefore difficult to model. Consequently, such decision issues are resolved through discussions, where argumentative logic and persuasive presentation are critical. In general, the discussion process involves both strict and defeasible reasoning. Strict reasoning is structurally coherent and logically consistent, and is thus not open to argumentation; defeasible reasoning includes structures of logic that are open to argumentation.

Defeasible reasoning arises due to perceptual differences among individuals about claims that lack a strong support base in terms of evidential data or strict reasoning. The resolution of the differences hinges on strengthening the support base and/or persuasive presentation. They develop a systematic framework for argument representation in modelling collaborative discussions. Secondly, they develop a connectionist architecture using their representational formalisms for argument analyses during the course of a discussion. Thirdly, the ideas are illustrated through connectionist models of practical discussions drawn from the published case study literature.

They define an argument structure as a simple set of assertions. Assertions can be of two types: positions or inferences. A statement of position is a claim. A statement of inference is a structural relationship among a set of positions and facts. Assertions are built up from a language, which is a triple S, R, Q, where S constitutes the sentences, R is a set of assertions built using sentences and Q is a set of assertion qualifications. A connectionist network formalism is used to model the debate or discussion. The connectionist network is defined as a 4-tuple with nodes, an activation function, a set of arcs and a set of weights. The network contains nodes, which represent claims, and arcs, which represent strict or defeasible support. The computational model accounts for actual power of reasoning support versus opposition, the activation levels of feasible units, as well as the simplicity of an argument. The cases analysed indicate that the computational model provides insight into the strength of support for various arguments. This approach does not provide a logic-based on analysis, leading to discrete valued assessments of arguments as either winning or losing. However, logical analysis of arguments surrounding business decisions most often leads to inferences that are inconclusive or undetermined. In contrast to the logic-based argument and analysis, the connectionist approach provides the means to assess the relative strengths of arguments in the discussion.

As mentioned before, the GAAM does not try to represent the dynamics of group decision making or dialogue. However, an individual GAS is a consensus representation of the structure of decision making within a domain. The connectionist model presented above by Raghu et al. may be a useful approach for developing the generic arguments with the domain. The next stage of our work will be to develop a full dialectical model based on the non-dialectical GAAM. The models that we have considered and most argumentation models tend to focus on the dialectic. They use propositions as their underlying non-dialectical model. This provides significant freedom but the use of GAAM structured propositions, we believe will realize other advantages in a dialectical model. It is important to appreciate that at this stage the GAAM is connected to a reasonig community in that the community constructs a GAS for a domain of discourse. However, without the full dialectical model, it does not permit the group to use the model for dialectical exchanges.

There are some similarities between the argument trees of the GAAM and conventional decision trees. Decision trees are rooted, usually binary trees, with simple classifiers placed at each internal node and a classification at each leaf. The outputs of the simple classifiers at the nodes determine a unique path from the root to a leaf of the decision tree. This path is known as the evaluation path. The classification associated with an object is the leaf reached by the evaluation path. Typically, the simple classifier at an internal node compares one of the input attributes against a threshold. The main difference is in the level of complexity. In a decision tree, there would need to be at least one decision node for each possible value of a node in the GAS. This means that a GAS serves as a more compact representation of reasoning within the domain.

Approaches that have been advanced to help individuals or groups reason with wicked problems include Problem Structuring Methods (PSM) outlined by Rosenhead (1989). Mingers and Rosenhead (2004) review PSM methods in numerous practical applications that involve multiple actors with conflicting interests engaged to solve a problem that involves considerable uncertainty. The methods broadly aim to help a group develop a model of the conflicting perspectives so that the issues become clearer and solutions more readily apparent. For instance, with soft systems methodology described by Checkland (1981) and Checkland and Scholes (1990), participants build conceptual models, for each relevant world view before comparing them. Along a similar vein, the Strategic Options Development and Analysis (SODA) approach advanced by Eden requires that each stakeholder generate a cognitive map, a model that describes the causal connection between key factors inherent in a decision. The maps are then compared and contrasted in a group session for the generation of a collective map. This provides an effective framework for the facilitation of group decision making and guides participants towards commitment to a portfolio of actions. According to Mingers and Rosenhead (2004), the cognitive maps of the SODA approach often have many hundreds of nodes interconnected in complex ways.

As Ackerman et al. (1997) illustrate, the process requires a great deal of effort on the part of facilitators and participants. The generation of models or maps by participants requires deep knowledge, creativity and considerable time, so does not readily scale up to widespread engagement of communities. Problem structuring methods are usually performed by small groups of participants in a decision making context. The methods typically provide a useful framework for a facilitator to manage the endeavors of a disparate group and are not designed to scale up to very large groups that encompass many members of a community.

Other approaches under the problem structuring methods banner include scenario modelling used for water allocation decisions by Young et al. (2000), Wang et al. (2008), Cai (2008), Chung et al. (2008), Bravo and Gonzalez (2009), and Li et al. (2009). With this approach, decision makers identify possible future scenarios and formulate allocation policies accordingly. Scenario maps can facilitate transparency, though the reasons for allocations under different scenarios are typically not made explicit in maps. The capacity for scenario modelling to scale up to facilitate active public participation has yet to be demonstrated.

SUMMARY

In this chapter, we have described the Generic Actual Argument Model. The model derives flexibility and power from: nodes whose generality is efficient in capturing many instance arguments that essentially have the same structure; a clear layout of the structure of reasoning; a clear delineation of inferences; capturing dialectical positions within a common structure. We have:

- Identified its basic set of propositions and how they are combined
- Identified the elements that formally control or represent the structure of reasoning
- Set out its reasoning mechanisms and how propositions are derived
- Discussed the extent to which derived propositions are valid and accepted and explored notions of argument strength that may suit different groups
- Set out the way in which the model supports discretion
- Clarified the boundaries of the non-dialectical model in supporting individual decision making as distinct from group decision making
- Discussed how the model supports the identification of points of similarity and difference in reasoning and is not altogether focused on defeat of another argument.

We have also noted that although it is Toulmin-based, it is quite different in its approach to modelling reasoning from other argument-based models. The salient features of the approach are its connection to a reasoning community, its mechanism for dealing with inconsistencies and its two levels of abstraction. The development of the complete dialectical model based on the GAAM is underway and this will provide a closer connection to the reasoning community.

The chapter illustrated the use of the GAAM with two examples, one drawn from refugee law and the other involving a group of water management novices determining how best to allocate water to different uses. The applications illustrate that the approach has some promise for supporting the work of participants in a reasoning community initially engaging in individual reasoning and later in collective reasoning. The Generic Argument Structure (GAS) shows some promise as an explicit representation of community reasoning however, the structure of the GAS seems to be at odds with the desire for inferences to be drawn holistically and perhaps intuitively.

REFERENCES

Afshar, F., Yearwood, J., & Stranieri, A. (2002). Capturing consensus knowledge from multiple experts. In *Proceedings of ES 2002, the Twenty-Second SGAI International Conference on Knowledge Based Systems and Applied Artificial Intelligence*. Cambridge, UK: Springer.

Ambler, S. (1996). A categorical approach to the semantics of argumentation. *Mathematical Structures in Computer Science, 6*, 167–188. doi:10.1017/S0960129500000931

Aristotle,. (1928). *The works of Aristotle. W. A. Pickard-Cambridge (Trans.)*. Oxford, UK: Oxford University Press.

Avery, J., Yearwood, J., & Stranieri, A. (2001). An argumentation based multi-agent system for etourism dialogue. In *Proceedings First International Workshop on Hybrid Intelligent Systems HIS 2001*, (pp. 497-512). Adelaide, Australia: ACM.

Ball, W. J. (1994). Using Virgil to analyse public policy arguments: A system based on Toulmin's informal logic. *Social Science Computer Review, 12*(1), 26–37. doi:10.1177/089443939401200102

Bayles, M. D. (1990). *Procedural justice: Allocating to individuals*. Dordrecht, The Netherlands: Kluwer.

Bench-Capon, T. J. M., Lowes, D., & McEnery, A. M. (1991). Argument-based explanation of logic programs. *Knowledge-Based Systems, 4*(3), 177–183. doi:10.1016/0950-7051(91)90007-O

Biswas, A. K. (2004). Integrated water resources management: A reassessment. *Water International, 29*(2), 248–256. doi:10.1080/02508060408691775

Branting, K. (1994). A computational model of ratio decidendi. *Artificial Intelligence and Law: An International Journal, 2*, 1–31. doi:10.1007/BF00871744

Branting, L. (2000). *Reasoning with rules and precedents -A computational model of legal analysis*. Dordrecht, The Netherlands: Kluwer Academic Publishers.

Buchanan, B., & Shortliffe, E. (Eds.). (1984). *Rule-based expert systems: The MYCIN experiments of the Stanford heuristic programming project*. Reading, MA: Addison Wesley Publishing Company.

Christie, G. C. (1986). An essay on discretion. *Duke Law Journal, 35*, 747–778. doi:10.2307/1372667

Clark, P. (1991). *A model of argumentation and its application in a cooperative expert system*. PhD Thesis. Glasgow, UK: University of Strathclyde.

Conklin, J., & Begeman, M. (1988). gIBIS: A hypertext tool for exploratory policy discussion. *ACM Transactions on Office Information Systems, 6*(4), 303–331. doi:10.1145/58566.59297

Dick, J. P. (1987). Conceptual retrieval and case law. In Proceedings of the First International Conference on Artificial Intelligence and Law, (pp. 106-115). New York, NY: ACM Press.

Dick, J. P. (1991). *A conceptual, case-relation representation of text for intelligent retrieval*. PhD Thesis. Ottawa, Canada: National Library of Canada.

Engisch, K. (1960). *Logische studien zur gesetzesanwendung* (2nd ed.). Heidelberg, Germany: Heidelberg Press.

European Union. (2004). *EU water initiative – Water for life*. Luxembourg, Luxembourg: Office for Official Publications of the European Communities.

Glymour, C., & Thomason, R. (1984). Default reasoning and the logic of theory perturbation. In *Proceedings of the AAAI Workshop on Nonmonotonic Reasoning*, (pp. 17–19). AAAI.

Gordon, T., & Karacapilidis, N. (1997). The zeno argumentation framework. In *Proceedings of the Sixth International Conference on Artificial Intelligence and Law*, (pp. 10-18). Melbourne, Australia: ACM Press.

Hua, G., & Kimbrough, S. (1988). On hypermedia-based argumentation decision support systems. *Decision Support Systems, 22*, 259–275. doi:10.1016/S0167-9236(97)00062-6

Jeffrey, P., & Gearey, M. (2006). Integrated water resources management: Lost on the road from ambition to realisation? *Water Science and Technology, 53*(1), 1–8. doi:10.2166/wst.2006.001

Johnson, P., Zualkernan, I., & Tukey, D. (1993). Types of expertise: An invariant of problem solving. *International Journal of Man-Machine Studies, 39*, 641–652. doi:10.1006/imms.1993.1077

Krause, P., Ambler, S., Elvang-Goransson, M., & Fox, J. (1995). A logic of argumentation for reasoning under uncertainty. *Computational Intelligence, 11*(1), 113–131. doi:10.1111/j.1467-8640.1995.tb00025.x

Loui, R., Norman, J., Altepeter, J., Pinkard, D., Craven, D., Lindsay, J., & Foltz, M. (1997). Progress in room 5: A testbed for public interactive semi-formal legal argumentation. In *Proceedings of the Sixth International Conference on Artificial Intelligence and Law*, (pp. 207-214). New York, NY: ACM Press.

MacCormick. (1978). *Legal reasoning and legal theory*. Oxford, UK: Oxford University Press.

Marshall, C. C. (1989). Representing the structure of legal argument. In *Proceedings of Second International Conference on Artificial Intelligence and Law*, (pp. 121-127). New York, NY: ACM Press.

Matthijssen, L. J. (1999). *Interfacing between lawyers and computers: An architecture for knowledge based interfaces to legal databases*. Dordrecht, The Netherlands: Kluwer Law International.

McDermott, D., & Doyle, J. (1980). Non-monotonic logic. *Artificial Intelligence, 13*, 41–72. doi:10.1016/0004-3702(80)90012-0

Prakken, H. (1993b). *Logical tools for modelling legal argument*. PhD thesis. Amsterdam, The Netherlands: Vrije University.

Raghu, T., Ramesh, R., Chang, A.-M., & Whinston, A. (2001). Collaborative decision making: A connectionist paradigms for dialectical support. *Information Systems Research, 12*(4), 363–383. doi:10.1287/isre.12.4.363.9705

Raz, J. (1990). *Practical reason and norms* (2nd ed.). Oxford, UK: Oxford University Press.

Reiter, R. (1980). A logic for default reasoning. *Artificial Intelligence, 13*, 81–132. doi:10.1016/0004-3702(80)90014-4

Rittel, H. J., & Webber, M. M. (1973). Dilemmas in a general theory of planning. *Policy Sciences, 4*, 155–169. doi:10.1007/BF01405730

Robert, C. (2001). *The Bayesian choice*. Berlin, Germany: Springer Verlag.

Rowe, G., Reed, C., & Katzav, J. (2003). *Araucaria: Marking up argument*. Paper presented at the European Conference on Computing and Philosophy. Glasgow, UK.

Stranieri, A., Yearwood, J., & Meikle, T. (2000). The dependency of discretion and consistency on knowledge representation. *International Review of Law Computers & Technology, 14*(3), 325–340. doi:10.1080/713673364

Stranieri, A., & Zeleznikow, J. (1998b). Split up: The use of an argument based knowledge representation to meet expectations of different users for discretionary decision making. In *Proceedings of Innovative Applications of Artificial Intelligence IAAI, 1998*, 1146–1152. Washington, DC: American Association of Artificial Intelligence.

Stranieri, A., & Zeleznikow, J. (2000a). Copyright regulation with argumentation agents. *Information & Communications Technology Law, 10*(1), 109–123. doi:10.1080/13600830124950

Stranieri, A., & Zeleznikow, J. (2001). Webshell: The development of web based expert system shells. In *Proceedings of ES2001-The Twenty-First SGES International Conference on Knowledge Based Systems and Applied Artificial Intelligence*, (pp. 245-258). London, UK: Springer Verlag.

Toulmin, S. (1958). *The uses of argument*. Cambridge, UK: Cambridge University Press.

van Dijk, T. A. (1989). Relevance in logic and grammar. In Norman, J., & Sylvan, R. (Eds.), *Directions in Relevance Logic* (pp. 25–57). Dordrecht, The Netherlands: Kluwer Academic Publishers. doi:10.1007/978-94-009-1005-8_2

Verheij, B. (1999). Automated argument assistance for lawyers. In *Proceedings of the Seventh International Conference on Artificial Intelligence and Law, ICAIL 1999*, (pp. 43-52). ACM Press.

Waismann, F. (1951). Verifiability. In Flew, A. (Ed.), *Logic and language*. Oxford, UK: Blackwell.

Walton, D. (1996a). *Argument structure: A pragmatic theory*. Toronto, UK: University of Toronto Press.

Walton, D. N., & Krabbe, E. C. W. (1995). *Commitment in dialogue: Basic concepts of interpersonal reasoning*. Albany, NY: State University of New York Press.

Yearwood, J., & Stranieri, A. (1999). The integration of retrieval, reasoning and drafting for refugee law: A third generation legal knowledge based system. In *Proceedings of the Seventh International Conference on Artificial Intelligence and Law. ICAIL 1999*, (pp. 117-137). ACM Press.

Yearwood, J., & Stranieri, A. (2000). An argumentation shell for knowledge based systems. In *Proceedings of IASTED International Conference on Law and Technology*, (pp. 105–111). IASTED.

Yearwood, J., Stranieri, A., & Avery, J. (2001). Negotiation and argumentation based agents to facilitate ecommerce. In *Proceedings of the International Conference on Advances in Infrastructure for Electronic Business, Science and Education on the Internet, SSGRR 2001*, (pp. 100–109). SSGRR.

Zeleznikow, J., & Stranieri, A. (1995). The split up system: Integrating neural networks and rule based reasoning in the legal domain. In Proceedings of the Fifth International Conference on Artificial Intelligence and Law, ICAIL 1995, (pp. 185-194). New York, NY: ACM Press.

Chapter 5
Communicating Reasoning and Dialectics

ABSTRACT

In this chapter, we consider the part that the communication of reasoning plays in contributing to the actions of reasoning communities. Communications distinguish group processes from individual processes and will introduce factors that enhance performance as well as factors that inhibit performance.

INTRODUCTION

The term "dialectic" has its origins in the philosophy of Plato, as the logical method of philosophy in the Socratic dialectical method of cross-examination. It is usually understood as an exchange of propositions (theses) and counter-propositions (antitheses) resulting in a synthesis of the opposing assertions, or at least a qualitative progression in the direction of the dialogue. The aim of the dialetical method is to try to resolve disagreement through rational discussion.

Motivated by a desire to organise communication within multi-agent systems, McBurney, Parsons, and Wooldridge (2002) specify a *Dialectical System* as consisting of:

1. A set of topics of discussion;
2. The syntax for a set of defined locutions concerning these topics;
3. A set of rules which govern the utterance of these locutions;
4. A set of rules which establish what commitments, if any, participants create by the utterance of each locution;
5. A set of rules governing the circumstances under which the dialogue terminates.

There seems to be a natural tendency for individuals to adopt a dialectical approach to the discussion of issues. When the number of individuals involved in the discussion becomes greater than two, it is often difficult to track discussion.

DOI: 10.4018/978-1-4666-1818-3.ch005

In its most liberal form the discussion can become chaotic, but often it is the case that there is a polarization between two large subgroups which can lose the advantages of having a diverse and rich contribution, capturing the diversity present in the group. Van de Ven and Delbeq (1971) found that groups where each group member generates ideas alone without interacting with other members were significantly superior to interacting groups. These results were based on three measures of performance: the number of unique ideas generated per person, the mean total number of ideas, and the quality of the ideas. Furthermore, in Electronic Brainstorming Systems (EBS) research, individuals working alone have been found to be as productive (in terms of the number of unique ideas) as EBS groups where individuals interact with each other (Hymes & Olson, 1992; Pinsonneault, Barki, Gallupe, & Hoppen, 1999). The lesson for communication within groups between individuals is that, in general, it is more effective for individuals to work alone in the generation of their ideas and reasoning before there is engagement with the wider group.

We have argued in Chapter 2 for the advancement of a more structured approach to reasoning within a reasoning community. In terms of communication, we envisage that individuals may engage in:

- Inter-individual reasoning communication;
- Communication of reasoning to the pool; and
- Communication of reasoning to the community based on their knowledge of the reasoning pool.

These levels of communication can pertain to the tasks that are associated with individual reasoning described in Chapter 3: fact finding or information seeking, inquiring, organising, or structuring and making claims or arguments. In considering these three levels of communication we shall concentrate in this chapter first on

the communication and reasoning that goes into developing the structured pool of reasons and then on how individual communication based on the pool structure proceeds. Inter-individual reasoning communication can involve information seeking dialogue, inquiry, narrative, persuasion, and deliberation, however based on the studies by van de Ven, Hymes and Pinsonneault we shall not concentrate on communication between individuals at an early stage but assume that individuals largely work alone in developing their individual reasoning.

The layout of arguments advanced by Toulmin (1958) has been enormously influential, however most studies that have applied the structure in computer-based systems have ultimately modified the original layout. In Stranieri et al. (2001) the variations are explained by drawing a distinction between argument models that are dialectical (in that their focus is to represent the exchange of views between participants) and those that are non-dialectical. Non-dialectical models use argumentation concepts to structure and organize knowledge and do not represent an exchange or discussion.

The Generic/Actual Argument Model (GAAM) described in the previous chapter is advanced as a non-adversarial, non-dialectical model for organizing knowledge within a community so that decisions can be effectively made in a transparent fashion and various elements of the decision may be supported by machine or human inference. The GAAM is a two-level model comprising generic arguments and actual arguments. Generic arguments provide a template that organizes all arguments plausibly advanced within a discourse. Actual arguments represent positions that discourse participants hold.

The Generic/Actual argument model has been applied to the development of numerous knowledge-based systems as illustrated throughout this text. In communities where there are multiple decision makers or the framework is used as the basis of deliberation for discussion on an issue, there is a need to identify the avenues for effective discourse and the necessary protocols for supporting this discourse. In this chapter, a dialectical model based on the GAAM is advanced and its application to deliberative dialogue is discussed. The discussion concentrates on the dialectical aspects that relate to the use of the GAAM framework by a group of reasoners.

Walton and Krabbe (1995) classified human dialogues into six basic types based on the objectives of the dialogue, the objectives of the participants and the information available to participants at the start of the dialogue. These are:

- **Information-Seeking Dialogues** where one participant seeks the answer to a question from another participant who is believed to know the answer;
- **Inquiry Dialogues** where the participants collaborate to answer some questions whose answers are not known by the participants;
- **Persuasion Dialogues** where one participant is trying to persuade another to accept a proposition;
- **Negotiation Dialogues** where the participants bargain over the division of a scarce resource. Each participant may be seeking to maximize her share of the resource;
- **Deliberation Dialogues** where the participants collaborate to decide on a course of action in some situation;
- **Eristic Dialogues** in which participants vent perceived grievances and injustices.

Formal models have been proposed for information-seeking dialogues (Hulstjin, 2000), inquiry dialogues (McBurney & Parsons, 2001), persuasion dialogues (Amgoud, Maudet, & Parsons, 2000; Walton & Krabbe, 1995), negotiation dialogues (Amgoud, Parsons, & Maudet, 2000; McBurney, van Eijk, Parsons, & Amgoud, 2003; Hulstjin, 2000; Sadri, Toni, & Torroni, 2001) and deliberation dialogues (Hitchcock, et al., 2001).

Reasoning communities that are effective are likely to be those whose interactions are characterised by deliberative dialogue (Wilhelm, 2000). Deliberation is distinguished from other types of dialogue and reasoning by several characteristics. Firstly, it focuses on action, or what is to be done in some situation by an individual or group of individuals. Secondly, there are frequently no commitments by any individual on the issue or basic question. Although individuals may hold a position on the issue there is no attempt to persuade others to agree to this position. Thirdly, there is a mutual concern or focus and although individual participants may evaluate proposals according to varying criteria, these differences are not based on personal interests that they seek to incorporate in the community decision. Reasoning communities are diverse in their goals, however in general they focus on outcomes that are optimal for the community as a whole. The decisions may be suboptimal for individuals within the group. Many reasoning exist to capitalize on the strength that they have through the range of talent and abilities they have across individuals and so the reasoning to action may be compelling in the case of the group if not in the case of any individual.

Deliberative discourse is often advanced as an ideal for modern democratic states with advanced Internet technologies. However, the extent to which this form of dialogue spontaneously occurs within groups is unclear. In his content analysis study of a number of Internet discussion groups Wilhelm (2000) found very little evidence for deliberation. Workshop methods such as the Search Conference advanced by Emery and Purser (1996) aim to facilitate deliberative dialogue largely because this form of group interaction is not the norm and can so easily be thwarted by power imbalances, organizational rigidity or numerous other factors.

McBurney, Hitchcock, and Parsons (Hitchcock, et al., 2001) present a formal model for deliberation dialogues grounded in Harald Wohlrapp's (Wohlrapp, 1998) theory of retroflexive argumentation for non-deductive argument and fully articulate the locutions and rules of a formal dialogue game for this model. In their discussion of deliberation dialogues, they say "Proposals for actions to address the expected need may only arise late in a dialogue, after discussion on the governing question, and discussion on what considerations are relevant to its resolution." The considerations relevant to resolution of the issue would be the relevant facts, factors, and reasons. Therefore, for example, in the case of the GAAM this would relate to the Generic Argument Structure (GAS) for the particular governing question within a domain that was the focus of the reasoning community. The reasoning community is structured in-line with their thoughts, so that the governing issue is identified and then each individual gathers the factors and facts considered relevant to the issue before coalescing to an agreed pool of relevant factors and reasons. The first part of this chapter will focus on the dialogue to establish the structured pool of reasons for some of the approaches to collective reasoning already discussed but with a particular focus on the GAS. The second part of the chapter will study the characteristics of deliberation dialogue that are based on the GAAM as well as briefly consider other models. We will assess the discourse by some of the models that have been proposed in the aforementioned literature. In particular, we consider the extent to which there is compliance with McBurney, Hitchcock and Parsons' eightfold way of deliberation dialogue (Hitchcock, et al., 2001).

In the next section, we discuss discursive communities and then a brief review of dialectical commnication. Then a brief review of the GAAM is provided prior to a description of the split between non-dialectical and dialectical notions of modelling reasoning. We briefly review the way in which dialogue to develop a GAS may proceed. A dialectical system based on the GAAM is developed and then an example of a dialogue based on the deliberative dialogue structure is presented.

The chapter concludes with some discussion and remarks and a brief look at other approaches.

ON-LINE AND OFF-LINE COMMUNITIES

The World Wide Web is usually seen as an information repository and resource. However, more recently, it is seen to act as a communication medium and as a forum for a liberal exchange of information and personal expression. As such, it has considerable potential for supporting group reasoning and decision-making. A large range of possible scenarios can be imagined, from a small panel of jurists considering a current case to a virtual community discussing a particular issue with an aim of reaching agreement or at least understanding of their differences. Key structural considerations need to be addressed to move towards implementations of systems to provide effective support. Some of the important questions are:

- What rules and tools would an on-line community need in order for it to engage in effective, meaningful debate so that decisions are generally accepted by its members?
- Can on-line communities produce a better-informed and more responsible constituency?
- Can on-line, and increasingly off-line as well, communities govern themselves online?

Our sense of how traditional communities operate is well developed as their existence has been documented over thousands of years. In contrast, on-line communities are only a few decades old, and the large difference evident between the two leaves us without the full benefit of the lessons of experience. For example, members of self-organizing, on-line communities come to one another and communicate as equals, without many of the social cues present in physical encounters. Much of the effective social glue that binds physical communities is lacking in their on-line counterparts. As well as this, various physical constraints that keep traditional geo-communities together in times of significant disagreement and conflict are also missing.

Although open communities on the Web are usually formed by those who share like values and a desire to use their shared on-line spaces for communication, virtual communities rarely achieve long-term peaceful existence, the ability to adequately inform themselves as a group or discuss and decide important issues. Greater anonymity on-line encourages both valuable conversations among those who would not normally interact off-line and the recognition and respect of views that would otherwise never be heard. It also fosters an irresponsibility that deeply undermines on-line discussions. Off-topic comments, disagreements about process, and much pointless discussion without decision-making are common. As a consequence, many on-line groups have resorted to moderators and filtering.

Governance of on-line communities requires the consent of the participants to a greater degree than physical communities. However, unlike off-line jurisdictions, on-line groups may have no convincing means by which to force their members to remain involved. This is a difference from ordinary communities in that not even the presence of members of self-organizing, on-line communities is assured. At any time, without providing reasons, a member can simply leave the community, sacrificing their social and intellectual investment usually without penalty.

One of the claims advanced in this book is that on-line discussions can be regulated for the benefit of all participants with the use of a normative reasoning structure -the coalesced reasoning. The structure captures important elements of reasoning within the field of discourse of concern

to the community and, by and large, is acceptable to the community. The structure can be created and maintained by the community itself or it may be created maintained by a social institution. The structure represents a shared understanding of the field of discourse and acts as a way of enhancing community identity.

Participants express their claims and beliefs with the use of the normative structure. The structure provides a mechanism for organizing the claims made by potentially thousands of participants. Supporting evidence for claims advanced by participants, typically expressed using links to documents, can be coherently organized by linking the evidence into the appropriate node within the structure. In this way, documents are efficiently collected and collated within the reasoning context of their use.

In moving between communities, documents play an important role, bringing people from different groups together to negotiate and coordinate common practices. Such negotiations are particularly significant in institutions, bureaucracies, and corporations that comprise many different communities. The direction of the institution as a whole may depend on the successful outcome of communication and negotiations among its constituent groups. Both the means and a willingness to come to a shared understanding are vital to the effectiveness of such institutions. Within on-line communities the views, thoughts and arguments are put forward as documents albeit possibly less structured (as comments on a news group, say). It becomes a key requirement within the on-line community to collectively develop the broad terms of reference of the discourse or in fact the key elements and agreed structure of the discourse. An explicit structure for the cooperative product of the group's deliberations can make this a more useful resource for the communication of reasoning and ultimately the formulation of individual and community reasoning. As we have already discussed in Chapter 2, this requirement is met to differing extents by IBIS, Delphi, ConSULT, and the GAAM. However, it is important to capture a normative structure that is based on a shared understanding of the domain of discourse.

How do we move on from the collection of heterogeneously structured documents and comments that make up the discourse provided by electronic media such as news groups or bulletin boards? Many on-line publications enable readers to respond directly to an article and to have that feedback appear directly below the article in a kind of threaded discussion format. A perfect example of this is ZDNet's Anchordesk. Publications can implement this process as a stand-alone feature or they can integrate it with existing discussion boards. CoNote is a computer-supported, cooperative work system designed to facilitate communication within a group via the use of shared annotations on a set of documents reported by Davis (1995). Google have added this idea to their collaborative authoring in Google Docs, which is a Web environment for storing, authoring, and collaboratively working on documents. The owner of a document can allow a community of people access to editing and annotating the document so that the document can be collectively crafted and discussion of the ideas and content can proceed. The central idea underlying CoNote and Google Docs is that shared annotations provide an effective forum for groups whose work involves frequent reference to some set of documents. The key difference is that the documents being annotated provide a context for the group discussions. This context enables people to find relevant discussions more easily. The shared annotations model also provides a more structured forum than tools for shared authoring, because the documents play the role of a (relatively) fixed context for discussions.

Seen in this way, shared documents within communities are in many ways the grounds for disagreement or agreement. Documents are the beginning rather than the end of the process of deliberation, providing a shared context for constructing meaning. Huizinga (1972) was particularly critical of the teaching of writing in the United States. Writing was presented to students as the outcome of deliberation whereas, Huizinga maintained, it was really just another part of the deliberative process. This view of the document as a medium or resource for negotiation and deliberation suggests that one avenue for technological development lies in improving the means for deliberation and negotiation.

In this chapter, we study the characteristics of deliberation dialogue that are based on the GAAM and we will assess the discourse by some of the other models that have been proposed in the literature. In particular, we consider the extent to which the models comply with the eightfold specification of a deliberation dialogue proposed by McBurney, Hitchcock, and Parsons (Hitchcock, et al., 2001). In general terms, this chapter also describes the extent to which the dialectical system based on the GAAM satisfies this specification.

DIALECTICAL ASPECTS OF REASONING

Argumentation has been used in reasoning in two distinct ways: with a focus on the use of argumentation to structure reasoning (i.e. non-dialectical emphasis) and with a focus on the use of argumentation to model discourse (i.e. dialectical emphasis). Dialectical approaches typically automate the construction of an argument and counter-arguments normally with the use of a non-monotonic logic where operators are defined to implement discursive primitives such as attack, rebut, or accept. Carbogim, Robertson, and Lee (2000) present a comprehensive survey of defeasible argumentation.

Dialectical models have been advanced by Cohen (1985), Fox (1986), Vreeswijk (1993), Dung (1995), Prakken (1993b, 1993a), Prakken and Sartor (1996), Gordon (1995b), Fox and Parsons (1998), Farley and Freeman (1995), Poole (1988), and many others. In general, these approaches include a concept of conflict between arguments and the notion that some arguments defeat others. Most applications that follow a dialectical approach represent knowledge as first-order predicate clauses but engage a non-monotonic logic to allow contradictory clauses. Mechanisms are typically required to identify implausible arguments and to evaluate the better argument of two plausible ones.

In applications of argumentation to model dialectical reasoning, argumentation is used specifically to model discourse and only indirectly used to structure knowledge. Concepts of conflict and of argument preferences map directly onto a discursive situation where participants are engaged in dispute.

COMMUNICATION TO ESTABLISH IBIS, DELPHI AND ConSULT MODELS

IBIS

Using an IBIS-based approach to assist a reasoning community involves building a representation of the reasoning towards the issue using the IBIS grammar. As discussed in Chapter 3, most IBIS-based approaches involve a facilitator in soliciting from the participants the elements of the IBIS grammar (questions, ideas, arguments—pro, con) before individuals can formulate their reasoning within this framework. Communication involved in developing this structure involves the facilitator first clearly identifying the issue/question through iterative dialogue with the group. Either agreement on a single issue is reached or multiple issues emerge for consideration. Once the issues are established then ideas are contributed. Communication is primarily from participants to facilitator who lists the relevant ideas and connects them to the relevant issue, but there may be discussion between participants that refines the ideas before they are represented in the IBIS structure. Similarly, with arguments for each idea,

the facilitator prompts for arguments pro and con each idea and as participants communicate these arguments, they may be discussed and refined before representation in the IBIS structure. At the end of these communications, an agreed IBIS structure serves as a template for individual and group reasoning to conclusions about the issue and the format of this structure can now act as a template for communicating reasoning on an issue.. The nature of the communication of each individual to the structure is heavily influenced by the IBIS grammar itself. These communications then become quite predictable in structure although the incidental inter-participant dialogue may be somewhat more free from and involve information-seeking dialogue, inquiry, persuasion and deliberation.

Delphi

The Delphi method can be used to structure a group communication process to deal with a complex problem. The Delphi Method is based on the Dialectical Inquiry approach. It helps to build consensus about a particular complex topic. In computer Delphi, there is no necessity for the contributors to be together. A panel of experts formulates a set of hypotheses (or theses) about the topic in question which are distributed to the participants. Their anonymous comments are then integrated into modified hypotheses. The iterative process continues until consensus is achieved on the hypotheses.

The method of communication used here is close to Socratic dialogue, not between participants, but between each participant and the expert team. The team is referred to as expert because they have to understand enough to rework the hypotheses on the basis of the communication received from the participants (maybe antitheses) and present new, revised hypotheses to the group. There is very little formal structure that is used in this technique to represent knowledge. The summarization and recasting of hypotheses is done by human intelligence and the whole process relies on human integration of multiple individual communications into a group or consensus view on the issue.

In work on the effectiveness of Delphi-structured communication for an idea generation task, Van de Ven and Delbeq (1974) found that Delphi groups generated more unique ideas than non-structured interacting groups but did not differ significantly in terms of satisfaction. This is in contrast to the results from van de Ven and Delbecq (1971) and Hymes and Olson (1992) who found that individuals generated more ideas than interacting groups. Therefore, the Delphi's structuring of communication provides the group with an improvement in the process. The key point here is to identify that this is not free, inter-individual communication of reasoning in the early stages but structured communication of individual reasoning and is closer to individual reasoning being communicated to the group pool of reasoning.

Dividing the Delphi approach into communication involving the explicit representation of a structure to support the reasoning community in reasoning and then individual or group reasoning using this structure is not appropriate. There is a more integrated approach here, which shows improvement over 'normal' groups interacting at the reasoning stage. The process aims to achieve consensus and individuals may only see summaries by the experts of the group communications rather than an explicit representation to which they contribute.

ConSULT

In ConSULT individual reasoning is contributed and captured as arguments (Toulmin style), these arguments are discussed (IBIS style) and then the pool of reasoning is used with a Borda voting technique to move participants to a consensus based on their shared understanding. Individuals, therefore, communicate with the ConSULT

system, representing their reason in Toulmin-style arguments. Anyone in the group can see these arguments presented in this form but their response to these arguments is made in an IBIS fashion with an individual participant presenting reasons for and against the other contributed propositions. All of these reasons can be seen by each individual in the information sharing stage. The communication process follows Hitchcock's high-level, five-stage model for deliberation dialogues: opening of the dialogue, sharing of the information, making proposals or counter-proposals, confirming the accepted proposals, and closing the dialogue.

As with Delphi, it is difficult to delineate the communication of reasoning for the pool and individual reasoning or group reasoning from the pool. However, it is clear that, in ConSULT, the initial communication of reasoning is in the form of Toulmin arguments and this provides the base pool of reasons. The whole process of ConSULT is a deliberative communication process following Hitchcock's protocol.

THE GENERIC/ACTUAL ARGUMENT MODEL

Generic Arguments

As mentioned previously, the Generic Actual Argument Model (GAAM) uses a variant of the layout of arguments advanced by Toulmin (1958). Arguments are represented at two levels of abstraction: the generic and the actual level. The generic level is sufficiently general so as to represent claims made by all members of a discursive community. All participants use the same generic arguments to construct, by instantiation, their own actual arguments. The generic arguments represent a detailed layout of arguments acceptable to all participants, whereas the actual arguments capture a participant's position with respect to each argument. The actual arguments that one participant advances are more easily compared with those advanced by another in a dialectical exercise because, in both cases, the actual arguments have been derived from a generic template that all participants share.

Figure 1 represents the structure we call a generic argument that acts as a structured reasoning template for a discussion involving the legalisation of voluntary euthanasia. The generic argument differs from the Toulmin layout in that:

- Claims and data items are represented using a variable-values representation rather than a statement;
- Each data item includes a statement indicating its reason for relevance. This replaces the Toulmin warrant;
- A list of inference procedures that are used to infer a claim value from data values in place of the Toulmin warrant;

- Statements indicating reasons for the appropriateness of each inference procedure (optional);
- Reasons for the appropriateness of the inference procedure;
- Context variables and values.

The claim in Figure 1 represents the point of the discussion; to ascertain whether Voluntary Euthanasia (VE) should be legalised. The generic argument structure, developed prior to the discussion, represents agreement amongst discourse participants on concepts deemed to be important to all. The generic argument does not reflect positions held by any participant but is intended to accommodate all positions regarded as reasonable.

Figure 1 illustrates that a claim on the legalisation of voluntary euthanasia is advanced on the basis of a position on three concepts: whether or

Figure 1. Generic argument for legalizing euthanasia

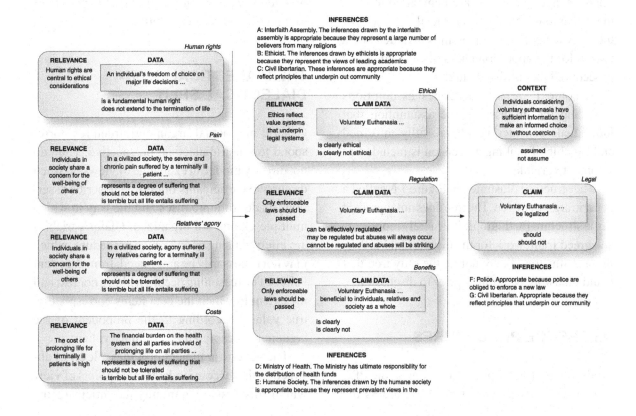

not voluntary euthanasia is regarded as ethical, the extent to which abuses can be curtailed and the extent to which benefits exist. A reason indicating why each of these concepts is relevant has been articulated to validate their inclusion. The process of drawing an inference from data values to claim values is seen as an exercise in mapping data to claim values. There are 24 different mappings possible. For example, an actual argument that advances the claims that VE is clearly ethical, it can be effectively regulated and is clearly beneficial therefore should be legalised represents one possible mapping. Two groups of mappings have been assigned a label (S. Police), which conveniently describe mappings that are consistent with inferences a police department might draw. A civil libertarian inference procedure describes mappings that are consistent with inferences that a civil liberties group may raise.

Figure 1 illustrates that the human rights, pain and relatives' agony are data items used to infer a claim regarding the ethicalness of VE. Pain, relatives' agony and cost are items used to infer the extent to which VE is beneficial. A reason for the relevance of each data item is included and a reason for the appropriateness of each inference procedure label is also included.

A context variable describes assumptions regarding the discussion. The assumption that individuals considering VE are fully informed and capable of making a decision is included as a context variable.

The structure illustrated in Figure 1 is called a generic argument tree. The tree does not represent a true structure for this topic but merely represents an agreed framework for the discussion. Further, the tree illustrated may not be the only tree that could plausibly be defined prior to discussion.

INFERENCE PROCEDURES

Trudy Govier (1987) provided a view of the PPC (premise, premise, conclusion) structure as the basic argument structure that can be filled by a variety of different argument schemes. At one level, this is the essence of the Toulmin structure as well as the GAAM. The GAAM takes this a step further by regarding an inference as a function and permitting a variety of allowed inference functions in any inference slot as long as they are supported by the community attached to the GAS.

Actual Arguments

Actual arguments made are instances of a generic argument where each data slot has a value, an inference procedure can be chosen and executed to deliver a value for the claim slot. For example, participant A may construct an actual argument that claims that VE should be legalised by applying inference procedure T on data values *is clearly ethical, can be effectively regulated,* and *is clearly beneficial.* Inference procedure C is applied to leaf node values *is a fundamental human right, represents a degree of suffering that should not be tolerated for the individual and for relatives* to infer that VE is clearly ethical.

THE DIALECTICAL, NON-DIALECTICAL SPLIT

Generic and actual argument structures correspond to a non-dialectical perspective. They do not directly model an exchange of views between discursive participants but rather describe assertions made from premises and the way in which multiple claims are organized. Claim variables are inferred using an inference procedure, which may not necessarily be automated, from data item values. The reasoning occurs within a context and the extent to which the data items correspond to true values, according to the proponent of the argument, is captured by certainty values.

The generic argument provides a level of abstraction that accommodates most points of view within a discursive community and anticipates the creation of actual arguments by participants as instantiations of a generic argument. However, it is conceivable that, given the open-textured nature of reasoning, a participant will seek to advance an actual argument that is a departure from the generic argument. This is a manifestation of discretion and can be realized with the introduction of a new variable (data, claim, or context) value, with the use of a new inference procedure or with a new claim value reason.

This framework including the generic/actual distinction, the clear separation of inference procedure from other components and the inclusion of reasons for relevance and context, introduces a structure that represents knowledge applicable to a discursive community.

Situations will arise where an argument needs to be made for which no generic argument exists. In these cases, a new argument specific to that situation is created. Ultimately, the series of actual arguments made in a case is built and represents the full argument in that situation. Some of the arguments are instances of generic arguments, others are newly created.

DIALOGUE FOR DEVELOPING A GAS

Within a community, a GAS provides a constant reminder of the agreed upon, shared understanding and interpretative assumptions. Between communities, it can provide a public face to the elaboration and explanation as well as the possibility of encouraging participation. The GAS can be developed in two ways. Participants to a dialogue can collectively deliberate on a structure that will suit as the desired normative structure. Alternatively, a social institution can be charged with the advancement and on-going maintenance of a GAS. Once a GAS is developed for the community, then discourse using the structure can proceed.

An example of the latter approach can be imagined in a futuristic legal setting. The social institution charged with the maintenance of the GAS would be the Court that has jurisdiction over the subject matter of the discourse. For example, a future Family Court may advance a GAS. All concepts that are relevant for a Family Court judgment and precisely how each relates to others is explicitly represented in the GAS. Claims made by all parties to a dispute are made as actual arguments, instantiated from the GAS. In this way, points of divergence can more readily be identified and information systems can more easily be integrated to support reasoning. Ultimately, a court judgment is also represented as an instantiation of the GAS ensuring a transparency of reasoning that is well beyond current practice.

Discursive communities that have no social institution that can be appropriately charged with the maintenance of a GAS can develop their own GAS. The construction of the generic argument structure can be carried out through structured dialogue between GAAMtalk (a Web version of our argumentation tool) (Yearwood & Stranieri, 2002) and the participants. The basis of this structured dialogue is the repeated use of a meta-generic argument structure. It sets the structure of reasoning and debate for the community on the particular matter for deliberation. As a step toward achieving this, Afshar et al. (2002) describe ConSULT, a system that enables a community to engage in a Delphi-like communication and a Borda preferendum vote in order to agree on a generic argument structure.

The meta-generic arguments are:

1. The top-level generic argument claim is: <PREFIX><VALUE><SUFFIX>{is/is not} the top-level claim. At this stage <VALUE> is left unspecified;

2. <VALUE SET> {is/is not} the agreed set of values for the top-level claim;

3. <PREFIX><VALUE><SUFFIX>{is/is not} a data item for the claim;

4. <REASON FOR RELEVANCE> {is/is not} a reason for the relevance of the data item;
5. <BACKING> {is/is not} is the backing for the <REASON FOR RELEVANCE>.

These can be organised into a tree with the top-level claim that, 'the GAS that emerges,' is the currently agreed GAS for the discourse. Each of the above meta-generic arguments then acts as grounds for this top-level claim. The subject of Argument 1 is moved, seconded, and voted upon. Once the generic form of the top level claim is established the grounds on which such a claim will be made are adduced. "<PREFIX><VALUE><SUFFIX> {is/is not} a data item for the claim," has to be moved and seconded. The support for the data item is then measured. In the case that the support is judged to be sufficient, the reasons supporting the claim (a document) are stored as <REASON FOR RELEVANCE>. <BACKING> is then dealt with in a similar fashion and then the discourse will move onto the next grounds or data item in turn. The appropriate meta-generic arguments are iteratively applied until there is agreement not to go any further.

The collaborative development of the generic structure provides a framework for the development of actual arguments. It involved the contribution of reasons (these are attached as documents) as to why data items are relevant and participants are now in a position to construct their actual arguments. The structure can be displayed as a tree in one of the Windows of GAAMtalk and the contents of each node displayed as each node is traversed.

Once a generic argument structure has been established, participants can start to use the structure to develop their actual arguments. Points of diversion identified between participants' arguments can be discussed by focusing on the particular issue (whether it be a claim value reason or a new data item). Once these points of disagreement are identified the strength of each argument can be gauged.

INDIVIDUAL REASONING FROM A GAS

Dialectical arguments are those that focus not only on support by reasons but also attack by counter-arguments. In a standard view, arguments express how a conclusion is supported by premises. This is largely the notion supported by the GAAM. However, the GAAM sets out a structure for a domain of reasoning that permits reasoning towards different conclusions. In considering how arguments are supported or attacked by other arguments, dialectic argumentation frameworks resort to operators that describe support and attack. Attack operators may be further classified as rebut or undercut or other more specific classifications of attack that relate to the particular argumentation structure or argumentation theory. For example, in Verheij's CumulA, defeat of an argument can be represented in terms of Pollock's (1987) undercutting and rebutting defeat but also by sequential weakening and defeat by parallel strengthening. In the argument mediation system ArguMed Verheij (1999), only undercutters are used. In the GAAM approach, the structural point at which there is divergence can be identified and is suggestive of dialectical operators that describe these discrepancies.

In the GAAM, a GAS encourages participants to construct actual arguments that are structured by the GAS. This structure then provides a basis for the comparison of arguments and the basis for the dialectical exchange that may occur around participants' reasoning. The particular elements of an actual argument that need to be considered, assuming that the actual arguments comply with the GAS, relate to data, inference and claim or conclusion (assuming the same context variable values). These are data item values, selection of an inference procedure and claim value or conclusion. If one or both of the actual arguments deviates from the domain GAS then the comparison of actual arguments becomes more complex.

Consider two actual arguments A_1, and A_2. Based on the structure of actual arguments described above we can investigate the different types of dialectical operators that may be suggested by the ways in which the two actual arguments differ. Actual arguments can differ in their data item values, their inference procedures and their claim values as well as the certainty values on each of these. Leaving aside the certainty values, Table 1 summarises the different types of dialectical operators that are suggested.

Complete Agreement occurs when both arguments make identical claims, from the same premises in the same way. These arguments are labeled identical. *Agreement* occurs if the very similar premises are used to infer the same claims using the same inferences. The arguments are said to be equivalent. A *Questionable divergence* occurs when different claims are reached with the same inference applied to very similar premises.

Divergent inference occurs when the same or similar premises lead to different claims because a different inference is used. In terms of divergence or attack, it is the inference procedure as the connection between the premises and the conclusion that is the point of divergence and in the extreme case the inference procedure reasons may attack each other and so would constitute a Pollock undercut.

Divergent premises occur when different premises lead to different claims despite the same inference. Different claims can also arise from different premises and inferences (Divergent premise and inference).

A *mistake* occurs when two arguments use identical premises and inferences but somehow arrive at different claims.

An actual argument supports another as *supportive by premise* if both use the same premises to advance the same claim though this is done using different inference. *Supportive by inference* occurs when the same claim is inferred using the same inference though premises differ. *Supportive by claim* describes those arguments that advance the same claims though premises and inferences are different.

A GAS Provides a Theory of Normativity

At a fundamental level, any actual argument that is instantiated from the GAS should be admissible from the point of view of the associated community. Any argument that is not an instantiation of

Table 1. Dialectical operators suggested by comparing actual argument components

Dialectical Operator	Data of A_1, A_2	Inference Procedure of A_1, A_2	Claim values of A_1, A_2	Type
Complete Agreement	Same	Same	Same	Identical
Agreement	Similar	Same	Same	Equivalent
Questionable divergence	Similar	Same	Different	Questionable
Divergent inference	Same or similar	Different	Different	Different premise
Divergent premise and inference	Different	Different	Different	Different argument
Mistake	Same	Same	Different	Not possible
Supportive by premise	Same	Different	Same	Reinforcement
Supportive by inference	Different	Same	Same	Insensitive inference procedure
Supportive by claim	Different	Different	Same	Support

the GAS may become admissible if the argument can be viewed as an instantiation of a changed GAS by the agreement of the community. Good or admissible arguments are those that comply with the *norm* of the GAS. A 'bad' argument may be one that cannot be made to conform to any close approximation to the GAS. In attempting to model the usual dialectical positions, it is necessary to agree on a definition of which claim-value pairs constitute opposites. We do not attempt to make this definition here, as it would be a matter for the associated community.

In the following $\neg C$ refers to the opposite (defeater) of C. We make the following definitions.

A statement $C = C_p C_{vk} C_s$ is Γ-*justified* if and only if it can be deduced from Γ.

A statement $C = C_p C_{vk} C_s$ is *universally* Γ-*justified* if and only if it has at least one derivation from Γ and $\neg C$ has no derivation from Γ.

A statement $C = C_p C_{vk} C_s$ is *unjustified* if it has no derivation in G and it is *defeated* if it is unjustified and at least one $\neg C$ has a derivation.

In a GAS where there are only computational inference procedures, the status of any admissible proposition is automatically computable. The question of whether one proposition defeats another is not attempted here as the strength of individual arguments can be defined in different ways and computed by one of the mechanisms discussed above.

In the dialectic view, although the starting points of the participants are asymmetrical, the regulating system of rules for the discussion is not. According to Slob (2002), dialectic logic aims at an inter-subjective understanding of normativity based on the assumption that participants *would* accept the rules if they were explicitly stated, *would*-normativity. However this also allows *would not*. Faced with losing a discussion a participant may simply withdraw his commitment. According to Johnson and Blair 'many people evaluate arguments by one "standard" only:

does it support my view or not?' They insist that this is not a logical standard of evaluation but a purely idiosyncratic one (Johnson & Blair, 1983, p. 30). The usual way that dialecticians overcome this is to try to regulate the basic agreement of participants by means of a modest understanding of rationality. Dialectical rationality is a logical ideal, deriving its normativity from the idea that ultimately people would come to agreement in matters under dispute if they were given sufficient time and information. Slob argues that the main problem for a dialectical notion of rationality is that it cannot perform its evaluative task. The perspective of a rational observer is only useful if it transcends the limited perspectives of the discussants and in this case there is no impact on the participants, but this would mean that, if there is an influence, the observer becomes part of the discussion and therefore loses this external position and therefore the capacity to perform the evaluative task.

This means that there is no *shared* standard for evaluation available. Slob proposes a solution based in the similarity of dialectic and rhetoric characterised by Perelman and Olbrechts-Tyteca (1971). He proposes leaving the setting of the audience-orientation limits to the participants themselves. His dialogical rhetoric distributes burden of proof over both participants. This is a shift from the pure dialectic, one-sided burden of proof to a more symmetrical requirement. It allows both participants to apply their own, perhaps idiosyncratic, standard. The argumentative force of the conclusion is the result of the moves that are established during the discussion.

Dialogue

In a dialogue the participants of a community reasoning on an issue modelled by a GAS may start anywhere in the tree (GAS). This can be viewed as a claim, an inference slot or their actual arguments associated with the claim slot. The object of a dialogue is to identify whether there is agreement on the claim or where in the associated argument, differences may be considered for reconciliation. If there is agreement, then the dialogue ends and another dialogue, starting at some other point in the GAS (outside the subtree underneath the agreed claim), can occur. If there is not agreement, then the participants move to exchanges on each of the claims that are the data for the inference slot. If the claim is a leaf of the GAS then the participants are *irreconcilable on data*. If they agree on all of the data items then they may differ on the context variable values and in this case they are *potentially reconcilable through agreement on context variable values* otherwise they are *potentially reconcilable through agreement on inference*. If there are data items that they differ on, then each of these can be used as the starting point for a new dialogue.

EXAMPLE

We consider one of Trudy Govier's examples (1992) on 'conductive argument': the question of legalizing voluntary euthanasia for terminally ill patients. She gives 4 points for and two against: responsible adults should be able to choose whether to live or to die; that patients could be saved from unbearable pain; that social costs would be reduced; that relatives would be saved from unbearable agonies; (against) that we are never sure that a cure might be discovered and that we risk abuse. The example has been modelled slightly differently using the GAAM and is presented in Figure 1. A sample dialogue between participants X and Y is as follows:

1. The discussion commences with X and Y agreeing to use the generic argument as a template.
2. X proposes the actual argument claim for the argument labeled *Ethical* in Figure 1, that Voluntary Euthanasia (VE) is clearly not ethical. Y also believes this. At this point, X

and Y have, as their point in common, the claim that VE is clearly ethical. They both assert this.

3. Y selects a new node to discuss: the node concerning the regulation of VE and proposes that VE *may be regulated though abuses will always occur*. This is the argument labeled *Regulation* in Figure 1. X is concerned that *abuses will be prominent*. This is a Point of Difference at a leaf node so is listed as potentially reconcilable on data. Y selects a new node for discussion.
4. The argument labeled *Cost* in Figure 1 concerning the financial burden of terminally ill individuals is selected by Y. Y proposes that the financial burden on the State of keeping terminally ill patients alive *is so high that others will suffer if funds are not re-directed*. X agrees and adds a Point of Agreement.
5. X proposes that VE is clearly beneficial to the individual and society by creating an actual argument from the generic benefit argument labeled *Benefit* in Figure 1. Y proposes that the benefit *is not so clear*. The difference is required to be justified. The set of actual arguments for child nodes of the benefit argument are examined by X and Y.
6. Y re-selects an earlier node: that concerning the regulation of VE and this time retracts the earlier hard-line claim and softens it to claim that *although abuses will occur, by and large VE can be regulated*. This claim is removed from the Point of Difference list. Y selects a new node for discussion.
7. Both X and Y agree that the individual's pain should not be tolerated in the argument labeled *Pain* in Figure 1. The relatives' agony is similarly intolerable and costs should be borne by the health system. However, the irreconcilable difference at the node concerning *Benefit* remains despite agreement on all three-child nodes. This is because X has adopted an inference procedure consistent with that advanced by the Humane Society,

whereas Y has used a different mapping. X and Y are therefore potentially reconcilable on inference. There are still nodes to discuss.

8. At the root node labeled *Legal*, X asserts that VE should be legalised. Y disagrees. Both have agreed that VE is ethical and that it can be regulated although abuses will occur. Y was not clear of the benefits of VE whereas X remains certain. There are no nodes that have not been discussed so the dialogue is called a complete dialogue and ends.

The discussion has identified numerous points of difference and of agreement upon which both parties should deliberate. The generic argument structure has provided a template to structure the dialogue without resorting to combative metaphors or unduly constraining the content or flow of the discourse.

Dialogue involving the use of a generic argument structure involves steps more formally defined in the addendum of this chapter.

The dialogue procedure avoids differences that lie in the sub-tree of an agreed claim. A top-level claim is fully discussed when a set of dialogues that covers the GAS has occurred between participants. We will call this a *complete dialogue*.

This approach to dialogue suggests a particular approach to deliberation that allows interaction between participants punctuated with deliberation and the possibility of revision. It is also flexible in the selection of arguments that cover the GAS. The procedure can be organised to add claims that participants agree on to their individual commitment stores (Singh, 2000). These claims do not need to be revisited. The alternative (monolithic) approach would be to have each participant deliberate and present their complete actual argument that covers the whole GAS. This has the advantage of enforcing consideration of all items in the GAS as well as encouraging complete independence on all arguments in the tree. The former dialogue approach may support less independence and more interaction in the deliberation process.

Dialogue with a Non-Static GAS

The dialogue above is defined for a static GAS but the GAS in fact can change over time and often the change is prompted by participants using a GAS in a deliberative discussion rather than developing a GAS. We could refer to this situation as a variable GAS situation. A dialogue using a variable GAS would differ from the above in item (4b). At this stage, the participants would have different data item sets. Only the case of one participant having data items additional to the shared GAS need be considered.

If a participant is not using some of the data items in the common GAS then these can simply be taken to have default values. If C_0 is an additional data item for participant P_1 and if $POD=\emptyset$ for all the GAS data items then P_1 can provide P_2 with an *RR* (*reason for relevance*) and a *B* (*backing*) although these are part of the GAS construction dialogues. At this stage C_0 is identified as the point for reconciliation. If $POD\neq\emptyset$ then each $C_i \square POD$ can be used to start a new dialogue.

Baker's (1998) main hypothesis is that argumentative interactions impose "a special type of interactive and interactional pressure on participants (to resolve the verbal interpersonal conflict, to be internally coherent, to preserve face,...) that may force meanings and knowledge to be refined." Therefore, it is that participants in a discussion with an incomplete GAS may use their discussion to further elaborate the GAS.

Multi-Participant Dialogues

One of the advantages of the dialogue above is that it can be easily modified to suit many participants. Consider the following.

Complete Dialogues

McBurney, Hitchcock, and Parsons (Hitchcock, et al., 2001) present a formal framework for deliberation dialogues grounded in Harald Wohlrapp's

(1998) theory of retroflexive argumentation for non-deductive argument and fully articulate the locutions and rules of a formal dialogue game for this model. They define: questions, actions, goals, constraints, perspectives, facts, and evaluations as mutually exclusive types that are used in their eight-stage model of deliberation dialogue. The eight stages are: *open, inform, propose, consider, revise, recommend, confirm,* and *close*. They assess their protocol by comparison with human deliberation dialogues, by measuring it against normative principles for deliberation, specifically, Alexy's rules for discourse ethics (Alexy, 1990) and Hitchcock's Principles of Rational Mutual Inquiry (Hitchcock, 1991), and by deliberation outcomes. Constraints, perspectives, and evaluations are more relevant to the dialogue for establishing a GAS and are not discussed further here. Actions will be taken to correspond to the values of the top-level claim of the GAS.

We now consider how a complete dialogue based on the GAAM implements the eight-stage model for deliberation dialogues. We use the same set of locutions with their form adapted to suit the constructs of the GAAM. They are illustrated in Addendum 3.

In a manner similar to McBurney et al., we can conclude that the above supports each of the eight stages of their formal model for deliberation dialogues. Furthermore, the dialogue structure above satisfies Alexy's rules for discourse ethics to the same extent. It also satisfies all but four of Hitchcock's eighteen Principles of Rational Mutual Inquiry. We would also argue that H5 (Orderliness) is satisfied by virtue of the systematic approach of the dialogue structure.

COMMUNICATING INDIVIDUAL REASONING WITH THE GAAM

The GAAM makes the following contributions as a framework to support deliberative discourse and reasoning within reasoning communities.

1. It abstracts claims into a more general (and computationally useful, variable-value) form that allows for the expression of a range of views. In doing so, a more general 'matter in question' is captured. This transformation of a specific claim into a more general issue or matter in question sets the scene for the next stage -the finding or adduction of the premises that would be considered relevant to arguing towards a conclusion on the matter in question.

2. At a common sense level, the criterion used to decide upon premises (again generalised claim slots) is relevance to inferring a conclusion. This is, however, not the full story as relevance is subjective in nature. The question, 'relevant from whose point of view?' may be legitimately asked. However, the GAAM supports a GAS that connects, or is associated with, a community of reasoners or decision-makers. It does this in a number of ways:

    a. the set of premise slots linked to a claim slot by an inference slot is supposed to allow the presentation of actual arguments that are inclusive of the broad range of perspectives in the community. This requirement is in practice an approximation to the theoretical requirement of capturing the different frames (perspectives) on the matter in question from the various positions of the participants in the community. This is supported by Wohlrapp (1998), "In general, a conclusion of an argumentation is plausible if it contains a unification of the different frames given to the MIQ (Matter In Question) by the positions."

    b. the set of premise slots is open to agreement by the community and can be added to at any time.

    c. there are several ways of making an inference from the premise slots to the claim slot rather than a unique inference.

3. It separates the structure of reasoning from the details of the inferences. The structure is determined as in (2) above. Permissible inference procedures are determined by the members of the community. Why should the model propose and suggest a choice of many inference procedures within an inference slot? At a philosophical level, this is a move away from deductive monism but it is also a move away from the standard dialectical normativity and dialectical rationality. There is no outside, rational observer. The participants in general agree on the GAS (premises, structure and inferences) and in specific decide on the way that these are used in deliberative dialogue. At a more pragmatic level, it is concerned with permitting the expression of different reasoning functions on the premises. One manifestation of this is allowance for different weighing of premises in inferences.

4. The dialogue structures presented in the previous sections for individuals using the structured pool (the GAS) permit freedom in the progression of the dialogue yet provide a procedure for identifying common ground, points of difference and identifies areas for reconciliation. In the case of a fully developed GAS, agreement can be reached by participants' reasoning leading to the same top-level claim by the dialogical process of component dialogues where reasoning for a particular claim is articulated followed by consideration of the other participant's reasoning on that claim and possible revision. When the GAS is variable, dialogue largely proceeds in a similar fashion with some additional proposals for premises (data items). Depending on the level of formality, there may be a need to resort to the judgment of the community on the admissibility of these into the structure.

COMMUNICATING INDIVIDUAL REASONING IN IBIS APPROACHES

Once an IBIS template has been established for an issue by a reasoning community, it forms the structured pool of reasons and product of cooperation. An individual can then represent and communicate their reasoning as ideas that they believe are supported and the (pro) reasons of support provided by the template. They may also provide reasons for not supporting other ideas, which may be the positions adopted by other individuals. If individuals agree on a position or idea that is most strongly supported, then a collective decision has been achieved. If there is disagreement on the position that is most strongly supported then the arguments in the structure are re-examined with a focus on the areas of conflict. There is, however, no means of representing the conflict between propositions within IBIS, so communication at the level of individual difference within IBIS is not supported.

The predominant hypothesis underlying computer systems based on IBIS is that, by making the structure of arguments explicit, diagrams can help users to construct more rigorous arguments that are easier to communicate (Golder & Coirier, 1996; Larkin & Simon, 1987; Scaife & Rogers, 1996). So it is the syntactic (not the semantic) structure of diagrammed arguments that helps reasoners to better formulate their statements.

The Zeno argumentation framework (Gordon & Karacapilidis, 1997) is a formal dialectical system based on IBIS. It does not contain any rules or constraints related to the validity of positions on an issue. In this system, discussion on an issue is represented as a dialectical graph based on the IBIS elements where a Dialectical Graph is defined as follows:

Definition: Let P, A and I be finite sets of positions, arguments and issues, respectively, such that the antecedents and consequents of all arguments in A are members of P. Then (P,A) forms a directed, finite graph in which the positions are nodes and the arguments in A are edges. Arguments link the positions as antecedent and consequent. The tuple (P,A,I) is called a dialectical graph.

A position is modelled as a primitive, atomic element in the Zeno model, similar to the way atomic propositions are primitive elements of propositional logic, but positions are different from propositions. A proposition is a context-independent, declarative statement having a truth-value, whilst a position records the performance of a speech act in a particular thread of discussion and its meaning is defined by its role in the discussion and is dependent on its location in the argumentation graph.

Prakken's concept of an Argumentation Framework (Prakken & Sartor, 1996) requires some representation of the idea of conflict between arguments. The IBIS model includes pro and con arguments, but they do not inform on the status or conflict of positions within the model. Zeno extends IBIS with a means of expressing preferences for positions and computes position labels, and so provides a means of specifying the status of propositions. In Zeno, preference expressions are a particular kind of position, with some internal structure and arguments about these are also supported. So it becomes possible to make a type of inference about the relative quality of alternative proposed solutions to an issue.

In Zeno, a set of proof standards (such as: scintilla of evidence, preponderance of evidence, no better alternative, best choice, and beyond reasonable doubt) is defined. For a dialectical graph and a proof standard for an issue, the main task is to determine which of the positions satisfy its standard. Several competing positions can satisfy the proof standard for an issue, and the users of the system may ultimately have to choose one when deciding the issue. Zeno uses a graph labelling system that is a type of *reasoning maintenance* system (Doyle, 1979).

The ability to qualify positions is a significant advance over the informal IBIS model. It transforms IBIS from a method to organize and index information into a medium for supporting debate. Participants can see whether their positions are currently "winning" or "losing" in the sense that the proof standard for the position is either satisfied or not.

COMMUNICATING INDIVIDUAL REASONING IN DELPHI AND ConSULT

In Delphi, individual communication of reasoning is part of the iterative process where essentially the pool of reasons is captured by a text summary of the reasoning of individuals and feedback on that reasoning. We shall consider the pool as the summarised reasoning after each iteration. An individual, based on the new version of the pool, may choose to make further contributions. In Delphi, these are in free, natural-language form. Based on these individual comments and further reasons, the facilitator detects whether there is agreement, general consensus or disagreement. At some point the facilitator's summary is accepted by all individuals and is taken as a representation of the community views or decisions.

ConSULT represents individual arguments within the pool as TAS, which each individual can see. Each individual then takes a position (IBIS style) on each of the claims in the Toulmin arguments in the pool and communicates the position. Again, each member of the community can see all of these communications.

OTHER DIALECTICAL APPROACHES

Verheij's (1996) CumulA's process-model is *free* in that it deals not only with forward argumentation or inference but also with the adduction of reasons or justification. *Premise-based* systems such as in Vreeswijk's model (1993, 1997) focus on inference or drawing conclusions from fixed premises. Issue-based systems such as IBIS (Rittel & Webber, 1973) focus on justification or adducing reasons for a fixed issue. The GAAM separates the adduction of reasons stage from the inference stage in that adduction is used (iteratively) to formulate the GAS and then, once the GAS has been developed, inferences can be made. In fact, the inference stage can be further split into two stages: the determination of admissible inference procedures and then the selection of an inference to a conclusion.

Prakken and Sartor (1996) present a formal framework and logical system for defeasible reasoning for assessing conflicting arguments. An important feature of their system is that priorities are not fixed, but are themselves defeasibly derived as conclusions within the system. This permits modelling debates about choice between conflicting arguments. The proof theory of the system is presented in dialectical style where a proof takes the form of a dialogue between a proponent and an opponent in an argument. An argument is *justified* if the proponent can make the opponent run out of moves in whatever way the opponent attacks.

SUMMARY

In this chapter, we have focused on the communication of reasoning in the framework of:

- Communication to establish the structured pool of reasons on an issue for the community
- Individual communication of reasoning based on the structured pool of reasons

Rather than focus on inter-individual communication of reasoning at an early stage, individuals can initially focus on their individual contribution to a structure for a pool of reasons and then par-

ticipate in a structured form of communication of their individual reasoning. A system can be used to identify points in common and points of difference and the basis for agreement, difference, and disagreement. A system like Zeno can be used to extend IBIS with a dialectical graph and a set of proof standards and then determine which positions satisfy the proof standards on an issue. This capability can be very useful in informing a reasoning community on the set of positions that meet some required standard for evidence that may have been determined at the engagement stage.

Systems that support communication and reasoning have been examined in this chapter and a detailed explanation of the GAAM has been provided to demonstrate how highly structured systems could operate. Inherent in the GAAM is a structured approach to reasoning. In a macro sense, the process of reasoning is structured into three stages: in the first stage, participants engage in the process of adducing premises for the matter in question—this is an iterative process that generates an agreed tree structure; in the second stage possible sets of inference from premises to conclusions are set out; in the third stage participants use the structure and choose inferences to present their actual reasoning.

We have relied on the work of Hitchcock, McBurney, and Parsons to demonstrate that these types of deliberation dialogues, which are supported by the GAAM, comply with criteria for normative principles for deliberation, specifically Alexy's rules for discourse ethics and Hitchcock's Principles of Rational Mutual Inquiry and indicated some additional aspects of *orderliness* over their framework.

The GAAM offers a dynamic template for structuring knowledge within a domain of discourse that is connected to, and regulated by, a community. It is the community-accepted GAS that acts to normatively influence both admissible reasoning and the progression of dialectical reasoning between participants. Around this structure can be woven dialogues that are orderly, but flexible, and that support deliberation. These dialogues may adhere to the two-level process of constructing the GAAM and then using it or to interweaving the development of a GAS with a discussion. These provide two different models that share a focus on a community-determined structure for reasoning.

We have demonstrated that there can be a range of ways that the GAAM can underpin a dialectical system to support deliberative discourse. The nature of the relationship determines the flexibility that the participants have in the discourse. In a very highly structured domain with an established reasoning community, with a stable GAS, participants are more confined to dialogue within the GAS. In a less developed arena where the GAS is less well developed, the dialogue and deliberations can proceed in either of two ways. In the first, community completion of the GAS would be required, followed by dialogue within the GAS structure. In the second, completion of the GAS could be interwoven with the formulation of each participant's reasoning.

REFERENCES

Afshar, F., Yearwood, J., & Stranieri, A. (2002). Capturing consensus knowledge from multiple experts. In *Proceedings of ES 2002, the Twenty-Second SGAI International Conference on Knowledge Based Systems and Applied Artificial Intelligence*. Cambridge, UK: Springer Verlag.

Alexy, R. (1990). A theory of practical discourse. In Benhabib, S., & Dallmayr, F. (Eds.), *The Communicative Ethics Controversy* (pp. 151–190). Cambridge, MA: MIT Press.

Amgoud, L., Maudet, N., & Parsons, S. (2000). Modelling dialogues using argumentation. In E. Durfee (Ed.), *Proceedings of the Fourth International Conference on Multi-Agent Systems (IC-MAS-2000)*, (pp. 31-38). Boston, MA: IEEE Press.

Amgoud, L., Parsons, S., & Maudet, N. (2000). Arguments, dialogue and negotiation. In W. Horn (Ed.), *Proceedings of the Fourteenth European Conference on Artificial Intelligence (ECAI-2000)*, (pp. 338-342). Berlin, Germany: IOS Press.

Carbogim, D., Robertson, D., & Lee, J. (2000). Argument-based applications to knowledge engineering. *The Knowledge Engineering Review, 15*(2), 119–149. doi:10.1017/S0269888900002058

Cohen, P. (1985). *Heuristic reasoning about uncertainty: An artificial intelligence approach.* London, UK: Pitman.

Doyle, J. (1979). A truth maintenance system. *Artificial Intelligence, 12*, 231–272. doi:10.1016/0004-3702(79)90008-0

Dung, P. M. (1995). On the acceptability of arguments and its fundamental role in non-monotonic reasoning, logic programming and n-person games. *Artificial Intelligence, 77*(2), 321–357. doi:10.1016/0004-3702(94)00041-X

Emery, M., & Purser, R. E. (1996). *The search conference: A powerful method for planning organisational change and community action.* San Francisco, CA: Jossey Bass.

Farley, A., & Freeman, K. (1995). Burden of proof in legal argumentation. In *Proceedings of Fifth International Conference on Artificial Intelligence and Law*, (pp. 156-164). ACM Press.

Fox, J. (1986). Knowledge, decision making and uncertainty. In Gale, W. A. (Ed.), *Artificial Intelligence and Statistics*. Reading, MA: Addison-Wesley.

Fox, J., & Parsons, S. (1998). Arguing about beliefs and actions. In Hunter, A., & Parsons, S. (Eds.), *Applications of Uncertainty Formalisms* (pp. 266–302). Berlin, Germany: Springer. doi:10.1007/3-540-49426-X_13

Frisby, D. (1978). Eine theorie des praktischen diskurses. In Oelmuller, W. (Ed.), *Normenbe-grundung-Normendurchsetzung. Berlin, Germany*. Paderborn.

Golder, C., & Coirier, P. (1996). The production and recognition of typological argumentative test markers. *Argumentation, 10*(2), 271–282. doi:10.1007/BF00180729

Gordon, T. (1995b). Zeno: A www system for geographical mediation. In M. Armstrong & K. Kemp (Eds.), *Collaborative Spatial Decision-Making, Scientific Report of the Initiative 17 Specialist Meeting, Technical Report*, (pp. 77-89). Santa Barbara, CA: Initiative 17.

Gordon, T., & Karacapilidis, N. (1997). The zeno argumentation framework. In *Proceedings of the Sixth International Conference on Artificial Intelligence and Law*, (pp. 10-18). Melbourne, Australia: ACM Press.

Govier, T. (1987). *Problems in argument analysis and evaluation*. Dordrecht, The Netherlands: Kluwer.

Govier, T. (1992). *A practical study of argument* (3rd ed.). Belmont, CA: Wadsworth.

Hitchcock, D. (1991). Some principles of rational mutual inquiry. In F. van Eemeren, R. Grootendorst, J. A. Blair, & C. A. Willard (Eds.), *Proceedings of the Second International Conference on Argumentation (AAAI 2000)*, (pp. 236-243). SICSAT.

Hitchcock, D., McBurney, P., & Parsons, S. (2001). A framework for deliberation dialogues, argumentation and its applications. In H. V. Hansen, C. W. Tindale, J. A. Blair, & R. H. Johnson (Eds.), *Proceedings of the Fourth Biennial Conference of the Ontario Society for the Study of Argumentation*. Windsor, Canada: University of Windsor.

Huizinga, J. (1972). *America: A Dutch historian's vision from afar and near*. New York, NY: Harper Torchbooks.

Hulstjin, J. (2000). *Dialogue models for inquiry and transaction*. PhD Thesis. Enschede, The Netherlands: University of Twente.

Hymes, C., & Olson, G. (1992). Unblocking brainstorming through the use of a simple group editor. In Proceedings of the Conference on Computer Supported Cooperative Work, (pp. 99-106). New York, NY: ACM Press.

Johnson, R., & Blair, J. (1983). *Logical self-defense*. Toronto, Canada: McGraw-Hill.

Larkin, J., & Simon, H. (1987). Why a diagram is (sometimes) worth ten thousand words. *Cognitive Science, 11*, 64–100. doi:10.1111/j.1551-6708.1987.tb00863.x

McBurney, P., & Parsons, S. (2001). Representing epistemic uncertainty by means of dialectical argumentation. *Annals of Mathematics and Artificial Intelligence, 32*(14), 125–169. doi:10.1023/A:1016757315265

McBurney, P., Parsons, S., & Wooldridge, M. (2002). Desiderata for agent argumentation protocols. In *Proceedings of the First International Joint Conference on Autonomous Agents and Multiagent Systems: Part 1*, (pp. 402-409). New York, NY: ACM Press.

McBurney, P., van Eijk, R. M., Parsons, S., & Amgoud, L. (2003). A dialogue game protocol for agent purchase negotiations. *Journal of Autonomous Agents and Multi-Agent Systems, 7*(3), 235–273. doi:10.1023/A:1024787301515

Perelman, C., & Olbrechts-Tyteca, L. (1971). *The new rhetoric: A treatise on argumentation* (Wilkinson, J., & Weaver, P., Trans.). London, UK: University of Notre Dame Press.

Pinsonneault, A., Barki, H., Gallupe, R. B., & Hoppen, N. (1999). Electronic brainstorming: The illusion of productivity. *Information Systems Research, 10*(2), 110–133. doi:10.1287/isre.10.2.110

Pollock, J. L. (1987). Defeasible reasoning. *Cognitive Science, 11*, 481–518. doi:10.1207/s15516709cog1104_4

Poole, D. L. (1988). A logical framework for default reasoning. *Artificial Intelligence, 36*, 27–47. doi:10.1016/0004-3702(88)90077-X

Prakken, H. (1993a). A logical framework for modelling legal argument. In *Proceedings of the Fourth International Conference on Artificial Intelligence and Law*, (pp. 1-9). ACM Press.

Prakken, H. (1993b). *Logical tools for modelling legal argument*. PhD Thesis. Amsterdam, The Netherlands: Vrije University.

Prakken, H., & Sartor, G. (1996). A dialectical model of assessing conflicting arguments in legal reasoning. *Artificial Intelligence and Law, 4*(3-4), 331–368. doi:10.1007/BF00118496

Rittel, H. J., & Webber, M. M. (1973). Dilemmas in a general theory of planning. *Policy Sciences, 4*, 155–169. doi:10.1007/BF01405730

Sadri, F., Toni, F., & Torroni, P. (2001). Logic agents, dialogues and negotiation: An abductive approach. In M. Schroeder & K. Stathis (Eds.), *Proceedings of the Symposium on Information Agents for E-Commerce, Artificial Intelligence and the Simulation of Behaviour Conference*. AISB.

Scaife, M., & Rogers, Y. (1996). External cognition: How do graphical representations work? *International Journal of Human-Computer Studies, 45*, 185–213. doi:10.1006/ijhc.1996.0048

Singh, M. P. (2000). A social semantics for agent communications languages. In F. Dignum, B. Chaib-Draa, & H. Weigand (Eds.), *Proceedings of the International Joint Conference on Artificial Intelligence (IJCAI 1999) Workshop on Agent Communication Languages*. Berlin, Germany: Springer.

Slob, W. H. (2002). How to distinguish good and bad arguments: Dialogico-rhetorical normativity. *Argumentation, 16*, 179–196. doi:10.1023/A:1015589400146

Toulmin, S. (1958). *The uses of argument*. Cambridge, UK: Cambridge University Press.

van de Ven, A. H., & Delbecq, A. L. (1971). Nominal versus interacting group processes for committee decision making effectiveness. *Academy of Management Journal, 14*, 203–212. doi:10.2307/255307

van de Ven, A. H., & Delbecq, A. L. (1974). The effectiveness of nominal delphi and interacting group decision making process. *Academy of Management Journal, 17*(4), 605–621. doi:10.2307/255641

Verheij, B. (1996). *Rules, reasons, arguments formal studies of argumentation and defeat*. Dissertation. Maastricht, The Netherlands: Universiteit Maastricht. Retrieved from http://www.metajur.unimaas.nl/ bart/proefschrift/.

Verheij, B. (1999). Automated argument assistance for lawyers. In *Proceedings of the Seventh International Conference on Artificial Intelligence and Law, ICAIL 1999*, (pp. 43-52). ACM Press.

Vreeswijk, G. (1993). Defeasible dialectics: A controversy-oriented approach towards defeasible argumentation. *The Journal of Logic and Computation, 3*(3), 3–27.

Vreeswijk, G. (1997). Abstract argumentation systems. *Artificial Intelligence, 90*, 225–279. doi:10.1016/S0004-3702(96)00041-0

Walton, D., & Krabbe, E. (1995). *Commitment in dialogue: Basic concepts of interpersonal reasoning*. Albany, NY: State University of New York Press.

Wilhelm, A. G. (2000). *Democracy in the digital age: Challenges to political life in the digital age*. New York, NY: Routledge.

Wohlrapp, H. (1998). A new light on non-deductive argumentation schemes. *Argumentation, 12*, 341–350. doi:10.1023/A:1007791211241

Yearwood, J., & Stranieri, A. (2002). Generic arguments: A framework for supporting online deliberative discourse. In *Proceedings of the Thirteenth Australasian Conference on Information Systems (ACIS 2002)*, (pp. 337-346). Melbourne, Australia: ACIS.

Yearwood, J., & Stranieri, A. (2006). The generic actual argument model of practical reasoning. *Decision Support Systems, 41*(2), 358–379. doi:10.1016/j.dss.2004.07.004

Appendix 1: Formal Description of Single Participant Dialogue with a GAS

Define an actual argument A associated with an inference slot I in a GAS G as a tuple $(I_j, C_{1_{i_1}}, ..., C_{ni_n}, C_{n+1_{v_{n+1}}})$.

Within a GAS G, the set of *points in common* from the arguments of two participants P_1 and P_2 is the set $PIC = \{C \in C : C_v^{P_1} = C_v^{P_2}\}$ and the set of *points of difference* is the set $POD = \{C \in C : C_v^{P_1} \neq C_v^{P_2}\}$.

Definition A *dialogue* based on a GAS G is a finite nonempty sequence of moves where $move_i = (Player_i, C_i \in A)(i > 0)$, such that:

1. $A \in A(G)$; An actual argument is an instantiation of a generic argument structure
2. $Player_i = P_1$ iff i is odd; and $Player_i = P_2$ iff i is even; *In the sample dialogue above Player X is odd and Player Y is even.*
3. $Player_i = Player_1$, then A^1;
4. If $Player_i = P_2$, and $C_{n+1_{v_{k2}}}^2 = C_{n+1_{v_{k1}}}^1$ then $PIC = \{C_{n+1}\}$ and $POD = \varnothing$; If players advance identical claim values then the claim is assigned to the Points in Common Set. For instance, after Steps (1) and (2) in the sample dialogue both X and Y propose the claim that VE is clearly ethical. So this claim value is in the Points in Common Set $PIC = \{Ethical_{is}\}$ otherwise $C_{n+1_{v_{k2}}}^2 = C_{n+1_{v_{k1}}}^1$ and $PIC=\varnothing$ and $POD = \{C_{n+1}\}$ So, compare data. If players advance claim values that are contrary then the claim is assigned to the Points of Difference set and the data items for the claim are compared.

   a. If C_{n+1} is a leaf node of G then P_1 and P_2 are *potentially reconcilable on data. After Step (3) in the sample dialogue,* $POD = \{\text{Re}gulation_{abuses\_will\_occur}\}$ This claim is a leaf node so X and Y are potentially reconcilable on data.

   b. $PIC = \varnothing$ and $POD = \varnothing$ For each $C_i \in signature(I) \subset C$, P_1 and P_2 compare $C_{i_{v_{k1}}}^1$ and $C_{i_{v_{k2}}}^1$. After Step (5) the $POD = \{Benefit_{clear}, Benefit_{notsoclear}\}$. The data item values related to claims of Pain, Relatives' agony and Costs are elicited from X and Y and compared. If $C_{iv_{k1}}^1 = C_{iv_{k2}}^2$ then $PIC = PIC \cup \{C_i\}$ at step (7) in the example X and Y agree that the individual's pain should not be tolerated and the relatives' agony is similarly intolerable. They also agree that costs should be borne by the health system. These claims are added to the PIC set else $POD = POD \cup \{C_i\}$; If the players disagree on any of the child nodes then the claim value disagreements are added to the POD set.

   c. If $POD = \varnothing$ then compare CVV^1 with CVV^2. If $CVV^1 \neq CVV^2$ then P_1 and P_2 are *potentially reconcilable through agreement on context variable values* on C_{n+1} of A^i else P_1 and P_2 are *potentially reconcilable through agreement on inference* on C_{n+1} of A^i. *At Step (7) in the sample case, X and Y disagree on the Benefit claim. The difference derives from a difference in inference procedure so the two players are potentially reconcilable through agreement on inference.*

   d. If $POD = \varnothing$ then a new dialogue can start for each C_i in POD.

Appendix 2: Formal Description of a Multi-Participant Dialogue with a GAS

Definition An *m-participant dialogue* based on a GAS G is a finite nonempty sequence of moves where $move_i = (Participant_i, C_i \in A)(i > 0)$, such that:

1. $A \in A(G)$;
2. For $Player_i, ...Player_m, C^1_{n+1_{v_{k1}}} = ..C^j_{n+1_{v_{k_j}}} = ...C^m_{n+1_{v_{k_j}}}$ then $PIC = \{C_{n+1}\}$ and $POD = \emptyset$ otherwise $C^1_{n+1_{v_{k1}}} \neq C^j_{n+1_{v_{k_j}}}$ for $i, j \in \{1, ...m\}$ and $PIC = \emptyset$ and $POD = \{C_{n+1}\}$; So, compare data.

    a. If C^1_{n+1} is a leaf node of G then $P_1, ...P_m$ are *irreconcilable on data*.

    b. $PIC = \emptyset$ and $POD = \emptyset$. For each $C_h \in signature(I) \subset C, P_1, ..., P_2$ compare $C^1_{hv_{k1}}, ...C^m_{hv_{kn}}$. If $C^1_{hv_{k1}}, ...C^m_{hv_{kn}}$ then $PIC = PIC \cup \{C_h\}$ else $POD = POD \cup \{C_h\}$

    c. If $POD = \emptyset$. then compare $CVV^1, ..., CVV^2$. If $CVV^i \neq CVV^j$ then P_i and P_j are *potentially reconcilable through agreement on context variable values* on C_{n+1} of A^i else P_i and P_j are *potentially reconcilable through agreement on inference* on C_{n+1} of A^i.

    d. If $POD = \emptyset$. then a new dialogue starts for each C_h in POD.

Appendix 3: GAAM Dialogue as a Complete Dialogue

- **open dialogue** (P_i, G): Participant P_i proposes opening the dialogue to consider the matter in question (top-level claim) of G. A dialogue begins with this move.
- **enter dialogue** (P_i, G): Participant P_j indicates a willingness to join the dialogue.
- **propose** $(P_i, type, N_h, v_{ki})$:Participant Pi proposes a value v_{ki} for $N_h \in G$ where type $\in \{cliam, context\ var iable, \inf erence\}$
- **assert** $(P_i, type, N_h, v_{ki})$: Participant Pi asserts a value v_{ki} for $N_h \in G$ where type $\in \{cliam, context\ var iable, \inf erence\}$ This is a stronger locution than **propose**(..)and results in the tuple $(type, N_h, v_{ki})$ being inserted into the commitment store of $(P_i, CS(P_i)$
- **prefer** (P_i, a, b): Participant P_i indicates a preference for action option a over action option b. This is not used in these dialogues as it relates to some form of evaluation. It may be used in determining agreement between a set of participants that have reasoned towards different actions (values for the top-level claim in G).
- **ask_justify** (P_j, P_i, C_h, v_{ki}): Participant P_j asks participant P_i to provide a justification for the value v_{ki} for claim C_h.
- **move** $(P_i, action, a)$: Participant P_i proposes that each participant pronounces on whether they assert a as the action (top-level claim value) decided on by the group. This locution inserts $(action, a)$ into $CS(P_i)$.
- **retract** $(P_j, locution)$: Participant P_j expresses a retraction of a previous locution, locution which may be one of **assert, move**. The retraction will cause a deletion from $CS(P_i)$

- **withdraw dialogue** (P_i, G): Participant P_i announces her withdrawal from the dialogue to consider the matter in question of G.

Once a dialogue opens and another participant enters, the progression of the dialogue is quite structured. Consider the progression below:

1. **open dialogue** (P_i, G)
2. **enter dialogue** (P_j, G)
3. **propose** $(P_i, claim, C_h, v_{ki})$ and **propose** $(P_j, claim, C_h, v_{ki})$
   a. If $v_{ki} = v_{kj}$ then **assert** $(P_i, claim, C_h, v_{ki})$ and **assert** $(P_j, claim, C_h, v_{ki})$, select another claim not in $CS(P_i) \cap CS(P_j)$ if there are none then move agreement on the top-level claim.
   b. Otherwise, **ask justify** (P_j, P_i, C_h, v_{ki}).
      - Then for each claim C_c that is a child of C_h, **propose** $(P_i, claim, C_h, v_{ki})$ and **propose** $(P_j, claim, C_h, v_{ki})$,
      - if $v_{ki} = v_{ki}, \forall i$ i then consider context variable values, **propose** (P_i, CVV, cv_c, v_{ki}) and **propose** (P_j, CVV, cv_c, v_{ki}),
      - if $v_{ki} = v_{ki\,j}$ then consider choice of inference procedures **propose** (P_i, I, I_c, I_{ki}) and **propose** (P_j, I, I_c, I_{ki})
   c. If either participant does not revise their claim with a propose then this claim still remains a point of difference.
   d. Otherwise for some child claim $C_c v_{ki} \neq v_{ki}$, so return to the third step with this claim
4. At any stage a participant may **retract** $(P_j, locution)$
5. At any stage any participant may **move** $(P_i, action, a)$
6. At any stage any participant may **withdraw dialogue** (P_i, G)
7. A dialogue terminates when less than 2 participants have not withdrawn.

Chapter 6
Narrative Reasoning

ABSTRACT

A large proportion of our knowledge and indeed our reasoning is not received or communicated as formal reasoning or informal reasoning but, in fact, as stories. When we focus on this as a reality, it demands that we consider what can be said about reasoning that is conveyed and represented in stories and how it relates to other forms of representing and communicating reasoning. Given that stories are so commonly used, is it possible that they are a form of coalesced reasoning that a community can use, or do they confuse and detract from the main concerns and aspirations of reasoning communities?

The paradigmatic mode of human decision making and communication is "good reasons" which vary in form among communication situations, genres, and media (Fisher, 1995).

INTRODUCTION

There are two main approaches that people use to organize and make sense out of their experiences: logical thinking and stories or narrative thinking. Both of these approaches have a long history of providing useful structures for organizing experiences and being able to make sense of

them. Narrative reasoning can provide a valuable approach to complex reasoning involved in problem solving and decision-making. Often, there are areas that require clear practical reasoning that may be poorly understood and even less clearly available for learning by some form of logical analysis and representation.

Much of our attempt to understand our world has taken the form of stories and narrative myths. These myths and stories have often passed on, in a compressed form, reasoning that has been important practically as well as in a literary sense. McCloskey (1990) describes stories and metaphors as the two ways of understanding

DOI: 10.4018/978-1-4666-1818-3.ch006

things and suggests that they can work together to provide answers. Narrative reasoning addresses situations that find difficulty in being addressed with the sequential form of verbal reasoning. The situations often involve multiple causes and multiple effects. Many social phenomena are like this and it would be fair to say that the great body of our accumulated social wisdom is expressed as narrative. Narrative reasoning could be viewed as an efficient way of dealing with complexity. Whereas verbal reasoning relies on long chains of logical steps, each small enough to be considered proven, narrative reasoning addresses situations that cannot be addressed in this way. For example, we could analyse the social information in the movie Jurassic Park as the verbal representations: the amazing world of the dinosaurs recreated as a theme park; the fallacy of man trying to control the development of biological species. There are many other interpretations and lines of reasoning that are captured.

In both logical reasoning and narrative reasoning, cause and effect relations are established between factors and used in sequential patterns. Both aim to organize and make sense of human experience in a way that can guide problem solving and decision-making. Whilst we recognize the product of logical or analytical reasoning as laws or rules, which are largely context-free and testable, the product of narrative reasoning is a story, which is highly contextual and testable mainly through personal and interpersonal experience.

In this chapter, we briefly review models of stories and narrative. From this, we extract a simple story model and some of the important aspects of narrative models. These are combined with a model of reasoning (the Generic/Actual Argument Model) to produce a way of generating stories from reasoning that convey the reasoning.

The literature has suggested that human beings process information in two ways: analytically and narratively. People in areas such as law and the sciences are more familiar and aware of analytic argument, but legal discourse can also take the form of narrative. Some of the differences between what

might be called analytic reasoning and narrative can be gleaned. Arguments and more formal reasoning tend to convince others by being grounded in the facts and sound deductive reasoning from the facts. They try to appeal to a notion of truth and rules. However often this is achieved through norms that are abstracted from life experiences. Narratives are convincing because of their plausibility or likeliness. A narrative's likeliness arises out of reasoning based upon common, shared or well understood experience and knowledge of how things really are in the world. There is a strong connection to the specifics of a situation and its credibility.

Conventional, analytical reasoning and argument tends to deconstruct experience, narrative attempts to reconstruct it. For example, in constructing an argument we might collect a number of propositions that could be regarded as facts and then map out abstract propositions that are rules or abstract propositions of the domain (for example, the law) that can be put together to reach the desired conclusion. However, if we were trying to weave a convincing story to persuade others on action to a desired conclusion, then this will look very different from an analytical argument. Narrative sequence treats narrative facts as they are found in life, embedding them in particular context-rich settings. The narrative's concrete details are not connected through abstract propositions but through natural associations that 'ring true.' Events and facts that are linked in these associations resonate and have effect because they are familiar and reflect the world of another individual—the reader or listener. Their world is a situated world of cultural norms, values, and conventions and they will interpret and test the narrative's authenticity, credibility, and point against their own experience of the world. A narrative presentation of a case requires the reader's involvement by asking them to draw upon their personal experience and normal expectation when reading and interpreting the text.

In this chapter, it is argued that stories are an important way in which some members of a reasoning community encapsulate their reasoning and that some stories capture very pertinent and important reasoning lessons. We also show that stories generated from reasoning can be used to enhance understanding and acceptance of the reasoning from which they are built. We also discuss how stories can be used to assimilate evidence and reason to complex decisions and contend that reasoning augmented with stories assists in making high quality decisions.

The chapter is organised as follows; the next section provides some background on narrative including a characterisation of narrative reasoning. The following section reviews some of the work on stories and story models. Narrative coherence and means for generating simple stories from reasoning are then discussed. The notion of narrative information systems is outlined before the chapter ends with a description of some narrative learning environments that assist novices to become expert decision makers.

NARRATIVE

The terms narrative and story have varied in their interpretation by different people. For example, the word story has been used in everyday speech as any explanation of events, people, and things. It is also used to refer to a more abstract description of a causal or temporal linkage between events, people, and things. Story can be thought of as a system of associations between elements composed of events, people, and things. Chatman (1978) describes story as:

Story, in my technical sense of the word, exists only at an abstract level; any manifestation already entails the selection and arrangement performed by the discourse as actualized by a given medium. There is no privileged manifestation (p. 37).

Branigan's (1992) work with modern cinematic narratives uses the narrative scheme:

1. Introduction of setting and characters;
2. Explanation of state of affairs;
3. Initiating event;
4. Emotional response or statement of goal by the protagonist;
5. Complicating emotions;
6. Outcome;
7. Reactions to outcome.

The order here is important because they progress from the beginning of the narrative through to the end.

Bruner (1990, p. 77) identifies four features of a text that marks it as narrative:

- **Sequence in time:** Narrative has a clear beginning, middle and end although narratives do not need to present events in sequence; they are frequently rearranged for dramatic effect. It is critical that the events or actions in a narrative are understood to happen in a sequence.
- **Focal actor or actors:** Narratives are always about someone or something. There is a protagonist and frequently an antagonist, as well. The characters provide a thread that ties the events in a narrative together.
- **Identifiable narrative voice:** A narrative is something that someone tells, so there should always be an identifiable voice doing the narrating.
- **Canonical or evaluative frame of reference:** Narratives carry meaning and cultural value because they encode, implicitly or explicitly, standards against which actions of the characters can be judged. White (1981) argues that what distinguishes narrative from a mere chronicle is this sense of closure, and that this closure is provided by the moral context that gives meaning to the events.

Narrative Reasoning

Narrative reasoning differs from formal reasoning or formal logic in many ways. As we know, a story generally deals with individuals whilst formal reasoning deals with rules that apply to whole sets of individuals. Formal reasoning analyses movements and causes whilst narrative deals with motives and reasons. Narrative has a point of view rather than "being objective" and presenting a 'view' from nowhere. Narrative contains dialogue rather than only declarative sentences. It relies on context and not simply data alone. As such, it is open-ended and metaphorical rather than determinate and literal. It is situated at a particular time rather than being timeless, and may deal with emotions and emotional reasoning. Most fundamentally, narrative reasoning exploits the notion of "common knowledge," where two or more people know something and each understands that the others know it as well.

In "story logic," how the storytellers characterize an event or person is crucial. If a man scratches his forehead, it may indicate that he is worried, that he has an itch, or that he is sending a signal or many other things depending on the many perspectives we might have and on the many human contexts in which we might find ourselves. Unlike formal logic, story logic is not open to substitutions as is the case in the predicate calculus. For example, Oedipus is attracted to the woman Jocasta, not to the extensionally equivalent person who is his mother.

Narrative Rationality

The essential components of the narrative paradigm according to Fisher (1985) are:

- Humans are essentially storytellers;
- The fundamental mode of human decision making and communication is "good reasons" which vary in form among situations, genres and media of communication;
- The production and practice of good reasons are ruled by history, biography, culture and character;
- Rationality is determined by the nature of persons as narrative beings, their awareness of *narrative coherence*, whether a story "hangs together," and their constant habit of testing *narrative fidelity*, whether or not the stories they experience ring true with the stories they know to be true in their lives;
- The world as we know it is a set of stories that we must choose among in order for us to live life in a process of continual re-creation.

Fisher (1994) argues that many forms of discourse (including scientific discourse) is amenable to interpretation through the narrative paradigm and its attendant logic, *narrative rationality*. Narrative rationality entails a re-conceptualization of knowledge, one that permits the possibility of wisdom. It recognizes that discourse rarely presents an incontestable truth and provides means by which reason can be assessed. He argues that reason is to be found in the warrants that are provided for accepting the advice offered through the narrative communication and these are often value laden. Narrative rationality includes tests of values and "reasons." The two major considerations in narrative rationality are coherence and fidelity. Coherence has three aspects:

- **Argumentative or structural coherence;**
- **Material coherence:** comparing and contrasting a story with other relevant stories from other disciplines allows the identification of factual errors, omission of important arguments and other distortions;
- **Characterological coherence:** regard for the intelligence, integrity and goodwill (ethos) of the author, the values he or she would advance in the world.

Fisher adds that in each of these aspects of coherence, values such as consistency, completeness and character are manifest.

Fidelity considers the qualities that are not revealed by considering matters of coherence and entails two lines of assessment. Firstly, assessing the elements of the communication that we would usually call its "reasons." The determination of whether items that purport to be fact are indeed facts and whether some have been omitted or misrepresented, assessing the soundness of the reasoning by using standards from formal and informal logics as well as identifying whether the key issues have been addressed. Secondly, addressing questions related to values -what are the implicit and explicit values in the story and are they appropriate?

Stories

Most stories or narrative texts have a predictable structure or pattern of events that create the properties of a story. There are both *basic elements* in stories and *abstract story structures*. While the basic elements are generally agreed upon, it is the abstract story structures that have provided the greatest area of debate. *Abstract story structures* refer to those structures that can be abstracted from stories but are not explicitly represented within stories. Most story models include these basic components: *objects, events, causality,* and *time*. There is one component that can be considered an object but is important enough to be singled out. This special type of object is called a *character*. There are structures for each of these basic elements. Structures for objects are typically based on the spatial proximity of objects.

Such a cluster of objects is usually called a *scene* (Black & Wilensky, 1979). Structures for events are classified in terms of their influence on objects and on the episode in which they occur. The influence that an event has is related to the number of objects that the event affects. An event that affects objects in many scenes is called a *global*

event. The *episode* in which events occur refers to the sequence of events that occur in a particular scene. Structures for causality have generally been disregarded in non-computational models. In Schank's influential script model, causality has four types: result causation, enable causation, initiation causation and reason causation. There are three *structures for time* that are identified: story, discourse and iconographic. Story time is monotonically related to normal time whilst discourse time is the order in which events are presented to the audience. Iconographic time refers to the period when the story is set. *Structures for characters* in stories depend on their role in the story. There are five basic roles (although other sets have been used): protagonist, antagonist, helper, hinderer and neutral. The protagonist is the main character and the antagonist is the main opponent of the main character.

Many abstract structures have been proposed such as plots and episodes. Top-down approaches provide a framework that is filled in progressively as the story unfolds. *Bottom-up* approaches provide a number of units that are matched to elements of a story and are connected together to provide a representation of the story. *Event-scene* structures are those that relate the objects of a scene and can be classified as to whether events are dependent or independent of the scene. *Event-character* structures are those that relate to the interactions between events and characters. These can be classified as those that affect every character or those that affect the main character.

Event-character structures link specific events to characters' goals, which in turn cause other events and outcomes for those events. The first such structure was proposed by Rumelhart (1975) who tried to formalize the work of Propp (1968). Rumelhart's episode schemata attempt to describe various events in every story in relation to a character's goals. Many event-character structures are variations of story grammars. Story grammars have been criticized due to their inability to distinguish between stories and non-stories such as procedural exposition (Black & Wilensky, 1979). Criticism has also been levelled at the limited way in which these grammars represent stories as little more than a set of coherent sentences. Mandler and Johnson (1977) and Mandler (1984) have used a grammar that captures quite complex story structure. It is described by the rewrite rules in Table 1.

Event-main character structures are more general than story grammars. They outline a sequence of discrete stages of situations, events and character goals in a literary manner. These structures allow the identification of the main character or protagonist.

Event-scene dependent structures consist of a sequence of actions that are triggered when a particular set of conditions occurs in a scene. These are commonly known as scripts in Artificial Intelligence (AI) and based on the Memory Organization Packet (MOP) (Schank & Abelson, 1977) representation of human memory. The main

problem with scripts is that the event sequences are hard wired and the number of scripts required to model stories would be very large.

Event-scene independent structures are completely independent of the scene. These are generally called *themes* (Brinker, 1993) and they capture recurrent or implicit ideas across a number of situations and stories. A theme in literary theory encapsulates a wide range of intra-story structures but has been used with a much narrower meaning in computational story models. For example, BORIS was a story understanding program that included Thematic Abstraction Units (TAU) (Dyer, 1983) which share similarities with other representational systems such as Schank's Thematic Organization Packets and Lehnert's Plot Units. TAUs allow BORIS to represent situations, which are more abstract than those captured by scripts, plans, and goals. They contain processing knowledge useful in dealing with the kinds of

Table 1. Rewrite rules for the base structure of simple stories

Rewrite Rules	
STORY	→ Setting and EPISODE
EPISODE	→ $\left\{ \begin{array}{l} \text{BEGINNING Cause DEVELOPMENT Cause ENDING} \\ \text{EPISODE(} \left\{ \begin{array}{l} \text{AND} \\ \text{THEN} \end{array} \right\} \text{EPISODE)}^n \end{array} \right\}$
BEGINNING	→ $\left\{ \begin{array}{l} \text{Beginning Event} \\ \text{EPISODE} \end{array} \right\}$
DEVELOPMENT	→ $\left\{ \begin{array}{l} \text{COMPLEX REACTION Cause GOAL PATH} \\ \text{Simple Reaction Cause Action} \\ \text{DEVELOPMENT(} CauseDEVELOPMENT \text{)}^n \end{array} \right\}$
COMPLEX ACTION	→ Simple Reaction Cause Goal
GOAL PATH	→ Attempt Cause Outcome
OUTCOME	→ $\left\{ \begin{array}{l} \text{Outcome Event} \\ \text{EPISODE} \end{array} \right\}$
ENDING	→ $\left\{ \begin{array}{l} \text{Ending Event} \\ \text{EPISODE} \end{array} \right\}$

planning and expectation failures that characters often experience in narratives.

Bottom-up story structures use discrete units that are matched to elements in a story and are connected to produce a representation of the story. The units can be characterized as either event-character or event-scene. Event-character structures have been proposed at three levels: uniform goal structures, goal hierarchy structures and goal relationship structures. An event-character uniform goal structure that relates events to the positive or negative effect on the goals of an actor was developed by Lehnert (1982).

In Lehnert's structure a story is a configuration of plot units, and each plot unit is itself a configuration of smaller entities called *affect states*. Affect states do not describe emotional states in the detail that an inference mechanism would require, they merely distinguish between 'positive events' denoted '+', 'negative events,' denoted '−' and mental events, denoted by 'M' that are neutral. As a story progresses, there is a linear sequence of affect states for each character. Causality is made explicit by links between affect states. There are four types of links: motivation— a link running from a negative event to a mental state; actualization—a link from a mental state to a positive event; termination is not used when an event is terminated but when the affective impact of the event is displaced; equivalence between events and states indicates a separation of multiple perspectives of a single affect state.

There are fifteen legal pair-wise configurations of these linkages between affect states that give us what are called primitive plot units, each of which has been given a name. Using these, larger plot units can be built and many of these involve more than one character. Cross-character links can occur between any pair of affect states and they have interpretations by convention.

An *event-character* goal hierarchy structure views stories from the point of view of characters dealing with various types of conflict. In the *points* structure used in the story understanding

program PAM (Wilensky, 1982), a story has three levels: the story itself; the important content of the story; and the points. The *points* are a template for the important content of the story in terms of the goals of the characters. The notion of a story *point* competes with the idea of story grammars as a way to characterize story texts. A story grammar defines a story as having a certain form, whereas a story point model defines a story as having certain content. The form of a story is viewed as being a function of the content of the story. Wilensky (1982) claims that understanding a story is more about understanding the point of what the text is about rather than understanding the structure of a text.

An *event-character* goal relationship structure based on the Aristotelian theory of drama, interprets the actions of characters in relation to their goals, relationships and norms (Sgouros, 1999). This model has been used to generate interactive stories.

Narrative Models in Jurisprudence

The narrative theory of Bennett and Feldman (1981) describes the structure of a story as consisting generally of a *setting—concern—resolution* sequence.

The setting usually includes the time, place, and some of the characters. The concern is an action that given the setting creates a climactic (eventful, ironical, suspenseful) situation. For example, if someone is rock-climbing (as was the case in one of our stories) and slips and falls, slipping and falling are the concern. If the story ended at this point, the audience would be left wondering: what happened to the climber? Was he hurt or killed? A complete story will provide an answer to these questions. This stage is the resolution. The central action is the structural element that creates the central question the story must resolve. The resolution normally resolves both the predicament created by the problem and the questions listeners might have had about the outcome. In the rock-climbing story, the resolution consisted of telling the audience that the climber was taken to the hospital for treatment.

They argue that it is not the weighting of the individual elements of the story, each in terms of the evidence for that element, which renders a case persuasive or not, but rather the plausibility of the story structure taken as a whole. In order to test their hypothesis, they set up an experiment where two groups of undergraduates told stories to the rest of the class. One group told true stories involving themselves and the other group told false stories involving themselves and the audience rated the truth of each story. They found that that there was no statistical association between the actual truth status of the stories and their perceived truth status. Furthermore, they found that the structure of a story had a considerable impact on its credibility; as structural ambiguities in stories increased, credibility decreased and vice versa. In a good story, all elements are connected to a central action and nothing is left standing on its own. The context provides a full and compelling account of why the central action should have developed in the way that it has. If this is not the case, then the story contains ambiguities. There are two types of ambiguities: missing elements and contradictory elements.

Narrative Coherence

Wagenaar, van Koppen, and Crombag (1993) proposed the theory of anchored narratives moving on from the work of Bennett and Feldman (1981) where the task of the judge was seen as determining the *plausibility* of the stories presented by the prosecution and the defence. This narrative theory has its basis in cognitive psychology and contends that evidence derives its meaning from a story context.

According to Pennington and Hastie (1992), coherence refers to consistency, completeness, and plausibility. Pennington and Hastie's Story Model

is based on the hypothesis that jurors impose a narrative story organization on trial information, in which causal and intentional relations between events are central (Bennett & Feldman, 1981; Pennington & Hastie, 1981). Meaning is assigned to trial evidence through the incorporation of that evidence in one or more stories describing what happened. The Story Model includes: evidence evaluation through story construction; representation of decision alternative by learning verdict category attributes; reaching a decision through classification of the story into the best-fitting verdict category. The factors that govern which story will be accepted, which decision will be selected and the degree of certainty with which the decision will be made are: *coverage, coherence, uniqueness,* and *goodness-of-fit.* For Penington and Hastie, coherence refers to consistency, completeness, and plausibility which are very close to what Fisher says are the values that underpin coherence. Pennington and Hastie (1986) conclude again that a narrative *story sequence* is the most effective "order of proof" at trial. Jurors instructed to make a final global judgment were more likely to adhere to an explanation-based judgment strategy that will lead to higher confidence in verdicts than a cumulative, item-by-item updating judgment strategy. They also concluded that Bayesian approaches do not provide a valid description of jurors' typical judgment processes

Pennington and Hastie (1993) show that a typology of formal and informal inference forms originally proposed by Collins is an appropriate framework to represent inferences that occur in the over arching explanation-based process. They use the Johnson and Caldwell murder case where the story of a juror reaching a not guilty verdict is compared with the story of another juror who reaches a decision of first degree murder. The function of the story in this process is to organise and make sense of the evidence. These stories could be analysed using narrative rationality. Associated with the juror story that leads to a decision of first degree murder is suspicion whereas the story with the not guilty decision is more open.

NARRATIVE COHERENCE IN LAW

Narrative is understood broadly as actions arranged in a time sequence and forming a meaningful totality (Twining, 2002). This is in very strong alignment with the Story model of Pennington and Hastie for making sense of evidence by jurors in decision-making.

Normativists within legal philosophy have come to see *narrative coherence* as contributing to the construction of justification (Jackson, 1990) both justification of factual conclusions reached by the judge and justification of solutions to difficult problems of discovery of law. The latter is represented by Dworkin's theory of "law as literature." Neil Mac-Cormick understands narrative coherence as "a test of the truth or probability in questions of fact and evidence upon which direct proof by immediate observation is unavailable."

FROM STORIES TO REASONING

Is there a means of translating between reasoning expressed as narrative and some more explicit means? Essentially, it would be nice to have a mapping from stories to the reasoning that they contain. This means that we are interested in extracting from a story a different (or explicit) representation of the reasoning towards the claims that the story makes. Such a mapping $R : S \to A, R(S) = AA$ where S is the set of stories, S is a story and AA is the actual argument that represents its reasoning would be very difficult in general because a story may often contain more than one chain of reasoning and make more than one point. Furthermore, there is often an intertwining of story elements to support these points. In the first instance, it would make sense to consider only stories that make a single point. However even this is difficult because we do not yet have good insight into the links between story structure and reasoning.

The use of memory as a measure of language comprehension, in particular, has continued into modern times (Mandler & Johnson, 1977; Stein & Glenn, 1979; Thorndyke, 1977). A consistent finding is that some narrative events are more memorable than others. Events that are best recalled introduce the protagonist, provide a spatial-temporal context in which the story occurs, initiate goal states within the protagonist and describe the consequences of the protagonist's goal directed action.

Trabasso and vanden Broek (1985) assess, in a comparative reanalysis of both the Omanson (1982) and the Stein and Glenn (1979) corpuses, the relative contributions of story grammar category, causal chain, and causal connectivity factors to recall and other measures of story understanding (summarising and judging the importance of individual events); secondly, they provide a theoretical account of the identified variables and their influence on the comprehension of stories.

Causal network representations of the stories were derived for prediction of data on immediate and delayed recall, summarization, and judged importance of events. Properties of the networks were compared in multiple regression analyses with other factors, notably the story grammar categories of the events. Whether or not the event was in a causal chain and the number of its causal connections were both found to account for substantial proportions of common and unique variance in all four measures. The story grammar category of events also contributed unique variance but overlapped substantially with the causal factors. The concreteness, serial position, and argument overlap of an event failed to account uniquely for the data. A recursive transition network model is discussed that integrated story grammar, causal chain, causal network and hierarchical problem solving approaches to story representation.

Read (1987) proposes a model of causal reasoning based on Schank and Abelson's (1977) (Scripts, Plans, Goals, Goal Relations, and

Themes) analysis of knowledge structures. He argues that a central attributional problem is to explain extended sequences of behaviour. To do this, people must interrelate actions in a sequence and construct a coherent scenario from them.

An event may be remembered, summarised, or judged to be important because of its causal and logical relations, its role in an episodic structure, or its level in a hierarchy or any combination of these factors. In most instances of stories, these factors co-vary but Trabasso and van den Broek's work shows them to be independent in their own right.

Trabasso, van den Broek, and Suh (1989) proposed an analytic model incorporating a general recursive transition network for representing narratives by Trabasso and van den Broek (1985) and a taxonomy for labelling causal relationships by Warren, Nicholas, and Trabasso (1979). In the network, nodes represent the conceptual category of a clause's content, labelled arcs between two nodes represent the causal relation between a pair of conceptualizations. These nodes represent setting, reactions, goals, attempts, and outcomes. The labels on the arcs denote enabling, psychological, motivational, and physical causal relations. The node labels reflect their structural functions as well as their content, and resemble, to a large extent, those of story grammars (Johnson & Mandler, 1980; Rumelhart, 1975; Stein & Glenn, 1979). Trabasso uses a crucial test for the identification of a causal relationship. It is the counterfactual test as to the necessity of one category to another category in the circumstances of the story. The test has the form: *If A had not happened in the circumstances of the story, then B would not have happened.* A judgment that the counterfactual is true in the circumstances of the story leads to a decision that A is the cause of, or a condition for, B. The criterion of necessity in the circumstances, originally proposed by Hart and Honore (1959) and discussed by Mackie (1980), has been used extensively by Trabasso and colleagues in highly reliable identification of causal relations in stories with initial identification by intuition or the Graesser (1981) approach of asking of why-or how-questions about each state or action.

Whilst there has been some success in representing stories using story grammars, there is no clear way to move from the grammar to a representation of reasoning. Recursive transition network models move closer to a reasoning structure in the sense that there is some representation of causality but it is still not clear how this might be mapped to an explicit reasoning structure. This work, largely carried out by the cognitive psychologists, provides a first step in establishing structures of causality from narrative. Without considering its automation, the next stage would be the representation of the overall narrative as a tree or trees of reasoning including the use of both local and global coherence. Correira (1980) describes a technique for building story trees based on the theory of macrostructures by Kintsch and van Dijk (van Dijk, 1977). Rules are conceptually and notionally derived from the Horn clauses. Each rule consists of sets of causally, temporally, or thematically related propositions. The work goes a large way to demonstrating that stories can be generated from story trees based on macrostructures and also that stories generated can be parsed and summaries generated which capture the story.

For the moment our attention lies in the other direction; mapping reasoning to narrative. In the next section, we introduce a representation of reasoning that has been deployed in numerous applications in order to illustrate a reasoning to narrative mapping described in the following section.

TRANSFORMING REASONING INTO A STORY

We consider the inverse problem: given an explicit representation of some reasoning towards a claim, can a story be generated that contains this reasoning or makes this reasoning point? This tries to find a mapping $N : A \rightarrow A, N(AA) = S$, where A is the set of actual arguments, S is the set of stories, AA is an actual argument and S is a story.

In mapping reasoning into a narrative expression, we are trying to preserve the message contained in the reasoning but achieve an alternative channel or expression, which may facilitate its comprehension by people through their natural ways of interpreting narrative. There is evidence that causal explanations of actions, events, and states play a central role in our understanding of narrative (Black & Bower, 1980; Trabasso & Sperry, 1985; Graesser, 1981). The importance of causal explanations is also supported by theories of causal attribution in social psychology (McLauchlin, 1990; Pennington & Hastie, 1986; Read, 1987), and with theories of planning and reasoning in AI (Schank, 1986).

We choose to represent reasoning using the Generic/Actual Argument Model (GAAM) (Yearwood & Stranieri, 2006). In fact other representations could be used but would require the addition of contextual information and multiple inferences. The GAAM has the advantage that it captures a range of actual arguments and is richer in contextual information that supports the construction of narrative. It is arguable that any PPC (Premise, Premise, Conclusion) representation or decision tree representation could be used with suitable augmentation but this is not explored fully here. One of the important features is the separation of the inference from the structure of the reasoning. The particular inference made in any actual argument is captured by the choice of an inference procedure that is applied to data item values. In the first instance, we consider a simple situation that involves one reasoning step, that is, just one inference as represented in a generic argument tree. So the formal situation is $I(d_1...d_{k_i}) = c_i$ where d_1 is the value of the first data item, c_i is the claim value inferred and I is the inference procedure.

In the first instance, we have chosen to use a narrative model in conjunction with the GAAM representation of the reasoning to allow the design of narratives that reflect domain reasoning. An essential feature of all narrative models is that of sequence. For example, from the story grammar of Mandler and Johnston (Table 1) we see that a story consists of Setting and EPISODE and EPISODE is BEGINNING Cause DEVELOPMENT Cause ENDING. At this level it agrees with the narrative model of Bennett and Feldman. The narrative model that we use here is based on the story structure sequence of Bennett and Feldman (1981) and represents a narrative as an ordered quadruple (G, S, C, R) where G is a Generic Argument Structure (GAS) for the domain augmented with some narrative information. The setting S is obtained from the reasoning context made explicit through the GAS corresponding to the (reasoning expressed as the) actual argument. C (the Concern) corresponds to the data values for the data items in the actual argument sub-tree. R (the Resolution) is generated from the claim value of the actual argument.

Example 1: Crying Child

Informally, consider the reasoning presented in Figure 1 where the reasoning of a parent surrounding a situation where a child cries is represented as a simple generic argument.

Consider the particular reasoning (actual argument) of a parent whose child starts to cry and in response cuddles and reassures the child. This might correspond to a simple story:

A parent notices his child start to cry. He cuddles and reassures her.

Clearly, the setting involves two characters, the parent, and the child. A concern is established by the child crying and as the reasoning indicates this is the trigger for the parent to make a decision.

Figure 1. Generic argument for parent reasoning about child crying

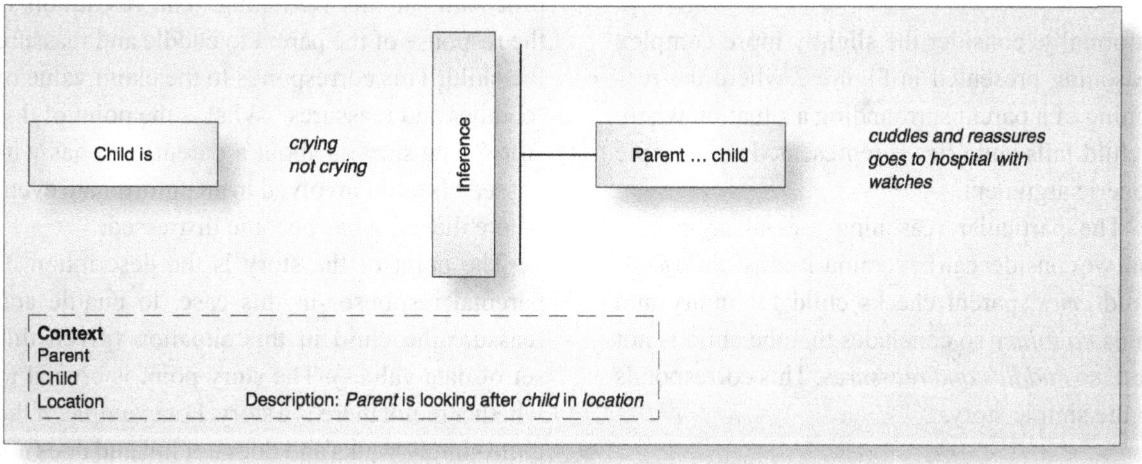

Therefore, a particular set of data values establish a concern. The generic argument indicates choices of (*cuddles and reassures, goes to hospital with, continues watching*), which is resolved by the parent cuddling and reassuring the child. Therefore, the resolution corresponds to the choice of a particular claim value. The story point is that the recurrent goal of the parent to keep the child safe and happy is disturbed by the action (event) of the child crying and the reasoning of the parent is towards re-establishing the subsumption state in which the child is safe and happy by cuddling and reassuring the child. The generic argument also provides a reason for an inference procedure and in this case the reason for the inference procedure is the role of the parent in keeping the child safe and happy (not shown in Figure 1). Therefore, the story point will contain values for a goal state for the child that meet the requirements of being safe and happy. The concern is established by selecting the data item value for the child as *cries*, which conflicts with at least one of the values of the variables in the story point that represent safe and happy.

What are the features of the mapping $N : A \rightarrow S, N(AA) = N$? We start by describing how $N=(S,C,R)$ is obtained from AA for this simple situation. There is not a unique story cor-

responding to the reasoning. In order to give a unique specification for N we have to specify particular values for many of the variables that occur in the generic argument corresponding to AA. In this case AA corresponds to the single generic argument (which might be part of a larger tree of generic arguments) shown in Figure 1. S is obtained by selecting values for the context variables: Parent, Child, and Location and with these values instantiating the *context description*. Therefore, for parent *John*, child *Emma*, and location *playground* the context description becomes, John is looking after Emma in the playground. C is a choice of data value for the data item, so in this case (AA) it would be *crying* which would produce the concern expressed as 'Emma is crying.' The resolution R is then simply the claim value of the generic argument that is specified in the actual argument. In this case *cuddles and reassures* which would be expressed as 'John cuddles and reassures Emma.' This mapping produces the story 'Emma's parent John, is looking after Emma in the playground. Emma is crying. John cuddles and reassures Emma.' Notice that if the child had not been crying, both the reasoning and the story are less interesting because there is less of a concern.

Example 2: Child Falls and Cries

Informally, consider the slightly more complex reasoning presented in Figure 2 where the reasoning of a parent surrounding a situation where a child falls and cries is represented as a simple generic argument.

The particular reasoning (actual argument) that we consider can be summarised as: child *falls*, child *cries*, parent checks child for injury and finds *no injury* so concludes that the child is not hurt, so *cuddles and reassures*. This corresponds to the simple story.

A parent hears the child cry and notices that she has fallen. He picks the child up and checks for injury. Finding no injury, he gives her a reassuring cuddle and lets her know that she is OK.

This simple story is already a slight embellishment of the essential story, which comprises a setting where there is a parent and a child. A concern is established when the child falls, cries and the parent checks for injury. The concern is resolved by the parent cuddling and reassuring the child. At this very basic level, the setting describes the characters, scene and temporal aspects and the narrative voice or narrator. The concern is created by having the child fall and cry with the parent checking for injury. This corresponds to the setting of values for the data items of the inference procedure in this reasoning. The resolution is the response of the parent to cuddle and reassure the child. This corresponds to the claim value of 'cuddles and reassures.' What is the point of this story? The story is about a parent who has witnessed his child involved in an unfortunate event where the child has become distressed.

The point of the story is the description of parental response -in this case, to cuddle and reassure the child in this situation (given this set of data values). The story point is crucial to whether or not there is a story. For example, if the child simply walks and does not fall and does not cry and the parent does not check for injury and simply continues to watch the child then there is not a very interesting story because only a weak concern arises. The recurrent goal of the parent to keep the child safe and happy by watching the child during activity is fulfilled but this is against a background of the possibility of something happening to the child.

This is simply a description of the recurrent goal of the parent keeping a watchful eye on the child. In the simple story this recurrent goal state is terminated by the child falling and the goal of the parent then is to re-establish the subsumption state.

Notice again that the concern corresponds to the selection of data values *falls* or *cries* or *injury* which each conflict with one of the values

Figure 2. Generic argument for parent reasoning about child falling

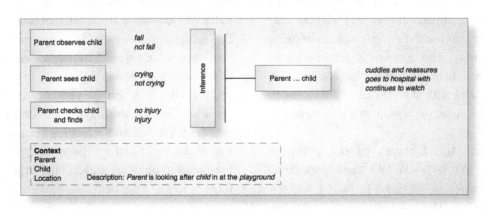

of the variable in the story point where the goal of the parent to keep the child safe and happy is represented. The selection of data values for not falling, not crying and no injury do not establish such a strong concern.

In Example 1 where the activity of the child (walking) is not explicitly represented, there is only one data item and we do not have to be concerned with the sequencing of events beyond the natural sequencing represented by the reasoning itself. That is, the story events follow the reasoning sequence. In the case (Example 2) where the child is engaged in some activity (walking), the generation of a story requires the sequencing of the events: walking, crying and checking for injury. So how is the sequence of events determined? Recall that the representation of an actual argument (actual reasoning) in the GAAM requires not only a selection of values for each data item but also the selection of an inference procedure. Each inference procedure has attached to it a set of reasons for the inference procedure. In this example, Inference 1 might correspond to one particular ordering of data items and Inference 2 another ordering. Let Inference 1 correspond to the (child action, child behaviour, parent action) order and Inference 2 correspond to the (child behaviour, child action, parent action) order. The point of the above story is about the response of a parent who witnesses the child action as an unfortunate event, then the distressed behaviour. The sequencing of events that is important to the reasoning is obtained from the inference procedure corresponding to the story point and its reasons. If we consider Inference 2, then for data of the child crying and falling the inferred parental response might be simply to continue watching. The corresponding story point would be about a parent who sees a crying child, fall and quickly checks for injury and continues to watch. This set of data and claim values corresponds to a particular inference (and inference procedure). The order of events that is crucial to the reasoning is encoded in the inference procedure and can be obtained from the slot in the generic argument that holds the reasons for the inference procedure.

$N=(S,C,R)$ is obtained from *AA* for this example as follows. In this case *AA* corresponds to the single generic argument (which might be part of a larger tree of generic arguments) shown in Figure 2. *S* is obtained by selecting values for the context variables as before. *C* is a choice of data values for the data items, so in this case (*AA*) it would be *fall, crying, no injury* which could produce a range of concerns depending on the order in which these happen. Therefore, it is at this stage that an inference procedure has to be specified so that the order in which data items are considered can be obtained from the reasons for the inference procedure. Inference 1 is the inference procedure that orders (child action, child behaviour, parent action). So the concern would be expressed as 'John observes Emma fall, John sees Emma crying, he picks her up and checks her for injury but there is no injury.' The resolution *R* is then simply the claim value of the generic argument that is specified in the actual argument. In this case *cuddles and reassures* which would be expressed as 'John cuddles and reassures Emma.' This mapping produces the story 'Emma's parent John, is looking after Emma in the playground. John observes Emma fall, he sees her crying and picks her up to check for injury but finds no injury. John cuddles and reassures Emma.' Again, in this example which is based on only one inference slot we have been able to describe how elements of the actual argument along with the appropriate generic argument component can be used to construct a story corresponding to the reasoning.

Generating Abstract Story Structures

In the discussion above, we have used the Wilensky notion of story points. The story point emerges as the reason for the inference itself—the actual claim value given the data values that have been used in the reasoning. The concern arises as the data values that are used in the reasoning and can be made more explicit by examining the degree of conflict that occurs between these values and conditions that the character goals would imply or require. The plot is the sequence of events and actions that constitute the data item values followed by the inference to the claim value or resolution. These character goals and values are usually present in the generic argument as the reason for the inference procedure. The extent to which these can be automatically processed depends on the extent to which this knowledge base is encoded.

It should also be pointed out that the (S, C, R) model would be classed as an event-character structure and in fact seems to encode more semantics than the story grammar models because the concern C signifies more than, say, DEVELOP-MENT in the Mandler and Johnson grammar. In dealing with more involved reasoning examples, the (S, C, R) model is too simple and we find that a concern C can consist of nested sub-trees of concerns with their resolutions. One such example is considered next.

A More Involved Example

To explore a more complex piece of reasoning that spans more than a single inference we will consider the story of Anju who is an applicant for refugee status in Australia. Australia is a signatory to the United Nations Convention on the Status of Refugees and so there are laws and guidelines that set out, to some degree, the basis for determining refugee status.

The members of the Refugee Review Tribunal of Australia represent a community of decision-makers. From consultations with members of this community, we have been able to represent the reasoning that they use in determinations on refugee status as a tree of *generic arguments*. This tree comprises approximately 300 nodes and it sets out the structure of reasoning for these determinations. In determining refugee status, one component of the reasoning is concerned with establishing

whether the applicant has a well-founded fear of persecution. A well-founded fear of persecution depends on a number of relevant data: the incidents of harassment that have occurred in the past; the credibility of the applicant's story; practices and policies in the country or region that target the applicant; whether these practices and policies have changed recently and whether or not the applicant could be relocated within the country of origin. Each one of these in turn depends on other nodes in the tree. This approach simply sets out a tree structure for reasoning in this domain where each node has a label that indicates the issues or facts that are used to construct reasoning. Figure 1 represents the structure we call a generic argument that acts as a structured reasoning template for reasoning involving refugee status in Australia. In particular, it presents the structure of reasoning relating to the aspect of refugee status dealing with establishing a "well-founded fear of persecution." The generic argument differs from the Toulmin layout in that (although not all of these are shown in Figure 1):

- Claims and data items are represented using a variable-value representation rather than a statement;
- Each data item includes a statement indicating its reason for relevance. This partly replaces the Toulmin warrant (not illustrated in Figure 1);
- It includes a list of inference procedures that are used to infer a claim value from data values in place of the Toulmin warrant (not illustrated in Figure 1);
- There are reasons for the appropriateness of the inference procedure;
- Context variables and values are specified (not illustrated in Figure 1).

The claim in Figure 1 represents the reasoning towards a claim on well-founded fear (either *has* or *does not have*). The generic argument structure, developed from experts on refugee law, represents agreement on the structure of reasoning used in making decisions on refugee status. The generic argument does not reflect positions held by any participant but is intended to accommodate all positions regarded as reasonable. It illustrates that a claim of well-founded fear is advanced on the basis of a position on five data items: whether the applicant can be relocated to avoid harassment; the credibility of the applicant's story; the extent to which practices/policies that target the applicant are prevalent; the overall impact of the past incidents of harassment and whether or not there have been changes in the policies/practices. A reason indicating why each of these factors is relevant has been articulated to validate their inclusion and is part of the GAAM. The process of drawing an inference from data values to claim values is seen as an exercise in mapping data to claim values.

Although not shown in Figure 1, a reason for the relevance of each data item is included and a reason for the appropriateness of each inference procedure is also included. Reasons for the relevance of data items may come from guidelines, policies, or statutes in the area or indeed agreement of the reasoning community. Reasons for inference procedures can come from the agreed validity of the inferences, agreed rules or agreed principles and values that underpin the way in which data values are mapped to claim values. Context variables describe the circumstances and assumptions regarding the reasoning. Context variables are shown in the generic argument of Figure 2.

Anju was a Sikh born in India in the 1970s. She had thirteen years of education there before she travelled to Australia in the 1990s and married a Muslim. Her culture does not approve of marriage into other religions. She feels that her relatives in India would have nothing to do with her if she returned because she has done something that is culturally unacceptable. If she were to return to India now, at the very least she would face taunt-ing and social ridicule over her marriage. She has recently divorced her husband and is being supported by relatives. She feels that it would be difficult to live in India without the support of relatives.

The members of the Refugee Review Tribunal of Australia represent a community of decision-makers. From consultations with members of this community, we have been able to represent the reasoning that they use in determinations on refugee status as a tree of *generic arguments*. This tree comprises approximately 300 nodes and it sets out the structure of reasoning for these determinations. In determining refugee status, one component of the reasoning is concerned with establishing whether the applicant has a well-founded fear of persecution. A well-founded fear of persecution depends on a number of relevant data: the incidents of harassment that have occurred in the past; the credibility of the applicant's story; practices and policies in the country or region that target the applicant; whether these practices and policies have changed recently; and whether or not the applicant could be relocated within the country of origin. Each one of these in turn depends on other nodes in the tree. This approach simply sets out a tree structure for reasoning in this domain where each node has a label that indicates the issues or facts that are used to construct reasoning.

GENERALIZING THE STRUCTURE

The Toulmin argument structure represents reasoning as arguments constructed from sentences, which are claims and data. The reasoning that represents the position of the applicant (Anju) and the reasoning of the RRT member would be represented as two separate Toulmin diagrams, however both arguments can subscribe to the same generic argument. Figure 1 sets out the section of a more complete tree that represents reasoning towards a claim on 'well-founded fear.' Each claim and data item are generalised to a sentence with a variable-value component that can accommodate the claims of both the applicant (Anju) and the member. In fact, a range of claims can be accommodated. Anju's actual argument is captured by the selection of claims (indicated with the lighter shading) in Figure 1.

THE CASE AS AN ACTUAL ARGUMENT

Anju's actual argument is captured within this generic argument structure by the selection of values for each data and claim item as shown in Figure 1. The argument could be expressed as:

Anju has a well-founded fear of persecution because: the incidents of harassment that have occurred in the past certainly constitute persecution due to a convention reason, namely religion; her story that she came to Australia in the 1970s and married a Muslim is completely credible; relocation within her country of origin is not feasible; practices/policies of harassment that target her are likely because her religion <u>does not approve of marriage into other religions</u>*; these practices have traditionally* <u>been ostracism especially by relatives</u> *and recently there has not been any change to this practice.*

The underlined sections of the text above come from arguments lower in the argument tree which have not been shown in Figure 1. For example, data for the claim that incidents taken together constitute persecution would be based on nodes containing a description of each incident. The incidents of taunting and ridicule over her marriage and the fact that these have a religious basis would be described in these data items. The severity of the incidents would also be captured as a data item. The fact that practices of harassment do exist also stem from an argument underneath the **Practices that target Applicant** claim with

a data item that simply allows for a description of the practice. This node would contain the fact that Sikhs do not approve of marriage into other religions and that there is a practice of ostracism (see Figure 3). The reasoning presented in this example is more complex because it spans two levels of the argument tree.

FROM ACTUAL ARGUMENT TO NARRATIVE: ANJU'S STORY

This actual argument is based on reasoning about refugee status in Australia. Australia is a signatory to the United Nations Convention on the Status of Refugees and the laws regarding refugees are based on this to a large extent. This knowledge is captured in a GAS G developed from knowledge acquisition with members from the Refugee Review Tribunal of Australia. In capturing the actual argument made by Anju the following context variables are also captured (as part of the generic argument). As part of the process of generating a narrative, the system will prompt for additional information to enhance the generation of a narrative. These context and narrative variables are shown in Table 2.

This assignment (Table 2) constitutes S. The concern of the story (C in the (G,S,C,R) tuple) is a selection of data values for the data items in the sub-tree as follows, selected values are in bold typeface: the incidents of harassment that have occurred in the past **[certainly]** constitute persecution due to a convention reason; her story is **[completely credible]** (R_1) as [C_1 -**she came to Australia in the 1970's and subsequently married a Muslim**]; relocation within her country of origin **[is not feasible]** (R_2) because [C_2 -**she needs the support of her relatives**; practices/policies of harassment that target her **[are likely]** (R_3) because [C_3 -**her religion does not approve of marriage into other religions**; these practices have **traditionally been ostracism especially by**

Figure 3. Practices/policies argument for Anju

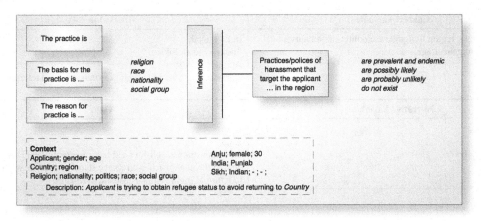

relatives] and recently there **[has not]** been any change to this practice. The concern *C* here spans two levels of inference, the level shown in Figure 1 and in three of the sub-trees, Credibility, Relocation and Practices that Target Applicant (Figure 3).

The end of the story (*R* in the (*G,S,C,R*) tuple) is generated from the claim value; the applicant, Anju, **[has]** a well-founded fear of persecution, which is Anju's inference. The story point is the reason for Anju's inference, namely, that she cannot go back to India without being ostracised by her relatives.

The story generated from Anju's actual argument is:

S *I am an Indian born Sikh from the Punjab region, living in Australia. I am trying to get refugee status to avoid returning to India.*

C *Incidents of harassment that have occurred in the past constitute persecution due to a convention reason. My story is completely credible as I married a Muslim. Relocation within India is not feasible because I need the support of my relatives. Practices and policies of harassment that target me are likely because my religion does not approve of marriage into other religions. These practices have traditionally been ostracism especially by*

relatives and recently there has not been any change to this practice. **C** *C_1 -I came to Australia in the 1970s and subsequently married a Muslim -this is true [completely credible - R_1]. C_3 My religion does not approve of marriage into other religions and C_3 there are practices of taunting and ostracism especially by relatives. R_3 These practices of harassment are likely. Incidents of harassment that have occurred in the past certainly constitute persecution due to a convention reason. C_2 I need the support of relatives so relocation within India is not possible R_2. There has not recently been any change to the practice of harassment.* **R** *I have a well-founded fear of persecution.*

The story point is the reason for the inference that she has a well-founded fear of persecution based on likely harassment because her religion does not approve of marriage into other religions. In this case, the full effect of the story point is captured across two levels of inference in the argument tree.

Essentially the story generated has the top level form (S, C, R) where C is $([R_1, C_1], [R_3, C_3], C_{Incidents}, [R_2, C_2], C_{Change})$ where the nested sub-trees of the main concern C are shown. The way in which this is sequenced

Table 2. Context variable values for Anju's actual argument

Context Variable	Value
Country of origin; region Religion;race;politics;nationality;social group Applicant;gender;age Description	India;Punjab Sikh;-;-;Indian;Sikh Anju;female;30 Applicant is trying to get refugee status to avoid returning to Country
Narrative Variable	**Value**
Narrative voice Protagonist Protagonist goals Character	Anju Anju To demonstrate a well-founded fear of persecution (This is a sub-goal of the goal to achieve refugee status so that she will not have to return to India.) Anju's husband -a Muslim

into a story is open to selection. In most cases, the setting *S* will be used first and the order of presenting the events that make up the concerns and their resolutions can be altered within constraints. These constraints are those that impact on the reasoning and therefore the story point. A natural structure is an hierarchical story, where the episodes are embedded. Notice that in this case the tree is traversed bottom up starting from the deepest point.

FROM ACTUAL ARGUMENT TO NARRATIVE: THE MEMBER'S STORY

Similarly, the member's story could be generated from the member's reasoning as follows. The narrative voice in Table 2 would change to be the member and all other values would remain unchanged.

These assignments would constitute *S*. The concern of the story (*C* in the (*G,S,C,R*) tuple) is a selection of data values for the data items in the sub-tree as follows. (Selected values are in bold typeface): the incidents of harassment that have occurred in the past **[to a minimal extent]** constitute persecution due to a convention reason; her story is **[partially credible]** (R_1) as [C_1 -**she has married a Muslim**]; relocation within her country of origin **[is likely to lead to protection]** (R_2) because [C_2 -**she can be away from**

her relatives; practices/policies of harassment that target her **[are likely]** (R_3) because [C_3 -**her religion does not approve of marriage into other religions**; these practices have **traditionally been ostracism especially by relatives**] and recently there **[has not]** been any change to this practice. The concern *C* here spans two levels of inference, the level shown in Figure 1 and in three of the sub-trees, Credibility, Relocation, and Practices that Target Applicant (Figure 3).

The end of the story (*R* in the (*G,S,C,R*) tuple) is generated from the claim value, the applicant Anju **[does not have]** a well-founded fear of persecution, which is the member's inference.

The story generated from the member's actual argument becomes:

S *Anju is an Indian-born Sikh who married a Muslim.*

C *If she were to return to India, there are practices of harassment that would be applied to her because she married outside her religion. She is likely to be ostracised by her community and her relatives. This is still practised but relocation would offer protection as she would be away from her relatives.*

R *Her fear of persecution if returned to India is not well founded.*

Note that the story point is the member's reason for the inference that Anju does not have a well-founded fear of persecution on the basis of possible ostracism by her community if returned to India because she could relocate.

OVERVIEW OF THE NARRATIVE MAPPING

The mapping from reasoning represented as an actual argument which has an underlying generic argument has involved the following aspects:

- A recursively nested version of the Bennett and Feldman story model (this is equivalent to the recursive nature of episodes in story grammars); in the examples above, the story output is generated by bottom-up traversal through the argument tree (depth first) with a breadth-first sequence following the sequence specified in the reason for each inference procedure or if the sequence is not specified passing control to a sequencing module with user input
- A mapping of reasoning components to story elements
- Input on narrative components.

The correspondence between the reasoning elements and story elements that is used in the generation of narrative is shown in Table 3 and has been illustrated by the three cases described. Notice that no reasoning components correspond to characters. Characters are often not present in reasoning and so the protagonist and other characters and their goals are not explicit in the mapping but need to be introduced as narrative components. Data items may be events that have outcomes and these usually correspond to or make up concerns. Coherence is not a story component but is an aspect of the story that is controlled or insured by the relevance of the data items in the GAS. The plot of the story emerges as the sequence of considerations and practical actions that make up the data item values and finish with the outcome of the inference, the claim value. The GAS itself may cover many aspects of reasoning and may correspond to the theme of the reasoning.

Figure 4 shows the components of the system that achieve the generation of these narratives from the reasoning that is represented as actual arguments, which come from a generic argument of the GAS. The Selector uses the actual argument components as well as context elements from the generic argument and other narrative elements that may be user specified to provide the components for the Narrative Structure Model. These are then sequenced into the narrative by the Sequencer module following the rules that have been applied in the examples above.

ANALYSIS OF THE STORIES

We approach the evaluation of the stories in terms of their capacity to express and elucidate reasoning and to assist a decision maker. As stated

Table 3. Correspondence between reasoning elements and narrative elements

Reasoning Component	Story Component/Aspect
Context	Setting
Data item	Necessary circumstance (event)
Data values	Concern
Claim value	Resolution
Data relevance reasons (that form the basis of the GAS)	Coherence
Inference (practical actions that make up the inference)	Plot
Reason for inference procedure Reason for inference	Sequencing of events, principles, goals Story point

Figure 4. Overview of a system for generating narrative from reasoning

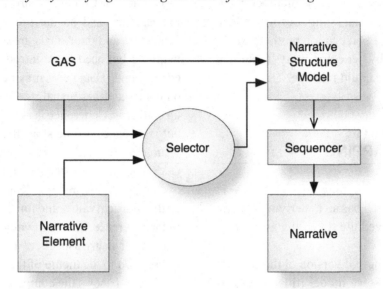

earlier, we look to see whether the stories express the reasoning towards a decision in a way that connects with our story background, rings true, and helps to appreciate the overall nature of the reasoning. To a large extent the assessment is subjective but we focus our discussion of this on coherence, storiness, and the impact of multiple stories on understanding and decisions.

We can note that the stories provide good summaries of the reasoning. Using Fisher's notions of structural and material coherence and fidelity (Fisher, 1985), we argue that structural coherence is achieved largely by the fact that each of these stories is strongly linked to the domain GAS. Each of the generated stories is generated from actual arguments that are structured by the GAS and this is a graph of items that are related by relevance to each other. The mapping that we have implemented takes as a basis the structure of reasoning set out in the GAS and events are ordered according to breadth-first, upward traversals of the tree that respect data ordering necessary in each inference procedure. If the applicant's reasoning does not fit well with the GAS (in the case, say, of reasoning that is outside the guidelines of the UN conven-

tion), then there would be less control over the mapping from data to reasoning to narrative and consequently coherence. Material coherence is also supported by the abductive structure of the GAS as relevant data and facts, in the main, have to fit into this structure. Therefore, data which are outside the structure stand out in the reasoning and consequently may stand out in the narrative, especially if there are elements that do not ring true with other stories in the domain. Of course, it is also supported by using the narrative model to control the formation of the stories. Material coherence between the two stories can now be used to identify factual errors, missing arguments and other distortions.

Characterological coherence is enforced to some extent by the GAS because this controls the elements that go into the story. In the case of Anju's generated story, this control helps to frame the story in the relevant way for the member and, in the case of the member's generated story, it helps to frame the story to reduce the likelihood of an appeal. Even so, Anju's story engages attention in terms of her honesty, her situation, and her concern for personal happiness.

Testing for fidelity of the applicant's story is concerned with the truth qualities not revealed by considering matters of coherence. The facts and reasons given in Anju's story are quite clear and none of the facts are in dispute. It is clear also that the main area of divergence between her story and the member's concerns the different reasoning (inference) involving the possibility of relocation. Anju's says that she needs the support of her relatives and so we can understand that relocation away from them will be a problem. Her dilemma is that, in India, she could neither be near her relatives or far from them. This difficulty in her story becomes the prominent situation with which an audience (reader) can identify. In the same way the member is forced to weigh this predicament against the alternatives that the UN convention may allow.

The values behind her reasoning are those relating to the need for a support group and her honesty. These values, to a large extent, determine the inferences that she makes in presenting her case for refugee status. On the other hand, the member has to be seen to apply the spirit of the United Nations Convention on the Status of Refugees fairly and therefore weighs the fact that there are others whose need is a real fear of actual persecution, not simply the hardship of being away from one's relatives. The values that underpin this reasoning are related to fairness, justice, and humanity.

The two stories generated seem to expose a more holistic picture of the reasoning. Comparing the stories, we find that the tension between the support from relatives and the harshness in their ostracism of Anju is a key element. This gives the story generated from Anju's reasoning a greater element of storiness than the member's story. The stories make us consider what our options may be if we had engaged in actions that would warrant being ostracised by our own relatives. This engages an understanding of Anju in not wanting to be ostracised and at the same time being already ostracised by being in another country. In response to those who say that the reader of the stories is not left with expectations and questions during the story, we might ask them to consider the two stories in sequence as segments of a larger story in which Anju narrates her story first and then narrates the member's story. In this enlarged story, Anju's story becomes one data item and the members another, which creates concern that would have to be resolved by a decision to return to India.

Anju's story and the members differ in their underlying values. The reasoning that they use is different because of these different values. In terms of the GAAM, we would say that their choice of inference is determined by their values. The values not only determine the reasoning but also determine qualities such as honesty and fairness that come through in the stories.

Although we are not so concerned with the level of entertainment or drama offered by the stories, we are concerned that the essence of being a story or storiness is present. Whilst we have already commented on the level of concern generated by various data item values earlier and the effect that this may have on interest and drama some comments on storiness should be made. Bailey (1999) suggests that storiness is represented as the expectations and questions that a reader may have as the story unfolds. Expectations are logical inferences made by the imagined reader of the story from the story so far and questions are reader response phenomena emergent from specific patterns of expectations. Putting the two stories together with the member's story following the applicant's (Anju) story, in fact makes a story with a good level of storiness. In the refugee domain this is in fact what happens, applicants hope that their story of potential persecution if returned to their country of origin will have an outcome that avoids return. The contrast between their reasoning and that of the member carries many expectations and questions. The different ways in which inferences can be made based on the same facts is, in this case the feature that creates questions and expectations that contribute to the storiness.

Arguably, the most important contribution of the ability to generate stories automatically from reasoning is the opportunity for the decision-maker to see their reasoning set alongside the applicant's reasoning, both being in a narrative form. In our example, Anju's story, at first glance, connects more with us as a story than the member's. This would also be apparent to the member. A layperson may tend to be more convinced by the applicant's story and not understand why the member has reasoned in this way. The two stories ignite a further deliberation response in the member that invite him to again consider the reasoning to his decision. The focus of this deliberation will be directed towards the differences between his story and Anju's and should focus around the different claims about relocation. There would be a strong suggestion for the member to consider, in more detail, reasons for relocation and communicate these in his reasoning explaining the severity of harassment required to be classed as persecution. In a domain where the inferences are not expressed as explicit rules, it is important to communicate the reasons for a decision. Whilst members of the tribunal are required to communicate reasons for their decision, the ability to see both stories corresponding to the reasonings can suggest further points of deliberation. It is recognised that deliberation can lead to improved decisions (Swank & Wrasai, 2002). The combination of multiple stories and multiple representations of the reasoning contribute to expert decisions as Geoffrey (2005), in research on clinical reasoning and expertise, points out. That work indicates that the nature of expertise lies in the availability of multiple representations of knowledge and that in terms of learning reasoning the critical element may be deliberate practice with multiple examples, which, on the one hand, facilitates the availability of concepts and conceptual knowledge (i.e. trans-

fer) and, on the other hand, adds to a storehouse of solved problems.

One important aspect of the correspondence between reasoning and story is the alignment between the stories and with the data. In the example above, the member's story, derived from their reasoning is not misaligned with the story generated from Anju's reasoning. The stories are different in their outcomes not because of discrepancies in the evidence but because of the different perspectives of the reasoners. The story generated from Anju's reasoning exposes the dilemma that she faces by needing the support of her relatives but not being able to get it. This is not sufficient to be judged as persecution.

In cases where the stories are not aligned, the discrepancies between them are highlighted. The discrepancies may be in the facts that make up the setting or events, the reasoning or values. In coming to a decision, the decision maker would need to be comfortable with and understand the basis for the difference in the stories.

NARRATIVE INFORMATION SYSTEMS

Returning to Aristotle's configuration of *praxis*, *logos,* and *mythos*, our approach above has concentrated on producing a mapping between *logos* and *mythos* but there is a good interest in the complete mapping from *praxis* through *logos* to *mythos* especially if this is seen as the realization of a narrative information system or the production of narrative from an information system. Goble and Crowther's (1994) proposed models support the medical record as a coherent story reconstructed from the sequence of recorded events within the medical record. They propose one representation, which unifies all four models by a three-space approach, each space acting as a schema for the space below. Their three spaces (category, individual, and occurrence) assist a temporal summarisation of a patient's medical record and despite the difficulties of recording retrospective or contradictory observations facilitate the production of a narrative of the events in the medical record. Their model does not account for the reasoning to a clinical decision expressed in narrative form. This part of the reasoning is precisely what our approach is able to achieve but of course requires a rich representation of the reasoning. As knowledge-based systems become more common it would be viable to produce stories that reflect the clinician's reasoning and have these form part of the patient information and patient medical record.

Interpretation and subjective implication are key dimensions of narrative use within organizations. The relationship between narration, sense-making and negotiation of meaning is often emphasized (Weick, 1995; Wenger, 1998). A narrative allows the recognition of meanings for cues, events, and situations which are difficult to interpret or for which there exist competing frameworks of interpretation. Zack (1999) classifies these as two of the types of organizational ignorance: ambiguity—not having a conceptual framework to interpret information; equivocacy—having several contradictory conceptual frameworks.

Soulier and Caussanel (2002) argue that narration can be a way of dealing with ambiguity and equivocacy. The starting point is usually a cue or event that is considered surprising and does not relate to the framework of interpretation of the agents. Narration of the situation produces "naive explanations" that result from causal attributions. Their approach is to use a story model based on the following components:

- **Situation:** description of the situation;
- **Complication:** description of the events which make intrigue;
- **Resolution:** development of the story; and
- **Result:** the result that closes the story.

Each of these components is a list of narrative elements coming from analysis of the narrative broken down into simple assertions. The model also represents theme and scenes. The model can be used as a base for enriching the structure and narrative by opposing different views of the agents involved in the situation. In this way, a negotiation around the narrative of the story is engaged in order to reach a consensual model.

INTERACTIVE NARRATIVE ENVIRONMENTS FROM REASONING

Critical Care Nursing

Advances in critical care technologies and practices over recent decades have led to decision-making settings that are complex and demand extensive nursing training. Monitoring and responding to ventilated patients' gaseous exchange is a central role for ICU nurses. Horn (1986) argued that there are too many factors or possible solutions for a human to remember at once, even when the problem is broken down into smaller pieces. Decisions must be made under pressure, and missing even a single factor could be disastrous. The decision making involved in determining the actions a nurse should perform when a low oxygen alarm sounds with a mechanically ventilated patient is typically taught informally 'on the job' in conjunction with some classroom exercises. In practice, nurse educators aim to impart knowledge of three aspects of practical reasoning to novices:

- **Action:** What action to perform next. For example an action an ICU nurse has to learn to perform is to check the shape of the pleth wave. This is a wave displayed on a monitor that is derived from an infrared finger probe detecting the level of oxygen in the blood stream.
- **Incorrect Action Consequence:** This is the consequence of performing an incor-

rect action. For example, changing the finger probe is the correct action when the oxygen alarm is sounding and the pleth wave is noisy. A noisy pleth wave often indicates that the probe is not reading accurately. Checking the blood pressure at this time has a consequence that is relatively minor in that it diverts the nurse's attention from effective troubleshooting. Other situations have more serious consequences. The severity of each consequence is captured on a scale from 1-10 illustrated in brackets in Figure 5.

- **Omission consequence:** This is the immediate consequence of failing to perform the action when it should be performed. Failing to administer pure oxygen to the patient when the alarm has sounded and the pleth wave is accurate results in a possible state of insufficient oxygen.

Reasoning involving the action and consequences following a low oxygen alarm in an Australian hospital has been modelled using decision trees described in Stranieri et al. (2004). In that study, reasoning was modelled using a decision tree in order to implement a decision support system that represented best practice in critical care nursing. The decision tree structure has been converted to an argument tree representation shown in Figure 5 for the IILE.

The data items (extreme left) represent possible events or causal factors in ICU situations. There are three claim variables (extreme right):

1. Actions an ICU nurse may take at a point in time in a given situation,
2. Consequence that follows if the action is not correct, and
3. Consequence of failing to perform the correct action for the situation.

Arrows represent inference procedures that will be invoked to infer a value on each claim variable for any set of input data items. After initialisation, the IILE functions using a SET-INFER-NARRATE-cycle illustrated in Figure 6.

A prototype IILE with partial functionality has been implemented and evaluated to date. The prototype permits a restricted set of context variables and does not infer the severity of incorrect actions or omission consequences but, more simply, presents canned text about the errors to the learner during the narrative phase. The learner has initial input into the story by setting context variable values such as the name and gender of the patient and nurse. Figure 7 illustrates the main screen for the prototype. On the left is a list of all actions available to the nurse. The top pane on the right provides the narration to date. Beneath that, the learner is prompted to set data item values for the 'Check the signal indicator or pleth wave' action that was selected prior to the display of the screen in the SET phase. Once an action is selected and a data item value set, the system invokes the inference procedure in the argument tree to determine what the correct next action should be (INFER). If the next action the learner selects is not correct, two segments of text are generated for the NARRATE phase; a segment explaining why the action was incorrect and another explaining the consequences associated with the non-performance of the correct action.

Figure 8 illustrates a screen that presents the narrator's voice back to the learner following the setting of the pleth wave to accurate. The learner is about to select the next action to infer is to check the leads. However, behind the scenes, the INFER phase has determined that the correct action to perform next is to increase oxygen. Figure 9 depicts the NARRATE phase screen that displays the incorrect action text explaining why checking the leads was not appropriate and the omission text explaining why increasing the oxygen was more important. The NARRATE, SET, INFER cycle continues until a pre-defined end state is reached. These end states depict recovery or es-

Figure 5. ICU argument tree

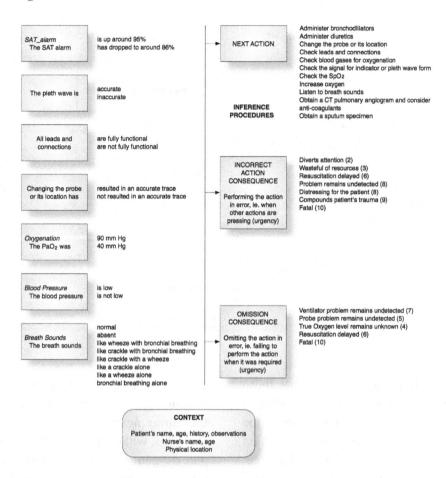

calation of the concern to a point where a doctor is called.

Table 4 illustrates a similar example though differs from the prototype sample above in that the IILE exerts control of events to dramatise the impact of an error and produce a more dramatic story. Initially, at Steps 1 to 7, the learner propels the narrative on sufficiently so the IILE does not intervene but acts only as a narrator providing the learner with an alternate description of the learners experiences. At Step 8, the learner erroneously elects to check the breath sounds instead of checking the leads. The noisy pleth wave typically indicates that the finger probe is not accurately picking up a signal so checking the breath sounds is unnecessary. The IILE infers the next

action given the situation (i.e. 'alarm,' 'noisy pleth wave,' and 'wheezing breath sounds') is still that leads should be checked. The consequence of not doing this (omission consequence) is that the true oxygen level is not known. The severity of this is rated at 4.

In order to make a dramatic impact of the learner's error, the IILE commences to direct the narrative by attempting to set events that would extend the current situation and lead to the maximum omission consequence (i.e. death rated at 10) or the maximum incorrect action consequence (i.e. death rated at 10). The IILE performs a search, essentially by scanning inference procedures backwards, from claim to data-item values, in a goal-driven search. The search aims

Figure 6. Narrate, set, infer cycle

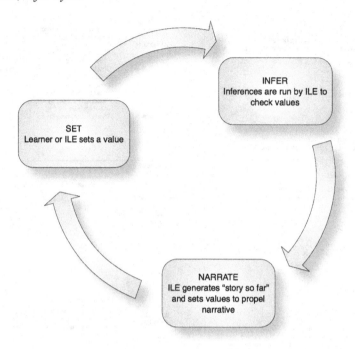

to find a set of data items that subsumes those currently set (alarm, noisy pleth wave, wheezy breath) and an omission consequence equal to the target (death). The search ends with the addition of the value is inadequate set for the data item Oxygenation to the currently set items. That is, the forward inference on the set (alarm, noisy pleth wave, wheezy breath, and oxygenation inadequate) results in the next action being to increase oxygen to 100% (Step 9) and a consequence that failing to do this would be fatal. The IILE therefore sets the data item Oxygenation as inadequate. The narration at Step 10 informs the learner of the consequence of performing the last action erroneously. Further, the narrator also informs the learner that the story has taken a twist in that the patient now has insufficient oxygenation. When the SAT alarm begins sounding, Flo checks the pleth wave and notices it is noisy. She immediately checks the breath sounds and hears a wheeze. However, this is not the best thing for her to do because it has diverted her attention from the real problem and she does not know the true oxygen level. As it happens, Jim has taken a turn and has a very low oxygen level. At Step 11, the learner again errs by checking the endotracheal tube without increasing the oxygen level to pure oxygen and suctioning. The IILE detects that this is the second error with a fatal consequence and triggers a resolution sequence that will leave the patient dead. Finally, the narrator describes the resolution by informing the learner of the mistakes made and actions that should have occurred. As it happens, Jim has taken a turn and has a very low oxygen level. Flo checks the endotracheal tube but has not increased the oxygen intake to 100% O2. Jim has entered seizure due to the low oxygen and has died. Early on, as soon as Flo noticed a noisy pleth wave, she should have checked the leads instead of the breath sounds. Failing to do this meant that she did not know the true oxygenation which as it happens was critically low. She will do better next time.

In order to make a dramatic impact of the learners error, the IILE commences to direct the narrative by attempting to set events that would

Figure 7. SET phase screen prompting the learner to set pleth data item values

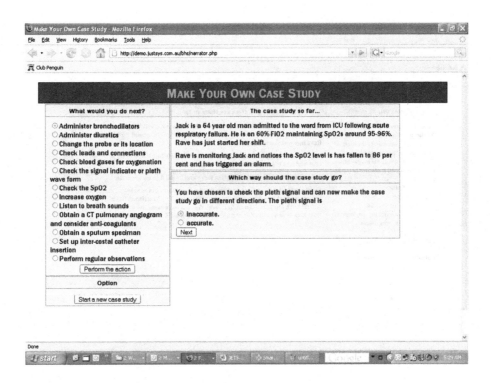

Figure 8. NARRATE phase screen after pleth set to accurate

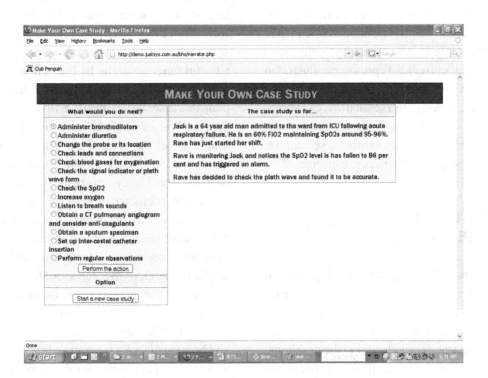

Figure 9. NARRATE phase screen after an incorrect action

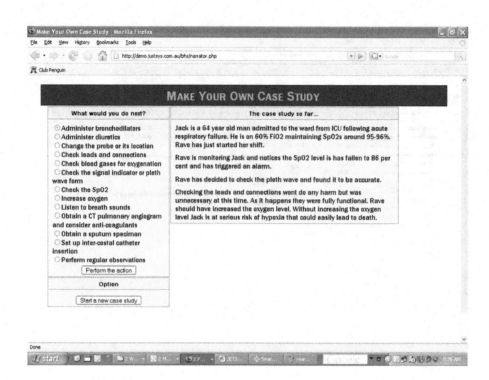

extend the current situation and lead to the maximum omission consequence (death rated at 10) or the maximum incorrect action consequence (death rated at 10). This functionality has not been included in the current ILE prototype illustrated in the screens above. In the next example, a short scenario is generated from a session driven entirely by the IILE. This simulates the presentation of case studies of best practice central to second tier learning as a step towards expert learning.

AUTOMATED CASE STUDY GENERATION

In problem-based learning and learning through cases considerable resources go into the construction of problems/cases and related resources for supporting learners in enabling users to learn through understanding and solving the problems. The construction of cases depicting past or hypo-

thetical scenarios in a non-interactive format is important for the early stages of the transformation from novice to expert. The automated generation of case narratives from a strong domain model is a useful function of the IILE in a non-interactive mode of control. In the automatic generation of plausible case studies, the IILE first establishes the setting of the narrative by executing the initialisation phase of the cycle. Following that, the IILE selects actions based on inferences drawn from best practice. The cycles are illustrated in Table 5. The events, depicted as predicate-like clauses in Table 5 are feasibly converted to natural language below with relatively standard natural language generation techniques (from the rich resources stored in the GAAM). Jim is a 60-year old man admitted to the intensive care unit with acute respiratory failure. He has been intubated for the last 3 days. His CXR shows bilateral patchy infiltrates and he is on 60% FiO_2 maintaining SpO_2s around 95-96%. You are caring for this patient when the

Table 4. Emergent narrative example

NAR	1	patient name(jim), patient age(jim,60), patient cxr(jim, bilateral patchy infiltrates), patient Fio2(jim,60%), patient spo2(jim, 95-96%), nurse(Fio).
SET	2	Set(ILE,SAT Alarm,sounding)
INF	3	infer(Check pleth)
NAR	4	nurse(observes,SAT Alarm, sounding)
SET	5	Set(learner, Pleth, noisy)
INF	6	infer(Check leads)
NAR	7	nurse(observes, Pleth, noisy)
SET	8	set(learner, Check breath, like a wheeze) set(ILE, Oxygenation, inadequate)
INF	9	infer(Increase oxygen to 100% and suction)
NAR	10	nurse(observes, Breath, wheeze), narrator(tells, Incorrect action consequence, Diverts attention), narrator(tells, Omission consequence, True oxygen level unknown), narrator(tells, Oxygenation, inadequate)
SET	11	Set(learner, Check ETT function, functional)
INF	12	infer(Increase oxygen to 100% and suction)
NAR	13	narrator(resolution,Patient dies), narrator(tells, Oxygenation, inadequate), narrator(tells, Check breath instead of Check lead,), narrator(tells, Incorrect omission consequence, Unknown oxygen level)

SAT alarm begins sounding. You notice that the pleth wave does not appear accurate but is noisy. You check leads and connections and see that they are fully functional. Changing the probes or their position has not resulted in an accurate trace. You take blood gas samples to check saturation and find that these values are adequate. You conclude that oxygenation is adequate despite the probe readings, but proceed to apply the OxyMax procedure. OxyMax is necessary to accurately detect oxygen levels in some patients. You continue to monitor Jim closely.

RESULTS AND DISCUSSION

The basis of this system and its functionality has been illustrated using two examples. The IILE allows the user to interactively interrogate or select actions within a setting and receive feedback in the form of a narrative. The learner is engaged in the respiratory treatment of the patient and tries to act in the way that is best for the patient. To this end, they select actions to perform and the IILE responds through the narrator to receive feedback and commentary to improve the users understanding. The system uses knowledge to recognize incorrect actions or omitted actions by the learner and makes subsequent events occur for dramatic impact on the learner through the narrative. As the narrative emerges from the interaction between the learner and the IILE, it provides supportive commentary as the learner reasons correctly but causes increased concern for the learner as reasoning mistakes or omissions are made. The IILE is capable of automatically generating a narrative based on knowledge that has been captured on reasoning to complex practical decisions. A Web-based version of this design has been built and used as an instructional aid. There are some differences from this design in that the system does not propel the story to a dramatic end but simply narrates what has happened with the narration including advice about the consequences of incorrect actions, omissions as well as consequences of these actions.

The impact of the ILE on learning outcomes amongst student nurses was evaluated in a trial involving three groups of third year nursing students at the University of Ballarat described in

Table 5. Automated generation of plausible case example

Phase	Step	Events
NAR	1	patient name(jim), patient age(jim,60), patient cxr(jim, bilateral patchy in□ltrates), patient Fio2(jim,60%), patient spo2(jim, 95-96%), nurse(Fio).
SET	2	Set(ILE,SAT Alarm,sounding)
INF	3	infer(Check pleth)
NAR	4	nurse(observes,SAT Alarm, sounding)
SET	5	Set(IILE, Pleth, noisy)
INF	6	infer(Check leads)
NAR	7	nurse(observes, Pleth, noisy)
SET	8	Set(IILE, Leads, fully functional)
INF	9	infer(Change probe)
NAR	10	nurse(observes, Leads, fully functional)
SET	11	Set(IILE, Change probe, not resulted in an accurate trace)
INF	12	infer(Check oxygenation)
NAR	13	nurse(observes, Change probe, not resulted in an accurate trace)
SET	14	Set(IILE, Oxygenation, adequate)
INF	15	infer(Continue to monitor)
NAR	16	nurse(observes, oxygenation, adequate), narrator(resolution,Continue to monitor)

(Yearwood, Avery, & Stranieri, 2006). Briefly, the study involved the use of three groups of student nurses. One group used the IILE in a tutorial, another used decision tree flowcharts, and the third, a control group, used a conventional tutorial format. Results from a test common to all groups was used as an objective measure of learning outcomes and subjective ratings of student interactions in the classroom were used as a measure of engagement. T-tests revealed that students who used the flowcharts and those that used the IILE performed significantly better on the common test than the control group. Further, the measures of student engagement clearly favoured the IILE.

SUMMARY

In this chapter, we have focused on the ways in which presenting reasoning via a story generated from the reasoning can be used to assist, in particular, novices in a reasoning community.

Stories have been used for reasoning in the following ways:

- To make sense of evidence a constructed story is assessed for coherence and plausibility and possibly compared with other stories to see if it 'rings true';
- To convey and express reasoning; and
- To connect with human understanding.

We have used the GAAM to capture the actual reasoning of a decision maker in the framework of the accepted reasoning of a community, and the context of their reasoning. These are mapped into a story through a story model that makes explicit the concern as a set of conditions, which set up a conflict for the protagonist to resolve. The concern is closely aligned with a decision or inference that needs to be made and captures the point of the story. These inferences generally satisfy the criterion of necessity in the circumstances. Sufficiency in the circumstances does not lead to these interesting inferences. The mapping from reasoning to story is developed and demonstrated through its application to examples of increasing complexity and demonstrates a realization of the second component of Aristotle's progression from praxis to mythos. The GAAM, together with the mapping to the story model, can be used to generate stories from reasoning. The stories generated can be used to re-express the reasoning in narrative forms that help to portray a whole that can be evaluated for coherence and fidelity. Furthermore, the automation of story generation from reasoning (expressed more formally) support each other and demonstrate subtle differences and nuances peculiar to different narratives that can be important to deliberation and high quality decisions. An important feature is the ability to capture not only the context of the reasoning but also the possibility of alternative inferences from the same data. Whilst the GAAM has been used to represent reasoning, most other representations of reasoning could be used but would need to be augmented with the relevant contextual information and choice of inferences and outcomes. The embellishment of the stories by some form of discourse elaboration technique could be implemented to go beyond the minimalist form presented here.

Stories are a natural way in which human beings choose to present their reasoning. Whilst it is difficult to automatically extract the reasoning that they contain, it is arguable that they should be included in the pool of reasons because they act as compressed cases or case studies that can help engage a wider range of reasoning participants. We have suggested that structured representations of the reasoning pool can assist a reasoning community in coalescing their reasoning. The precise way in which stories can be integrated into this structure is not yet clear. However, linking stories to chains of reasoning or particular elements of the structure may have advantages for integrating the two approaches.

Poletta (2006) found that members of all demographic groups who saw themselves as having opinions or experiences that they believed were unlikely to be shared were more than five times as likely to tell stories to make their points as to give reasons. They also found that participants were more likely to engage narrative claims: to request clarification or further elaboration of a point, expand on it, question its generalizability or relevance, agree or disagree with it, or acknowledge its impact on their opinions. They claim that narrative's openness to interpretation allowed deliberators to advance compromise and third positions without antagonization and that this 'give and take' fostered deliberation. The motivation for being part of a reasoning community is the belief that an individual can achieve better justified judgments than they would alone and the motivation for the community to exist is the belief that it can support the achievement of better justified decisions on the issues that it considers. Poletta's findings suggest that stories are a means of both including a broader cross-section of community as well as bringing into the reasoning resources a great wealth of human experience that may or may not be readily integrated into the other reasoning structures of the community.

REFERENCES

Bailey, P. (1999). Searching for storiness: Story generation from a reader's perspective. In M. Mateas & P. Sengers (Eds.), *Narrative Intelligence: Papers from the AAAI Fall Symposium*. North Falmouth, MA: AAAI.

Bennett, W., & Feldman, M. (1981). *Reconstructing reality in the courtroom: Justice and judgment in American culture*. Newark, NJ: Rutgers University Press.

Black, J., & Bower, G. (1980). Story understanding and problem solving. *Poetics, 9*, 223–250. doi:10.1016/0304-422X(80)90021-2

Black, J., & Wilensky, R. (1979). An evaluation of story grammars. *Cognitive Science, 3*, 213–230. doi:10.1207/s15516709cog0303_2

Branigan, E. (1992). Narrative comprehension and film. In Buscombe, E. (Ed.), *Sightlines*. New York, NY: Routledge.

Brinker, M. (1993). Theme and interpretation. In Sollors, W. (Ed.), *The Return of Thematic Criticism* (pp. 21–37). Boston, MA: Harvard University Press.

Bruner, J. (1990). *Acts of meaning*. Boston, MA: Harvard University Press.

Chatman, S. (1978). *Story and discourse: Narrative structure in fiction and film*. Ithaca, NY: Cornell University Press.

Correira, A. (1980). Computing story trees. *American Journal of Computational Linguistics, 6*(3-4), 135–149.

Dyer, M. (1983). *In depth understanding: A computer model of integrated processing for narrative comprehension*. Cambridge, MA: MIT Press.

Fisher, W. (1985). The narrative paradigm: An elaboration. *Communication Monographs, 52*, 347–367. doi:10.1080/03637758509376117

Fisher, W. (1994). Narrative rationality and the logic of scientific discourse. *Argumentation, 8*, 21–32. doi:10.1007/BF00710701

Fisher, W. (1995). *Narration, knowledge and the possibility of wisdom, rethinking knowledge: Reflections across the disciplines*. Albany, NY: State University of New York Press.

Geoffrey, N. (2005). Research in clinical reasoning: Past history and current trends. *Medical Education, 13*(4), 418–427.

Goble, C., & Crowther, P. (1994). Schemas for telling stories in medical records, in M. Jarke, J. Bubenko, & K. Jeffery (Eds.), *Proceedings of the 4th International Conference on Extending Database Technology (EDBT)*. Cambridge, UK: Springer-Verlag.

Graesser, A. (1981). *Prose comprehension beyond the word*. New York, NY: Springer Verlag. doi:10.1007/978-1-4612-5880-3

Hart, H., & Honore, A. (1959). *Causation in the law*. Oxford, UK: Clarendon Press.

Horn, M. V. (1986). *Understanding expert systems*. Toronto, Canada: Bantam Books.

Jackson, B. S. (1990). Narrative theories and legal discourse. In Nash, C. (Ed.), *Narrative in Culture: The Uses of Storytelling in the Sciences, Philosophy and Literature* (pp. 23–50). London, UK: Routledge.

Johnson, N. S., & Mandler, J. M. (1980). A tale of two structures: Underlying and surface forms in stories. *Poetics, 9*, 51–86. doi:10.1016/0304-422X(80)90012-1

Lehnert, W. G. (1982). Plot units: A narrative summarization strategy. In Lehnert, W. G., & Ringle, M. H. (Eds.), *Strategies for Natural Language Processing* (pp. 375–414). Hillsdale, NJ: Erlbaum.

Mackie, J. (1980). *The cement of the universe: A study of causation*. Oxford, UK: Clarendon Press.

Mandler, J. (1984). *Stories, scripts and scenes: Aspects of schema theory*. Hillsdale, NJ: Lawrence Erlbaum Associates.

Mandler, J., & Johnson, N. (1977). Remembrance of things parsed: Story structure and recall. *Cognitive Psychology, 9*, 111–151. doi:10.1016/0010-0285(77)90006-8

McCloskey, D. N. (1990). Storytelling in economics. In Nash, C. (Ed.), *Narrative in Culture: The Uses of Storytelling in the Sciences, Philosophy and Literature* (pp. 5–22). London, UK: Routledge.

McLauchlin, M. (1990). Explanatory discourse and causal attribution. *Text*, *10*, 63–68. doi:10.1515/text.1.1990.10.1-2.63

Pennington, N., & Hastie, R. (1981). Juror decision-making models: The generalization gap. *Psychological Bulletin*, *89*, 246–287. doi:10.1037/0033-2909.89.2.246

Pennington, N., & Hastie, R. (1986). Evidence evaluation in complex decision making. *Journal of Personality and Social Psychology*, *51*, 242–258. doi:10.1037/0022-3514.51.2.242

Pennington, N., & Hastie, R. (1992). Explaining the evidence: Tests of the story model for juror decision making. *Journal of Personality and Social Psychology*, *62*, 189–206. doi:10.1037/0022-3514.62.2.189

Pennington, N., & Hastie, R. (1993). Reasoning in explanation-based decision making. *Cognition*, *49*, 123–163. doi:10.1016/0010-0277(93)90038-W

Polletta, F. (2006). *It was like a fever: Storytelling in protest and politics*. Chicago, IL: University Of Chicago Press.

Propp, V. (1968). *Morphology of the folktale*. Austin, TX: University of Texas Press.

Read, S. J. (1987). Constructing causal scenarios: A knowledge structure approach to causal reasoning. *Journal of Personality and Social Psychology*, *52*(2), 288–302. doi:10.1037/0022-3514.52.2.288

Rumelhart, D. E. (1975). Notes on a schema for stories. In Bobrow, D. G., & Collins, A. (Eds.), *Representation and Understanding: Studies in Cognitive Science* (pp. 185–210). New York, NY: Academic Press.

Schank, R. (1986). *Explanation patterns: Understanding mechanically and creatively*. Hillsdale, NJ: Erlbaum.

Schank, R. C., & Abelson, R. P. (1977). *Scripts, plans, goals and understanding: An inquiry into human knowledge structures*. Hillsdale, NJ: Lawrence Erlbaum.

Sgouros, N. (1999). Dynamic generation, management and resolution of interactive plots. *Artificial Intelligence*, *107*, 29–62. doi:10.1016/S0004-3702(98)00106-4

Soulier, E., & Caussanel, J. (2002). Narrative tools to improve collaborative sense-making. In *Meaning Negotiation: Papers from the AAAI Workshop*, (pp. 5-9). Menlo Park, CA: AAAI Press.

Stein, N. L., & Glenn, C. G. (1979). An analysis of story comprehension in elementary school children. In Freedle, R. (Ed.), *New Directions in Discourse Processing* (pp. 53–120). Norwood, NJ: Ablex.

Stranieri, A., Yearwood, J., Gervasoni, S., Garner, S., Deans, C., & Johnstone, A. (2004). Web-based decision support for structured reasoning in health. In *Proceedings of the Twelfth National Health Informatics Conference*, (p. 61). Brisbane, Australia: Health Informatics Society of Australia.

Swank, O. H., & Wrasai, P. (2002). *Deliberation, information aggregation and collective decision making*. Retrieved from http://papers.ssrn.com/sol3/papers.cfm?abstract_id=635285.

Thorndyke, P. W. (1977). Cognitive structures in comprehension and memory of narrative discourse. *Cognitive Psychology*, *9*, 77–110. doi:10.1016/0010-0285(77)90005-6

Trabasso, T., & Sperry, L. (1985). Causal relatedness and importance of story events. *Journal of Memory and Language*, *24*, 595–611. doi:10.1016/0749-596X(85)90048-8

Trabasso, T., & van den Broek, P. (1985). Causal thinking and story comprehension. *Memory and Language, 24*, 612–630. doi:10.1016/0749-596X(85)90049-X

Trabasso, T., van den Broek, P., & Suh, S. Y. (1989). Logical necessity and transitivity of causal relations in stories. *Discourse Processes, 121*, 1–25. doi:10.1080/01638538909544717

Twining, W. (2002). *The great juristic bazaar: Jurists texts and lawyers stories*. London, UK: Ashgate.

Wagenaar, W. A., van Koppen, P. J., & Crombag, H. F. M. (1993). *Anchored narratives: The psychology of criminal evidence*. Hempstead, UK: Harvester Wheatsheaf.

Warren, W. H., Nicholas, D., & Trabasso, T. (1979). Event chain and inferences in understanding narratives. In Freedle, R. O. (Ed.), *New Directions in Discourse Processing*. Hillsdale, NJ: Erlbaum.

Weick, K. (1995). *Sensemaking in organizations*. Thousand Oaks, CA: Sage.

Wenger, E. (1998). *Communities of practice: Learning, meaning and identity*. Cambridge, UK: Cambridge University Press.

White, H. (1981). The value of narrativity in the representation of reality. In Mitchell, W. (Ed.), *On Narrative* (pp. 1–4). Chicago, IL: The University of Chicago. doi:10.1086/448086

Wilensky, R. (1982). Points: A theory of the structure of stories in memory. In Lehnert, W. G., & Ringle, M. H. (Eds.), *Strategies for Natural Language Processing* (pp. 345–374). Hillsdale, NJ: Erlbaum.

Yearwood, J., Avery, J., & Stranieri, A. (2006). *Interactive narrative by thematic connection of dramatic situations*. Paper presented at the Narrative and Interactive Learning Environments (NILE 2004). Edinburgh, UK.

Yearwood, J., & Stranieri, A. (2006). The generic actual argument model of practical reasoning. *Decision Support Systems, 41*(2), 358–379. doi:10.1016/j.dss.2004.07.004

Zack, M. (1999). Managing organizational ignorance. *Knowledge Directions, 1*, 36–49.

Chapter 7
Ontologies and the Semantic Web

ABSTRACT

We mentioned in Chapter 2 that there are fundamental elements that underlie why reasoners might disagree. One of these fundamental elements is the set of concepts that are related to, or necessary for, communication and reasoning in the domain of discourse. It is important that participants in a reasoning community make explicit the concepts that they are employing and have ways of dealing with the evolution of concepts. In finding a way to apply a concept to a new case, the concept itself is altered in a way that is determined by what the community interprets as the necessary impact from this new case. In this chapter, we illustrate that the "evolved" concept then becomes the one that will be applied to future cases. Not only is it important that concepts and their meaning and interpretation are explicit and up-to-date, but also that there is an agreement on and commitment to this explicit formulation of concepts.

Words exist because of meaning. Once you've gotten the meaning, you can forget the words. Where can I find a man who has forgotten words so I can talk with him?

Chuang Tzu

INTRODUCTION

In philosophy, an ontology refers to a systematic description of what exists. In computer science and artificial intelligence, the focus of existence

DOI: 10.4018/978-1-4666-1818-3.ch007

is restricted to things that can be represented. If knowledge about the concepts or 'things' in a domain is represented using a declarative formalism, then the set of objects or concepts of the world that is being represented is called the universe or domain of discourse. The set of objects and the relationships between them form the basis of an ontology as an explicit specification of this conceptualization. In such an ontology the names of entities, the classes, relations, functions, and other objects are specified using formal rules that define the interpretation as well as human-readable text describing what the names mean. Gruber (1993) refers to an ontology as 'a specification of a conceptualization.'

Ontologies have become important in domains where it is necessary to have explicit representations of knowledge that everyone in the reasoning community accepts. Ontologies form the basis of the Semantic Web that will allow software applications and software agents to make intelligent and intended use of the information captured in semantic Web documents (ontologies). The Semantic Web will not be a monolithic ontology but rather a distributed system of ontologies that capture knowledge across any range of domains so that it can be used by a range of applications and agents.

Ontologies are designed and used for enabling knowledge sharing and reuse. In this sense, an ontology is a specification that is used for making ontological commitments. That is, an agreement to use a vocabulary in a way that is consistent with the total specification of the ontology. So within a reasoning community, we commit to an ontology or ontologies so that we can share knowledge with and amongst ourselves and, in the case of the existence of the Semantic Web, with software agents. A common ontology defines the vocabulary that forms the basis of communication (queries and assertions) between participants and agents of the reasoning community. The participants and agents committed to a set of ontologies need not share a knowledge base; each may know things the other does not, and commitment to an ontology does not require that a participant or agent be capable of answering all queries that can be formulated in the shared vocabulary.

People use natural language to communicate and exchange knowledge and so, when we think of reasoning communities that are composed entirely of people, we expect that natural language is the default for communication and probably also the expression of reasoning. Whilst the usual dictionary definitions of words form the basis of the use of words and terms in communication and informal reasoning, it is frequently the case, for example in legal situations that terms need to be precisely defined and agreed upon. In order to

decrease ambiguities, the field of terminology has emerged and is concerned with communication and correct usage in specific domains using specific vocabularies or indeed formal vocabularies. Terminology systematically studies the labelling or designating of concepts particular to one or more subject fields or domains of human activity through analysis of terms in context.

In this chapter we consider why some very specific reasoning communities, mainly in the sciences, have developed ontologies and what the development of the semantic web might mean for reasoning communities. Under what circumstances should reasoning communities consider moving to the formality of building ontologies?

ONTOLOGIES

In computer science and especially in artificial intelligence, ontologies play an important part in representing knowledge, usually about restricted parts of the real world. In knowledge management the representation and organization of knowledge is studied as well as the transfer of knowledge between systems and between agents. These areas are based on formal models for the representation of knowledge and the management and organization of knowledge has been studied in various contexts. When multi-agent systems are used, in order to communicate, the agents involved usually have to represent knowledge using an agreed knowledge model, otherwise there needs to be considerable effort in meaning negotiation (Avery & Yearwood, 2002). The purpose of these models is to facilitate effective communication between the agents or systems by providing a method for an unambiguous representation of the knowledge to be transferred. These restricted knowledge models for a specific domain are often called domain models.

Two types of knowledge models have emerged to date (but currently both fall under the umbrella of ontologies): ontologies and terminologies (Guarino & Giaretta, 1995). Whilst ontologies range from simple taxonomies based on inheritance and part-whole knowledge to complex, formal concept systems that attempt to formalise common-sense knowledge, terminologies are restricted to natural language definitions for specific domains.

One of the simplest notions of a possible ontology is a controlled vocabulary. These were frequently used by librarians in the classification of articles. Catalogues are also example of a controlled vocabulary. Another basic type of ontology is a glossary, which is simply a list of terms and meanings. The meanings are specified typically as natural language statements. This provides a kind of semantics that humans can read and understand. However, interpretations of the meanings are not without ambiguity and these specifications are not adequate for computer systems and software agents.

Thesauri provide additional semantics through the in-built relations that they expose between terms such as synonym and hyponym. In general, thesauri do not provide an explicit hierarchy although, with narrower and broader term specifications, a simple specialization hierarchy might be deduced. Yahoo's term hierarchy provides a basic notion of generalization and specialization. It has a small number of top-level categories. Yahoo does provide an explicit hierarchy, but this hierarchy is not a strict subclass or *is-a* relationship.

There are stronger ontologies that include strict subclass hierarchies. In these systems if A is a superclass of B, then an object that is an instance of B means that the object is an instance of A. Strict subclass hierarchies are necessary for exploitation of inheritance.

Even more involved ontologies can have a frame structure. Therefore, classes would include property information. For example, the 'mp3 player' class may include properties of "price" and "type." Properties are more useful when they are specified at a general class level and then inherited by subclasses. Furthermore, properties can have value restrictions, so restrictions on the values

that designate the property can be prescribed. For example, the "price" property could be restricted to have values that are numbers in a specified range.

As ontologies need to express more information, their expressive requirements grow. Some languages allow for the statement of arbitrary logical statements. Very expressive ontology languages allow the specification of first-order logic constraints between terms and more detailed relationships such as disjoint classes, disjoint coverings, inverse relationships, and part-whole relationships.

van Heijst, Schreiber, and Wielinga (1997) classify ontologies along two dimensions: the subject and the structure of a conceptualization. Along the dimension of subject, there are categories such as conceptualization, application ontologies, domain ontologies, generic ontologies, and representation ontologies. Domain ontologies give a view of a particular domain such as medicine or law. Generic ontologies specify very general concepts such as time and space. Representation ontologies specify knowledge representation formalisms, for example, the frame ontology used in Ontolingua (Gruber, 1993).

The second dimension, the structure of conceptualization, captures ontologies that range from simple taxonomies to networks including axioms associated with concepts and relations. van Heijst et al. (1997) distinguish three categories with increasing complexity:

- Terminological ontologies such as lexicons and taxonomies,
- Information ontologies that specify the record structure of databases, and
- Knowledge modelling ontologies that specify conceptualizations of knowledge.

One indicator of the complexity of an ontology is the nature of the set of conceptual relationships. Usually, specialization/generalization is the most basic relation to be found in an ontology. This relation can use inheritance mechanisms for a concise and efficient representation. Another standard relation is the 'part-of' relation. For example, arm is 'partof' body. Ontologies can have a predefined set of relations, for example, WordNet (Felbaum, 1998) has the synonym and hyponym relations, others define the set of relations explicitly in the ontology itself (Mahesh & Nirenburg, 1995). Another indicator of complexity can be the granularity of the concepts. Some ontologies are language-dependent and use words as conceptual primitives, while others choose more complex situations/events as the basic building blocks.

Other dimensions for a classification of ontologies have been proposed. Fox and Gruninger (1998) define an ontology as a vocabulary plus a specification of the meaning of this vocabulary. This allows ontologies to be distinguished based on the degree of formality in the specification of meaning. Therefore, informal ontologies use natural language in the specification of meaning, semiformal ontologies provide weak axiomatizations such as taxonomies, and formal ontologies define the semantics of the vocabulary by a formal language with an axiomatization that is complete and sound.

There is general agreement that every natural language processing application that seeks to represent and manipulate meanings of texts needs an ontology that serves as a semantic lexicon. Such ontologies are used to represent the text meaning in a language-independent form as well as to resolve ambiguities. Important applications in this area are machine translation and query formulation in natural language. Examples of ontologies that have mainly been developed for natural language processing include WordNet (Felbaum, 1998), and SENSUS (Knight & Luk, 1994).

If ontologies can be used to capture the meaning of all terms within a vocabulary then there are several potential applications in terms of natural language processing. The lexical ontology, WordNet, is a machine-readable ontology for the English language and there are several endeavours to develop applications to enhance information

retrieval based on the use of this ontology. World-Net allows the expansion of terms in the query to their synonyms, hyponyms, and/or semantically related concepts. However these approaches have not yet been effectively used to achieve enhanced retrieval of relevant documents and certainly not to achieve the retrieval of documents that answer the query in terms of its meaning. Other approaches perform content matching of queries and documents by indexing the documents and the queries with concepts rather than words. Guarino (1998) use a combination of both approaches in OntoSeek that indexes queries and documents by words but measures the similarity between queries and documents in terms of semantic similarity between the underlying concepts. OntoSeek uses the SENSUS ontology to represent both user queries and resource descriptions. McGuinness (1998) has developed FindUR for knowledge-enhanced search. To carry out query expansion, it explicitly uses background knowledge that is captured and organized in ontologies. FindUR increases recall and precision under certain conditions, such as short document length and limited content areas, and there is some evidence that query formulation is easier than for many other semantically based search engines. (KA)^2 is an initiative that focuses on the distributed development of an ontology that captures knowledge about the researchers, their topics and products in the knowledge acquisition community. Other examples of ontologies and applications would also include areas of library science Dublin Core (http://dublincore.org/), ontology-enhanced search eCyc (http://www.e-Cyc.com/), and FindUR (McGuinness, 1998), and e-commerce (Amazon.com, Yahoo Shopping). The Cyc ontology, an ontology of common sense knowledge is still being developed and now contains over 300,000 concepts.

The database and information systems communities also have many different approaches that use ontologies. In these communities, middle-ware technologies play an important role. Middle-ware links data resources and application programs by accessing and retrieving relevant data from multiple heterogeneous resources, transforming these data into a common representation and transmitting this knowledge to application programs. The Extensible Mark-up Language (XML) enabled a new level of interoperability for heterogeneous IT systems. However, although XML enables separation of data definition and data content, it does not ensure that data exchanged is interpreted correctly by the receiving system. That is, XML does not, of itself, capture semantics. This motivates data management to support unambiguous definition of data elements for information exchange. Using a common reference model improves this process. This is now part of the field known as knowledge management in enterprises and the technology of organizational and group memories, where ontologies play a crucial role for structuring, sharing and reusing knowledge (Vasconcelos, Kimble, Gouveia, & Kudenko, 2000).

From a knowledge engineering perspective, ontologies allow sharing and reuse of knowledge across different applications and domains, hence development costs can be reduced. Knowledge-based systems that are based on ontologies are easier to integrate in distributed environments -for example, the integration of decision support systems into medical record systems. There is a tension in ontological development between the use of very large ontologies whose coverage is large and more specific domain ontologies. Swartout, Patil, Knuth, and Russ (1996) use the SENSUS ontology to build a new domain ontology. SENSUS serves as a broad coverage, skeletal ontology to which domain-specific terms are linked. The advantage is that building the new ontology is easier, more cost effective, and potentially more reusable than building it from scratch. It also has the advantage that ontologies built in this way share the same structure.

In summary, there are several reasons for developing an ontology and these include:

- Sharing a common understanding of the structure of information among people but more usually among software components within or external to a system
- Enabling reuse of domain knowledge and avoiding re-inventing and re-representing the knowledge. More importantly it is to establish or introduce standards and most importantly to share ontologies among different domains
- Making domain assumptions explicit and providing a representation that is simple to update and extend. This can also make it easier to understand and update legacy data
- Separating domain knowledge from operational knowledge
- Enabling inferencing and reasoning on data. For example, understanding interrelationships between data can allow software to reason against the data to infer new information (If A "is a" B and B "is a" C then A "is a" C).

Defining an Ontology

We have already alluded to Gruber's definition of an ontology so what is it that has to be done to define or build an ontology? We start from a position of concentrating on a particular domain rather than think of building an ontology of everything. An ontology is an explicit definition of our domain of interest. The ontology must capture the concepts of this domain, the properties of these concepts as well as the relationships between concepts. That is we need to define:

- Concepts;
- Properties and attributes of concepts;
- Constraints on properties and concepts;
- Individuals or instances of concepts.

In defining these elements there is a responsibility to ensure that the definitions are shared by all agents that will be using the ontology so that the ontology is the basis for a common vocabulary and a shared understanding of this vocabulary that is developed in the ontology. Remember that the basis for an ontology is a conceptualization. An ontological analysis of a particular domain provides a conceptualization along with a vocabulary to refer to the entities in the conceptualization. The conceptualization consists of the identified concepts (objects, events, states of affairs, beliefs) and relationships that are assumed to exist and to be relevant. In medicine, for example, an ontological analysis might arrive at concepts such as "disease," "symptom," "therapy," and relationships like "causes" and "treats" where "disease causes symptom" and "therapy treats disease." Furthermore, an ontology specifies the conceptualization explicitly in a formal language, usually as a First Order theory. This means that the intended meaning of the vocabulary is formally defined. Such an explicit and formal definition enables artificial agents to reason about the relevant domain.

The process of defining an ontology involves:

- Defining the terms in the domain and the relations among them
  - The concepts in the domain are objects or Classes
- Arranging the concepts in a hierarchy (Sub-Class / Super-Class)
- Defining attributes of the classes (Properties) and any constraints on their values and relations
- Defining individuals and Instances.

When an object model is used the object model allows for:

- Inheritance, importing and typing
- Explicit statements, rather than definitions buried in code
- All users of the model to use properties and constraints.

Ontologies as a shared understanding to which there is a commitment are a standards-based representation of information models. The Resource Description Framework (RDF) defines a data model as a series of resources and their interrelations. The model consists of a set of statements and each statement contains a subject, predicate, and object. All resources are defined using unique URIs (Universal Resource Indicators) and objects can be resources or literal strings. Resources can be both subjects and objects in statements and this allows for easy linking between statements. These statements are machine-readable.

Examples of Ontologies

Ontologies vary in their complexity as shown in Figure 1. Terminologies are closer to the taxonomy end of the scale and are not as costly to build and potentially more important. They are available in many forms, some as freeware on the Web, and many exist as internal information and knowledge organization structures within companies and other organizations. Some collaborative efforts, which are generating large simple ontologies, already exist, for example the DMOZ topic ontology (www.dmoz.com), which leverages volunteer editors and has many thousands of classes in a taxonomy. Additionally, some more sophisticated ontologies are available. For example, the unified medical language system (UMLS—http://www.nlm.nih.gov/research/umls/) and developed by the national library of medicine is a large ontology of medical terminology.

At a base level, ontologies provide a controlled vocabulary. This by itself can provide a good level of consistency and great leverage since users, authors, agents and databases can all use terms from the same vocabulary. In addition, software can implement interfaces that encourage the use of these controlled terms. The result is that people use the same set of terms. Despite this standardization, some of the terms may still be used with different senses, but common term usage works

Figure 1. Ontologies of differing complexity

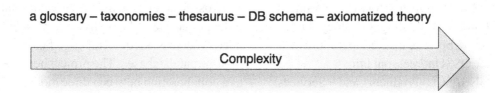

to aid interoperability. Simple taxonomies may be used for site organization and navigational support. Many websites take advantage of this and expose the categories on the page as the top levels of a generalization hierarchy of terms. The categories are usually clickable and expand into the subcategories.

Taxonomies may also be used as 'umbrella' structures from which to extend content. Some freely available ontologies are attempting to provide the high level taxonomic organization from which many efforts may inherit terms. The UNSPSC (Universal Standard Products and Services Classification, www.unspsc.org), is one such categorization scheme. It was jointly produced by the United Nations Development Program and Dun and Bradstreet and was aimed at providing the infrastructure for interoperability of terms in the domains of products and services. It provides a classification scheme (with associated numbers). For example, Category 5000000 Food, Beverage, and Tobacco Products has a subclass family 50100000 called 'Fruits and vegetables and nuts and seeds,' which in turn contains a subclass 50101500 called 'Vegetables,' which in turn has a subclass commodity 50101538 called 'Fresh Vegetables.' Many e-commerce applications can make use of such umbrella organization structures and in fact a number have chosen to be compliant with the UNSPSC. Most applications need to extend these ontologies, but when applications need to communicate between several content providers, it is convenient to use a shared, upper-level ontology.

From an information retrieval perspective, taxonomies can be used to provide search support. Query expansion methods may be used to expand user queries with terms from more specific categories in the hierarchy. This approach was exploited in work on FindUR and it was found that under certain conditions (such as short document length and limited content areas), query expansion can improve search outcomes. Additionally they may be used to sense a need for disambiguation support. If the same term appears in multiple places in a taxonomy, an application may traverse the taxonomy to a more general level in order to find the sense of the word. For example, if an ontology contains the information that Apple is an instance of a computer company and also an instance of a fruit, an application may choose to clarify by querying a user searching for Apple on whether they are interested in computers or fruit. Figure 1 shows a range of levels of complexity of an ontology.

Criteria for the evaluation of the quality of an ontology might be completeness, accuracy and cognitive adequacy.

Some common examples of ontologies are:

- Web Classifications -Yahoo categories
- On-line shopping catalogues -Amazon product catalogue
- Domain specific standard terminology

- ○ Unified Medical Language System (UMLS)
- ○ BPMO -Open Source Business Process Modelling Ontology http://www.bpiresearch.com/Resources/REOSSOnt/reossont.htm
- ○ UNSPSC -Products and Services classification hierarchy -eClassOWL contains more than 75,000 ontology classes on 25,658 types of products and services, plus 5,525 properties for describing products and services instances, and 4,544 value instances for typical enumerative data types. http://www.heppnetz.de/eclassowl/
- ○ FEF -Financial Exchange Framework http://www.financial-format.com/fef.htm
- Web services ontology -http://www.daml.org/services/swsf/1. 0/swso/.

Figure 2 shows some of the concepts as classes in an ontology about refugee law. The concepts shown on the left of the pane, which is a window in the Protege tool for building ontologies, are: asylum seeker, refugee, boat person, persecution, well-founded fear. On the right of the pane some of the slots (properties) of these classes are shown. In the press, the terms asylum seeker and refugee are often confused and in the context of refugee law are more strictly defined.

THE GENE ONTOLOGY

The Gene Ontology project started because geneticists investigating genes of different types of organisms wanted to link the data in their different databases. This is a common computational activity that has to take place through the use of human intelligence to map from one database schema to another. It is done to achieve machine-to-machine communication, however, it is ultimately humans

from different research communities who want to share a common vocabulary to communicate and do cross-species research. The Gene Ontology (GO) project is a collaborative effort to address the need for consistent descriptions of gene products in different databases. The project began in 1998 as a collaboration between three model organism databases, FlyBase external link (Drosophila), the Saccharomyces Genome Database external link (SGD) and the Mouse Genome Database external link (MGD), but since then has grown to include many databases. The Gene Ontology project provides a controlled vocabulary to describe gene and gene product attributes in any organism.

Currently biologists, individually or in small groups, spend time and effort in searching for all of the available information about each small area of research and this can be hampered by the variations in terminology that may be in common usage at any given time. For example, in searching for new targets for antibiotics, a scientist might want to find all the gene products that are involved in bacterial protein synthesis, and that have significantly different sequences or structures from those in humans. If one database describes these molecules as being involved in 'translation,' whereas another uses the phrase 'protein synthesis,' it will be difficult for a human and impossible for a computer without knowledge about both schemas and how to translate between them (inter-schema knowledge), to find functionally equivalent terms.

The GO project has developed three structured, controlled vocabularies (ontologies) that describe gene products in terms of their associated biological processes, cellular components, and molecular functions in a species-independent manner. There are three separate aspects to this effort: first, the development and maintenance of the ontologies themselves; second, the annotation of gene products, which entails making associations between the ontologies and the genes and

Figure 2. Part of a refugee ontology displayed in a protege window

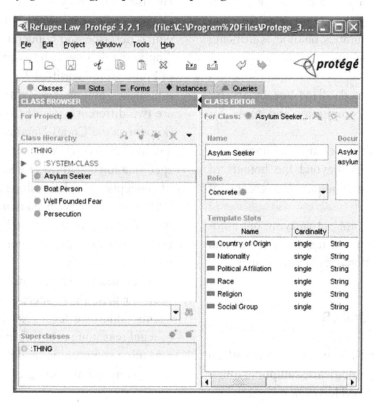

gene products in the collaborating databases; and third, development of tools that facilitate the creation, maintenance, and use of ontologies.

The use of GO terms by collaborating databases facilitates uniform queries across them. The controlled vocabularies are structured so that they can be queried at different levels: for example, you can use GO to find all the gene products in the mouse genome that are involved in signal transduction, or you can zoom in on all the receptor tyrosine kinases. This structure also allows annotators to assign properties to genes or gene products at different levels, depending on the depth of knowledge about that entity.

(http://www.geneontology.org/GO.doc.shtml)

The Gene Ontology, like other biomedical ontologies, has been found to be necessary to enable more efficient reasoning to occur on the large amounts of data that have been collected about genes and gene products by many different scientists across the world and stored in different databases. The amount of information contained in these databases challenges the ability of a single individual to effectively harness it in reasoning processes. In effect, it is the bounded rationality of individuals and indeed in this case the bounded rationality of groups of individuals that creates the need for the ontology and the tools to maintain the ontology, search databases and assist reasoning. Simple human agreement on concepts and relations is not sufficient with knowledge on this scale. Automatic tools based on formal and machine understandable representation are necessary.

In these areas of large-scale scientific reasoning, where there are large amounts of data and large reasoning communities, ontologies are being used at a number of levels:

- To provide a standardized vocabulary for the reasoning community and tools for maintenance;
- Tools to permit reasoning on databases of evidence that are beyond the bounds of rationality of individuals and groups of individuals;
- These tools are not yet carrying out automated reasoning on these databases and making new inferences autonomously.

LEGAL ONTOLOGIES

Legal theories usually contain elements of an ontology and have ontological assumptions either implicitly or explicitly. However, a legal theory is normally framed around some specific theoretical goal which is beyond the ontology itself (Breuker, Valente, & Winkels, 2005). For instance, Hart's theory (Hart, 1961) is concerned with an explanation of how legal systems evolve whilst Kelsen (1991) tries to demonstrate the difference between laws and morals. Both propose specific views on the primitive concepts that are used to represent law. The extraction of the ontological view proposed by each of these approaches is difficult. Breuker and Winkels (2003) describe the ontological views contained in these works and consider the primitive concepts that they have proposed to represent legal knowledge. Their work then looks at how these can be translated into an ontology.

Building ontologies by manually extracting ontological views and translating these to ontologies is a very expensive process. Lame (2003) considers ways of automating the ontology building process.

He uses text analysis to extract concepts and relations among these concepts from legal texts, which describe and conceptualize a legal field. Applying this approach to very codified versions of French law, identified 2,580 relevant relations established among 3,762 different terms. There are two different types of Codes in French Law (known as the Codes Napoleon): the Civil code and the Penal code, and these are very close to a specification that allows for automatic extraction of concepts and relationships between concepts. Although there have been many legal ontologies built, there does not seem to be evidence of their use to the extent that ontologies are used in the biomedical sciences.

The building of legal ontologies seems to have been for theoretical interest in having software agents undertake legal reasoning. The practice of legal reasoning is still firmly based on human reasoning communities and it is not apparent that there is any use of ontologies to assist in this area.

TERMINOLOGY

Terminology is an interdisciplinary research field that has emerged from linguistics and cognitive science. According to Sager (1994), Terminology is:

A theory concerned with those aspects of the nature and the functions of language, which permit the efficient representation, and transmission of items of knowledge in all their complexity of concepts and conceptual relationships.

The science of terminology studies the representation of knowledge through linguistic sign systems. Its underlying objects that are terms and concepts. Terms are lexical units that denote concepts and concepts are pieces of knowledge that act as aids for human cognitive processes of modelling the world. Terms are often used in special languages for specific domains, and are used to express highly specialized knowledge in a concise and unambiguous form.

Terminological science focuses on human communication and precise and appropriate terminologies provide important facilities for human communication. They are becoming more important because of the rapid increase in knowledge in all fields and the growing need for information dissemination. Information dissemination needs to occur both between specialists and between specialists and non-experts. As computer systems have been more widely applied in information processing and more systems underpin complex monitoring and decision-making tasks, there is an increased need for accurate and precisely defined terminology. Furthermore, the user community should be in agreement on the terminology as a level of ontological commitment.

Terminological acquisition can be achieved through the use of both written and spoken corpora, however this process is expensive because it is time-consuming, requires human intelligence and is error-prone. Usually, the process starts from a collection of text documents that humans scan for relevant terms. Advances in text processing have provided tools and automatic methods for corpus exploration. Currently corpus-based terminology can be acquired with the use of software applications to explore the corpus for terminologically relevant information. This corpus-based terminology acquisition improves the quality of terminological research and its output. It permits exhaustive search for new terms, has decreased risk of making errors or missing relevant terms, and has the capacity to provide more contextual information to the user by providing direct links between the terms in a term bank and the corpus.

A terminology management system provides tools that help people to trace the life cycle and evolution of terms. That is, the system should allow the acquisition, maintenance, modification, and dissemination of the terminological information. A core part of any terminology management system is the representation of terminological information in a term bank. The information stored in terminological databases is:

- Concept-related information -definition and class;
- Administrative data;
- Terms and term-related information -grammatical and lexical information;
- Concept-related descriptive elements -notes, cross-references, and bibliographical information.

The information required for this is represented as free text in natural language. Therefore, this means that the traditional view of terminology science, where conceptual knowledge is described by means of natural language definitions and explanations, is upheld. This representation means that these terminologies are necessarily limited to human users, and providing computational support for the maintenance of and the navigation through the database becomes difficult.

THE SEMANTIC WEB

The Semantic Web provides a common framework that allows data to be shared and reused across application, enterprise, and community boundaries. It is a collaborative effort led by W3C with participation from a large number of researchers and industrial partners. It is based on the Resource Description Framework (RDF).

(W3C)

At present, the Semantic Web is still largely a vision although if we define it to be the set of OWL documents on the Web then it is developing at a modest rate. In 2008 there were approximately 1.5 million semantic Web documents (RDF) and about 250,000 of these are OWL documents and this has grown from a few hundred since 2003.

The Semantic Web is about common formats for integration and combination of data drawn from diverse sources. The original Web mainly concentrated on the interchange of documents and, through standards like XML (the Extensible Markup Language), there is the possibility of applications communicating if they share the same XML schema. The Semantic Web is an attempt to move beyond the simple interchange of documents and the requirements of having standard schemata. It is really a language for recording how the data relates to real world objects. That allows a person, or a machine, to use data from one database, and then move through an unending set of databases which are essentially about the same thing although they may not use the same language, schema or standard. The Semantic Web is currently one of the major endeavours of the World Wide Web Consortium (W3C). It aims to add to the existing Web, meta-data and methods that will provide Web-based systems with advanced capabilities that allow sophisticated inter-operability that might be called understanding between systems.

The Semantic Web can be understood in terms of a transition from XML to RDF. XML is a standard for developing Document Type Definitions (DTDs) or schemata for languages. The specification is a grammar for the language to be used. So XML can specify the syntax for structured documents but does not specify any semantic constraints. XML Schema is a language for restricting XML document structure and includes data-types.

The Resource Description Format (RDF) provides a data model for objects and relations between them. It also provides semantics for the data model and machine-readable metadata. RDF Schema (RDF-S) extends RDF to provide a vocabulary for describing properties and classes of RDF resources. The Web Ontology Language (OWL) adds more vocabulary for defining full ontologies. It allows for the specification of:

- Relations between classes

- Constraints -cardinality, necessary/sufficient conditions
- Equivalence
- Rich property typing
- Logic constructs (Description Logic) to allow inferencing and reasoning.

OWL is designed for use by applications that need to process the content of information instead of just presenting information to humans. OWL facilitates greater machine interpretability of Web content than that supported by XML, RDF, and RDF Schema (RDF-S) by providing additional vocabulary along with a formal semantics. (W3C Recommendation)

The Semantic Web is a set of distributed ontologies that are not centrally controlled. It is inevitable that there will be ontologies that represent objects in different ways and so this entails conceptual disagreement and difference.

REASONING

Just as the current Web is inherently heterogeneous in data formats and data semantics, the Semantic Web will be inherently heterogeneous in its reasoning forms. It is likely that no single form of reasoning will be realistic for the scope of the Semantic Web. At this point in the development of the Semantic Web, the reasoning layers that sit above the ontology layers (see Figure 3) are not well specified. Ontology reasoning in general relies on monotonic negation which is the negation used in classical logic and mathematics. (So if a consequence, $\neg F$ follows from a set of premises S then with monotonic negation $\neg F$ also follows from $S \cup F$.) On the other hand, databases, Web databases, and Web-based information systems employ non-monotonic reasoning. Therefore, for example, flights not mentioned in a timetable do not exist when using non-monotonic negation. Constraint reasoning is used in dealing with time, while forward and/or backward chaining is the reasoning of choice in coping with database-like views.

Most current ontologies are what Fürst and Trichet (2006) call *lightweight ontologies*. These lightweight ontologies integrate terminological knowledge and some properties that are used to structure this knowledge. However, to reason on the Web, ontologies need to capture the whole knowledge of the domain. They have to become *heavyweight* ontologies. This means that they have to include all axioms that are needed to represent the semantics of the domain. The RuleML initiative (Boley, Tabet, & Wagner, 2001) and the SWRL initiative (O'Connor, Knublauch, Tu, Grosof, Dean, Grosso, & Musen, 2005) are founded on the requirement for the use of rule-like

expressions that can be thought of as the axioms of the domain.

The advanced capabilities hoped for in most Semantic Web application scenarios primarily call for reasoning. There is the general reasoning underlying the Semantic Web technologies, such as Description Logics, Hybrid Logics, and others like F-Logic and LP semantics. Some specialized reasoning capabilities are already offered by Semantic Web languages currently being developed such as the OWL family together with Triple, RDQL, SPARQL, OWL-QL, or ontology-based application-specific languages and tools like the Business Process Execution Language (BPEL). These languages, however, are developed mostly from functionality-centred perspectives that focus on ontology reasoning or access valida-

Figure 3. Layers of the semantic web

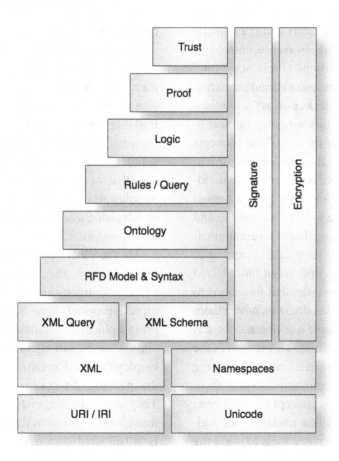

tion or application-centred perspectives that are concerned with Web service retrieval and composition. A perspective centred on the reasoning techniques such as forward and backward chaining, tableau-like methods and constraint reasoning, would complement the functionally-centred and application-centred perspectives and provide full reasoning capability for Semantic Web systems and applications.

Whilst there are languages for reasoning at the ontological level within the semantic Web, developing the full capability of reasoning that we would like is not yet available.

THE SEMANTIC WEB AND REASONING COMMUNITIES

What might a fully functional Semantic Web contribute to Reasoning Communities? Both ontologies and terminologies are formal ways of specifying an agreed vocabulary and of capturing the meaning of the concepts. In a sense, ontologies focus on building a definition of the concepts and seeking to have agreement or shared understanding on these and their properties as well as the relationships between them. In this way they purport to represent the meaning of the terms and concepts in a domain and users of the ontology commit to this understanding so that it is a shared understanding. In many instances an ontology is a formal specification that can be used by a machine and indeed provide the meaning that different applications can understand. In most cases, ontologies are not for human consumption but more to aid humans in the reasoning tasks that they need to undertake in quite complex domains where there are different teams of people working and there is a need for common semantics. This is seen in the use of ontologies like the Gene Ontology by large and diverse reasoning communities where there is a need for agreement on concept vocabulary as well as a need for a machine readable ontological specification for automated tools to make the

required adjustments across a range of databases. The Semantic Web is seeing the development of many ontologies that can be used to improve the interoperability of systems and machines. This will definitely aid the development of software agents and systems that can make use of large amounts of data stored in different databases in an intelligent way and eventually see the development of reasoning capability. However, in the first instance, it will be a challenge to have tools to assist human reasoning communities to make use of the Semantic Web infrastructure to support their reasoning.

While most important decisions require careful analysis of the factors influencing a decision, there has been little work on tools to capture and assess validity of a heterogeneous set of facts and claims that bear on a decision. Good decision-making requires two components that can be recognised as specializations of Semantic Web approaches: sound reasoning about the factors involved and bearing on the decision and clear judgments about the reliability of the information sources in which the reasoning is grounded. Chklovski, Gil, Ratnakar, and Lee (2003a) proposed TRELLIS, as a vehicle for investigating the problem and a tool that supports making decisions, when there are possibly conflicting or unreliable information sources. They collect and classify argumentation acts that occur in real arguments, and outline ongoing work on extending how argumentation and decision making over heterogeneous sources can be supported.

On the other hand, terminologies tend to be extracted from the linguistic use of the terms. Perhaps Wittgenstein's definition of meaning is more appropriate here. Sect. 43 of Wittgenstein's Philosophical Investigations says that: "For a large class of cases—though not for all—in which we employ the word 'meaning' it can be defined thus: the meaning of a word is its use in the language." They are more linguistically focussed and, although there are formal terminologies, their use is still directed towards humans. So terminologies are increasingly used as human-understandable specifications of a vocabulary.

Either approach has value for a reasoning community engaging in a complex issue. It is very likely that the usage of terms will determine the quality of the reasoning in the reasoning pool. There are a number of levels of support that can be associated with ontological or terminological support for a reasoning community:

- An agreed common vocabulary where the terms have an explicit natural language definition that is accepted by the community -a terminology
- An agreed set of concepts and relationships between them that is explicitly represented -formally or semi-formally -a weak ontology
- A formal ontology description and tools for maintenance and use of the ontology
- A Semantic Web ontology
- A formal ontology and automated reasoners on the ontology.

SUMMARY

Clearly, ontologies are playing an important role in allowing communities to tackle problems that are large and complex. For these problems, committing to an ontology and the further development of that ontology by the reasoning community allows the use of tools that can draw on information across a range of databases and even carry out automatic reasoning of a specified nature. The Semantic Web allows the development of distributed ontologies in a way that they can be reused. At this stage, it is not clear that the semantic Web provides or will provide useful support for human reasoning communities. Currently, the Semantic Web, through the Web Ontology Language, OWL, provides a

framework for developing ontologies and this is being used in large-scale areas requiring reasoning of a large number of individuals that can be considered to be one large community. Ontologies on the Semantic Web are really developed for machines and machine applications or software agents that understand these ontologies can be used as reasoners or participants in the reasoning community or by human participants to provide support in their human reasoning.

Many of the examples of reasoning communities presented in this book are not of this scale and it is not clear that an investment in an ontology is necessary. The use of a terminology (as a form of ontology) can solve most of the problems relating to commitment on the precise meaning of concepts on which reasoning in the community rests.

If we let ontologies subsume terminologies then it is reasonable to say that a reasoning community can benefit from an appropriate level of ontological commitment and that this can reduce the potential for terminological misunderstanding to act as a source of disagreement.

REFERENCES

Avery, J., & Yearwood, J. (2002). A foundation for strange agent negotiation. In *Papers from the AAAI Workshop on Meaning Negotiation*, (pp. 72-77). Menlo Park, CA: AAAI Press.

Boley, H., Tabet, S., & Wagner, G. (2001). Design rationale of RuleML: A markup language for semantic web rules. In *Proceedings of the Semantic Web Working Symposium (SWWS 2001)*. Amsterdam, The Netherlands: IOS Press.

Breuker, J., Valente, A., & Winkels, R. (2005). Law and the semantic web. *Lecture Notes in Computer Science, 3369*, 36–64. doi:10.1007/978-3-540-32253-5_4

Breuker, J., & Winkels, R. (2003). Use and reuse of legal ontologies in knowledge engineering and information management. In *Proceedings of the Workshop on Legal Ontologies and Web-Based Legal Information Management: Organised in Conjunction with the Ninth International Conference on Artificial Intelligence and Law*. New York, NY: Springer.

Chklovski, T., Gil, Y., Ratnakar, V., & Lee, J. (2003a). Trellis: Supporting decision making via argumentation in the semantic web. In *Proceedings of 2nd International Semantic Web Conference (ISWC)*. Berlin, Germany.

Felbaum, C. (1998). *Wordnet: An electronic lexical database for English*. Cambridge, MA: MIT Press.

Fox, S. M., & Gruninger, M. (1998). Enterprise modelling. *AI Magazine, 19*(3), 109–121.

Fürst, F., & Trichet, F. (2006). Reasoning on the semantic web needs to reason both on ontology-based assertions and on ontologies themselves. In *Proceedings of the World Wide Web Conference*. Edinburgh, UK: Aalborg University Press.

Gruber, T. R. (1993). A translation approach to portable ontologies. *Knowledge Acquisition, 5*(2), 199–220. doi:10.1006/knac.1993.1008

Guarino, N. (Ed.). (1998). Formal ontology in information systems. In *Proceedings of the First International Conference (FOIS 1998), Frontiers in Artificial Intelligence and Applications*. Amsterdam, The Netherlands: IOS Press.

Guarino, N., & Giaretta, P. (1995). *Towards very large knowledge bases: Knowledge building and knowledge sharing*. Amsterdam, The Netherlands: IOS Press.

Hart, H. L. A. (1961). *The concept of law*. Oxford, UK: Clarendon Press.

Kelsen, H. (1991). *General theory of norms*. Oxford, UK: Clartendon Press. doi:10.1093/acp rof:oso/9780198252177.001.0001

Knight, K., & Luk, S. (1994). Building a large-scale knowledge base for machine translation. In *Proceedings of the 12th National Conference on Artificial Intelligence (AAAI 1994)*, (Vol 1), (pp. 773-778). Seattle, WA: AAAI.

Lame, G. (2003). Using text analysis techniques to identify legal ontologys components. In *Proceedings of the ICAIL 2003 Workshop on Legal Ontologies & Web Based Legal Information Management*. New York, NY: ACM Press.

Mahesh, K., & Nirenburg, S. (1995). A situated ontology for practical nlp. In *Proceedings of the IJCAI-95 Workshop on Basic Ontological Issues in Knowledge Sharing*. Ottawa, Canada: University of Ottawa.

McGuinness, D. L. (1998). Ontological issues for knowledge enhanced search. In N. Guarino (Ed.), *Proceedings of the First International Conference on Formal Ontology in Information Systems*, (pp. 302-316). Trento, Italy: IOS Press.

O'Connor, M., Knublauch, H., Tu, S., Grosof, B., Dean, M., Grosso, W., & Musen, M. (2005). Supporting rule system interoperability on the semantic web with SWRL. In *Proceedings of the International Semantic Web Conference*, (pp. 974-986). Berlin, Germany: Springer-Verlag.

Sager, J. C. (1994). Terminology: Custodian of knowledge and means of knowledge transfer. *Terminology, 1*(1), 7–16. doi:10.1075/term.1.1.03sag

Swartout, B., Patil, R., Knuth, K., & Russ, T. (1996). Towards distributed use of large-scale ontologies. In B. Gaines & M. Musen (Eds.), *Proceedings of the 10th Workshop on Knowledge Acquisition for Knowledge-Based Systems*. Banff, Canada: ACM.

van Heijst, G., Schreiber, A., & Wielinga, B. (1997). Using explicit ontologies in kbs development. *International Journal of Human-Computer Studies, 46*(2/3), 183–292. doi:10.1006/ijhc.1996.0090

Vasconcelos, J., Kimble, C., Gouveia, F., & Kudenko, D. (2000). A group memory system for corporate knowledge management: An ontological approach. In *Proceedings of the First European Conference on Knowledge Management,* (pp. 91-99). Bled, Slovenia: Bled School of Management.

Chapter 8
Pragmatic Approaches to Supporting Reasoning Communities

ABSTRACT

Apart from work toward developing ontologies, very little has been done towards developing highly structured reusable reasoning repositories that might support reasoning communities into the future. Pragmatic approaches that have been deployed are surveyed in this chapter. They include approaches for identifying types of problems, techniques for organising text, and approaches for facilitating the sharing of information.

INTRODUCTION

Apart from the work towards developing ontologies in many areas and the work to develop machine-readable knowledge bases in some domains there is currently very little done towards developing highly structured reusable reasoning repositories that might support reasoning communities into the future. Within academic reasoning communities, the literature (of academic disciplines) is large and there are periodic review articles that act to coalesce the knowledge. These academic repositories are almost universally in text. The approaches and tools that academics and technically focused groups use to approach reasoning are a mixture of document databases, bibliographic software tools and search engines. For more broadly based communities that are concerned with current important issues, the literature relevant to the issue seems to grow in ways that are influenced by factors other than reasoning. It is often not clear that the resolution of major issues is achieved in a way that values the broadest consideration of all relevant factors by a reasoning community that can adequately cover these relevant areas and do so in a way that allows all elements of a reasoning process to be represented as completely as they should be represented. The reality is that currently the reasoning on an issue is:

DOI: 10.4018/978-1-4666-1818-3.ch008

- Initiated and carried out by a reasoning community that may or may not have the capacity or expertise to adequately cover all aspects that pertain to the issue
- Assisted by using expert knowledge and search engines to collect a range of text documents relevant to the issue
- Captured by the production of a range of text documents on various aspects of the issue
- Likely to raise questions that require further investigation to provide answers that are needed in order to make decisions on the issue.

This reflects the natural tendency for individual reasoners to contribute their views and reasons in words, often as arguments in text or as narrative. A pragmatic approach would allow these contributions as text or narrative to be as free form as individuals within the community desire.

This chapter considers possible approaches using currently available technologies for supporting the reasoning community in accessing relevant knowledge, organising the knowledge, creating a community pool of reasons, and developing reasoned solutions in a less structured way than the techniques proposed earlier in this book.

WELL-STRUCTURED PROBLEMS

The tools that a reasoning community uses or would have on its wish list depend on the nature of the problem or issue being considered. In Chapter 2, problem-structuring methods were briefly considered. These are approaches that help to clearly define the problem, its component questions and the way in which these fit together to provide a solution or decision on the problem. Well-structured problems are those where there is already a known model of reasoning, an algorithm or set of requirements that once dealt with will provide a reasoned decision or solution that

the community is likely to accept. The tools that are currently used are the tools that exist for a range of tasks mainly related to managing and manipulating documents. These tools might be pragmatically used by a reasoning community to help in gathering and building the repository of documents that describe and support reasoning within the community. Once this repository is developed then various editing tools and search tools are required.

ILL-STRUCTURED PROBLEMS

Ill-structured problems are those that require definition and understanding. For example most design problems would be ill-structured problems because there can be many criteria that the design should meet. The exact way in which it meets these criteria and provides a satisfactory solution to objectives that may be difficult to specify may allow a great range of possible solutions. How to commercialise some intellectual property or product of research also has many of the attributes of an ill-structured problem. Goals have to be set and given that the technology or product is new it may not be known precisely how markets will respond. The tools required for these problems would be a broader range of tools that encompass those used for well-structured problems but should also include tools that can assist in the structuring of the problem or the structuring of reasoning in the domain. These tools can include modelling and simulation tools to help develop, visualize and study possible scenarios.

TOOLS FOR DEFINING THE REASONING COMMUNITY

Some reasoning communities come together naturally but others are formed to provide the best possible reasoning to a solution on an issue. In many circumstances, membership is designed to achieve desired outcomes that match particular political or organizational agendas. Whilst these communities would not meet the principles that we propose for reasoning communities they do exist.

In many cases, it would seem reasonable that a reasoning community on an issue should at least have representation by individuals who have knowledge and expertise in the areas that are relevant to the issue. Therefore, for example, in reasoning about what forms of energy should be developed to supply a nation's energy requirements for the next 50 years one would expect to see representation from individuals that have expert knowledge in solar energy, nuclear energy, geothermal energy as well as other relevant factors such as environmental concerns. In other cases, such as ethics committees, membership is sought from a broad spectrum of people with a background in research, science, law, or religion, as well as lay people. For example the National Health and Medical Research Council (NHMRC) of Australia in their National Statement on Ethical Conduct in Research Involving Humans, 1999, stipulates that the membership of a human ethics committee should include:

- A chairperson
- A layman, not affiliated with the institution
- A laywoman, not affiliated with the institution
- A lawyer
- A minister of religion
- At least two medical graduates with research experience
- At least one allied health professional (such as a nurse or clinical psychologist).

In the case of a jury under legal systems that derive from the British system of justice the requirement is that the jury be representative so that the accused has "the lawful judgement of his peer" (as stated in Magna Carta). This is usually interpreted as the judgement of representative citizens of the state. Whilst this is the basic qualification,

there are, however exclusions. For example, qualified legal practitioners are ineligible and anyone who has been convicted of an indictable offence is disqualified. There are also situations that might require additional criteria to ensure that the jury is in fact representative of the community. For sex offences, it may well be appropriate to require that the jury have an approximate sex balance by ensuring that neither sex should constitute more than two thirds of the jury.

There are issues, pertaining to attributes of membership, to be considered in some complex cases where it may be appropriate to consider a rider to the general criteria for membership. In these cases, a jury simply chosen at random from the community may not be in a position to understand the technical issues sufficiently to enable it to apply basic community values such as honesty and fair dealing to the matters of the case. Jurors in these types of cases may need to have reached a certain minimum education standard in order to enable them to judge in accordance with the appropriate standards for society. This then presents as a risk that these juries may, in judging the accused, reflect the standards of an educated elite rather than the standards of the general community. Perhaps this risk must be accepted in the interest of having a jury that understands the issues.

TECHNIQUES FOR ASSISTING INDIVIDUAL COALESCING

Techniques for Organising Text

To organizations, communities, groups, or individuals seeking to track their reasons for making certain decisions and learn from experience, fact-finding tools, as well as well structured documentation are important. Most important decisions require careful analysis of the factors influencing a decision and there is a need for tools to capture and assess the validity of heterogeneous sets of facts and claims that bear on a decision.

Sound decision-making requires:

- The location of relevant documents,
- The ability to identify and locate assertions about trustworthiness of sources used in a decision, and
- Storing and retrieving reasoning and arguments in structured form, which would allow for re-use of relevant parts of the reasoning.

This functionality, while requiring specific tools, could be enabled by the ontological markup and protocols of the Semantic Web. TRELLIS (Chklovski, Gil, Ratnakar, & Lee, 2003b) allows users to add their observations, viewpoints, and conclusions as they analyse information by making semantic annotations to documents. Users can associate specific claims with particular locations in documents that are used as sources or backing for analysis, and then structure these statements into an argument on an issue. Because evidence is often incomplete and may be biased, TRELLIS includes specific tools for indicating trustworthiness of a source with respect to a particular purpose. TRELLIS is based on Semantic Web enablement in the following ways:

- It uses Semantic Markup of arguments rather than handle arguments in fully textual form. TRELLIS supports construction of argument trees which can be searched, imported, and otherwise processed by both machines and humans,
- Rating of information sources. It collects reusable semantic markup (reliability and trustworthiness for a given context) of documents from users,
- Easy adoption path. Users of TRELLIS are allowed to mix arbitrary natural language with semantic markup structuring clauses.

Other tools can assist in locating passages within texts relevant to aspects that an individual reasoner has identified as relevant. Passage retrieval is different from document retrieval in two key and related ways. In passage retrieval the information need is a specific one and what constitutes a passage can be flexible in order to best meet this need. Kaszkiel and Zobel (1997) compare many approaches and passage lengths in trying to determine a best approach to passage retrieval. They find that overlapping windows of fixed size can yield good results. Subsequently, Clarke and Cormak (2000) have used the MultiText approach to identify passages that are defined by the coverage of the keywords in the user query. Text can also be automatically segmented based on change of topic within the text (Hearst, 1997; Choi, 2000) and this can be done even across paragraphs. These tools can be used to segment texts into topic-based passages with reasonable accuracy. Whilst there are ways of automatically segmenting text by topic there seem to be few robust tools commercially available for this task.

Text Classification and Clustering

Libraries have traditionally organised documents into classes based on their subject matter or content. So we expect to find similar documents in the same classes. The Dewey decimal system is a mechanism for organising the classification of documents. It attempts to organize all knowledge into ten main classes, which are then further subdivided. Therefore, each main class then has ten divisions, and each division is then further divided into ten sections. The advantage of using decimals for its categories is that this allows both purely numerical and hierarchical classification. Classification is principally by subject, with extensions for subject relationships as well as other attributes.

The task of document classification is to put documents related to or relevant to the class into that class. Historically this was a manual task carried out by librarians; however, automatic text classification algorithms have been available for some time. Whereas human beings use their intelligence in this process, many automatic text classification systems employ statistical analysis of the presence and frequency of words used in the documents to classify documents. Automatic document classifiers require a set of pre-defined classes and a set of labelled documents that adequately cover and provide examples of all classes. Various machine-learning processes can then be applied with the training examples used to 'supervise' the learning process for building the classifier (Sebastiani, 2002; Joachims, 1998).

Text categorization and document classification can be useful to reasoning communities in automatically assigning documents or texts to categories. This means that the reasoning community has to know the categories of interest or relevance on the issue. For example, in considering the issue of future energy sources, one class might be solar energy and a document classifier would be able to automatically assign documents from the community's general collection on energy to the specific class of solar energy. The same classifier could simultaneously assign documents to many of the other classes that the community might have identified as being relevant to the issue. The use of automatic classification tools requires the community to pre-define its categories of interest. This is consistent with structuring the reasoning (or at least the documentary evidence to support the reasoning) on an issue that we have previously argued as being beneficial.

An automatic classification tool can be quite accurate in the assignations that it makes, however it usually requires training examples for each of the pre-defined categories. An alternative approach is to consider tools that automatically cluster documents based on their text content. Document clustering groups similar documents together into clusters and each cluster is dissimilar to the other clusters. Clustering forms natural groupings of documents that maximize intra-cluster similarity and minimize intercluster similarity. There are many approaches to clustering and the results

can be problematic nevertheless quite useful (Jain, Murty, & Flynn, 1999; Kazuaki, 2004). One of the problems with a resulting clustering is the interpretation of the clusters. Therefore, in a large collection of documents, a clustering algorithm will result in groupings of documents but it is then a separate task to understand what each grouping means.

Clustering might be used differently from classification by a reasoning community. It is more likely to be used in the problem-structuring phase. So if, for instance, the community wanted to see what categories of energy there were that should be considered from the perspective of what is available in the literature then it might cluster the energy documents and examine the cluster to see what topics they suggested. Many studies also suggest that document clustering can be a better way of organizing the retrieval results obtained from search engines and can be an effective way of directing a user towards relevant documents among the retrieved set than the ranked list approach used by most search engines (Leuski, 2001).

Automatic Summarization

An important impact of the development of the World Wide Web is a dramatic shift, within society in general, from information scarcity and inaccessibility to a situation of information overload and ease of access. This has brought with it problems of selection from this large body of information and also problems associated with comprehension of large quantities of information. There is more than can be read in the time available and yet we need to reason to decisions based on the information available. There is, therefore, a need for automatic summarization tools. In the late 1990s, in recognition of this need there was a strong increase in research and development devoted to automatic text summarization. The United States (through DARPA), the European Community, and Pacific Rim countries identified text summarization as a critical research area. The main focus of research in the 1990s was the automatic summarization of text documents but as the World Wide Web has evolved there is now also a need for automatic summarization of multimedia information. A useful overview of automatic summarization can be found in Mani (2001).

Text summarization is the process of distilling the most important information from one or more sources to produce an abridged version for a particular context. Here, context refers to the purpose of the summary as well as the audience. Karen Sparck Jones defines a summary as: *'a reductive transformation of source text to summary text through content reduction by selection and/or generalization on what is important in the source'* (Sparck-Jones, 1998). The basic process model is a three-stage model:

- Interpretation -source text *interpretation* to source text *representation*
- Transformation -source representation *transformation* to summary text representation
- Generation -summary text *generation* from summary representation.

In DeJong's FRUMP (Jong, 1982), for example, the source and summary representations are conflated. Luhn (1958) pioneered automatic abstracting and summarization with a surface-level approach, exploiting features such as term frequency and positions of the most important sentences. Virtually all of the work done so far can be categorized as either: *text extraction* or *fact extraction*. In text extraction, some of the source text is transferred and used to constitute the summary text. In fact extraction, what is being sought to be extracted from source documents is what gets transferred to the summary. So text extraction is flexible and tuned to the source while fact extraction tends to be rigid and finds individual instances or manifestations of specified important notions.

Originally, much of the work on automatic indexing of documents and automatic abstracting was done to support information retrieval, particularly in scientific and technical areas. Our expectations and hopes for automatic summarization have now changed so that we might, for instance, like to ask for a summary of all the literature on climate change or we might like to summarize news articles from the Chinese Press on the Chinese response to the Kyoto Treaty. A significant need to support the practice of evidence-based medicine is the need for a capability to summarize the most recent literature on a particular disease or treatment. In reasoning communities where the issue under consideration is one on which there is a significant body of literature then automatic summarization tools would certainly be of assistance.

Currently the most available text summarizer is the tool provided within Microsoft Word. This tool employs *shallow approaches, which* basically represent the text at a syntactic level and produce extracts by extracting sentences based on the importance of the words in them and synthesizing these sentences into the summary. It is questionable whether this tool could be used in a reliable way to help with providing summaries of documents that give support to individual or coalesced reasoning. However it is possible that such a summarization tool could be used in conjunction with other tools such as information retrieval tools in a pragmatic way to support individual reasoning tasks and to some extent group reasoning.

For example, an individual reasoner may consider a summary of a number of documents to get the gist of the content rather than reading the whole corpus. On the basis of such a summary an information retrieval tool could be used to locate the particular section of the document or documents that contain the issue of interest from the summary.

When a community or individual is establishing the major relevant sub-issues on an issue then a query might be posed to a search engine. The return of a large number of documents is likely and it may be very useful to have the salient points of this large collection of documents automatically extracted. Goldstein, Mittal, Carbonell, and Kantrowitz (2000) and Radev, Blair-Goldensohn, and Zhang (2001) describe multi-document summarization methods for summarizing the information in hit lists retrieved by search engines. McKeown et al. also consider the problem of providing summaries of on-line medical literature to physicians (Elhadad, Kan, Klavans, & McKeown, 2005).

TEXT MINING

Search engines are used on a daily basis to find information in collections of text documents. This search is for information that we think or know exists and is really locating it in the vast volume of information that is in the collection. Text mining is the discovery of new, previously unknown information by automatically extracting textual information from different written resources in a collection or across collections. A key element is the linking together of the extracted information to form new facts or new hypotheses to be explored further by more conventional means of experimentation. So text mining is different from what we are familiar with in Web search. In search, the user is typically looking for something that is already known and has been written by someone else.

The goal of data mining is to discover or derive new information from data, finding patterns across datasets, and/or separating signal from noise. Text mining aims to discover useful patterns in text. Its methods have being successfully used on text documents or text collections to carry out a number of mining tasks. Some text mining approaches rely only on statistics such as the frequency of words or phrases, while others employ much stronger techniques which require the availability of additional resources such as natural language processing tools; availability

of lexicons; ontologies of concepts; frameworks such as FrameNet (Fillmore, Johnson, & Petruck, 2003), PropBank (Palmer, Kingsbury, & Gildea, 2006), or VerbNet (Kipper, Dang, & Palmer, 2000); enriched sources such as links between the text units or other non-textual data. We do not yet have computer programs that can interpret text although good progress is being made in natural language processing and computational linguistics. It is unlikely that this capability will be available for a long time. Nevertheless, there are still results that can be achieved from the currently available text mining technology.

For example, Swanson has shown how reasoning can be done from literature in a text mining sense. He has been able to hypothesize causes of rare diseases by looking for indirect links in different subsets of the biomedical literature. Some of these have subsequently received supporting experimental evidence (Swanson, 1987; Swanson & Smalheiser, 1997). This is indicative of an approach that could be quite useful in a reasoning community because we have advocated at least a repository of reasons in a reasoning community. As this repository and its associated backing literature grows then it is useful to have techniques that look for links across sections of the literature or in other literature to suggest new inferences. The reasoning community then has the task of assessing these new hypotheses.

Automated text mining capability is not yet able to achieve these types of knowledge discovery and hypothesis generation but the potential for this to be developed into tools that assist the reasoning process is certainly one that should be developed.

Reasoning from Narrative

We pointed out in Chapter 6 that although there has been some cognitive science work done on recursive transition network models for the representation of causality from textual narrative and that these move closer to a reasoning structure in the sense that there is some representation of causality, it is still not clear how this might be mapped to an explicit reasoning structure. This work, largely carried out by cognitive psychologists, provides a first step in establishing structures of causality from narrative. An important feature of this work is the use of the counterfactual test as to the necessity of one event to another event in the circumstances of the story. The test has the form: If A had not happened in the circumstances of the story, then B would not have happened. A judgment that the counterfactual is true in the circumstances of the story leads to reasoning that A is the cause of, or a condition for, B.

The parsing required for automatic interpretation or extraction of reasoning from narrative is not currently available. Pragmatically, however, the place that narrative holds in the reasoning processes of individuals and groups needs to be recognised. Consider the interaction between a doctor and a patient. The literature surrounding doctor-patient interaction and decision making indicates that there is a range of models that may be adopted (Emanuel & Emanuel, 1992). The traditional (paternalistic) model is one where the reasoning and decision making is primarily done by the doctor based upon the symptoms described by the patient. The more recent, partnership model is one where the doctor and the patient both play significant roles in the reasoning and the decision-making. It is arguable that in either of these models we have a reasoning community of two participants. In the case of a model where the patient is supported in their reasoning by relations and friends the number of participants may be larger. The patient usually describes their symptoms and problems in a narrative form. A dialogue ensues where both the doctor and the patient ask questions and provide information. The doctor then contributes their understanding of the problem and diagnosis, the recommended treatment and the likely prognosis. This is the second narrative. This is usually followed by some more dialogue, possibly with the patient rejecting some of the methods of treatment and

finding out more about others. The third narrative is the joint narrative where patient and doctor agree on the problem and diagnosis, agree on a treatment, and agree on the likely prognosis. The level of engagement and joint contribution determines how much the third narrative is built from the two initial narratives. So where has the reasoning occurred? A well-informed patient may have some ideas about possible causes of their symptoms and may have developed through their own individual reasoning (experience and a limited medical knowledge) a possible diagnosis and may have reasoned to a set of possible treatments. In some cases, they are seeking confirmation and a clear selection of a treatment option. This is still likely to be presented as a narrative describing symptoms and likely causes. A doctor, upon hearing the narrative description of the symptoms, will use their medical knowledge (coalesced in their training and from experience) to identify possible diagnoses and treatments. The full extent of this reasoning is not apparent to the patient. Some aspects of it may be provided to the patient as they ask questions. The doctor provides a summary of their reasoning in narrative form to the patient. The participating patient will seek detail and further understanding. Finally, the agreed reasoning is captured or coalesced between the two participants but articulated and communicated as a narrative. It is also interesting to note that in subsequent consultations the doctor will often retrieve the patient's medical notes and recap in narrative form at the start of the consultation.

The doctor-patient reasoning community described involves reasoning, but the explicit manner in which the reasoning is communicated is as a sequence of at least two individual verbal, narratives followed by a number of iterations, which characterize the coalescing of reasoning and finally a collaborative product, or coalesced reasoning, which is usually in the form of a narrative. If we try to obtain a more explicit or symbolic representation of the reasoning then we would need to have processes for converting the narrative to our favoured reasoning representation scheme. One way of thinking about the processes in this reasoning community is as follows. The patient narrative creates through the counterfactual test a possible explanation of causes. The doctor reflects this individual patient experience on their larger medical knowledge and case experience and locates the (partial) narrative against this wider background to create a new (doctor) narrative. The counter factual test can be applied now to this narrative to provide a stronger explanation of causes. An iterative process of patient-doctor communication refines the reasoning and arrives at the coalesced reasoning, which is verbalized and agreed in narrative form.

The doctor-patient example exemplifies a small practical reasoning community. In most reasoning communities of this size, it would seem that narrative would be the default means for expressing reasoning, communicating reasoning and finally coalescing reasoning. The exceptions to this rule tend to exist in small reasoning communities where both participants are experts in their field and the problem under discussion requires a formal representation. Even in these cases, narrative is frequently the means of developing the ideas behind the formal reasoning.

INFORMATION RETRIEVAL SYSTEMS

Information retrieval is the science of finding information within databases. When the databases are structured relational information retrieval systems use exact matching techniques for matching the query with information in the database. When the databases are semi-structured or unstructured, as in the case of free text, then other approaches involving inexact matching are used. Text retrieval is the study of retrieving information from databases of text documents. Information retrieval systems are probably the most commonly used software systems other than an operating system and are commonly referred to as search engines. In general information retrieval systems may be used to retrieve information of any type including text, images, or video.

Generally text or document retrieval systems index the collection of documents by the words in the documents but they might also index phrases of might index n-grams. The most common approach is the bag-of-words approach where the document is represented by the index terms without regard to the order in which they occur in the document. In the vector space model (Salton, 1971) a document is represented as a vector of term weights where the weight for each term indicates the importance of the term in the document or the probability of the term given relevance. A query is then represented as a vector and matched against document vectors using a matching function such as the cosine measure. The relatedness of a document to the query is given by the score on this matching function and is used as the basis for returning a ranked list of 'relevant' documents. Search engines on the World Wide Web also use the linking information between documents to add to the assessment of relevance of the document. Therefore, more frequently linked (cited) documents have a greater chance of being more highly ranked in terms of relevance to the query.

In general, search engines based on the above statistical approaches have tended to outperform those that have tried to use more semantic approaches that aim at representing meaning. This is due primarily to the limited ability to provide adequate semantic representations of documents at this stage. Whilst many users of search engines are sometimes frustrated with the presence of irrelevant documents in the ranked list, the speed and general precision of these tools is impressive. Better retrieval can usually be retrieved by query revision and relevance feedback.

Question Answering Systems

Question answering systems as textual information retrieval systems have recently attracted a large amount of interest. From an information retrieval point of view, there are two major approaches to specifying information needs: 1) keyword-based queries, and 2) natural language questions. While the former is subject to resolution by systems known as Search Engines, the latter has been the impetus for Question Answering systems evolving in a way that allows direct communication with users in a more convenient and comprehensive fashion through a natural language. Having received natural language questions, such systems perform various processes to return actual direct answers to the requests eliminating the burden of query formulation and reading many irrelevant documents to reach the desired answers by users.

Information seekers or QA system users usually want brief answers to specific questions, (for example: "How old is the President? Who was the second person on the moon? When was the storming of the Bastille?" rather than whole documents (Ofoghi, Yearwood, & Ghosh, 2006). In a typical pipelined architecture of a question answering system, there are four main procedures: 1) question analysis and query formulation to find the answer type of the question and formulate the best representative query for the next two information retrieval procedures, 2) document retrieval using the query already formed, 3) passage retrieval from the most related documents, and 4) answer extraction and scoring from the most related text snippets retrieved by the passage retrieval process. To effectively answer specific information needs, a common starting assumption is that the part of the text which is most similar to the queries will be a rich source of candidate answers from which the actual answer may be obtained. However, considering the main goal of QA systems, relatedness of the passages may not be the best criterion and specificity may be more desirable than having short texts actually containing the answers. This phenomenon creates new limitations and necessitates more precise text understanding processes to approach more effective QA systems whose end-to-end effectiveness cannot go beyond the accuracy of each building block of the entire system.

Two early question-answering systems are SHRDLU and ELIZA. SHRDLU, a very domain-specific system, simulated the operation of a robot in the "blocks world," and focused on asking the robot questions about the state of the world. ELIZA was a much more general system that was supposed to be able to converse on any topic by using simple rules that detected important words in the person's input. It was very rudimentary in the way that it answered questions but led to an understanding of the complexity of question answering systems.

The annual Text Retrieval Conference (TREC) includes a question-answering track. Systems participating in TREC are expected to answer questions on any topic by searching a corpus of text that varies from year to year. TREC has fostered research and development in open-domain, text-based question answering. The best systems achieve percentages in the high 70s for correct answers to factoid questions.

START was the world's first Web-based question answering system and has been operating since 1993. It has been developed by the InfoLab Group at the MIT Computer Science and Artificial Intelligence Laboratory. Currently, the system can answer millions of English questions about places, movies, people, and definitions. Aranea is another Web-based factoid question answering system that has performed well in TREC. It is the successor of the askMSR system that was developed at Microsoft Research.

The QA systems discussed above mainly focus on factoid questions and so could be useful in the fact finding phase of the reasoning process. QA systems that can answer 'why' type questions are not well advanced as this is a much more difficult task that might involve the automatic identification of cause and effect textual units or discourse within.

SEMI-STRUCTURED APPROACHES

Wikis

A Wiki is a website that enables the addition, deletion, and editing of content. It is a collaborative technology for organizing information on Web sites. A particular feature of the Wiki is that it is a group communication mechanism that allows the organization or structure of contributions to be edited as well as the content itself.

Wiki technologies are collaborative authoring environments developed in 1994 by Ward Cunningham. The characterising feature of a Wiki is the capability for readers of a Web page to edit the page so as to readily add text and links to other pages within the Wiki and to external websites. This enables the Wiki to be used as a vehicle for sharing of knowledge amongst a community of users. A prevalent application of Wiki technology is the online encyclopaedia Wikipedia developed by Jimmy Wales. Contributors to Wikipedia edit a page, adding or deleting freely. Volunteer moderators assigned to some of the 1,800,000 pages in Wikipedia during 2007 check that changes made are relevant and appropriate.

More recently, Wiki technology has been used for traditional knowledge management applications. For example, in a government tax office in Australia, a Wiki is deployed so that case officers can more readily share knowledge about legislative interpretations, cases, and scams. In this deployment, editing main pages is restricted to authorised editors in order to keep the content reflective of management policies and views. Case officers make suggestions on discussion pages set up for this purpose. In another application, a University research centre has deployed a Wiki accessible only to group members that is almost totally unmoderated. Researchers add or delete information about conferences, journals, grants, and projects freely. In this way, information is readily shared amongst the researchers in the research centre.

Wikis used for organisational knowledge management must be structured in some way. The encyclopaedic structure characterised by a page per concept is not well suited to most organisational needs. In an organisational setting, pages may be created to map directly to sections of regulations governing work practices. For instance, a legal office may create pages in a Wiki that correspond to sections of the relevant act. Alternatively, pages may be created to map to known problems or key concepts. For example, officers may be expected to consult the Wiki to discover the latest organisational policies on superannuation by presenting pages that enable the reader to progressively drill down to the policy of interest.

Wiki technology can support the work of reasoning communities in a number of ways yet stops short of being a true group coalescing tool. Wiki technology does not facilitate the early engagement phase of a reasoning community. The selection of participants, agreement on a decision-making protocol and agreement on a communication protocol are tasks not supported by Wiki technology. There is nothing in the use of a Wiki that can identify appropriate participants for a community. Wikipedia is open to all participants. In organisational contexts participants are typically defined by management or in an ad-hoc way by other participants. Similarly, a Wiki does not facilitate deliberations regarding a decision-making protocol to be used. Typically, group decision making does not occur as such in a Wiki community. Rather, the Wiki is built up as a resource that individuals draw upon as background knowledge for their own individual reasoning.

Although Wiki technology does not support the Engagement phase of the work of a reasoning community, the device can best be seen to act as a background knowledge repository for individual reasoners and an artefact of a communication protocol, during the individual coalescing phase. Individual reasoning involves the identification and understanding of relevant background knowledge as precursor to the fixing of beliefs and assertion of claims to other participants. Seen in this light, Wiki pages are very convenient repositories for knowledge relevant to a reasoning community. For instance, collaborating researchers form a reasoning community in order to identify a journal for the publication of results. Each researcher, as individual reasoner, consults an internal research Wiki to discover lists of journals with which others within the laboratory have had some experience. The informal comments about each journal form crucial background knowledge for each researcher as they individually determine their preferred option prior to a group discussion.

Wiki pages can also be seen to be artefacts of a strict communication protocol. Contributors to a Wikipedia community implicitly agree to confine all communication between themselves to the pages of the Wiki. It is not expected that, and hardly possible for, a contributor to make email, phone or other contact with other contributors. Implicitly, contributors have agreed to broadcast their views and assertions in the form of additions or deletions to a Wiki page that all can see. Further, contributors have agreed to constrain the expression of their views to assertions that build on the assertions that the previous contributor has advanced.

A WIKI AS A GROUP COALESCING TOOL

The pages in a Wiki cannot necessarily be regarded as an artefact of a group coalescing process. A Wiki page in a current state represents the individual views of the last contributor. The last contributor to a page has implicitly agreed however to build on the views of the previous contributor and can change a page without consultation or coalescing views of others. A group coalescing process differs in that an attempt is made to take stock of all contributions and produce a document that merges all perspectives into one artefact.

A Wiki page that reflected a group coalescing process can be expected to reflect a summary of the assertions and associated reasons advanced by previous contributors to that page. Although there is nothing inherent in the Wiki technology to prevent a Wiki page containing this content, typically Wiki pages are not used in this way.

Weblogs

A Weblog or 'blog' is a website where entries are contributed over time but displayed in reverse chronological order. The ability for readers to leave comments in an interactive format is an important part of many blogs. Most blogs are primarily textual although images and video can be supported. As well as their use as online diaries, they also can be used as technical discussion sites and repositories of the most recent discussions on technologies or issues. The content can be controlled or moderated and even structured by the blog owner. This is often a feature that makes blogs more useful and accessible.

WEBLOG AS AN INDIVIDUAL'S COALESCING TOOL

From a reasoning point of view a Weblog can be seen as a log of the development of an individual's reasoning. It could be used as a trace of the coalescing of the individual reasoning although it does not explicitly represent the reasoning. In a similar fashion, it could be used to trace the reasoning of a small group of contributors to the Weblog. An individual moderator may coalesce the reasoning of individuals so a Weblog can provide some support for this process although there is little explicit in the technology itself to support the coalescing process.

SUMMARY

This chapter has briefly covered some technologies and tools that have not been designed explicitly to support the group reasoning process in the way that we describe in this book but could pragmatically be used to assist various parts and stages of the processes of a reasoning community. Some of these tools, such as search engines and Wikis, are already almost indispensable. Others such as automatic summarization tools are becoming increasingly necessary but are not widely used because of the quality of the result. These pragmatic approaches do not support the work of reasoning communities in a systematic way but they can certainly be exploited in the tasks required. In discussing these approaches and tools it can be seen that there are opportunities for adapting some of these tools to better support the tasks of reasoning communities. So Wikis or Blogs may be better able to support reasoning communities if the role of the moderator were to include responsibility for coalescing and the coalesced reasoning was explicitly represented in some more highly structured form.

REFERENCES

Chklovski, T., Gil, Y., Ratnakar, V., & Lee, J. (2003b). Trellis: Supporting decision making via argumentation in the semantic web. In *Proceedings of 2nd International Semantic Web Conference ISWC 2003*. Berlin, Germany: Springer.

Choi, F. Y. Y. (2000). Advances in domain independent linear text segmentation. In *Proceedings of the 1st Meeting of the North American Chapter of the Association for Computational Linguistics (ANLP-NAACL-00)*, (pp. 26-33). San Francisco, CA: Morgan Kaufmann Publishers.

Clarke, C. L. A., & Cormak, G. V. (2000). Question answering by passage selection (multitext experiments for trec-9). In E. Voorhees & D. Harman (Eds.), *Ninth Text Retrieval Conference (TREC 9)*, (pp. 673-683). Gaithersburg, MD: National Institute of Standards and Technology (NIST). Retrieved from http://trec.nist.gov/pubs/trec9/papers/mt9.pdf.

Elhadad, N., Kan, M.-Y., Klavans, J. L., & McKeown, K. (2005). Customization in a unified framework for summarizing medical literature. *Artificial Intelligence in Medicine*, 33(2), 179–198. doi:10.1016/j.artmed.2004.07.018

Emanuel, J., & Emanuel, L. (1992). Four models of the physician-patient relationship. *Journal of the American Medical Association*, 267(16), 2221–2226. doi:10.1001/jama.1992.03480160079038

Fillmore, C. J., Johnson, C. R., & Petruck, M. R. (2003). Background to framenet. *International Journal of Lexicography*, 16(3), 235–250. doi:10.1093/ijl/16.3.235

Goldstein, J., Mittal, V., Carbonell, J., & Kantrowitz, M. (2000). Multi-document summarization by sentence extraction. In Proceedings of ANLP/NAACL 2000 Workshop on Automatic Summarization, (pp. 40-48). East Stroudsburg, PA: Association for Computational Linguistics.

Hearst, M. A. (1997). Texttiling: Segmenting text into multi-paragraph subtopic passages. *Computational Linguistics*, 23(1), 33–64.

Jain, A. K., Murty, M. N., & Flynn, P. J. (1999). Data clustering: A review. *ACM Computing Surveys*, 31(3), 264–323. Retrieved from http://www.citeseer.ist.psu.edu/jain99data.html doi:10.1145/331499.331504

Joachims, T. (1998). Text categorization with support vector machines: Learning with many relevant teatures. In *Proceedings of the European Conference on Machine Learning*, (pp. 137-142). Berlin, Germany: Springer-Verlag.

Jong, G. D. (1982). Information extraction. In Lehnert, W., & Ringle, M. H. (Eds.), *Strategies for Natural Language Processing* (pp. 149–176). Mahwah, NJ: Lawrence Erlbaum.

Kaszkiel, M., & Zobel, J. (1997). Passage retrieval revisited. In N. J. Belkin, A. D. Narasimhalu, & P. Willett (Eds.), *Proceedings of 20th Annual International ACM SIGIR Conference on Research and Development in Information Retrieval*, (pp. 178-185). Philadelphia, PA: ACM Press.

Kazuaki, K. (2004). Techniques of document clustering: A review. *Library and Information Science, 49*, 33–75.

Kipper, K., Dang, H. T., & Palmer, M. (2000). Class-based construction of a verb lexicon. In *Proceedings of the AAAI-2000 Seventeenth National Conference on Artificial Intelligence*. AAAI.

Kling, R. (1991). Cooperation, coordination and control in computer-supported work. *Communications of the ACM, 34*(12), 83–88. doi:10.1145/125319.125396

Leuski, A. (2001). Evaluating document clustering for interactive information retrieval. In *Proceedings of the ACM CIKM 2001 Tenth International Conference on Information and Knowledge Management*, (pp. 33-40). New York, NY: ACM Press.

Luhn, H. P. (1958). The automatic creation of literature abstracts. *IBM Journal of Research and Development, 2*, 159–165. doi:10.1147/rd.22.0159

Mani, I. (2001). *Summarization evaluation: An overview*. Retrieved from http://citeseer.ist.psu.edu/mani01summarization.html.

Ofoghi, B., Yearwood, J., & Ghosh, R. (2006). A hybrid question answering schema using encapsulated semantics in lexical resources. *Advances in Artificial Intelligence, 4304*, 1276–1280.

Palmer, M., Kingsbury, P., & Gildea, D. (2006). The proposition bank: An annotated corpus of semantic roles. *Computational Linguistics, 31*(1), 71–106. doi:10.1162/0891201053630264

Radev, D., Blair-Goldensohn, S., & Zhang, Z. (2001). Experiments in single and multidocument summarization using mead. In *Proceedings of the Document Understanding Conference*. New York, NY: ACM Press.

Salton, G. (1971). *The SMART retrieval system: Experiments in automatic document processing*. Englewood Cliffs, NJ: Prentice-Hall.

Sebastiani, F. (2002). Machine learning in automated text categorization. *ACM Computing Surveys, 34*, 1–47. doi:10.1145/505282.505283

Sparck-Jones, K. (1998). Automatic summarising: Factors and directions. In I. Mani & M. Maybury (Eds.), *Automatic Text Summarization*, (pp. 1-12). Cambridge, MA: MIT Press. Retrieved from http://www.citeseer.ist.psu.edu/jones98automatic.html.

Swanson, D. R. (1987). Two medical literatures that are logically but not bibliographically connected. *Journal of the American Society for Information Science American Society for Information Science, 38*(4), 228–233. doi:10.1002/(SICI)1097-4571(198707)38:4<228::AID-ASI2>3.0.CO;2-G

Swanson, D. R., & Smalheiser, N. R. (1997). An interactive system for finding complementary literatures: A stimulus to scientific discovery. *Artificial Intelligence, 91*, 183–203. doi:10.1016/S0004-3702(97)00008-8

Chapter 9
Tools and Applications for Reasoning Communities

ABSTRACT

In this chapter, technological innovations that aim to support reasoning communities are presented. These include decision support systems, group decision support systems, online dispute resolution systems, and tools for the representation of argumentation. Future directions and an analysis of requirements for enhanced tools are made.

INTRODUCTION

Rene Descartes observed in his *Meditations*:

Some years ago I was struck by the large number of falsehoods that I had accepted as true in my childhood, and by the highly doubtful nature of the whole edifice that I had subsequently based on them. I realized that it was necessary, once in the course of my life, to demolish everything completely and start again right from the foundations if I wanted to establish anything at all in the sciences that was stable and likely to last.

Descartes was one of the 17th century philosophers who delved into the nature of reason with the objective of establishing a sound and intellectual foundation. He was one of the "Continental Rationalists," along with Gottfried Leibniz and Immanuel Kant, who thought that the senses alone were inadequate for the task of determining knowledge. They considered reason superior to experience and sought to establish their philosophies on the basis of more certain principles. There were also the "British Empiricists," such as Bacon, Thomas Hobbes, John Locke, David Hume, and Mary Wollstonecraft, who maintained that all

DOI: 10.4018/978-1-4666-1818-3.ch009

knowledge has its foundation in sensory experience and developed their thought on that basis. Immanuel Kant worked to combine these two approaches and in so doing developed a uniquely influential system of philosophy which saw the culmination of the 'The Age of Reason' (The Enlightenment). This is somewhat captured by "All our knowledge begins with the senses, proceeds then to the understanding, and ends with reason. There is nothing higher than reason"—Immanuel Kant, *Critique of Pure Reason.*

It can be argued that the age of reason dawned during the seventeenth century and we have seen the use of reasoning adopted in more formal and overt ways across almost all areas of human activity. In more recent times, advances in computing technologies (particularly the Internet) and the emergence of sophisticated reasoning paradigms have enabled the development of decision-support systems, which provide an individual or a community with support in the decision-making process. The manner in which decisions are made is determined, in part, by how the problem can be modelled. For example, if a problem can be modelled mathematically, then the decision-making process can be represented very formally and often as an optimization problem. For non-mathematical problems, a second important factor is whether reasoning or voting is used as the basis for choosing a solution from a set of candidates.

In this book, we have argued for a better understanding of the communities that engage in collective reasoning and for tools to support these communities in the processes of reasoning and decision-making. In this chapter, we consider the range of decision-support tools that are currently available, with an emphasis on tools that support reasoning. The tools are discussed in terms of their domains of application, the nature of the support that they provide and some evolving areas of application.

DECISION SUPPORT SYSTEMS

There is a large literature on systems for supporting decision making (DSS) and systems for groups making decisions (GDSS). There are also many domains of application. Traditionally, there have been many systems deployed in areas such as engineering, medicine, and environmental sciences. However, new domains of application are opening. For example, post September 11, 2001, police have become interested in the use of DSSs to support decision making involving security and emergencies. In this and the next section, we consider some applications in some domains and, in particular, from the point of view of supporting reasoning to a decision.

The sections below will illustrate that despite a large amount of work in the area of DSS there has not been large scale penetration and acceptance. It is clear from a reasoning community perspective that DSSs do not help the Engagement phase or individual coalescing but do assist individual reasoning a little. There is almost no assistance in group coalescing because the systems have not been developed with this over-arching view in mind. Furthermore, arguably, they do not help in the decision-making phase because they largely ignore the group.

Medicine

In the domain of medicine, the traditional applications of decision-support systems have been in the area of support for physicians. The adoption of decision support appears to occur mostly in narrowly defined and highly specialised areas (for example, cardiac problems, pharmaceutical design and development) rather than in general medicine. Identified reasons for this include: general medicine is not a well-defined domain and many problems in the area have many aspects to them, not simply symptoms; experienced clinicians can outperform existing systems leading to a lack of trust and a reduced perception of need; and whether a system is used or not, the final responsibility for diagnostic outcome lies with the doctor. On the other hand, in western countries, patients have an increased capacity to be actively involved in decision making about their health and treatment. This means that it is the patients, rather than the physicians, who are in need of decision support. Consequently, we are seeing a change of direction in the aspects of decision making in health care that are supported by technology.

Ridderikhoff and van Herk (1999) investigated the phenomenon of the failure by physicians to adopt Clinical Decision-Support Systems (CDSSs), even amongst those physicians who perceived the need for diagnostic support devices. To do this, they asked a group of 20 physicians to solve a number of patient problems with the help of a Diagnostic Decision Support System (DDDS) in a realistic environment. To use the DDSS, the doctor enters a set of symptoms and the system presents the doctor with as many explanations for the present symptom configuration as possible. Next to the name of the diagnostic hypothesis the number of matching symptoms is shown, which gives a hierarchy of diagnostic possibilities. The system has two capabilities: a knowledge-based diagnostic component and an encyclopaedia (a component that enables the doctor to question the database) to find a range of diagnoses with similar sets of symptoms.

The results indicated that while the use of a DDSS was not an obstacle in diagnosing symptoms, the support part of the system turned out to be problematic. This component was meant to stimulate the user's thoughts and to prompt the revision of conclusions. However, the critiquing function of the system was not appreciated by the participants, and only rarely influenced their diagnostic judgment.

Dreiseitl and Binder (2005) examined the attitudes of physicians to the use of DSSs and their reactions when the systems provided alternative/contradictory diagnoses to those made by the physicians. The study involved 52 dermatologists who rated the malignancy of 25 lesion images and who had to make a recommendation for each as to whether it should be excised or not. This is a domain where even experts only perform at 70-90% correctness. A black-box diagnostic system (one that provides no reasoning for the diagnosis) was used in parallel. After viewing the system's recommendations, the dermatologists then had the option of revising their own opinions. It was found that only 24% of decisions were revised when these were different from those provided by the system. Willingness to change was found to be significantly negatively correlated with the level of the physician's experience (rated on a 6-point scale from novice to expert) and confidence in their own diagnoses. Because it was found that the least experienced physicians were more likely to accept the system solutions than were more experienced physicians, the authors stressed the need for quality assurance and validation of diagnoses. Because CDSSs can be prone to error, following CDSS recommendations may lead to incorrect diagnoses, for which the physician will be held accountable. For this reason, careful evaluation of the performance of physicians versus computer-supported physicians is required to assess the value of CDSSs for routine clinical use. Dreisitl and Binder stressed the need for systems that provide reasons for their diagnoses, which was a feature of first and second-generation systems (for example CASNET, MYCIN, and INTERNIST-1 from the 1970s, and DX-plain and QMR in the 1980s). They also noted that more recent systems have focused on data-driven approaches. Examples of such systems are Pathfinder (Heckerman, Horvitz, & Nathwani, 1992), Pap-Net (Mango, 1994), and Hepaxpert (Adlassnig & Horak, 1995), the last being a knowledge-based, data-driven system. They also noted that reasoning paradigms such as Case-Based Reasoning (CBR) may provide a viable approach to providing explanations (Reategui, Campbell, & Leao, 1997; Stamper, Todd, & Macpherson, 1994).

Kaplan (2001) reviewed the literature on Clinical Decision Support Systems (CDSS), with a focus on evaluation. These studies ranged in the manner in which they were implemented. The most prevalent research design is to focus on the performance of the systems in controlled settings as compared with human diagnosticians (accuracy of diagnoses). Kaplan suggests that other approaches have been underrepresented and that there is a lack of experiments in realistic settings. This has resulted in a dearth of literature about why doctors do/do not make greater use of CDSSs in clinical (real-world) settings. The review was conducted using a very broad definition of computer support systems (not simply diagnostic systems) to ensure that a range of evaluation techniques was included. This is in line with the guide published by the Journal of American Medical Association to using articles evaluating the clinical impact of a CDSS (Randolph, Haynes, Wyatt, Cook, & Guyatt, 1999). A total of 140 studies that were identified using Medline were reviewed. With regard to usefulness of CDSSs, Kaplan reported that while there was a general view that systems have the potential to improve patient care and to change clinical practice, there is little evidence that clinicians do change the thinking behind their practice or that the systems aid in diagnosis. Results on the latter point were equivocal. It was shown that despite their assumed benefits, CDSSs are still not generally adopted in real-world settings. Thus, there is a dearth of information that could be useful in understanding why CDSSs may or may not be effective. This leads to the making of less informed decisions about these and other medical informatics applications. Kaplan notes that over the past 50 years, there has been little change in comments concerning implementation issues and barriers to system use, which may be partly due to the fact that system evaluations often ignore issues concerning user acceptance or changes in workloads and work practices. Because different study designs answer different questions, Kaplan concludes that it would be useful for evaluation

studies to include a range of methodological approaches and research questions to broaden understanding of clinical acceptance and use of informatics applications. Wyatt (1997) found that most evaluations of Clinical Decision-Support Systems (CDSSs) focused either on improved clinical practice or improved patient outcome. However, the benefits of CDSSs are difficult to evaluate simply on these measures because the systems are, by nature, very complex and hence the effects of their use are difficult to predict. Wyatt outlined the need for full evaluation of CDSSs to ensure that full costs and potential side effects (such as increased workload) are identified. He outlined a set of measures that he believed should be used routinely.

Woolf et al. (2005) examined the need for better decision-support systems for patients confronted with making decisions about their treatment. They noted that typically supporting patients in their decision-making is not done well by either hospitals or physicians. The need for support coincides with societal changes in expectations of what medicine can and should deliver. There has been a dramatic change in roles from the situation where the clinician played a paternalistic role and was assumed to be the informed expert, to the current situation (at least in Western countries) where the patient now expects to be a more active player in the decision-making process. That is, formerly patients were only involved in two decisions: whether or not to consult a physician and, if they did, whether or not to accept/act upon the advice given by the physician. Nowadays, however, the patient has a greatly expanded role in the decision-making process for a variety of reasons including increased patient autonomy, broader access to information, expanding clinical options, rising costs, ascendancy of chronic illness, complex tradeoffs, and greater accommodation of personal values. This has led to the need for the patient to have support in their decision-making, which has in turn led to a change in the roles played by health experts. The authors describe decision making in terms of themes and components. The themes of informed decision-making that the authors address are: the patient's role in decision making; the clinical issue or nature of the discussion; the alternatives for management of the patient's condition; the potential benefits and risks of proposed management options; the uncertainties; the patient's understanding; and the patient's preferences. The components of shared decision making are: understanding the risks associated with the condition; understanding the options, including the risks, benefits, alternatives, and uncertainties; weighing personal values regarding potential benefits and harms; participating in decision making at the level desired.

Another problem with existing health systems is that the systems are not well equipped to inform patients in a manner that is timely, easily understood, and jargon-free, nor do they encourage people to consider consequences, to ask questions, to clarify values, or to express preferences. In other words, as patients and consumers of health services demand a greater and more flexible level of participation in the decision process, the constitution of the reasoning community in the area of health is undergoing substantial changes. There are clearly difficulties in having health systems that are able to meet the consequential needs for consumer understandable information.

Woolf et al. also found that, on their own, decision aids (information sources such as print-based information and medical websites) are not sufficient for helping patients with decision making. While these aids provide patients with the ability to access medical information (for example, Medline, libraries), there are several inherent problems. Information may be biased (which is typically not acknowledged); there is the potential for information overload and patients are not necessarily able to locate the critical information that they need; there are physical (access) and economic impediments for some patients in accessing the information; and there is a need for

strong literacy and numeracy skills if patients are to be able to make use of the information provided.

Kuziemsky and Jahnke (2005) made similar observations about existing DSSs in health. They argue a need for DSSs that can enhance health care delivery in a range of contexts. To do this, the systems must be able to:

1. Link a patient's history with guidelines to provide patient-specific decision support,
2. Reconcile issues of workflow and how they will be impacted by a DSS,
3. Be applied to support different levels of clinical practice expertise and care givers in different roles,
4. Be continuously updated with new evidence, and
5. Be monitored and evaluated in terms of their effectiveness on an ongoing basis.

They say that to develop systems that are closer in operation to real medical reasoning, a wider range of decision-making processes should be involved. They discuss three approaches: the hypothetico-deductive approach (which currently dominates in the area of health care DSSs), the argumentative approach (Dickinson, 1998) and a model for making managerial health care decisions in complex, high velocity environments described by Reay (2000). The hypothetico-deductive approach is an iterative process for data collection and hypothesis generation. It involves a sequence of steps consisting of data collection, data interpretation, and hypothesis generation. Rather than being data-driven, Dickinson's approach is based on argumentation and highlights three different types of reasoning (inductive, deductive, and abductive). The third model, Reay's framework, focuses on the transfer of knowledge from the research arena to accepted clinical practice. It identifies how new information can be: recognized and accessed, appraised, adapted for use in another setting, and applied and integrated into the practices of an organization. The key points and omissions of each model are described. Kuziemsky and Jahnke contend that there is a need for systems that not only support physicians in their decision-making, but that are capable of communicating and sharing the information. In our view, this would be analogous to having the system actively participating as an agent in the reasoning community. To this end, they present a framework for a multimodal DSS that incorporates each of the three methods of decision-making. The DSS framework contains four major components: ontology, guideline base, literature base, and evidence base. The framework has been used to design a DSS for palliative care, which is not yet fully implemented, but which the authors claim could be applied in different con-texts/modes. At a base level, an expert caregiver may only want to access the guideline base because they possess the tacit knowledge required to supplement the rules. However, novice caregivers or experts who want more detail than is provided by the guideline base can find additional supporting material by accessing the detailed management and education tables from the categorization scheme. The historic cases can also be used as a set of teaching cases. Because the DSS also supports different types of reasoning, it can be used to support both diagnosis and management functions.

These studies show that there are major changes occurring in the constitution of reasoning communities engaged in medical decision making. The communities are becoming more diverse, in terms of both their medical expertise and their personal stake in the outcome of the decision-making process. As a consequence, there is a need to develop systems that are based on models of reasoning and decision making which are appropriate for use by all members of the reasoning community. Most importantly, systems must be able to provide an explanation of the reasoning behind particular decisions or outputs. In the studies where decision support systems could have been considered as an extra agent participating in a reasoning community it appears that experienced clinicians rarely heeded

the input from the DSS and the researchers in these studies consistently suggest the need for the DSS to provide its reasoning for the system to act in a useful way alongside experienced clinicians. This observation is very much in line with the notion of a reasoning community as opposed to the notion of a decision-making community. There are clearly problems at the systems level in terms of the provision of information that is appropriate to the needs of the reasoning community. However, it is anticipated that these problems will be resolved with the emergence of new models of decision making that take greater account of the characteristics and needs of the particular reasoning community.

Ecology and Environmental Science

There has been a growing focus on reasoning and decision making in the areas of ecology and environmental science as well as resource and energy allocation. The types of problems encountered in these domains tend to be multi-criteria and frequently multi-objective decision problems. There are a number of approaches that fall under the umbrella of Multi-Criteria Decision Analysis (MCDA) and these are well covered in (Figueira, Greco, & Ehrgott, 2005). A feature of much current work is on the integration of multiple perspectives that have to be taken into account in these issues. From our point of view, the reasoning communities are necessarily diverse in terms of economic, social, environmental, and cultural perspectives.

Examples

Ceccaroni, Cortes, and Sanchez-Marre (2004) describes the OntoWEDSS system, which helps to improve the diagnosis of faulty states of a wastewater treatment plant. OntoWEDSS augments rule-based reasoning and case-based reasoning with a domain ontology. It provides support for complex problem-solving and facilitates modelling knowledge for reuse. The authors detail how they addressed the following issues:

- Modelling information about wastewater treatment processes;
- Clarifying terminology in the domain;
- Incorporating knowledge from the ontology into the reasoning process; and
- Designing and developing a decision-support system for diagnosing faulty states of a wastewater treatment plant.

The system was successful in at least 73% of its diagnoses. The authors contend that the approach is of general interest because the system's architecture, which is underpinned by an ontology, could be applied not only to wastewater treatment plants but to other environmental domains.

Qin, Huang, Huang, Zeng, Chakma, and Li (2006) have developed a DSS for managing sites that have undergone subsurface contamination by petroleum products. Because contamination can be widespread, decisions must be made regarding the remediation alternatives in order to identify a feasible set of options. To this end, the DSS has been designed to support mathematical modelling of the problem, risk assessment, remediation-technique screening, and monitoring-program design. The system is supported by a visual-language software package, named NRSRM, which enables users to simulate and visualize contamination problems and proposed remedial actions. The system was evaluated using a contaminated site located in western Canada. It offered six remediation alternatives, each with associated information regarding the necessary activities including a cost analysis. The final decision was then left to the users.

Adriaenssens, De Baets, Goethals, and De Pauw (2004) applied fuzzy logic to highly variable, linguistic, vague and uncertain data or knowledge in the domain of ecosystem management. Adrianto, Matsuda, and Sakuma (2005) applied a multi-criteria participatory approach to the problem of assessing local sustainability

of fisheries. Ardente, Beccali, and Cellura (2003) developed software called ENDLESS to model recycling design strategies that are ecologically sustainable. The system uses multi-attribute decision-making. Phua (2005) also developed a decision-support system for forest conservation planning that incorporates a Geographic Information System (GIS) and uses a multi-criteria decision making approach. A categorisation of sustainability assessment tools can be found in Ness, Urbel-Piirsalu, Anderberg, and Olsson (2007), and Welp (2001) provides an overview of the use of decision support tools that are required to enable wider participation in the management of river basins based upon international conventions and policy documents including the EU Water Framework Directive. Related to these systems are those for managing disasters. Chang, Wei, and Tseng (1997) developed a GIS-based system to support decision making regarding chemical emergency preparedness and response in urban environments. Tamura, Yamamoto, Tomiyama, and Hatono (2000) showed that expected utility theory is inadequate for modelling events such as earthquakes, which have high consequences but low probability of occurrence. Another focus of system design has been the support of sustainable decision making in the domain of energy production. Examples include the production of bio-energy (Ayoub, Martins, Wang, Seki, and Naka, 2007), sustainable electricity production (Doukas, Patlitzianas, & Psarras, 2006; Yue & Yang, 2007) and nuclear energy (Lee & Koh, 2002).

Engineering

Engineering systems have become increasingly complex, expertise needed for the design, construction, and operation of these systems involves the effective collaboration of large teams of experts who are frequently geographically dispersed. For example, in the design of infrastructure and utility systems, one of the main sources of complexity is the large number of interacting and conflicting requirements of a diverse range of stakeholders. Reidsema and Szczerbicki (2002) reviewed software for Concurrent Engineering, which is a strategy for processing as many product development tasks in parallel and incorporating relevant life-cycle attributes as early as possible in the design phase. Its purpose is to reduce the duration of design projects and to provide better quality products. This entails a high degree of distributed cognitive processing and hence the distribution of appropriate knowledge to all participants is a very complex problem. Solution of the problem requires new approaches and tools (which are based on artificial intelligence methodologies) as well as the choice of an appropriate architecture.

Marashi and Davis (2006) proposed a methodology to help in the resolution of complex issues and to facilitate the evaluation of options during the design of such systems. The methodology is based on models of negotiation and argumentation. A measure of the success for different scenarios or design alternatives is derived from the process-based approach used to assemble and propagate evidence regarding the performance of the system and its components. An extension of the mathematical theory of evidence is used to deal with the reliability of information sources and experts' opinions. The framework helps in capturing the reasoning behind design decisions and in assessing the evidential support for each design option.

Liu and Wirtz (2006) addressed a similar problem, focusing on collaborative conflict resolution using a fuzzy inference engine. They created a model for resolving conflicts and managing a Toulmin-based argumentation network with many participants. The structured argumentation is represented as dialogue graphs. Based on this model, the authors developed a Web-based argumentation tool as a part of a collaborative engineering design system. It enables users to select the most favoured design alternative in the design argumentation from multiple perspectives in collaborative engineering design. The system

was used by the Solar Car Team from the University of Missouri-Rolla, a student design team, which won the competitions in the 2001 and 2003 American Solar Challenge.

Education

Various tools and techniques that have been developed to support decision-making have also been deployed in the domain of Education. Applications and tools that support reasoning in Education are treated in two parts: education with the aim of improving critical thinking, reasoning and argumentation skills and CSCL (Computer-Supported Collaborative Learning).

REASONING SKILLS

Many of the software packages (Araucaria, DiaLaw, Reason!Able, ATHENA, ArguMed) that have been developed to support argumentation have been tested in the area of (usually tertiary) education, particularly in domains such as legal reasoning and philosophy. Most authors agree that a single package is unable to achieve all the desired outcomes and suggest that a hybrid approach (combining verbal and graphical techniques) should be adopted. The educational studies are typically only pilot studies and lack deep evaluation of the learning that has taken place. There is also an absence of longitudinal studies to evaluate whether or not any effects are sustained beyond the period of intervention. Two notable exceptions to this are the work by Dan Suthers and Tim van Gelder. Van Gelder's software was designed specifically for educational purposes and has undergone several metamorphoses. Initially, Reason!Able was designed to help tertiary students develop critical thinking skills. The latest version of the software, Rationale, is aimed at students across all levels: primary, secondary and tertiary. Austhink, the company that developed Rationale, provides support for educators and students in the form of online documentation, downloadable software and an online forum. The software has a range of features: Grouping maps (which are useful for brainstorming, categorizing and creating structures of items), Reasoning maps (which identify contentions, reasons and objections and importantly reveal the relationship or structure between these claims), Analysis maps (which enable a more careful and rigorous analysis of an argument), Templates, Essay Planning, and Guides to the use of the software.

Whilst there are proponents of concept mapping and argument mapping to facilitate learning (van Gelder, 2001a; Twardy, 2004), there is little scientific evidence to suggest that there is a positive link. Dan Suthers at the Laboratory for Interactive Learning Technologies (LILT) uses Belvedere, which was developed to help secondary students to improve their critical thinking skills in science, as well as several other products including COLER (see Constantino-Gonzalez & Suthers, 2003), the Alvis (algorithm visualization technology) with Chris Hundhausen, and disCourse, a Web-based learning environment that supports discussion-oriented and project-oriented courses. Argument mapping is generally considered to be very useful in enabling the actors to keep track of the state of an argument by reducing cognitive load. This is particularly the case for novices.

In 1998, Lodder and Verheij (1998) conducted a trial with law students in the area of computer-mediated legal argumentation. Two approaches were used: graphical and verbal. Two systems were used to support the experiment: Lodder's DiaLaw (Lodder, 1998) (verbal) and Verheij's Argue! (Verheij, 1998) (graphical). The area of concern was Dutch tort law. DiaLaw is implemented in Prolog whereas Argue! takes the graphical approach and is a Delphi implementation of CumulA, which is a procedural model of argumentation with arguments and counterarguments (Verheij, 1996). Both systems are prototypes for the mediation of legal argument. DiaLaw is a two-person dialogue game, in which both players make moves. The goal of the game is that the proponent convinces the op-

ponent of the correctness of his own assertions, or the incorrectness of the opponent's assertions. Each move (statement) takes one of four forms: claim, question, accept, or withdraw. If a move is legitimate, the other player takes a turn. If the move is not legitimate, the player gets another chance. Students practised: making claims, defending claims (providing reasons) and denying the other player's claims.

In the Argue! System, arguments are assumed to be defeasible and the defeat of an argument is caused by a counterargument that is itself undefeated. Statements can be justified by adding reasons and can be used to draw conclusions. This is graphically depicted by arrows connecting the statement-boxes. One benefit of this approach is that students are forced to make arguments in an explicit reason-conclusion structure and experience how counterarguments can be used to defeat arguments. No data are available regarding student performance. The authors make the recommendation that neither system on its own can fully support the work (learning) and suggest the need for a hybrid approach.

Reed and Rowe (2001, 2004) and Rowe, Macagno, Reed, and Walton (2006) investigated the use of Araucaria in the teaching of critical thinking in philosophy. Araucaria is a software tool for representing argumentation in a diagrammatic form and is based on the Argumentation Markup Language formulated in XML. An argument takes the form of a tree structure. Araucaria supports argumentation schemes and diagrams show the type of inferential relations between premises and conclusions. To supplement standard classes in argumentation, Araucaria was used with 22 students of philosophy and required for assignment work. The aim of the study was to test Araucaria's effectiveness in aiding students in developing critical skills in the analysis of argumentation, particularly in identifying fallacious arguments. Students were required to identify and structure the chain of reasoning found in an actual case of argumentation. To carry out these tasks, the students were required to identify premises, identify partial and ultimate conclusions, and to distinguish between linked and convergent arguments. Students also had to learn to identify the argumentation schemes for the inferential steps. Assignments required students to construct argument diagrams, diagrams representing enthymemes and diagrams representing various types of emotional arguments.

After completion of the assignments, students provided feedback by completing a questionnaire about the usefulness of Araucaria in the development of critical thinking skills. Students were also able to provide comments. Student response was positive: almost 80 percent of them considered the program enjoyable, useful, and important for the purposes of the course. On the other hand, 57 percent of the students had problems in learning the software. So, again further study in areas broader than philosophy is warranted.

One domain where computer-supported argument mapping has already been extensively used is in teaching the general skills of reasoning and argument. For three years Reason!Able was the primary learning vehicle in a large, one-semester undergraduate subject (Critical Thinking) at the University of Melbourne. The subject has been intensively evaluated to determine the extent to which students actually improve their critical thinking skills. The data suggest that the approach based on computer-supported argument mapping was substantially more effective than traditional methods (van Gelder, 2001b). The software (Reason!Able) (van Gelder & Bulka, 2000) was designed with the purpose of enabling students to practise critical thinking skills. Results indicated that students who used the system showed more improvement in six months than would normally be seen over a three-year period. Correlational studies indicated that this improvement was not simply attributable to the time spent in practice; rather it seemed that the environment was responsible for the improvement. The author suggests that it is the visual representation of the argument that is most helpful to students.

ATHENA (Rolf, 2003) is a Java applet for enabling students to practise critical think-ing/argumentation skills. It has a similar interface and similar level of functionality to Reason!Able, but was developed independently. Similar to Reason!Able, it has been used with a range of tertiary students. While Reason!Able has been developed from a critical thinking perspective, Athena was designed to support professionals in argumentation. No data are available for comparing educational outcomes. However, the authors do note a major difference in intention of the two packages. The main difference between the approaches is that Reason!Able primarily is devoted to analysis, containing advisory functions, while Athena has relatively more emphasis on student production, for example, through different selective report functions. Reason!Able assumes a more definite structure and progress in a course of critical thinking. Through several tasks, the user is assumed to transfer his skills to non-educational contexts. Athena has fewer facilities for steering student learning. It is more geared to comprehensive students tasks, embedded in role-play, in order to promote efficient learning and transfer to professional tasks. These differences are gradual rather than absolute.

Twardy (2004) has used Reason!able with 135 first-year Philosophy students at Monash University in Melbourne to help them develop critical thinking skills. He evaluated the effectiveness of the teaching using the California Critical Thinking Skills Test (CCTST) developed by Peter Facione (1990, 1992). The test aims to evaluate the in-depth critical thinking ability of middle school students through adults. It was run both before and after the intervention. Twardy was interested in investigating whether the results that Melbourne University had been obtaining since Reason!Able was introduced into the curriculum was simply due to the founder effect. This was the reason for including Tim van Gelder in the study. The results in gain in performance for the Monash students were clearly above the expected gain for one whole year in university. Twardy attributes much of this gain to the use of argument mapping, which enabled the students to concentrate on developing arguments rather than keeping track of where the argument was up to. This reduces some of the cognitive load and hence results in improved performance.

COMPUTER SUPPORTED COLLABORATIVE LEARNING

Whilst "collaborative learning" has been embraced by the educational community, there had been little deep study of collaborative learning until IT became commonplace (particularly to support distance education in the tertiary sector). The focus of studies is now shifting to the cognitive aspects of Computer Supported Collaborative Learning (CSCL), rather than the social and affective domains. While most of these studies involve proprietary software (for example, BlackBoard) and do not investigate their use in supporting reasoning per se, they do provide good insight into how to measure the effectiveness of CSCL (Hathorn & Ingram, 2002; Rosenthal & Finger, 2006). There has been a proliferation of studies in this area in recent years. In general, it is found that whilst collaborative learning has become very fashionable, there are two main impediments. The first is that students do not understand what is required of them when they are asked to work "collaboratively." That is, the fact that students are working or sitting in groups does not guarantee collaboration. The second main problem is that of evaluating collaborative work. It is common to shift focus from evaluating what students have learned to what they have done. In most of these studies, tools were chosen that would support collaboration, although some used purpose-built tools.

Hathorn and Ingram (2002) worked with Kent State University Education graduate students from two locations, all of whom were studying the same unit with the same instructor. Four groups of students were given the same problem to work on (a cost-benefit analysis of distance education). The groups received different instructions. Two of the groups were told to collaborate on a solution, and the other two were told to have individuals select a role and discuss the problem from that point of view.

The purpose of the study was to measure collaboration within the groups. The authors distinguish between cooperation (division of task between group members) and collaboration where group members work interdependently to solve a problem. Similarly, they drew a distinction between participation, which refers to frequency of communication and interaction, which requires the evolution of an argument in that each statement should build upon previous statements. That is, interaction is like a threaded discussion. Equal participation is only one requirement of collaboration.

The study used a threaded Web discussion program called WebBoard. This was used for all discussions within the groups. Groups 1, 3, and 4 consisted of two females and one male, and Group 2 consisted of three females. In Groups 2 and 3, the group was instructed to collaborate. The instructions contained three requirements: a) they had to discuss all points together; b) they had to reach a consensus or compromise; and c) they had to write only one report. In Groups 1 and 4, individuals were asked to select one of three roles in the scenario (a faculty member, a student, or a local businessperson), and no instruction to collaborate was given. Computer-generated statistics were collated and the group responses were analysed to determine the level of collaboration.

Chi-square tests were used to determine whether there was an even level of contribution within the groups. Only Group 1 returned a significant result (uneven contributions). Group 1 had the lowest percentage of interaction statements that did not involve the instructor, whereas Group 2 had the highest. Based on the measures interdependence, independence, and synthesis, the groups were ranked according to the degree of collaboration they exhibited. The ranking of the final product (project) was conducted by three professors of education and the groups that produced the most successful outcomes exhibited more cooperative than collaborative behaviour. Overall, the results seem promising but the authors note the need for larger-scale studies. The study provides a useful framework for assessing collaboration and could be used in non-software-based studies. Similar results were obtained with elementary school students (Lipponen, Rahikainen, Hakkarainen, & Palonen, 2002).

Constantino-Gonzalez and Suthers (2003) used COLER which is a computer-mediated learning environment that includes a software coach, to help students collaborate while solving Entity Relationship modelling problems. COLER's coach is a pedagogical agent to facilitate collaboration. It does not tutor Entity Relationship modelling, but encourages students to discuss and participate during collaborative problem solving. The coach is implemented as a personal assistant for each student. There is no direct communication between different students' personal coaching agents, although group parameters are accessible through the local copy of the shared workspace. Students indicated that COLER did help them to collaborate. They mentioned that the chat is an important tool for communication and that giving an opinion when an object was added motivates them to reach agreement before moving on.

Suthers has mapped the evolution of CSCL (Suthers, 1999; Suthers & Hundhausen, 2002). His work has focused on the use of multiple representations of data to enrich the quality of discourse in a given domain. His conclusions are similar to those of van Gelder in that they support the use of non-verbal data representations to improve critical thinking.

GROUP DECISION SUPPORT SYSTEMS

Group Decision Support Systems (GDSS), as the name suggests, are systems designed to support groups of people, as distinct from individuals, in making decisions. The deployment of such systems has been enabled by the development of information and communication technologies. However, many of the systems that purport to be GDSSs do not yet support the group as a reasoning community in the way that we are suggesting reasoning and decision-making should be considered. At the lowest end are systems that simply support collaborative work, whereas GDSS focuses more on supporting decision making usually in terms of making rational choices from a range of options on an issue. Meetingware is a term used for systems that support and facilitate the meeting aspects of group interactions in meetings. A number of systems and electronic facilitators have been developed and are described in (Antunes, Ho, & Carrico, 1999; Antunes & Costa, 2003; Ho & Antunes, 1999; Antunes & Dias, 2001; Costa & Antunes, 2001; Antunes, Costa, & Pino, 2006; Kock & Antunes, 2007). Group Support Systems are also systems that provide support for groups to work on issues. Numerous studies have demonstrated how Group Support Systems (GSS) are superior in many cases to traditional, oral meetings. However, most GSS research has been based upon groups using English and existing systems are not easily adapted to handle other languages.

From the perspective of decision making, it may not be pertinent to go beyond collecting individual participant preferences on the options and either voting on these or having either a community or algorithmic revision process of the preference before combining to have a group selected option. In many cases, decision-making is achieved by using voting and/or an algorithmic approach. For example, FacilitatePro (http://www.facilitate.com/UsesFaceToFace.html) is a Web-based meeting system for facilitating group decision making. The suite of tools supports the following meeting steps: brainstorming (anonymous); categorizing ideas -a verbal discussion of the ideas is followed by organizing them into categories based on SWOT analysis: voting to generate a prioritized list of possible actions; documenting next steps and responsibilities to generate a report.

Other useful tools are Decision Explorer which is a concept mapping tool (http://www.banxia.com/demain.html), Group Explorer which is a concept mapping system with voting (http://www.phrontis.com/GE.htm) and Analytica which is a system that uses influence diagrams and Monte Carlo simulation of risk. Sharpe Decisions and Resolver are groupware systems with voting (http://www.sharpedecisions.com/ SDEW.htmland http://www.resolver.ca/products/resolverim.htm)

Group Support Systems are typically developed in well-defined domains, where an algorithmic approach is suitable for determining a solution. For example, within the health care industry, many decision-making approaches and tools are used. Hatcher (1994) explores the Analytic Hierarchy Process (AHP), which permits both subjective and objective information to be considered in a decision. The AHP assumes that preferences for different alternatives depend on separate criteria that can be reasoned about independently and captured in a numerical score. A reasoning community can determine the structure of the AHP and reason about the weights (numerical scores) attached to each criterion. The score for a particular criterion can be calculated from sub-criteria in the hierarchy. A weighted sum of these scores is used based on only pair-wise comparisons.

Tavana, Smither, and Anderson (2007) developed D-Side, which is a GDSS that uses multi-criteria decision making. It has been deployed by the Johnson Space Center to support management teams in making decisions regarding the allocation of capital improvement resources across twenty facilities. Five selection criteria were identified and a team of managers nominated weights for these. The AHP was then used to identify those facilities that were considered to be most critical in terms of the funding required. User evaluations of the system indicated that they were significantly more satisfied with this approach than they had been with the existing approach to decision making.

Jimenez, Mateos, and Ros-Insua (2005) use Monte Carlo simulation techniques in a group decision-support system based on an additive multi-attribute utility model for identifying a consensus strategy in group decision making problems where several decision makers or groups of decision-makers elicit their own preferences separately. They use Monte Carlo simulation techniques for identifying a consensus strategy in an iterative process. The objective of decision making during oil spill response management is to minimize pollution effects in coastal areas. Once spills occur, Liu and Wirtz (2006) approach this as a multi-group multi-criteria decision-making problem involving a variety of stakeholders and natural dynamic environments. However, not all coastal areas at risk can be saved due to a limitation of equipment or options. Thus, often preferences between different coastal areas or uses, respectively, have to be made in an operational way.

Many environmental issues are multi-criteria and multi-objective decision problems involving a range of stakeholders that can benefit from the use of decision support tools. For example, the Systems Analysis Laboratory at the Helsinki University of Technology is involved in a range of environmental decision making projects:

- Water Resources,
- Forest Resources,
- Nuclear Emergency, and
- Towards Electronic Democracy workshop: e-Participation in Environmental Decision Making

Fes, Giupponi, and Rosato (2004) have connected environmental tools and decision support methods, by using multicriteria analysis methods in a decision support system. Laukkanen, Palander, Kangas, and Kangas (2005) devise a voting theory based method called multi-criteria approval for group decision making in timber harvesting and Shih, Wang, and Lee (2004) use a multi-attribute approach where the final rankings of all possible alternatives is done collectively as a group after each individual has had an opportunity to make their own judgments, comparisons and rankings.

Hamalainen (2003) has produced software 'Decisionarium' (www.decisionarium.hut.fi), which is a public site for interactive multicriteria decision support. All of the tools are Web-based. Web-HIPRE supports value tree and AHP analysis including group models. The RICH methodology allows the decision maker to provide incomplete ordinal preference statements when considering the relative importance of attributes in a value tree. Opinions-Online is a platform for surveys voting and group collaboration. There are different ways for voting and multi-attribute scoring.

In recent years, there has been a move away from algorithmic approaches towards methods for supporting dialogue. Slotte and Hamalainen use a dialogue approach for the structuring of decisions, called Decision Structuring Dialogue (Slotte & Hamalainen, 2003). This is a facilitated process for group communication with specific rules and guidelines. The aim of such a dialogue is to aid group interaction, collective learning and collaborative investigation. Decision Structuring Dialogue is a method for structuring problems, elements of which can also be incorporated into other problem structuring methods. The approach was successfully used at a large Finnish Lake by a group of stakeholders with conflicting interests. This approach is quite consistent with the notions of a reasoning community.

Negotiation systems have also been developed using multi-agent system architectures. Morge and Beaune (2004) use multi-agent systems where each agent assists a user in multi-criteria decision making and negotiates according to this decision-modelling with other agents, each of them representing a user. Agents assist users in the debate to negotiate a joint representation of the problem and automatically justify proposals with this joint representation. Their approach uses the AHP.

Systems have also been developed to deal with conflict resolution. Zhuge (1998) presents an architecture and a decision model for Conflict Group Decision Support Systems (CGDSS). The decision model incorporates rule-based reasoning and voting-based decisions. Based on feedback from the conflict situation, it can support continuing, foreseeable, and adjustable decisions. Its use is demonstrated with a training example from an air force conflict group. INSPIRE is a Web-based system for the support and conduct of negotiations (Kersten & Noronha, 1999). The primary uses of the system are training and research; INSPIRE has been used at eight universities and training centres. In research, it is being used to study cross-cultural differences in decision making and the use of computer support in negotiation. INSPIRE negotiations are conducted through the exchange of offers and messages, which are two separate forms. They can be submitted together or separately. The negotiation ends when an agreement is made, that is, when both parties accept an offer. This acceptance is normally input via the system's menu.

None of the applications described here uses any form of reasoning or argumentation, rather their main focus is on decision outcomes and communication between the participants. However, it could be argued that recent developments in technology (particularly the Internet) rival the Gutenberg Press in terms of the potential they have to transform the ability of citizens to engage actively in decisions that directly affect their lives. As stated in the first chapter, the ancient Greeks recognised that full participation in democracy requires the citizenry to engage in sound reasoning. Decision making in two important domains, online dispute resolution and e-democracy, has now emerged as an important area of research and some of the developments in these areas are discussed next.

ONLINE DISPUTE RESOLUTION, CONFLICT RESOLUTION AND NEGOTIATION

In areas such as civil, commercial, family and labour disputes, it is becoming more common for the disputing parties to find alternative solution methods to litigation, which can be a drawn out and very costly process. Options include arbitration (where a neutral third party hears from both parties and then makes a decision) and mediation (where a neutral third party helps the disputants to reach a consensus). The major difference between these two options is that an arbitrator has the power to enforce a decision on the matter under consideration whereas a mediator does not. Both methods of dispute resolution provide an environment that is more private, less formal and less adversarial than that of litigation. In the case of Online Dispute Resolution (ODR), there is the added advantage that the disputants do not need to meet face-to-face nor even to engage in the dispute resolution synchronously. The advantages of ODR, which can be used asynchronously, over face-to-face meetings, include cost and time savings, avoidance of confrontation and the accommodation of living in different time zones. To date, the main area of application for these systems has been to e-commerce. For example SquareTrade, has been applied to the resolution of over one million disputes to do with online auctions. These on-line approaches have grown in popularity, so, there is a growing need for computer systems that can support the processes of arbitration and mediation, and it is also desirable to have these systems online. Research underpinning the development of these systems has

largely been conducted by the artificial intelligence community, particularly in the area of dialogue and argumentation (Zelenikow & Bellucci, 2003; Muecke & Stranieri, 2008). However, there are systems that use a mathematical model, rather than argumentation, to help disputing parties to come to a resolution. Approaches in this vein present a range of techniques, but online dispute resolution with argumentation is only just beginning to emerge in line with such areas as e-governance. Earlier systems (for example, SmartSettle and SquareTrade), though well deployed, are little more than fora for electronic haggling.

Dialogue-Based Systems Approaches

Walton and Godden (2005) showed how dialogue-based theories of argumentation can contribute to the construction of effective systems for dispute resolution. In particular, they consider the role of persuasion in online dispute resolution by showing how persuasion dialogues can be functionally embedded in negotiation dialogues, and how negotiation dialogues can shift to persuasion dialogues. The authors note that ODR can be seen as a negotiation since the primary issue can often be viewed as one of dividing up some property, asset or resource in such a way as to maximize the interests of the participants. As a result, the tendency has been to model ODR on negotiation-based models while neglecting the role that other types of dialogue can have in the ODR process. However, they contend that another approach is deliberation. They dispute the notion that negotiation is "communication for the purpose of persuasion," because they maintain that these are different dialogue types that have different goals, structures, and norms. Rather than dispute resolution being reduced to simple rounds of offers and counter-offers, they believe that these offers should be annotated with reasons for the purpose of conducting a dialogue.

Negotiation may be contrasted with persuasion dialogue and inquiry. The goal of an inquiry is to prove something, or to disprove it or show that it can be proved, by amassing and verifying all the relevant evidence. Persuasion dialogue is also about trying to find the truth of a matter, but the matter is a contested issue on which there is uncertainty and lack of knowledge. The viewpoints on either side of the controversy can only be evaluated by looking at the arguments on both sides and weighing up which side meets the burden of proof (Prakken, 1991). Negotiation is not primarily about finding the truth of a matter, and if a participant treats it that way, he or she will do poorly in the negotiation. In a persuasion dialogue, various kinds of moves are allowed, including the asking of questions, the answering of these questions, and the putting forward of arguments. In persuasion dialogue, the one party, called the proponent, has a particular thesis to be proved.

In comparing negotiation with persuasion, Walton and Godden use the models proposed by Mochol (2004) for three different types of dialogue: deliberation, negotiation, and argumentation. In Mochol's work, each of these design systems is composed of a set of three models: one describing the system components, a second depicting the use case of the system, and a third mapping the processes or activities involved in each system. A major problem with Mochol's model is that negotiations must end in agreement, which is not the case in practice. For this reason, they propose a modification to Mochol's model that includes rounds of offers and counter-offers, which will better allow it to capture the normative dialectical structure of the negotiation process. The motivations for this change are that the authors believe that ODR systems must be able to model the communicational activities of participants and reveal the internal structure of the negotiation process in such a way as to show how and where persuasion dialogues (including reasons for statements) might occur within it. They suggest that ODR systems must be able to manage and

regulate communication in such a way that basic cooperative principles are not violated, if they are to be effective as systems which support or facilitate the resolution of disputes.

Mediation-Based ODR Applications

The Internet is increasingly acting as the forum for commerce, which has resulted in an increasing number of disputes. Hence, there is a need for systems that can help in the resolution of these disputes. A number of websites have been established to address this need. Goodman (2003) examines and evaluates these websites. In particular, it examines and evaluates websites that use mediation techniques to help resolve disputes. It argues that cyber-mediation is in its early stages of development and that it will likely become an increasingly effective mechanism for resolving disputes as technology advances. The sites discussed are: Cybersettle at http://www.cybersettle.com; SettlementOnline at http://www.settlementonline.com; clickNsettle at http://www.clicknsettle.com now www.namadr.com; SmartSettle at http://www.oneaccordinc.com/; Internet Neutral at http://www.internetneutral.com; SquareTrade at http://www.squaretrade.com; WebMediate at http://www.webmediate.com.

Cybersettle, SettlementOnline, and clickNsettle are all fully automated, double-blind, online systems that are primarily used in the resolution of monetary disputes. Offers and counteroffers are sent by email. Cybersettle and SettlementOnline are both limited to three rounds of offers, however clickNsettle supports more rounds of offers but in a limited time period. CyberSettle has been involved in resolving disputes worth a total of more than one billion dollars. ClickNsettle (now myADR) handles cases worth more than $100 million per annum. SmartSettle is hosted by OneAccord Inc. The authors note "that lack of cooperation among decision makers is still a significant obstacle to overcome." SmartSettle goes through six phases: prepare, qualify interests, quantify satisfaction, establish equity, maximise benefits and secure commitment. InternetNeutral allows the parties to choose from a range of mediation alternatives, including e-mail, instant messaging, chat conference rooms, and/or video conferencing. SquareTrade, which aims to build trust via warranties, has been applied to the resolution of over two million disputes relating to online auctions. These disputes have arisen across 120 countries and involve five languages. WebMediate can resolve disputes either online (automatically using a secure, double-blind bidding process) or with the assistance of a professional mediator or arbitrator. Although almost all matters enter the system through the automated WebSettlement bidding process (which is appropriate for any monetary dispute), parties may also elect to submit their matter to WebMediation, in which a trained mediator assists the parties in resolving their dispute, or WebArbitration, in which the parties submit their dispute for decision by an experienced arbitrator.

The online systems discussed above have advantages that include: cost savings, convenience, asynchronicity, and avoidance of complex issues of jurisdiction. However there are also a number of disadvantages including: impersonality (not face to face), a limited range of disputes that can be handled by the existing systems, potential inaccessibility, concerns over confidentiality.

Argumentation-Based Approaches

Historically there have been many ODR systems: NEGOTIATOR PRO, INSPIRE, DEUS, LDS, SAL, MEDIATOR, PERSUADER, NEGOPLAN and GENIE. Bellucci, Lodder, and Zeleznikow (2004) integrate techniques from argumentation, artificial intelligence and game theory in the development of an environment for online dispute resolution system. Earlier research has shown that techniques from areas such as game theory, artificial intelligence, and social psychology have all been applied to the development of negotiation

decision support systems. However, no particular technique has been universally recognised to be best. Performance characteristics appear to be context-dependent and therefore the use of a hybrid approach is reasonable. They develop a generic framework for an ODR environment that builds on their earlier research. Bellucci and Zeleznikow integrated game theory and artificial intelligence to model the mediation process and identify possible trade offs (Bellucci & Zeleznikow, 2001; Zeleznikow & Bellucci, 2003). Lodder (1999) developed argumentation tools (DiaLaw) that support disputants to communicate about their conflict. Both the dialogue tool and the negotiation system are of a general nature and can be used in any jurisdiction, for basically any dispute. The environment is described in detail in Lodder and Zeleznikow (2005). In summary, the negotiation systems of Bellucci and Zeleznikow do not facilitate discussion, whilst the dialogue tools of Lodder do not suggest solutions. Both systems are useful in what they offer to the user, but the weakness of one application is the strength of the other.

Their ODR environment works in the following steps:

1. Calculate the Best Alternative to a Negotiated Agreement (BATNA)
2. Attempt to resolve the dispute through negotiation
3. Negotiation support through the use of compensation strategies and trade-offs and
4. Outcome of process.

Possible outcomes include: no resolution of issues, partial resolution (at which point, the parties may report partial success or no success) and complete resolution. The authors suggested that it is best to begin with the dialogue tool (rather than the negotiation tool) to encourage the parties to communicate. The authors conclude that the first step should be for parties to calculate their Best Alternative to a Negotiated Agreement, which is not yet supported in a generic tool. The reason for this is that this step is probably the most difficult one for the development of ODR applications, even though it is a really important one.

Computation-Based Negotiation

Tavana and Kennedy (2006) developed N-Site, a distributed consensus building and negotiation support system, which is used to provide geographically dispersed teams with agile access to a Web-based group decision support system. The framework integrates a database, a model base, Web resources, and intelligent resources with a Web-based user interface. Together, these components support data integrity, shared information space, and data communication. Data about alternative solutions, decision criteria, subjective weights, and probabilities of occurrence, are obtained from user input and Web resources. Four teams located in France, Mexico, the Ukraine, and the United States participated in the N-Site project. The N-Site participants were teams of MBA students at the ESCEM School of Management in France, the Universidad de las Americas in Mexico, the Lviv Institute of Management in the Ukraine, and La Salle University in the United States. Each team was required to research the problem using the World Wide Web. With this background, each team identified opportunities, threats and alternatives as a basis for developing a response to the Cuban Missile Crisis that confronted President Kennedy in October 1962. The Strategic Assessment Model (SAM) (Tavana, 2002) was used by each team to choose a strategy that best fitted the team's perspective. Lin's Maximum Agreement Heuristic (MAH) was used to produce a consensual ranking of the alternatives from the preferences of the teams. SAM and the Web enabled the teams to evaluate strategic alternatives and build consensus based on a series of intuitive and analytical methods including environmental scanning, the Analytic Hierarchy Process (AHP) and subjective probabilities. No argumentation was involved. The Web was used to achieve interaction among the international teams as they attempted to negotiate a decision framework and select a diplomatic response. The project was assessed with a Web-distributed survey instrument. Users were generally satisfied with the product in terms of usability and outcomes.

Ross, Fang, and Hipel (2002) developed a case-based reasoning system for conflict resolution called GMCRCBR. The system includes a DSS called GMCR II, which implements a methodology called the graph model for conflict resolution, which is detailed in related papers. Information on 104 conflict cases that have been analysed using the graph model for conflict resolution was collected and stored. The authors placed significant focus on case reuse and efficient retrieval. Their system has been used for a number of real world conflicts (Hipel, Fang, & Kilgour, 2005; Fang, Hipel, Kilgour, & Peng, 2003a; Fang, Hipel, Kilgour, & Peng, 2003b; Kilgour, 2003; Hamouda, Hipel, Kilgour, Noakes, Fang, & McDaniels, 2005; Noakes, Fang, Hipel, & Kilgour, 2005; Hamouda, Hipel, & Kilgour, 2004) particularly in the area of fishing rights and water resource management. The Conflict Analysis Group state that the most common uses of the GMCR II system are:

- As an analysis tool used by a decision maker in a conflict in which he or she is a participant
- As an analysis technique used by a consultant advising a decision maker who is a direct participant in the conflict
- As an analysis tool by an interested outsider ("third party") and not on behalf of any direct participant in a conflict
- As a coordination tool to enhance communication and facilitate mediation among decision makers in a conflict. In some situations, the GMCR could even be employed by an arbitrator; and
- As a simulation tool to help an interested person or group understand a strategic conflict by playing the roles of one or more

of the decision makers. For instance, prior to actual negotiation sessions, a negotiator could try out negotiating positions to identify those most likely to achieve desired results.

Whilst N-Site provides a database and shared information space, it allows participants to provide decision criteria, subjective weights, and probabilities of occurrence, which are used in a computational model. GMCR II, on the other hand, uses a case base where each case has been analysed using the graph-based model of conflict resolution. This case-base forms the repository on which other reasoning in new conflicts can be built.

The Reasoning Community in ODR

Lodder and Bol (2006) discussed the need for cooperation between lawyers and the IT community to ensure that the IT systems developed to support online negotiation are correct in terms of both legal principles and technical requirements.

Lodder and Bol (2006) was particularly interested in which parties may be involved (typically more than two players) in an online dispute using an ODR. Because members of current societies are used to spending large amounts of time online, Lodder contends that the widespread use of ODR systems is inevitable and that the main question for researchers to address is how this can best be achieved. He maintains that research needs to determine how to design systems that are easy to use, fair and efficient. Identifying the reasoning community that is involved in the dispute is fundamental for achieving successful resolution. For example if the dispute is one that involves property settlement during a divorce, then the ODR system might involve a mediator in the community as well as the husband and wife or it might involve other representatives. Problem resolution also needs to be based upon appropriate legal principles.

Schultz (2003) discussed the role of ODR and the conscious (or otherwise) assumption that government should not be involved. Schultz maintains that this is not appropriate as there are some things that are best done by governments such as providing an architecture of trust, accreditation of sites/providers, establishing clearing houses, providing a means for online appeals and the enforceability of negotiation and mediation outcomes.

ELECTRONIC DEMOCRACY

Government based on democratic principles has become increasingly prevalent in the last two centuries to the point that most nation states now are democratic. Key features of these states include the notion that a government, freely and fairly elected by the majority of people, rules on their behalf and by their consent. The protection of human rights, a respect for the rule of law, and the enshrinement of freedom of expression are ideals closely associated with democracy.

The form of government in the Greek city-states over two thousand years ago involved a direct democracy where citizens participated directly in debates that resulted in legislation and other decisions that affected the city. Although, participation in meetings of the Assembly was restricted to adult male citizens in Athens, according to (Manville & Ober, 2003) thousands of participants would dutifully attend monthly Assembly meetings. Debates often raged and ultimately decisions were made by a simple majority vote of a show of hands or counting of collared balls.

In contrast, representative democracy typical of most modern states, involves the appointment of representatives to engage in debates and make decisions on behalf of citizens. Direct democracy is regarded as infeasible as the population sizes increase whereas representative democracies have provided stable and effective government for millions. However, critics of representative democracy including Rousseau (1968) suggest that citizens are disempowered if removed from the means to direct the process of law making. Indeed, many democratic states report that participation by citizens is decreasing to alarming levels leading to widespread disenfranchisement, particularly for minority groups such as youth, the elderly, rural communities and certain disability groups (Macintosh, Robson, Smith, & Whyte, 2002; Chutimaskul & Funilkul, 2004).

Deliberative Democracy

Deliberative democracy (first coined by Bessette, 1994) combines elements of representative democracy with direct democracy by advocating some public deliberation about issues in decision-making debates. The Deliberative opinion poll model advanced by Fishkin (1991) exemplifies this form of democracy by involving a representative sample of participants to deliberate and ultimately vote on an issue. The deliberations and voting outcomes provide valuable insights, but do not supplant representative decision-making. Hundreds of initiatives similar to or inspired by deliberative opinion polls have been established in a number of countries. The sites vary according to their support for deliberation. Electronic petitions sites are a type of opinion poll where participants can signal their views on a topic though the capacity to access information and engage in deliberation is limited.

In his landmark work, John Dryzek lucidly argued for transformation of political processes to include the active and critical engagement of citizenry in deliberative processes in the modern, global world (Dryzek, 1990, 2002). In Australia, *GetUp* is a not-for-profit organization not affiliated with any political party. The organization elicits suggestions for issues from subscribers, collates information regarding the issue and provides an online bulletin board and voting mechanism. In a relatively short period of time, the subscription to GetUp has exceeded that of all political parties

in that country. The Australian Council for Trade Unions http://Rightsatwork.com.au campaign provides information regarding changes to industrial relations laws and encouraged online opposition. In three months, the email list grew from 4000 to 170,000 lodgements of opposition.

Initiatives in Europe include the Gov2u project http://www.gov2u.org/which is a generic but customizable, e-participation project that includes open source programs that facilitate the establishment of electronic participatory petitions. In Spain, over sixty municipalities are electronically implementing Gov2Demoss in the framework of the eConsensus project, which aims to foster public participation and consultation over the Internet; to improve the communication between councils and the citizens they serve; and to provide virtual fora to help citizens organize communities of interest and thus participate more effectively and constructively in public life.

In June 2007, the first e-community of Europeans was launched, creating the first multilingual social network, blogging platform, and fora for European citizens. With over 300,000 visitors per month and 30 000 subscribers on its newsletter cafebabel.com has changed the perspective of European citizens on Europe. It is a revolution in the field of Internet journalism.

In Japan, the Voicebank initiative (Yong, 2005) provides another example of an effective electronic petition site. Voicebank elicits opinions and concerns about government programs from citizens. The opinions and complaints are made available for all citizens and an online discussion of underlying issues often occurs. An electronic petition system in Thailand provides a link for citizens to lodge suggestions and complaints directly to the prime minister (Yong, 2005).

More recently, mobile technologies have been deployed to enable citizens, particularly in remote communities to voice their views and provide input into the decision-making process (Gross, 2000; Brucher & Baumberger, 2003; Cabri, Ferrari, & Leonardi, 2005). Further, a mobile system integrated into a geographical information system has been trialled in Portugal by (Carvalho, Rocha, & Oliveira, 2004).

A central tenant of deliberative democracy is the ideal that decision making ought to be informed by reasoned debate (Stromer-Galley, 2007). Electronic petition systems go some way toward this by providing easy access to information about an issue and the views of others. In reasoning community terms, this enables participants to perform individual coalescing and form their own views. Those views are then submitted to the community through the petition. The decision-making remains the province of the parliament or recipient of the petition. Some sites such as the Australian *GetUp* do not directly aim their petitions at a decision-making body.

Electronic petition approaches typically enable very little scope for participants to engage further with any opinions or to conduct deliberative discussions outside the petition forum. Electronic petition systems enable widespread access to information and spaces for discussion do not, in themselves, ensure that deliberation occurs. However, the identification of the nature of deliberation has been controversial.

According to Habermas (1984) decisions made by consensus following informed deliberation leads to outcomes that are just and invite compliance. This cannot be said of outcomes determined by a vote. In practice, decision-making is often not deliberative because participants do not start on a level playing field. Some participants have a greater voice, are more powerful, less inclined to hear others or are motivated by rewards outside the discussion. The perception that parliaments, local government councils, company boards, school boards and other decision-making bodies are not deliberative has possibly contributed to an unprecedented degree of public cynicism and mistrust of social institutions.

Although deliberation as an ideal may be intuitively appealing, the ascertainment of the extent to which deliberation occurs in a group is a difficult exercise. Approaches advanced to measure deliberation are presented in the next section.

Measuring Deliberation

The identification and measurement of deliberation is difficult despite its appeal as an ideal form of group communication to underpin democratic decisions. A clear definition of deliberation in a democratic context by Stromer-Galley (2007) provides a starting point:

deliberation as a process whereby groups of people, often ordinary citizens, engage in reasoned opinion expression on a social or political issue in an attempt to identify solutions to a common problem and to evaluate those solutions.

Niemeyer (2007), Stromer-Galley (2007) and Steenbergen, Bachtinger, Sporndliand, and Steiner (2003) present three different approaches for measuring the quality of a deliberation.

The Discourse Quality Index (DQI) of Steenbergen et al. (2003) and Steiner, Bachtiger, Sporndli, and Steenbergen (2004) provides an instrument that codifies interactions in order to rate the quality of discourse. The DQI was evaluated on parliamentary discourse in Britain and uses four criteria: the level of justification supporting claims, the extent to which justifications were egalitarian, the degree of respect paid to counter-arguments, and the extent to which proposals were based on a goal of reaching genuine consensus.

Stromer-Galley (2007) codifies dialogue using a different coding scheme that includes indicators for the extent to which reasons underpin opinions, the extent to which participants are engaged in the process and the extent to which discussion was on topic. She defined six key elements of deliberation:

- Reasoned opinion expression. Participants simply make assertions or provide reasons for their opinion

- References to external sources such as mass media and other materials. This is useful to ensure that all participants have access to the same background information. Claims based on the documents can be more readily understood when there is disagreement

- Expressions of disagreement. The free expression of disagreement is important to avoid undue influence of one view, the phenomena called "groupthink" by Janis (1972). Open expression of disagreement also ensures that participants justify their positions.

- Equal levels of participation. This ensures that all candidate solutions are identified, all parties must have equal opportunity to participate and all suggestions are considered

- Coherent topic and structure. Coherence is concerned with how much of the time is spent on-topic and with the structure of the deliberation

- Engagement between participants. Engagement between participants is necessary for discussions to evolve.

Niemeyer (2007) notes that measures of deliberation based solely on the quality of discourse unnecessarily ignore outcomes and that a more effective measure includes an assessment of the extent to which a participant's positions match their beliefs, a concept they label intersubjective rationality. Intersubjective rationality is measured by taking every pairing of participants and performing correlation statistics on their beliefs and their desired outcomes. The correlations are then plotted as illustrated in Figure 1, which might be indicative of low intersubjective rationality.

Points in the upper right quadrant represent those correlations where the pair of participants adopts similar positions taken on the basis of similar beliefs. In contrast, the correlations in the lower right quadrant represent correlations where

pairs of participants desire different outcomes though their underlying beliefs are similar. Figure 2 illustrates what the correlations might look like in the case of high intersubjective rationality. The deliberation amongst a group is more advanced if more pairings are in the top right or lower left quadrants. This demonstrates an alignment between beliefs and outcomes; an intersubjective rationality.

Yearwood and Stranieri (2007) examined the impact of different approaches to argument mapping on secondary school students reasoning in groups on a government policy issue. The researchers provided all students with the same background information regarding the Australian government's policy on the processing of asylum seekers and then divided them into seven groups to discuss the issue. Each group was provided with a different knowledge scheme to support their deliberations. These were the original Toulmin argument structure, IBIS (with and without the positions and arguments laid out), the GAAM (with and without the claims, relevance reasons and inference reasons laid out), and narrative reasoning. There was also a control group who received no support for their reasoning. Learning outcomes were measured with a test on the issue and group deliberation was subjectively measured by experimenter observation of the following features:

- The extent to which there was agreement on claims without the advancement of reasons or consideration of alternatives,

- The extent to which agreement was reached by disagreement with the alternative claims,

- The extent to which agreement was reached because of some other evidence or reason, and;

- The extent to which agreement was reached by a combination of other evidence data or reasons.

Figure 1. Low intersubjective rationality

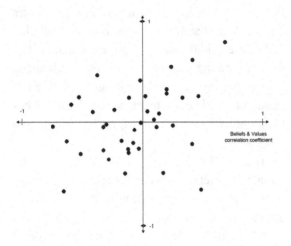

Some indicative results from the preliminary study are presented in Table 1. These results are inclusive but suggest that there are benefits to be gained by using techniques for structuring reasoning. Further work is being undertaken with greater emphasis on the groups acting according to the principles of a reasoning community.

In our view, efforts to measure the quality of deliberation, while important, are tangential to the goal of identifying effective technologies to support deliberation. The ability for large numbers of participants to engage in quality deliberative discussion, however this is measured, requires two key technological features:

- Advanced communication technologies. Existing Internet technologies provide the medium for unprecedented numbers of individuals across the globe to exchange views and information

- Schemes for organizing and structuring knowledge so that very complex issues and arguments can be organized in compact ways. Without this, participation in any discussion is restricted to a small number of highly specialized individuals because others will not have time to assimilate the large quantities of information that underpin most current issues.

The first requisite, advanced communication technologies, requires that there is widespread and affordable access to Internet and related technologies. Concerns that a digital divide between those with access to these technologies and consequent access to information and the opportunity to contribute to decisions, and those without this access will only result in a new underclass have been raised by numerous authors including Wilhelm (2000), Kampen and Snijkers (2003), Jaeger (2004), and Wright (2006). Although the ability to connect to the Internet is increasingly prevalent and affordable throughout many countries, access is still far from universal. Further, affordable access to information and communication technologies alone does not ensure empowerment and engagement. Educational, cultural, and other socio-political factors can impact significantly on the adoption of digital technologies to enhance participation (Wilhelm, 2000).

Digital divide issues aside, the second requisite for large numbers of participants to engage in reasoning involves schemes for organizing and structuring reasoning. This is needed because issues that attract the interest of large numbers of participants are invariably complex and involve

Figure 2. High intersubjective rationality

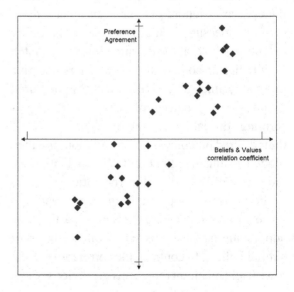

Table 1. Quality of reasoning when different argument techniques are used

GROUP	Rating of reasoning	Rating of group discussion
Unstructured	Reasoning was very poor with most students suggesting one of the solutions and modifying it to account for a health or language concern. Only two students mentioned reasons for their conclusion that were not simply a dislike of the other possible solutions	High. Discussion was based on single points of view put by individuals
GAAM	All students gave some reasons for their solution. Clear and balanced account of relevant factors	High. General discussion of issues.
TAS	3 out of the 4 gave reasons and 1 actually rated the importance of a particular factor as a reason. Little breadth of issues.	High
IBIS	3 students gave reasons for their choice the other 2 largely said that they liked their choice better than the other solutions without other reasons. Clear articulation	High, but focused on popularized discussion.

many claims, facts, and documents detailing evidence. For instance, an Environmental Impact Statement documenting arguments associated with the deepening of a shipping channel near the city of Melbourne totals more than 3000 pages (Melbourne Corporation, 2007). The executive summary alone exceeds 35 pages.

In another participatory decision making initiative in Australia, a forum known as the Energy Futures Forum engaged a variety of stakeholders including energy utilities and mining companies to identify plausible scenarios for generating energy needed by Australian industry and consumers (Morozow, 2006). A key feature of this forum was the inclusion of a deliberative democracy initiative called the Energy Futures Citizens Panels (EFCPs).

Twenty participants representing a cross-section of views on sources of energy formed each of three EFCPs held in different major Australian cities. Deliberations were conducted with a facilitator over a four-day period. A great deal of work was done in small groups who reported to the larger group. Facilitators helped groups by summarizing inputs and assisting with the production of each Panel's final PowerPoint presentation. The deliberations provided valuable insight for the drafters of the final report (Littleboy, Boughen, Niemeyer, & Fisher, 2006), though the issues were quite complex and intricate.

A detailed analysis of the EFCP panels led Dryzek and Niemeyer (2006) to observe that deliberation initially involves agreement on those values, beliefs and preferences that are relevant and legitimate to the issues at hand. It does not require consensus about which of them is right or how they should be prioritized, but it does require that all relevant perspectives be actively considered and understood. They call this agreement metaconsensus. Metaconsensus requires that participants understand each other and the pertinent factors without need for, and prior to, rational or simple consensus. Dryzek and Niemeyer (2006) claim that metaconsensus produces outcomes that are tractable and more legitimate than those where metaconsensus is low. It also eliminates irrelevant and strategic arguments.

Argument mapping methods such as Toulmin and its variants IBIS and GAAM can be seen to provide a diagrammatic representation of metaconsensus. In laying out positions and pro and con arguments, the IBIS map advanced by Rittel and Webber (1984) maps metaconsensus without prescribing a preference ranking or preferred solution. The version of the Toulmin structure deployed by van Gelder (2003) performs the same role by laying out assertions and reasons for or against them. The generic argument structure advocated by Yearwood et al. (2006) also performs the same role albeit in a different way as illustrated in the next section.

A central feature underpinning argument mapping methods and measures of deliberation is the use of reasons to underpin opinion. Somewhat surprisingly, Polletta (2006) found that discussion was indeed largely based on reasons however, if a view being advanced was unpopular or unorthodox, its advocate was far more likely to use personal story telling rather than reasons to advance their view. She attributes this to the power of storytelling for engaging with others in an inherently collaborative way. Listeners can identify, sympathize, and understand personal accounts in a qualitatively different way than they can when confronted with reasons.

Polletta (2006) cites a respondent in one of the online fora set up to foster participatory debate on the World Trade Center site who used a story to make the point that the new design must respect a sense of reverence the public has for the site:

Recently, someone I know came back for a visit. She and her family went to Manhattan and took the Circle Line for a ride and she said that when they reached the WTC site the entire ship got silent. It's this reverence that needs to be addressed.

It is difficult to imagine how an assertion depicting the need for a reverent site design backed by well-supported reasons could inspire the same sense of drama and impact that the short and simple personal account provides.

In addition to the use of stories for describing a view or making a point in a way that invites community unity rather than cold debate, Polletta (2006) notes that quite often participants in a discussion do not enter deliberations with fixed and certain opinions but rather do so with vaguely held notions and an openness to the views of others so that their own view may be cemented with some certitude.

The central lesson to draw from the varied approaches to measuring deliberation involves,

first of all, the acceptance that deliberation can be measured, it is desirable to measure it and that there may be more than one way to measure it. More research is required in order to determine the extent to which the different instruments correlate with each other though measuring different phenomena. It is quite possible, for instance, that deliberation measured using DQI results in deliberation ratings that are similar to those observed with intersubjective rationality. That said, the incorporation of quantitative measures of deliberation that include personal story telling metrics may be far more difficult to achieve.

The measurement of deliberation is of great interest to advocates of deliberative democracy though there is no suggestion that deliberation is restricted to public policy discussions involving large numbers of participants. We adopt the view that approaches to measure deliberation can be interpreted as approaches to measure the extent to which a reasoning community operates deliberatively. The nature of the processes at each phase of a reasoning community's work (engagement, individual reasoning, group coalescing, and decision-making can be identified to distinguish a deliberative reasoning community from less deliberative communities. Adopting this view facilitates the discernment of appropriate technologies to advance deliberation and, ultimately, the democratic ideal. This is discussed in the next section.

A REASONING COMMUNITY PERSPECTIVE ON DELIBERATIVE DEMOCRACY

A forum for deliberative democracy is an instance of a reasoning community. Like all reasoning communities, its processes comprise engagement, individual reasoning, group coalescing, and decision-making. Viewing deliberative democracies in this light enables a clear specification of elements in each phase that are essential for a community to operate as a deliberative democracy community. Table 2 summarizes essential elements. For instance, participants are best recruited to represent as broad a range of views and beliefs as possible for a deliberative democracy community. The communication protocol enables all views to be heard and encourages open expression. That all participants have easy access to relevant background information and work with schemes for the representation of their reasoning is particularly important for the individual reasoning phase of a deliberative community. Frequent and thorough group coalescing enables agreement on relevant features of a problem solution that is important to avoid individuals becoming overwhelmed by the complexity and size of policy issues. The spirit of deliberative democracy is more aptly captured with a decision-making protocol based on consensus than a resort to voting, regardless of how fair the voting algorithm is. Each of these points is elaborated upon in the next sections.

The Engagement Phase of a Deliberative Democracy Reasoning Community

The engagement phase of a reasoning community involves the recruitment of participants, agreement on a protocol for communication and another protocol for decision-making. The engagement phase also involves the articulation of the future audience that may re-use the community's reasoning. Features within each of these elements of the engagement phase can be identified that contribute to deliberative democracy to a greater extent than others.

For instance, the recruitment of participants for a deliberative democracy forum is ideally performed to include a broad range of stakeholder views, to ensure that all key views are represented and to ensure that participant demographics represent those of the broader community. Recruiting participants to ensure a broad range of views is important so that no opinion is left unheard and

also to ensure that the problem is viewed from many perspectives. For the World Trade Center discussion described by Polletta (2006), over 800 participants were selected to represent a cross section of views. They were assigned to 26 groups to discuss architectural designs, transportation, housing, and economic development options. This was done so that the solutions were guaranteed to be viewed from a range of pertinent perspectives.

The imperative to recruit participants so that the sample is representative of the broader community is more important in a deliberative democracy setting than in other reasoning communities. This taps into the democratic ideal that decisions are made by people who are affected by the decisions. In the Energy Citizen Panels study by Dryzek and Niemeyer (2006) participants were selected by random sampling from telephone directories and further stratified for age, gender, highest level of education and employment status. In the Bloomfield Track deliberations involving the controversial construction of an outback Australian road (Niemeyer & Blamey, 2003), indigenous participants were prevented from attending by floods.

Although not appearing as a criterion for the measurement of deliberation in existing schemes, the extent to which participants are selected to advance a broad range of perspectives is arguably as important as a criterion for measuring discourse quality once dialogue commences. In its extreme, discourse is conceivably extremely un-deliberative if adherents to controversial views are not invited to the table in the first place.

Communication protocols are agreed upon during a reasoning community's engagement phase. A communication protocol includes the following elements:

- The medium for communication. Options include online, face-to-face, email, telephone, sms, text
- The procedural regulation of discussion. This includes rules for turn taking, the ap-

Table 2. Elements of a deliberative democracy reasoning community

Reasoning Community Phase	Important Features for Deliberative democracy communities
Engagement	Recruitment of participants to ensure breadth of views Communication protocol characterized by respect, tolerance and listening
Individual reasoning	Ready access to all relevant background information Schemes for the explicit representation of reasoning
Group Coalescing	Frequent group coalescing endeavours Non-combative schemes for the explicit representation of meta-consensus
Decision Making	Universal participation in decision making Decision-making protocol based more on consensus than voting

pointment or not of facilitators or moderators and time or text limits on contributions.

• The regulation of content. This includes constraints on the content matter of contributions in addition to the manner in which the contribution is conveyed. Upper case email, for instance may be frowned upon because it is considered in the same vein as shouting.

Workshop methods such as the *Search Conference* advanced by Emery and Purser (1996) detail many aspects of a search conference that facilitate the respectful, engaging and collaborative communication that they claim to be essential for deliberation. For example, Search Conference interactions should take place face to face over one or more days to encourage participants to get to know each other. Seating arrangements should be chosen so that participants face each other. Facilitators are required to be well trained to bring quiet participants into discussion and regulate the behaviour of strongly assertive participants. In contrast, the Consult approach described by Afshar et al. (2006) advocates that deliberation can occur with an exclusively online medium provided the system mandates the supply of reasons to underpin suggestions, anonymity and an unbiased voting scheme. In a similar vein, group discussion using an email-based Delphi process is commonly believed to engage participants deliberatively.

The decision-making protocol is also determined in the engagement phase of the reasoning community life cycle. Deliberation is sometimes associated with consensual decision-making, however this is not necessarily the case. The final decision in the World Trade Center project was made by the City of New York. In the Energy Forum Citizens Panels managed by Dryzek and Niemeyer (2006), the panel views were aggregated with the use of the Hare, Condorcet and Borda preferential voting schemes. However, the voting scheme was not determined by the panellists but by the facilitators. The deliberation discussion facilitated by van Gelder (2003) in a workplace setting was made by consensus. His claim that the facilitated elicitation of a Toulmin-based diagram from a group of participants virtually ensures a consensual decision may be overstated, but this serves to highlight the need for further research in this field.

A reasoning community identifies the intended audience for the future re-use of their reasoning in the engagement phase. For Dryzek and Niemeyer (2006) this was predetermined by the experimenters who organized the fora in order to report to the national science and research organization, CSIRO. Participants were also aware that their deliberations would be reported in academic contexts with a view of formulating new research projects. The final report was distributed to the Australian federal government and four Australian universities.

The intended audience for future re-use of the reasoning performed within each citizen panel can easily be imagined to include new citizen panels discussing energy generation, anywhere in the world, though this was not advanced in the Dryzek and Niemeyer (2006) study. Future panels could benefit by having access to the claims, reasons and evidence from the Australian discussions, as a starting point. This would facilitate both individual reasoning and group coalescing. By adopting a reasoning community view, we more clearly see that there are several elements in the Engagement phase that can impact on the quality of deliberation. Further, existing measures of deliberation focus on some but not all of those elements that can feasibly have a significant impact on the quality of deliberation. Discourse based approaches to measuring deliberation by Stromer-Galley (2007) reference elements of procedural regulation of communication by including indicators such as equal levels of participation while being silent on the impact of the communication medium. Emery and Purser (1996) and Steenbergen et al. (2003) emphasize the importance of respect. Matching stated beliefs with desired outcomes (Niemeyer, 2007) side steps any impact on deliberation from Engagement issues.

The Individual Reasoning Phase of a Deliberative Democracy Reasoning Community

Participants in the individual reasoning phase perform two roles; to individually coalesce relevant knowledge and to deploy that knowledge to form beliefs, opinions, judgments, assertions, or claims. Polletta (2006) notes that many participants commence discussions without clear views of relevant factors, their own beliefs, or assertions. She identifies the importance of personal story telling in the task of making sense of the issue. In contrast, the intersubjective rationality approach for measuring deliberation by Niemeyer (2007) presumes that participants have clearly articulated

beliefs and desired outcomes. Further, implicit in intersubjective rationality is the view that participants form their beliefs and desired outcomes somewhat independently of group processing.

The feature of deliberative reasoning communities most pertinent to individual coalescing is the provision of reasons to underpin assertions. The extent to which reasons are provided can be found in all attempts to measure deliberative quality. For intersubjective rationality, the reasons are assumed to be the beliefs a participant holds. Two of the four criteria cited by Steenbergen et al. (2003) as indicative of deliberation are the level of justification and the content of the justification. The variation to the Toulmin structure that van Gelder (2003) has developed includes specific slots for reasons. Yearwood et al. (2006) used external observers to assess the extent to which reasons were provided by school students in discussing the government refugee policies. Polletta (2006) found that discussion was based heavily on reasons. Even when personal story telling was used rather than reasons to advance a view in her World Trade Center study, the events of the story can be seen to provide a reason to underpin the point of the story even though both point and reasons remain implicit in the narrative.

Although there is broad consensus that reasons are important for deliberation, there is far less clarity on what reasons are, and how a good reason can be discerned from a mediocre or a poor one. In our view an assessment of the quality of reasons cannot be made without reference to a representation of reasoning. In the classical syllogism and most logics, the reason for a new conclusion comprises the major and minor premises used to infer the conclusion. A poor major premise is one that is syntactically ill formed, semantically not relevant to the discussion, includes variables of questionable scope, or has a scope that is too narrow for the context of the discussion.

In the IBIS scheme, the reasons underpinning a position are the pro and con arguments. Arguments are represented as single statements in a natural language with all the nuances and shades of meaning that natural language permits, so judgments about well-formedness beyond grammatical correctness are difficult to make. Statements concerning the relevance of arguments are not represented. Precisely how arguments are weighed relative to others is also not specified, so assessments concerning their scope and relative importance are also difficult to make.

In the Toulmin model, a data item can first be advanced as a reason for a claim though both claim and data are expressed in natural language. Reasons that derive from data items for the claim that voluntary euthanasia is ethical include the assertions that termination choices are a basic right, the pain suffered by the terminally ill should not be tolerated and the suffering of loved ones witnessing a slow and painful death should not be accepted.

As illustrated in previous chapters, the GAAM model comprises a two-step representation; the most abstract representation is a Generic Argument Structure (GAS). The GAS is agreed upon by the reasoning community to be of appropriate relevance and scope to act as a template for the coalescing of knowledge and assertion of beliefs by each individual. The template is comprised of five main elements that support a claim:

- Data items and their values represented as variable-value pairs
- Reasons for relevance of a data item
- Reasons for the appropriateness of an inference procedure
- Reasons for the inference of a particular claim value from a given data item using a specified inference procedure
- The specification of context variables.

To reiterate, the specification of reasons is broadly accepted as an integral element of deliberative democracy. However, in our view, the way reasons are defined and conceptualized is intimately associated with the way in which reasoning is represented. The specification of reasons in a story format is quite different from the specification of reasons in the syllogism, Toulmin, IBIS, or the GAAM. Consequently, the measures of deliberative quality ought to include a notion of the representation of reasoning.

The Group Coalescing Phase of a Deliberative Democracy Reasoning Community

During the group coalescing phase, a reasoning community takes time out, as it were, to take stock of the individual reasoning advanced by each participant. The background knowledge discovered in addition to all claims and reasons are coalesced into a format that acts as a summary and a generalization of all views. Dryzek and Niemeyer (2006) observe that deliberation initially involves agreement on those values, beliefs and preferences that are legitimate and relevant to the issues. They call this agreement metaconsensus. Metaconsensus requires that participants understand each other and the pertinent factors without the need for consensus on outcomes.

In a small reasoning community such as a patient-doctor community, group coalescing is rarely performed at all. In a larger community involved with more complex issues, the specification of an explicit group coalescing is sometimes performed. The Search Conference technique of small breakout groups brainstorming an issue to present to the entire group enables the group to perform group coalescing, albeit indirectly. Claims, reasons and knowledge pertinent to the issue are elicited and distinguished from those that are not relevant. A Delphi facilitator engaged in organizing, abstracting and summarising input from participants is an agent actively engaged in group coalescing. Dryzek and Niemeyer (2006) claim that metaconsensus produces outcomes that are tractable and more legitimate than when metaconsensus is low. It also eliminates irrelevant and strategic arguments. van Gelder (2003) claims that the specification of an argument map goes a long way toward engaging participants to find a solution to a dispute. In our view, the group coalescing is a process that can be performed by participants or external personnel and produces, as an artefact, a representation of group reasoning or metaconsensus.

That group coalescing is performed frequently and represented explicitly is critical for deliberative democracy. Without constant coalescing, participants are readily overwhelmed by the complexity of knowledge, reasons, and claims in a large issue. Without some form of coalescing, deliberation can more readily degenerate into attacks on individual claims or onto individuals themselves. For instance, in the EFCPs, a facilitator was used to help the groups. The set of scenarios was modelled as a tree with 3 main branches (high carbon tax, late tax, no tax). In the Bloomfield Track study by Niemeyer and Blamey (2003), panellists were presented with five preferences and seven key factors to take into account as they deliberated. In particular, they agreed upon the set of relevant factors. For example, the impact of silt run-off on a nearby reef was removed from the list of environmental concerns after scientific evidence showed that this would be minimal.

Paradoxically, most of the approaches for representing individual reasoning are not readily applied to represent group coalescing. Personal stories are clearly not sufficiently generic. The syllogism or monotonic logics assume one truth so cannot represent multiple opinions. IBIS captures claims and reasons from a community in one map; however, the metaphor underpinning IBIS is combative.

By pitting arguments for a position against those against a position, IBIS focuses attention on points of disagreement between participants rather than identifying a shared understanding or metaconsensus. In our view, the Generic Argument Structure is a structure sufficiently general and abstract to represent different points of view

in a structure that focuses attention essentially on elements that are shared across a reasoning community; it is a representation of metaconsensus that can be used by participants in a reasoning community to instantiate their own claims and reasons in a standardized way. The Generic Argument Structure is not a representation of normative reasoning, rather, it is a representation of a normative structure of reasoning.

The Decision-Making Phase of a Deliberative Democracy Reasoning Community

In Athenian democracy, policy was ultimately decided by a simple majority vote of adult male citizens present at the discussion. Preferential voting schemes enable participants to rank their preferences and allow for more sophisticated aggregation of voting. Arrow (1963) identified four properties in social preference functions as follows:

- Universal Domain. The rationality of the outcome of a vote is maintained only if all voters use the same method for ordering preferences, and that method is acceptable to all the voters.
- Pareto Efficiency implies that the outcome is not rational if the voting system used does not consider voters' preferences.
- Non-dictatorship prohibits the outcome being dictated by one person.
- The independence from irrelevant alternatives entails that the order of preferences on the alternatives in the vote should not be affected by alternatives not being voted on.

According to Arrow's theorem (Arrow, 1963) it is impossible to construct a perfect system of voting that can satisfy all four fairness properties when there are more than two alternatives. List and Pettit (2002) note that the system known as the Borda Count system violates the fourth fairness condition though this is not regarded as necessarily disadvantageous. Niemeyer and Blamey (2003) compared three schemes, the Condorcet, Hare and Borda Count for the Bloomfield Track deliberation and found the final preferences differed for all three methods. Following further deliberation, the three methods were in complete agreement on rankings of the five solutions to the issue of sealing the outback road although there was a 7-5 split between two options.

Although voting schemes provide a fast, convenient mechanism for the determination of a final decision, there is a sense that resorting to a vote is not in keeping with the ideal of a deliberative discursive community as advanced by Habermas (1984). In that ideal, open dialogue unencumbered by power plays, false or missing information will lead naturally to a consensus. Once each participant is heard and rationality is exalted above other considerations, solutions can be agreed upon unanimously even if the solution goes against a particular individual's self-interest.

Features that characterize a deliberative democracy reasoning community from other reasoning communities can be identified at each phase of group reasoning. Currently, different measures of deliberative quality relate to some but not all of the features. In our view, this is an omission that can be clearly seen if a deliberative community is seen as an instance of a reasoning community. In the next section, other aspects of deliberative democracies are discussed.

Other Aspects of Electronic Democracy

Initiatives toward the advancement of electronic democracy do more than provide fora for deliberative democracy. The World Legal Information Institute (WorldLII) is a free, independent, and non-profit collaboration of a number of institutes dedicated to the provision of free access to public legal information throughout the world (World Legal Information Institute, 2007). Organisa-

tions such as the Australasian Legal Information Institute (AustLII), the British and Irish Legal Information Institute (BAILII), the Canadian Legal Information Institute (CanLII), the Hong Kong Legal Information Institute (HKLII), the Legal Information Institute (Cornell), and the Pacific Islands Legal Information Institute (PacLII) receive the text of judgments and statutes on a daily basis from thousands of courts and parliaments world-wide. Within a very short time frame, the text is automatically processed and uploaded to the relevant databases making the documents freely available to any Internet user. Other initiatives enhance the facility for citizens to voice their views to government. In Thailand, the Raking or Bell Ringing initiative provides an online avenue for complaints from citizens to be made directly to the prime minister. It operates as a feedback channel that augments the existing formal channels reminiscent of the traditional appeals directly to the ruler (Yong, 2005).

Initiatives to ensure that advanced communication technologies are readily accessible to all citizens include affordable access to the Internet, and a level of education and awareness to navigate effectively through the maze of information already available. This includes programs such as those envisaged by Macintosh et al. (2002) that aim to enhance participation by all age groups.

TOOLS TO SUPPORT REASONING

There is an emerging need for technologies to support reasoning communities whose members vary in their levels of expertise and background knowledge. Ideally, the systems need to be Web-based and to provide an interface that can both support the development of arguments and to provide visual information about the process. In this section, we detail three Web-based environments that can support diverse groups of users in reasoning and argumentation and describe some projects where they have been deployed. The first two environments use an IBIS-based model of argumentation, and the third environment is the one that we have developed and which is based upon the GAAM model of argumentation.

The Compendium Institute

As part of its commitment to social justice, the Open University in the United Kingdom has the mission of providing access to high-quality tertiary education to anyone who wishes to participate. It rose to prominence in the 1960s as one of the first universities to provide distance education by making use of improvements in communication technologies. Within the university is the Knowledge Media Institute (KMI), which is home to a number of projects aimed at developing technologies for improving knowledge modelling and use. The research team is led by Simon Buckingham-Shum and Albert Selvin.

Although education was the initial area of interest, some of KMI's tools have been deployed in a range of international projects. These projects are diverse in nature and have both made use of and led to developments in domains such as Cognition and Learning, Artificial Intelligence, Multimedia and Semantic Technologies. The Hypermedia Discourse programme has been running since 1995 and draws together elements of discourse theory and the use of hypermedia. It covers a number of projects including Compendium, the Digital Document Discourse Environment (D3E), Memetic, Open Sensemaking Communities, ScholOnto, and the Storymaking project. These projects and their relevance to our work are now outlined.

At the heart of the KMI's work is Compendium, which is a hypermedia software tool that is based upon the IBIS model of argumentation. It is a stand-alone product but can also be linked to various other tools. The developers describe Compendium as a knowledge management environment for supporting personal or group deliberations. The software is used to author and publish issue-based dialogue maps, which are concept networks that structure the issues and arguments in a discussion. These can be linked to relevant multimedia documents and Internet resources thereby enabling participants to follow the evolution of arguments and the evidence that is used to support them. Compendium has been applied to a number of projects involving participatory decision-making including the ECOSENSUS project in Guyana and the development of a draft Regional Plan for South East Queensland (SEQ) in Australia. In the latter application, members of the SEQ public were invited to submit comments, concerns, and questions on any issues in relation to the draft plan. Access was provided to the public via an online forum, multiple offline fora and written communications (including emails, posts, and faxes). More than 8000 formal written submissions were received via the ConsultQld online forum. Another domain of application of the Compendium software is in Design Rationale, which aims to develop effective methods and computer-supported representations for capturing, maintaining and re-using records of why designers have made the decisions they have. KMI also coordinates the GlobalArgument. net experiments, which map contemporary policy debates such as the Iraq invasion.

Memetic (Meeting Memory Technology Informing Collaboration) is an integrated set of tools to support the annotation and replay of Internet video conferences. It extends Compendium's capability for capturing the content of a meeting by integrating Compendium maps with the Access Grid video conferencing system to enable the generation of semantically indexed meeting replays. It uses index points of key moments (such as agenda items, decisions, actions, questions and ideas) to enable the user to jump to a particular point in a meeting replay.

The ScholOnto project was set up to address changes in how scholarly work is being undertaken and the results disseminated. The researchers believe that, rather than being published solely in prose, scholarly knowledge can be disseminated by use of the Internet, which also provides a means for enabling debate and analysis of ideas. To this end, they have developed a suite of experimental tools (including ClaiMaker and ClaimSpotter) for modelling scholarly literature as a network of claims, arguments and evidence. Claims are made by making connections between ideas, which can include counterarguments. The connections are based on an ontology of discourse/argumentation, which provides services for navigating, visualizing and analysing the argument network as it grows.

Related to the work on ScholOnto is the development of the Digital Document Discourse Environment (D3E). D3E is a toolkit for converting static HTML documents into discussion documents with navigational hyperlinks. Since 1996, D3E has been used at the Open University to publish the electronic Journal of Interactive Media in Education. The journal revolutionised the peer review process by enabling authors and reviewers to engage in a non-anonymous debate over submissions. The most interesting aspects of the process are co-published with the final multimedia articles. D3E was released as open source software, but it is no longer being supported.

Open Sensemaking Communities are collaborative tools for use by students and educators accessing the Open Educational Resources in the Open University's OpenLearn initiative. It has led to the publishing of thousands of hours of the university's distance learning resources on the Web. These materials are available for use free of charge.

The Storymaking project is aimed at developing a metadata scheme for annotating stories. The value of narrative as a means of reasoning has already been discussed (see Chapter 7). However, existing schemes for indexing stories can be inflexible and cannot take account of inherent ambiguities in stories. To address this, the KMI is developing expressive semantics for annotating stories that can reveal more interesting connections. The annotation schema is split into two dimensions: indexical dimensions, where the annotator is guided by an editor and relational dimensions, where the users work alone. The interface provides the user with a variety of ways to annotate a story, either in a freeform manner or guided by the underlying narrative scheme.

Zeno: A Mediating System for Group Decision Making

The Zeno system has already briefly been discussed in Chapter 2 as a system that implements the IBIS grammar. Work on Zeno began in 1995 (Brewka, Gordon, & Karacapilidis, 1995). The goal of the Zeno project was to design and implement a mediating system to support decision making in groups that was founded on a normative model of limited rationality. The system consists of the following four layers: Logic, Argumentation, Speech Act, and the Protocol layers. The initial prototype application for Zeno was developed to assist government and businesses with the retrieval, use and reuse of information, practices and knowledge in cooperative, distributed planning procedures requiring access to geographical information. Zeno participated in the Geographical Mediation Systems (GEOMED-F) feasibility project sponsored by the European Union.

Zeno was designed to be used in mediation systems, which are similar to discussion fora but with special support for argumentation, negotiation and group decision making. The dialectical graphs show the state of an argument at a particular point in time and emphasize the role of speech acts rather than their history. Participants make positions (rather than propositions), which are records of a speech act. Whilst propositions are declarative statements (true or false), a position is a statement whose veracity is context dependent. Each choice position of an issue is labelled either in or out to indicate whether or not it meets the proof standard selected for the issue. The authors state that there is no single standard that is appropriate for all issues. Rittel's IBIS model includes pro and con arguments, but they have no effect on the status of positions within the model. Zeno extends IBIS by including a means for expressing preferences and computing position labels, which overcomes this limitation. Given a set of preference expressions, it becomes possible to make inferences about the relative quality of alternative proposed solutions of an issue. A set of burden of proof standards was defined for this purpose. It is possible that more than one position may satisfy the proof standard for a particular issue. This enables interested parties to see whether their position is winning or losing at any point in time (Gordon & Karacapilidis, 1997).

Zeno has more recently been piloted in several e-democracy applications, including the Delphi Mediation Online System (DEMOS) project of the European Union (Gordon & Richter, 2002). In these applications, discourse is taken as dialogue about some language artefact, such as draft legislation, project proposals, or city plans. Similarly, a discourse support system is a system to support deliberation, consensus building, and conflict resolution with four main components:

- The actors (or participants in the dialogue) -the immediate reasoning community
- The document being discussed
- The dialogue about the document; and
- The norms that guide the dialogue and regulate any changes to the document -these come from the wider reasoning community.

A dialogue can comprise a variety of speech acts (questions, claims, and reasons). The norms also range in type (conventions, rules, laws) and can be in conflict and change with time. Therefore, the choice of norms and how to apply them is a source of difficulty in developing discourse systems. There are three main roles that can be adopted by the actors: readers, authors, and moderators. Readers are anyone with access to the dialogue document; authors can write to the document and moderators have the responsibility for editing the document and moderating the dialogue. Zeno was applied to an e-democracy

pilot application in the City of Esslingen, as part of the German Media@Komm project (Marker, Hagedorn, Trenel, & Gordon, 2002) and has also been used as a part of the foundation of the DEMOS system (Luhrs, Malsch, & Voss, 2001), which is an Internet-based e-democracy research and development project funded by the European Commission. The project aims to facilitate democratic discussions and participative public opinion formation to encourage all citizens to participate in such debates regardless of their interests, technical skills, or income. Pilot applications are being used in the cities of Bologna and Hamburg.

Zeno has also been used to support discourses between planners, contractors, clients, concerned parties and facilitators using the Internet. It can support participatory problem solving, consensus building, mediated conflict resolution, and consulting (Gordon, Voss, Richter, & Marker, 2001). Zeno has also been applied to education in the WINDS project, which is part of the European program on Information Society Technologies (IST). In WINDS, students and teachers from 20 European universities of architecture and civil engineering use Zeno to construct design rationales. As learning from precedents and reuse of designs is an important principle, teachers can create an associative network of concepts that indexes the elements of design rationales together with other learning material. There are a number of existing discourse support tools including: Descartes, D3E, Facilitate.com, MeetingWorks, Questmap, DRAMA, Decision Explorer, and Resolver. For a full discussion of mediation systems (see Gordon & Marker, 2002).

Araucaria and ArguMed are Toulmin-based tools with diagramming capability. Existing tools cannot model critical questions for modelling argument by expert opinion well. This has led to the development of a new argumentation framework, Carneades that combines a Toulmin model with diagramming. Improvements in software capability have led to changes in the original schemes for argumentation by expert opinion (Walton, 1997).

In Araucaria, each statement can be used as a premise in only one argument. In Carneades, a statement can be used as a premise in any number of arguments. This is the major difference between the two systems. The Carneades solution (Gordon & Walton, 2006) to the problem of critical questions is helped by its capability to support dialogue structures that enable implicit premises to be revealed dynamically as a dialogue proceeds.

e-Governance is about applying advanced information and communications technology to improve and support all tasks in governance. Governance, in the public context, is about how to manage, direct, or guide society in order to best serve public interests, that is, to achieve the common good. Gordon noted that most previous work in the area of governance had focused on organizational and communication issues related to the trend away from hierarchical towards networked forms of management and collaboration (Gordon, 2004). However, he maintained that there was a need for an approach that focuses on the central role of public policy, legislation, and regulations for guiding and directing society. He thought that placing the focus on the role of legislation would lead to increased awareness and appreciation of the potential of legal knowledge-based systems for governance. Further, he sees that the full potential of information and communications technology for improving the correctness, consistency, transparency, and efficiency of determinative processes of public administration will only be realized once systems that can support deep transactions are developed. The FOKUS Institute for Open Communications Systems of the Fraunhofer Gesellschaft, a non-profit association that aims to promote economic development by assisting companies to develop innovative products and services, founded an industry consortium consisting of all Legal Knowledge-Based System (LKBS) companies in Europe. The consortium aims to promote and develop advanced information and communications technology for improving the quality and efficiency of all tasks in the life cycle of legislation and regulations. This requires the use of appropriate industry standards to ensure the interoperability of eGovernance products. To this end, the consortium participates, wherever possible, in the activities leading to such standards.

Gordon (2005) sees governance as taking place in cycles. Phases of a cycle include: agenda setting, analysis, policy making/legislation, implementation and monitoring. E-governance is a particular application domain for any kind of information technology rather than as a particular kind of information technology per se. The agenda-setting phase, for example, should involve all players/actors. The use of DEMOS by the city of Hamburg is an example of a successful e-democracy application. Web logs (blogs) have enabled ordinary citizens to take an active role as commentator, rather than the more passive role of being consumers of information. At the analysis stage (brainstorming solutions), Gordon sees the need for Internet groupware, data mining packages and simulation software to help people understand possible outcomes of proposed solutions. He cites Araucaria as an example of software that has been designed to help people keep track of complex arguments. Legislative drafting could be assisted by the use of groupware to support discourse and rule-based systems for encoding the legislation. He sees knowledge-based systems as being particularly valuable in the implementation phase and other kinds of information technology (such as online databases of the full text of precedent cases) as having value in supporting attorneys and the courts.

In the Carneades model of argumentation legal rules are interpreted as reasoning policies, by mapping them in the semantics to argumentation schemes (Gordon, 2007). The system can be extended by employing models of other argumentation schemes. By entirely abandoning the relational interpretation of argumentation in favour of a purely procedural view, it is more in line with modern argumentation theory in philosophy.

Tools Based on the GAAM and Decision Graphs

We have developed a suite of tools to support decision makers and have applied them to a variety of projects in different domains. JustReason (Yearwood & Stranieri, 2000; Stranieri & Zeleznikow, 2000b; Stranieri, et al., 2001; Yearwood & Meikle, 2000) is a Web-based environment for modelling discretionary domains that has been applied to a number of projects

JustReason was developed over a decade based upon the results of a number of research projects. Initially, the Web shell used a combination of decision trees (for modelling procedural tasks) and argument trees (for modelling discretion). The decision trees use sentence fragments rather than the usual labels for concepts, arcs, and conclusions. The knowledge contained in the trees is mapped into sets called sequence transition networks that are stored in a relational database so that they can be retrieved for reuse. The shell also provides multiple inference mechanisms including neural nets, rule-based, and human. This provides flexibility that is not found in systems with a single inference mechanism and it enables decision makers from a variety of domains to produce reasoning-to-conclusion that can be reused in later situations.

A second shell, ArgumentDeveloper (Yearwood & Stranieri, 2000) was used to facilitate discussion/construction of arguments. It is based upon the GAAM (Yearwood & Stranieri, 2006) and enables the modelling of discretion. The latest version of the software was released in 2005. The current suite of tools includes:

- **justReason:** An open source inference engine. Knowledge that decision makers use is represented with decision trees and new structures we call argument trees following insights from artificial intelligence research. JustReason draws on knowledge bases (stored as standard relational database tables) and automatically produces Web pages that encode sequence of prompts that guide users to a conclusion;

- **justDraw:** A computer program that enables experts to draw decision and argument trees that represent their own reasoning steps. JustDraw automatically converts the drawings into SQL commands so that the knowledge bases can be implemented as relational databases ready to be drawn upon by justReason;

- **justForms:** A data entry form generator that integrates into justReason. This tool can be used by non-programmers to generate Web-based data entry forms so that applications that integrate decision support with intelligent data entry can be readily developed and maintained;

- **justReport:** A tool that generates reports in rich text format suitable for any word processor on any platform. The justReport tool enables developers or experts to create their own reports in a flexible way; and

- **justInfer:** A knowledge maintenance program that makes it easier for experts to evaluate their own inferences.

The flexibility of the JustReason approach is demonstrated by the diversity of its applications. To date, JustReason has been applied in a number of projects in copyright law, family law, refugee law, health, determining eligibility for government legal aid, career advice for the Technical and Further Education (TAFE) sector, e-commerce, e-tourism and education in law. These are now briefly described.

Copyright Law: RIGHTCOPY

Regulating copyright on the Internet is problematic because of jurisdictional and enforcement difficulties (Stranieri & Zeleznikow, 2000c; Stranieri & Zeleznikow, 2001). To overcome these problems, the authors developed knowledge-based systems that use an agent-based architecture that defines the actors, the knowledge shared by the agents and a protocol to interact with other agents. The shared knowledge is represented at two levels using GAAM. Three broad positions regarding responses to copyright in the digital age are outlined (complete overhaul, partial revision, and little or no change).

Family Law: SPLIT-UP

SPLIT-UP is a hybrid rule-based/neural net tool for modelling the reasoning that a judge of the Family Court of Australia performs in arriving at a percentage split of assets of a failed marriage (Zeleznikow & Stranieri, 1997c; Stranieri & Zeleznikow, 1998b; Stranieri, 1999). Reasoning in family law is represented using decision trees and argument trees. The main aim is to separate the layout or structure of reasoning from inferences. By doing this, it becomes easier to model inferences. The Split Up prototype was written with webShell. It represents reasoning as arguments consistent with the generic actual argument model of structured reasoning developed by the researchers. The original Split Up has been exposed to hundreds of cases decided by Family Court judges. Intended users include people going through a divorce, lawyers not familiar with family law, mediators, counsellors and accountants providing financial advice to a client going through a divorce.

A related study is the FAMILY LAW ORDERS system, which provides support for determining financial provision for divorce under Scots law.

Refugee Law: EMBRACE

EMBRACE is a decision support system designed to assist the Refugee Review Tribunal of Australia (RRT) in maintaining consistency of decisions, and preserve discretion of decision makers as well as making it easier to cope with high volumes of work in decreasing time frames (Yearwood & Stranieri, 1999; Yearwood & Meikle, 2000).

Education: ADVOKATE

The ADVOKATE system provides support for analysing eyewitness testimony to assess its reliability (Bromby, MacMillan, & McKellar, 2003). The prototype was built using the expert system shell justReason and was deployed on the Internet. It was designed to model eyewitness testimony. The system is not only a tool for use by practitioners in law, but is also capable of direct transfer into a learning environment. The system has been used by students taking a level 3 module in the law of evidence at Glasgow Caledonian University. The authors do not provide any evidence of their results.

Criminal Sentencing

Magistrates are often accused of being inconsistent in sentencing but baulk at the thought of rigid guidelines that stifle discretion and often result in unfair sentences (Hall, Calabro, Sourdin, Stranieri, & Zeleznikow, 2005). By modelling the way in which sentences are constructed, the system provides a way for magistrates to demonstrate consistency without losing discretion.

Health: The ICU Story

This project models decision-making processes in a health-care setting and demonstrates the need for professionals to make their reasoning both transparent and consistent (Stranieri, Yearwood, Gervasoni, Garner, Deans, & Johnstone, 2004). The researchers developed a method for representing complex and discretionary reasoning to model the decision-making processes that critical-care nurses deploy in responding to a low oxygen alarm. The approach enabled the rapid development of a Web-based decision support system. Two experienced intensive care unit nurses met a few times with a JustSys knowledge engineer to learn how to represent their knowledge of the best way that ICU nurses should respond to a ventilator alarm. A hospital IT employee uploaded the charts to the justReason knowledge base and set up a personal computer with open software to run justReason. The system can be accessed by any ICU staff member and is now being used to train novice ICU staff.

Career Advice

Options Career Exploration is a career exploration tool that was developed by JustSys for the TAFE Virtual Campus. Most websites that provide career advice engage a job seeker in hundreds of questions to build a psychological profile that is matched to suitable jobs. Most users find the questions tedious and users who have few job skills can become intimidated by this barrage of questions. By talking to career experts (who do not ask 200 questions), JustSys knowledge engineers designed a system that provides useful advice easily, without intimidation.

Ethics Applications

JustSys has developed an Advisory System for the electronic submission of applications for Human and Animal Research Ethics. It was specifically designed to help researchers to apply for Ethics Committee approval and to support Ethics committees in their decision-making.

Legal Aid: GetAid

The GetAid system helps to determine a client's eligibility for legal aid in Victoria. Lawyers at a government-funded legal aid organisation wanted to be able to apply for aid and have the application assessed for merit as easily and quickly as possible. By integrating legal aid guidelines with the practice heuristics of expert grants officers, JustSys knowledge engineers were able to build a system, GetAid. Lawyers access GetAid over the Web, lodge their application, and have an expert, prima facie determination made on the spot. The accuracy of this Web-based decision support system was evaluated favourably in a trial that compared GetAid determinations with grants officers on over 600 cases (Hall, Stranieri, & Zeleznikow, 2002; Hall, Hall, & Zeleznikow, 2003).

FUTURE DIRECTIONS

The review of the current state of tools to support reasoning communities is deliberately quite broad and considers a range of tools that pertain more to individuals than to communities. It particularly identifies that the concept of supporting reasoning, as distinct from decision-making or argument, is starting to emerge. At the same time, there is emergence and recognition of the fact that there are needs to support a range of different possible participants in reasoning in different ways in a reasoning community. Therefore, for example, we see a move to recognise and support the various roles that the patient may want to play in the reasoning and decision-making processes around the diagnosis and treatment of their health problems. Similarly, it is no longer permissible for water authorities to reason and make decisions on a purely utilitarian and economic basis. These decisions have to recognise and include the social, environmental, and cultural perspectives as well. There is also a stronger need for the broad range of stakeholders to be able to access the reasoning used in reaching these decisions. In many cases, whole communities need to be involved in the development of approaches to better manage scarce resources (such as water) at a time when greater strains are placed on them by factors like global warming and competing interests.

It is also apparent that there is a desire for both individuals and communities to make more use of approaches and tools that can lead to better reasoning and decision-making. There is also evidence of a need for tools that are Web-based and that have the ability to link to other tools. Some of these include: tools for communication, collaboration, visualization of reasoning, ontological support and tools to help organize, search and make sense of large information repositories.

We anticipate that the highest use will be in areas where discourse/reasoning is needed and that this will include many areas beyond the traditional areas of law, science, and education. The emerging areas are in financial planning and management, e-democracy, health, the environment, and group decision making in organizations.

WHAT IS NEEDED IN TOOLS

The 2003 Issues Paper by the Australian Administrative Review Council (2003) regarding the use of automated assistance in administrative decision-making systems noted that such systems were increasingly being used by both Commonwealth and state government agencies. In particular, the paper discussed the use of rule-based systems and neural net systems. The Issues Paper also noted a number of departments that, at the time, had not made and did not intend to make use of administrative decision support systems. However, some agencies did make considerable use of ADSSs (particularly risk assessment tools) including the Agriculture Fisheries and Forestry Australia (AFFA) and the Australian Tax Office (ATO). AFFA used a range of tools: the Ballast Water Decision Support System, the Vessel Monitoring System, systems used by the Dairy Adjustment Authority and the Australian Special Information Systems (including GIS capability). It also noted the development of the Quarantine Risk Indicator (QRI) project, which will determine the risk associated with goods of quarantine interest. The Australian Taxation Office used a neural network system called Netrisk, which is a debt risk-profiling application. The 2007 report discussed many of the same issues and included new case studies from both the department of Veterans' Affairs and Medicare (AGIMO, 2007). A major problem arises because systems are typically chosen to be used in a single agency and there is

little support for tracking and storing decisions for reuse. The AARC (2003) noted that: "the use of rule-based systems has evolved without consideration (other than on an agency-by-agency basis) of the administrative review questions that arise. For example, how is discretion exercised when a rule-base system is being used?"

The Issues paper makes some recommendations for the design of ADSSs so that they meet administrative law standards in discretionary domains and embody administrative law values and administrative justice. The two most important issues to address were the need for flexible, Web-based programs and the need for the decision makers to be able to exercise discretion (Stranieri, et al., 2000).

French and Turoff (2007) commented on the state of DSSs in the domain of disaster management. They contend that no existing system is able to provide the type of environment that is required to manage man-made or natural disasters. The authors also criticize the developers of the technology and suggest that artificial intelligence has been applied inappropriately. They suggest that the focus has been on applying artificial intelligence to the solution of a part of the problem without considering how it could contribute to a total environment. That is, DSSs need to be embedded in workflow systems rather than operating separately. The workflow systems themselves need to be flexible if they are to meet the requirements of a range of disaster scenarios. These requirements include tools for communication and visualization, identifying and balancing objectives as well as identifying issues and structuring problems, because it is necessary to manage both tacit and explicit knowledge. Often it is tacit knowledge that is particularly important in emergency situations because explicit knowledge is not available. This entails the need for collaboration tools, which to date have not been implemented in the domain of disaster management.

There is also clear recognition that there is little capacity for reuse in the systems that have been developed and it is appropriate that this is documented here. In this chapter, numerous systems with a range of approaches have been presented as efforts towards supporting individual reasoners and in some cases group reasoning. There is a notable lack of the ability in these approaches to represent the reasoning in ways that can be reused. Therefore, there is a clear need for approaches that allow reasoning communities to develop their reasoning repositories and coalesced reasoning in reusable ways.

Against a backdrop of global and societal drivers that include developments in ICT, global/online business, global threats, global phenomena models and citizens becoming more involved in decision making that affects them directly, there is a need to have a range of support for effective individual and group reasoning support. There is a growing need for better government, largely driven by the democratic need for transparency and consistency in decision-making. This requires reasoning approaches that can model multiple perspectives, multiple criteria and include discretion. This has led to the need for Web-based, accessible systems, particularly ones that can support dialogue. At the moment we see that designers of ODR systems believe that the systems should be knowledge-based and thereby contain and make use of the appropriate legal principles.

There is an emerging recognition of a need for approaches that can support groups in working cooperatively in making decisions. In most contexts, the reasons provided for this include a greater need for consistency of decisions and a greater need for transparency of the processes that led to them. These are only some of the indicators of the outcome of better overall reasoning. By beginning this chapter with a flashback to 'The Age of Reason,' we set the scene to look at what has happened since the seventeenth century in terms of the importance of reasoning. It seems that there is now a tendency to skirt around the notion of valuing better reasoning and seeking better outcomes,

better decisions, greater transparency and higher levels of consistency. What we are really seeing is a devolution of the need for better reasoning, not just at the philosopher or intelligentsia level as in the seventeenth century but at all levels of society. The groups and communities involved are reasoning communities and primarily value being reasonable. It is time to make this explicit and recognise a need for tools that can support this pervasive trend. In summary, these tools should:

- Capture reasoning in a reusable form
- Capture and represent multiple perspectives
- Capture and represent multiple criteria where these are relevant and necessary
- Clearly identify the participants of the reasoning community and its broader intended audience
- Support appropriate collaborative and communication mechanisms
- Provide structure for coalesced reasoning at both the individual and the group level; and
- Be interoperable with a number of resources and other tools, particularly those that support dialogue.

REFERENCES

Adlassnig, K., & Horak, W. (1995). Development and retrospective evaluation of hepaxpert-i: A routinely-used expert system for interpretive analysis of hepatitis a and b serologic findings. *Artificial Intelligence in Medicine, 7*(1), 1–24. doi:10.1016/0933-3657(94)00023-L

Adriaenssens, V., De Baets, B., Goethals, P., & De Pauw, N. (2004). Fuzzy rule-based models for decision support in ecosystem management. *The Science of the Total Environment, 319*, 1–12. doi:10.1016/S0048-9697(03)00433-9

Adrianto, L., Matsuda, Y., & Sakuma, Y. (2005). Assessing local sustainability of fisheries system: A multi-criteria participatory approach with the case of Yoron island, Kagoshima prefecture, Japan. *Marine Policy, 29*, 9–23. doi:10.1016/j.marpol.2004.01.004

Afshar, F., Yearwood, J., & Stranieri, A. (2006). A tool for assisting group decision-making for consensus outcomes in organizations. In Voges, K. E., & Pope, N. K. L. (Eds.), *Business Applications and Computational Intelligence* (pp. 316–343). Hershey, PA: IGI Global. doi:10.4018/978-1-59140-702-7.ch016

Antunes, P., & Costa, C. (2003). From genre analysis to the design of meetingware. In *Proceedings of the 2003 International ACM SIGGROUP Conference on Supporting Group Work*, (pp. 302-310). Sanibel Island, FL: ACM Press.

Antunes, P., Costa, C., & Pino, J. (2006). The use of genre analysis in the design of electronic meeting systems. *Information Research, 11*(3). Retrieved from http://www.di.fc.ul.pt/paa/papers/ir-06.pdf.

Antunes, P., Ho, T., & Carrico, L. (1999). A GDSS agenda builder for inexperienced facilitators. In *Proceedings of the 10th EuroGDSS Workshop*, (pp. 1-15). Delft, The Netherlands: Delft University of Technology. Retrieved from http://www.di.fc.ul.pt/paa/papers/egdss-99.pdf.

Antunes, P. C. C., & Dias, J. (2001). Applying genre analysis to ems design: The example of a small accounting firm. In *Proceedings of the Seventh International Workshop on Groupware, CRIWG 2001*, (pp. 74-81). Darmstadt, Germany: IEEE CS Press. Retrieved from http://www.di.fc.ul.pt/paa/papers/criwg-01.pdf.

Ardente, F., Beccali, G., & Cellura, M. (2003). Eco-sustainable energy and environmental strategies in design for recycling: The software end-less. *Ecological Modelling, 163*(12), 101–118. doi:10.1016/S0304-3800(02)00418-0

Arrow, K. J. (1963). *Social choice and individual values*. New York, NY: Wiley.

Ayoub, N., Martins, R., Wang, K., Seki, H., & Naka, Y. (2007). Two levels decision system for efficient planning and implementation of bioenergy production. *Energy Conversion and Management, 48*(3), 709–723. doi:10.1016/j.enconman.2006.09.012

Bellucci, E., Lodder, A., & Zeleznikow, J. (2004). Integrating artificial intelligence, argumentation and game theory to develop an online dispute resolution environment. In *Proceeding of the 16th IEEE International Conference on Tools with Artificial Intelligence (ICTAI 2004)*, (pp. 7490754). Los Alamitos, CA: IEEE Computer Society.

Bellucci, E., & Zeleznikow, J. (2001). Representations for decision making support in negotiation. *Journal of Decision Support, 10*(3-4), 449–479. doi:10.3166/jds.10.449-479

Bessette, J. (1994). *The mild voice of reason: Deliberative democracy & american national government*. Chicago, IL: University of Chicago Press.

Brewka, G., Gordon, T., & Karacapilidis, N. (1995). Mediating systems for group decision making: The zeno system. In *Proceedings of the KI-95 Workshop 4 -Computational Dialectics: Models of Argumentation, Negotiation and Decision Making*. Retrieved from www.tfgordon.de/publications/Brewka1995a.pdf.

Bromby, M., MacMillan, M., & McKellar, P. (2003). *Edu-KATE -A resource for learning the law of evidence*. Retrieved from http://www.caledonian.ac.uk/lss/global/contactmaps/staff/bromby/BILETA2003.pdf.

Brucher, H., & Baumberger, P. (2003). Using mobile technology to support edemocracy. In *Proceedings of the 36th Annual Hawaii International Conference on System Sciences*. Washington, DC: IEEE Computer Society.

Cabri, G., Ferrari, L., & Leonardi, L. (2005). A role-based mobile-agent approach to support e-democracy. *Applied Soft Computing, 6*(1), 85–99. doi:10.1016/j.asoc.2004.12.001

Carvalho, A., Rocha, R., & Oliveira, M. A. (2004). SINUP: Using GIS to support e-democracy. *Lecture Notes in Computer Science, 2739*, 341–344. doi:10.1007/10929179_61

Ceccaroni, L., Cortes, U., & Sanchez-Marre, M. (2004). Ontowedss: Augmenting environmental decision-support systems with ontologies. *Ontologies Environmental Modelling & Software, 19*, 785–797. doi:10.1016/j.envsoft.2003.03.006

Chang, N.-B., Wei, Y., Tseng, C., & Kao, C.-Y. (1997). The design of a GIS-based decision support system for chemical emergency preparedness and response in an urban environment. *Computers, Environment and Urban Systems, 21*(1), 67–94. doi:10.1016/S0198-9715(97)01009-0

Chutimaskul, W., & Funilkul, S. (2004). The framework of e-democracy development. *Lecture Notes in Computer Science, 3183*, 27–30. doi:10.1007/978-3-540-30078-6_5

Constantino-Gonzalez, M., & Suthers, D. (2003). Automated coaching of collaboration based on workspace analysis: Evaluation and implications for future learning environments. In *Proceedings of the 36th Hawaii International Conference on System Sciences HICSS-36*, (p. 32). Big Island, HI: IEEE Computer Society.

Costa, C., & Antunes, P. (2001). Meetings as genre systems: Some consequences for EMS design. In *Proceedings of Group Decision & Negotiation 2001*, (pp. 261-263). La Rochelle, France: Group Design and Negotiation. Retrieved from http://www.di.fc.ul.pt/ paa/papers/gdn-01b.pdf.

Dickinson, H. (1998). Evidence-based decision making: An argumentative approach. *International Journal of Medical Informatics, 51*, 71–81. doi:10.1016/S1386-5056(98)00105-1

Doukas, H., Patlitzianas, K., & Psarras, J. (2006). Supporting sustainable electricity technologies in Greece using MCDM. *Resources Policy, 31*(2), 129–136. doi:10.1016/j.resourpol.2006.09.003

Dreiseitl, S., & Binder, M. (2005). Do physicians value decision support? A look at the effect of decision support systems on physician opinion. *Artificial Intelligence in Medicine, 33*, 25–30. doi:10.1016/j.artmed.2004.07.007

Dryzek, J. (1990). *Discursive democracy: Politics, policy and political science*. Cambridge, UK: Cambridge University Press.

Dryzek, J. (2002). *Deliberative democracy and beyond: Liberals, critics, contestations*. Oxford, UK: Oxford University Press. doi:10.1093/019925043X.001.0001

Dryzek, J., & Niemeyer, S. (2006). Reconciling pluralism and consensus as political ideals. *American Journal of Political Science, 50*(3), 634–649. doi:10.1111/j.1540-5907.2006.00206.x

Emery, M., & Purser, R. E. (1996). *The search conference: A powerful method for planning organisational change and community action*. San Francisco, CA: Jossey Bass.

Facione, P. (1990). *Critical thinking: A statement of expert consensus*. Millbrae, CA: California Academic Press.

Facione, P. (1992). *The California critical thinking skills test and manual*. Millbrae, CA: California Academic Press.

Fang, L., Hipel, K., Kilgour, D., & Peng, X. (2003a). A decision support system for interactive decision making, part 1: Model formulation. *IEEE Transactions on Systems, Man and Cybernetics. Part C, 33*(1), 42–55.

Fang, L., Hipel, W., Kilgour, D., & Peng, X. (2003b). A decision support system for interactive decision making, part 2: Analysis and output interpretation. *IEEE Transactions on Systems, Man and Cybernetics. Part C, 33*(1), 56–66.

Fes, J., Giupponi, C., & Rosato, P. (2004). Water management, public participation and decision support systems: The mulino approach. In C. P. Wostl, S. Schmidt, A. Rizzoli, & A. J. Jakeman (Eds.), *Complexity and Integrated Resources Management: Transactions of the 2nd Biennial Meeting of the International Environmental Modelling and Software Society*. Osnabruck, Germany: IEMSS. Retrieved from http://www.iemss.org/iemss2004/sessions/dss2.html.

Figueira, J., Greco, S., & Ehrgott, M. (2005). *Multiple criteria decision analysis: State of the art surveys*. New York, NY: Springer.

Fishkin, J. (1991). *Democracy and deliberation: New directions for democratic reform*. New Haven, CT: Yale University Press.

French, S., & Turoff, M. (2007). Decision support systems. *Communications of the ACM, 50*(3), 39–40. doi:10.1145/1226736.1226762

Goodman, J. (2003). The pros and cons of online dispute resolution: An assessment of cyber-mediation websites. *Duke Law and Technology Review, 4*. Retrieved from http://www.law.duke.edu/journals/dltr/articles/2003dltr0004.html.

Gordon, T. (2004). *Egovernance and its value for public administration: Knowledge-based services for the public sector*. Paper presented at the Symposium on Knowledge-Based Services for the Public Sector. Bonn, Germany.

Gordon, T. (2005). Information technology for good governance. In D. Bourcier (Ed.), *Proceedings of the French-German Symposium on Governance, Law and Technology*, (pp. 87-95). Paris, France: University of Paris.

Gordon, T. (2007). Constructing arguments with a computational model of an argumentation scheme for legal rules: Interpreting legal rules as reasoning policies. In R. Winkels (Ed.), *Proceedings of the Eleventh International Conference on Artificial Intelligence and Law*. New York, NY: ACM Press.

Gordon, T., & Karacapilidis, N. (1997). The zeno argumentation framework. In *Proceedings of the Sixth International Conference on Artificial Intelligence and Law*, (pp. 10-18). Melbourne, Australia: ACM Press.

Gordon, T., & Marker, O. (2002). Mediation systems. In Marker, O., & Trenel, M. (Eds.), *Neue Medien in Der Konfliktvermittlung - Mit Beispielen Aus Politik Und Wirtschaft* (pp. 61–84). Berlin, Germany: Edition Sigma.

Gordon, T., & Richter, G. (2002). In Lenk, K., & Traunm¨uller, R. (Eds.). Lecture Notes in Computer Science: *Vol. 248–255. Discourse support systems for deliberative democracy*.

Gordon, T., Voss, A., Richter, G., & Marker, O. (2001). Zeno: Groupware for discourses on the internet. *K¨unstliche Intelligenz, 2*(1), 43–45.

Gordon, T., & Walton, D. (2006). The carneades argumentation framework: Using presumptions and exceptions to model critical questions. In *Proceedings of the First International Conference on Computational Models of Argument (COMMA 2006)*, (pp. 208-219). Liverpool, UK: IOS Press.

Gross, T. (2000). Technological support for e-democracy: History and perspectives. In *Proceedings of 11th International Workshop on Database and Expert Systems Applications*, (pp. 391-395). London, UK: ACM.

Habermas, J. (1984). *The theory of communicative action*. Cambridge, UK: Polity Press.

Hall, M. J., Calabro, D., Sourdin, T., Stranieri, A., & Zeleznikow, J. (2005). Supporting discretionary decision making with information technology: A case study in the criminal sentencing jurisdiction. *University of Ottawa Law & Technology Journal, 2*(1), 1–36.

Hall, M. J., Hall, R., & Zeleznikow, J. (2003). A process for evaluating legal knowledge-based systems based upon the context criteria contingency-guidelines framework. In Proceedings of the 9th International Conference on Artificial Intelligence and Law, (pp. 274-283). ACM Press.

Hall, M. J. J., Stranieri, A., & Zeleznikow, J. (2002). A strategy for evaluating web-based discretionary decision support systems. In *Proceedings of ADBIS2002 -Sixth East-European Conference on Advances in Databases and Information Systems*, (pp. 108-120). Bratislava, Slovak Republic: Slovak University of Technology.

Hamalainen, R. (2003). Decisionarium -Aiding decisions, negotiating and collecting opinions on the web. *Journal of Multi-Criteria Decision Analysis, 12*, 101–110. doi:10.1002/mcda.350

Hamouda, L., Hipel, K., & Kilgour, D. (2004). Shellfish conflict in baynes sound: A strategic perspective. *Environmental Management, 34*(4), 474–486. Retrieved from http://www.systems.uwaterloo.ca/Research/CAG/journals.html doi:10.1007/s00267-004-0227-2

Hamouda, L., Hipel, K., Kilgour, D., Noakes, D., Fang, L., & McDaniels, T. (2005). The salmon aquaculture conflict in British Columbia: A graph model analysis. *Ocean and Coastal Management, 48*(7-8), 571–587. doi:10.1016/j.ocecoaman.2005.02.001

Hatcher, M. (1994). Voting and priorities in health care decision making, portrayed through a group decision support system, using analytic hierarchy process. *Journal of Medical Systems, 18*(5), 267–288. doi:10.1007/BF00996606

Hathorn, L., & Ingram, A. (2002). Cooperation and collaboration using computer-mediated communication. *Journal of Educational Computing Research, 26*(3), 325–347. doi:10.2190/7MKH-QVVN-G4CQ-XRDU

Heckerman, D., Horvitz, E., & Nathwani, B. (1992). Toward normative expert systems: Part I: The pathfinder project. *Methods of Information in Medicine, 31*(2), 90–105.

Hipel, K., Fang, L., & Kilgour, D. (2008). Decision support systems in water resources and environmental management. *Journal of Hydrologic Engineering, 13*(9), 287–300. doi:10.1061/(ASCE)1084-0699(2008)13:9(761)

Ho, T., & Antunes, P. (1999). Developing a tool to assist electronic facilitation of decision-making groups. In *Proceedings of the Fifth International Workshop on Groupware, CRIWG 1999*, (pp. 243-252). Cancun, Mexico: IEEE CS Press. Retrieved from http://www.di.fc.ul.pt/ paa/papers/criwg-99.pdf.

Jaeger, P. (2004). The social impact of an accessible e-democracy: Disability rights laws in the development of the federal e-government. *Journal of Disability Policy Studies, 15*(1), 19–26. doi:10.1177/10442073040150010401

Janis, I. (1983). *Groupthink: Psychological studies of policy decisions and fiascos*. Boston, MA: Houghton Mifflin.

Jimenez, A., Mateos, A., & Ros-Insua, S. (2005). Monte Carlo simulation techniques in a decision support system for group decision making. *Group Decision and Negotiation, 14*(2), 109–130. doi:10.1007/s10726-005-2406-9

Kampen, J. K., & Snijkers, K. (2003). E-democracy. *Social Science Computer Review, 21*(4), 491–496. doi:10.1177/0894439303256095

Kaplan, B. (2001). Evaluating informatics applications -Clinical decision support systems literature review. *International Journal of Medical Informatics, 64*, 15–37. doi:10.1016/S1386-5056(01)00183-6

Kersten, G., & Noronha, S. (1999). Negotiation via the world wide web: A cross-cultural study of decision making. *Group Decision and Negotiation*, 8(3), 251–279. Retrieved from http://www.iiasa.ac.at/Publications/Documents/IR-97-052.pdf doi:10.1023/A:1008657921819

Kilgour, D. (2003). *Encyclopedia of life support systems*. Oxford, UK: EOLSS Publishers.

Kock, N., & Antunes, P. (2007). Government funding of e-collaboration research in the European union: A comparison with the united states model. *Journal of e-Collaboration, 3*(2), 36–47. Retrieved from http://www.di.fc.ul.pt/paa/papers/jec-07.pdf.

Kuziemsky, C., & Jahnke, J. (2005). Information systems and health care v -A multi-modal approach to health care decision support systems. *Communications of the Association for Information Systems, 16*, 407–420.

Laukkanen, S., Palander, T., Kangas, J., & Kangas, A. (2005). Evaluation of the multicriteria approval method for timber-harvesting group decision support. *Silva Fennica, 39*, 249–264.

Lee, Y., & Koh, K.-K. (2002). Decision-making of nuclear energy policy: application of environmental management tool to nuclear fuel cycle. *Energy Policy, 30*(13), 1151–1161. doi:10.1016/S0301-4215(02)00004-6

Lipponen, L., Rahikainen, M., Hakkarainen, K., & Palonen, T. (2002). Effective participation and discourse through a computer network: Investigating elementary students computer supported interaction. *Journal of Educational Computing Research, 27*(4), 355–384. doi:10.2190/MGTW-QG1E-G66E-F3UD

List, C., & Pettit, P. (2002). Aggregating sets of judgments: Two impossibility results compared. *Economics and Philosophy, 18*, 89–110.

Littleboy, A., Boughen, N., Niemeyer, S., & Fisher, K. (2006). *Societal uptake of alternative energy futures: Final report. Technical report.* Newcastle, UK: CSIRO Energy Transformed Research Flagship.

Liu, X., & Wirtz, K. W. (2006). Decision making of oil spill contingency options with fuzzy comprehensive evaluation. *Water Resources Management, 21*(4), 663–676. doi:10.1007/s11269-006-9031-5

Lodder, A. (1998). *DiaLaw -On legal justification and dialog games*. PhD thesis.

Lodder, A. (1999). *DiaLaw -On legal justification and dialogical models of argumentation*. Dordrecht, The Netherlands: Kluwer Academic Publishers.

Lodder, A., & Bol, S. (2006). *Towards an online negotiation environment: Legal principles, technical requirements and the need for close cooperation.* Retrieved from http://www.odr.info/papers.php.

Lodder, A., & Verheij, B. (1998). Opportunities of computer-mediated legal argument in education. In *Proceedings of the BILETA-Conference*. Dublin, Ireland: BILETA.

Lodder, A. R., & Zeleznikow, J. (2005). Developing an online dispute resolution environment: Dialogue tools and negotiation systems in a three step model. *Harvard Negotiation Law Review, 10*, 287–337.

Luhrs, R., Malsch, T., & Voss, K. (2001). Internet, discourses and democracy. In T. Terano (Ed.), *New Frontiers in Artificial Intelligence: Joint JSAI 2001 Workshop Post-Proceedings*. London, UK: Springer.

Macintosh, A., Robson, E., Smith, E., & Whyte, A. (2002). Electronic democracy and young people. *Social Science Computer Review, 21*(1), 43–54. doi:10.1177/0894439302238970

Mackie, J. (1980). *The cement of the universe: A study of causation.* Oxford, UK: Clarendon Press.

Mango, L. (1994). Computer-assisted cervical cancer screening using neural networks. *Cancer Letters, 77*(2/3), 155–162. doi:10.1016/0304-3835(94)90098-1

Manville, B., & Ober, J. (2003). *A company of citizens: What the world's first democracy teaches leaders about creating great organizations.* Boston, MA: Harvard Business School Press.

Marashi, E., & Davis, J. P. (2006). An argumentation-based method for managing complex issues in design of infrastructural systems. *Reliability Engineering & System Safety, 91*(12), 1535–1545. doi:10.1016/j.ress.2006.01.013

Marker, O., Hagedorn, H., Trenel, M., & Gordon, T. (2002). Internet-based citizen participation in the city of Esslingen: Relevance moderation – Software. In M. Schrenk (Ed.), *CORP 2002: Who plans Europe's future? Technical University International Symposium on Information Technology in Urban and Regional Planning and Impacts of ICT on Physical Space.* Vienna, Austria: Information Technology in Urban and Regional Planning.

Melbourne Corporation. (2007). *Channel deepening project environment effects statement.* Technical report. Melbourne, Australia: Port of Melbourne Corporation.

Mochol, M. (2004). Discourse support design patterns. In A. Lodder (Ed.), *Essays on Legal and Technical Aspects of Online Dispute Resolution,* (pp. 61-74). Amsterdam, The Netherlands: CE-DIRE: Centre for Electronic Dispute Resolution.

Morge, M., & Beaune, P. (2004). A negotiation support system based on a multi-agent system: Specificity and preference relations on arguments. In *Proceedings of the 2004 ACM Symposium on Applied Computing,* (pp. 474-478). New York, NY: ACM Press.

Morozow, O. (2006). *The heat is on: The future of energy in Australia. Technical report.* Melbourne, Australia: Commonwealth Scientific and Industrial Research Organisation.

Muecke, N., & Stranieri, A. (2008). An argument structure abstraction for Bayesian belief networks: Just outcomes in on-line dispute resolution. In *Proceedings of the Fourth Asia-Pacific Conference on Conceptual Modelling,* (Vol 67), (pp. 35-40). IEEE.

Ness, B., Urbel-Piirsalu, E., Anderberg, S., & Olsson, L. (2007). Categorising tools for sustainability assessment. *Ecological Economics, 60*(3), 498–509. doi:10.1016/j.ecolecon.2006.07.023

Niemeyer, S., & Blamey, R. (2003). *The far north Queensland citizens' jury. Technical report.* Canberra, Australia: Land and Water Australia.

Niemeyer, S. J. (2007). *Intersubjective rationality: Measuring deliberative quality.* Paper presented to Political Science Seminar, RSSS, ANU. Canberra, Australia.

Noakes, D., Fang, L., Hipel, K., & Kilgour, D. (2005). The pacific salmon treaty: A century of debate and an uncertain future. *Group Decision and Negotiation, 14*(6), 501–522. doi:10.1007/s10726-005-9005-7

Phua, M.-H., & Minowa, M. (2005). A GIS-based multi-criteria decision making approach to forest conservation planning at a landscape scale: A case study. *Landscape and Urban Planning, 71*(2), 207–222. doi:10.1016/j.landurbplan.2004.03.004

Polletta, F. (2006). *It was like a fever: Storytelling in protest and politics.* Chicago, IL: University of Chicago Press.

Prakken, H. (1991). A tool in modelling disagreement in law: Preferring the most specific argument. In *Proceedings of the 3rd International Conference on Artificial Intelligence and Law (ICAIL),* (pp. 165–174). ICAIL.

Qin, X., Huang, G., Huang, Y., Zeng, G., Chakma, A., & Li, J. (2006). NRSRM: A decision support system and visualization software for the management of petroleum-contaminated sites. *Energy Sources*, *28*, 199–220. doi:10.1080/009083190889951

Randolph, A., Haynes, R., Wyatt, J., Cook, D., & Guyatt, G. (1999). Users guides to the medical literature: How to use an article evaluating the clinical impact of a computer-based clinical decision support system. *Journal of the American Medical Association*, *282*(1), 67–74. doi:10.1001/jama.282.1.67

Reategui, E., Campbell, J., & Leao, B. (1997). Combining a neural network with case-based reasoning in a diagnostic system. *Artificial Intelligence in Medicine*, *9*(1), 5–27. doi:10.1016/S0933-3657(96)00359-4

Reay, T. (2000). *Making managerial health care decisions in complex high velocity environments*. Edmonton, Canada: Alberta Heritage Foundation for Medical Research.

Reed, C., & Rowe, G. (2001). *Araucaria: Software for puzzles in argument diagramming and xml. Technical report*. Dundee, UK: University of Dundee.

Reed, C., & Rowe, G. (2004). Araucaria: Software for argument analysis, diagramming and representation. *International Journal of AI Tools*, *14*(3-4), 961–980. doi:10.1142/S0218213004001922

Reidsema, C., & Szczerbicki, E. (2002). Review of intelligent software architectures for the development of an intelligent decision support system for design process planning in concurrent engineering. *Cybernetics and Systems*, *33*, 629–658. doi:10.1080/01969720290040786

Ridderikhoff, J., & van Herk, B. (1999). Who is afraid of the system? Doctors attitude towards diagnostic systems. *International Journal of Medical Informatics*, *53*, 91–100. doi:10.1016/S1386-5056(98)00145-2

Rittel, H. J., & Webber, M. M. (1984). Planning problems are wicked problems. In Cross, N. (Ed.), *Developments in Design Methodology* (pp. 135–144). New York, NY: John Wiley and Sons.

Rolf, B. (2003). Educating reason: From craft to technology. In *Proceedings 6th International Conference on Computer Based Learning*. Retrieved from http://www.athenasoft.org.

Rosenthal, S., & Finger, S. (2006). Design collaboration in a distributed environment. In *Proceedings 36th ASEE/IEEE Frontiers in Education Conference*. San Diego, CA: IEEE Press.

Ross, S., Fang, L., & Hipel, K. (2002). A case-based reasoning system for conflict resolution: Design and implementation. *Engineering Applications of Artificial Intelligence*, *15*(3-4), 369–383. doi:10.1016/S0952-1976(02)00065-9

Rousseau, J. J. (1968). *The social contract*. Harmondsworth, UK: Penguin.

Rowe, G., Macagno, F., Reed, C., & Walton, D. (2006). Araucaria as a tool for diagramming arguments in teaching and studying philosophy. *Teaching Philosophy*, *29*(2), 111–124.

Schultz, T. (2003). An essay on the role of government for ODR: Theoretical considerations about the future of ODR. *ADR Online Monthly UMASS*, *7*, 8.

Shih, H., Wang, C., & Lee, E. (2004). A multiattribute GDSS for aiding problem-solving. *Mathematical and Computer Modelling*, *39*(11-12), 1397–1412. doi:10.1016/j.mcm.2004.06.014

Slotte, S., & H¨am¨al¨ainen, R. (2003). *Decision structuring dialogue*. Technical Report E13. Helsinki, Finland: Systems Analysis Laboratory Research Reports. Retrieved from http://www. sal.hut.fi/Personnel/Homepages/RaimoH/publications.html.

Stamper, R., Todd, B., & Macpherson, P. (1994). Case-based explanation for medical diagnostic programs, with an example from gynaecology. *Methods of Information in Medicine, 33*(2), 205–213.

Steenbergen, M., Bachtinger, A., Sporndliand, M., & Steiner, J. (2003). Measuring political deliberation: A discourse quality index. *Comparative European Politics, 1*(1), 21–48. doi:10.1057/palgrave.cep.6110002

Steiner, J., Bachtiger, A., Sporndli, M., & Steenbergen, M. (2004). *Deliberative politics in action: Analysing parliamentary discourse*. Cambridge, UK: Cambridge University Press.

Stranieri, A. (1999). *Automating legal reasoning in discretionary domains*. PhD Thesis. Melbourne, Australia: La Trobe University.

Stranieri, A., Yearwood, J., Gervasoni, S., Garner, S., Deans, C., & Johnstone, A. (2004). Web-based decision support for structured reasoning in health. In *Proceedings of the Twelfth National Health Informatics Conference*, (p. 61). Brisbane, Australia: Health Informatics Society of Australia.

Stranieri, A., Yearwood, J., & Meikle, T. (2000). The dependency of discretion and consistency on knowledge representation. *International Review of Law Computers & Technology, 14*(3), 325–340. doi:10.1080/713673364

Stranieri, A., Yearwood, J., & Zeleznikow, J. (2001). Tools for placing legal decision support systems on the world wide web. In Proceedings of the 8th International Conference on Artificial Intelligence and Law (ICAIL), (pp. 206-214). St. Louis, MO: ACM Press.

Stranieri, A., & Zeleznikow, J. (1998b). Split up: The use of an argument based knowledge representation to meet expectations of different users for discretionary decision making. In *Proceedings of Innovative Applications of Artificial Intelligence IAAI, 1998*, 1146–1152.

Stranieri, A., & Zeleznikow, J. (2000b). Knowledge discovery for decision support in law. In S. Ang, H. Kremer, W. Orlikowski, P. Weill, & J. Degross (Eds.), *Proceedings of International Conference on Information Systems (ICIS 2000)*, (pp. 635-639). Brisbane, Australia: ICIS.

Stranieri, A., & Zeleznikow, J. (2000c). Tools for intelligent decision support system development in the legal domain. In *Proceedings of the 12th IEEE International Conference on Tools with Artificial Intelligence (ICTAI 2000)*, (pp. 186-189). Vancouver, Canada: IEEE Computer Society.

Stranieri, A., & Zeleznikow, J. (2001). Webshell: The development of web based expert system shells. In *Research and Development in Expert Systems XVIII: Proceedings of ES2001-The Twenty-First SGES International Conference on Knowledge Based Systems and Applied Artificial Intelligence*, (pp. 245-258). London, UK: Springer Verlag.

Stromer-Galley, J. (2007). Measuring deliberations content: A coding scheme. *Journal of Public Deliberation, 3*(1), 1–37.

Suthers, D. (1999). Effects of alternate representations of evidential relations on collaborative learning discourse. In C. M. Hoadley & J. Roschelle (Eds.), *Proceedings of the Third Conference on Computer Supported Collaborative Learning*. Mahwah, NJ: Lawrence Erlbaum Associates.

Suthers, D., & Hundhausen, C. (2002). The effects of representation on students' elaboration in collaborative learning. In Hoppe, H., Verdejo, F., & Kay, J. (Eds.), *Artificial Intelligence in Education*. Amsterdam, The Netherlands: IOS Press.

Tamura, H., Yamamoto, K., Tomiyama, S., & Hatono, I. (2000). Modeling and analysis of decision making problem for mitigating natural disaster risks. *European Journal of Operational Research, 122*(2), 461–468. doi:10.1016/S0377-2217(99)00247-7

Tavana, M. (2002). Euclid: Strategic alternative assessment matrix. *Journal of Multi-Criteria Decision Analysis, 11*(2), 75–96. doi:10.1002/mcda.318

Tavana, M., & Kennedy, D. (2006). N-site: A distributed consensus building and negotiation support system. *International Journal of Information Technology & Decision Making, 5*(1), 123–154. doi:10.1142/S021962200600185X

Tavana, M., Smither, J., & Anderson, R. (2007). D-side: A facility and workforce planning group multi-criteria decision support system for Johnson Space Center. *Computers & Operations Research, 34*(6), 1646–1673. doi:10.1016/j.cor.2005.06.020

Twardy, C. (2004). Argument maps improve critical thinking. *Teaching Philosophy, 27*(2), 95–116.

van Gelder, T. (2001a). How to improve critical thinking using educational technology. In G. Kennedy, M. Keppell, C. McNaught, & T. Petrovic (Eds.), *Proceedings of the 18th Annual Conference of the Australasian Society for Computers in Learning in Tertiary Education,* (pp. 539-548). Melbourne, Australia: The University of Melbourne.

van Gelder, T. (2001b). How to improve critical thinking using educational technology. In G. Kennedy, M. Keppell, C. McNaught, & T. Petrovic (Eds.), *Meeting at the Crossroads: Proceedings of the 18th Annual Conference of the Australasian Society for Computers,* (pp. 539-548). Melbourne, Australia: IEEE.

van Gelder, T. (2003). Enhancing deliberation through computer supported argument mapping. In Kirschner, P. A., Shum, S. J. B., & Carr, C. S. (Eds.), *Visualizing Argumentation: Software Tools for Collaborative and Educational Sense-Making.* London, UK: Springer Verlag.

van Gelder, T., & Bulka, A. (2000). *Reason!able (version 1.1).* Retrieved from http://www.goreason.com.

Verheij, B. (1996). *Rules, reasons, arguments: formal studies of argumentation and defeat.* Dissertation. Maastricht, The Netherlands: Universiteit Maastricht. Retrieved from http://www.metajur.unimaas.nl/ bart/proefschrift/.

Verheij, B. (1998). Argumed -A template-based argument mediation system for lawyers. In J. C. Hage, T. Bench-Capon, A. Koers, C. de Vey Mestdagh, & C. Grutters (Eds.), *JURIX: The Eleventh Conference on Legal Knowledge Based Systems,* (pp. 113-130). Nijmegen, The Netherlands: Gerard Noodt Instituut.

Walton, D. (1997). *Appeal to expert opinion: Arguments from authority. State College.* PA: Penn State University Press.

Walton, D., & Godden, D. (2005). Persuasion dialogue in online dispute resolution. *Artificial Intelligence and Law, 13,* 273–295. doi:10.1007/s10506-006-9014-0

Welp, M. (2001). The use of decision support tools in participatory river basin management. *Physics and Chemistry of the Earth. Part B: Hydrology, Oceans and Atmosphere, 26*(7), 535–539. doi:10.1016/S1464-1909(01)00046-6

Wilhelm, A. G. (2000). *Democracy in the digital age: Challenges to political life in the digital age.* New York, NY: Routledge.

Woolf, S., Chan, E., Harris, R., Sheridan, S., Braddock, C., & Kaplan, R. (2005). Promoting informed choice: Transforming health care to dispense knowledge for decision making. *Annals of Internal Medicine, 143*, 293–300.

World Legal Information Institute. (2007). *Website*. Retrieved from http://www.worldlii.org/.

Wright, S. (2006). Electrifying democracy? 10 years of policy and practice. *Parliamentary Affairs, 59*(2), 236–249. doi:10.1093/pa/gsl002

Wyatt, J. (1997). Quantitative evaluation of clinical software, exemplified by decision support systems. *International Journal of Medical Informatics, 47*, 165–173. doi:10.1016/S1386-5056(97)00100-7

Yearwood, J., Avery, J., & Stranieri, A. (2006). Interactive narrative by thematic connection of dramatic situations. In *Proceedings of NILE*, (pp. 98 – 110). NILE.

Yearwood, J., & Meikle, T. (2000). Design and development of a decision support system to support discretion in refugee law. In *Proceedings of ES2000, the Twentieth SEGS International Conference on Knowledge Based Systems and Applied Artificial Intelligence*, (pp. 243–256). SEGS.

Yearwood, J., & Stranieri, A. (1999). The integration of retrieval, reasoning and drafting for refugee law: A third generation legal knowledge based system. In *Proceedings of the Seventh International Conference on Artificial Intelligence and Law, ICAIL 1999*, (pp. 117-137). ACM Press.

Yearwood, J., & Stranieri, A. (2000). An argumentation shell for knowledge based systems. In *Proceedings of IASTED International Conference on Law and Technology*, (pp. 105–111). IASTED.

Yearwood, J., & Stranieri, A. (2006). The generic actual argument model of practical reasoning. *Decision Support Systems, 41*(2), 358–379. doi:10.1016/j.dss.2004.07.004

Yearwood, J., & Stranieri, A. (2007). *A study of frameworks for structured reasoning on reasoning quality and knowledge*. Unpublished.

Yong, J. S. (2005, July). *e-Government in Asia: Enabling public service innovation in the 21st century*. Times Media.

Yue, C. D., & Yang, G. (2007). Decision support system for exploiting local renewable energy sources: A case study of the Chigu area of Southwestern Taiwan. *Energy Policy, 35*(1), 383–394. doi:10.1016/j.enpol.2005.11.035

Zeleznikow, J., & Bellucci, E. (2003). Family-winner: Integrating game theory and heuristics to provide negotiation support. In *Proceedings of Sixteenth International Conference on Legal Knowledge Based System*, (pp. 21-30). Amsterdam, The Netherlands: IOS Publications.

Zeleznikow, J., & Stranieri, A. (1997). Splitup: An intelligent decision support system which provides advice upon property division following divorce. In *Proceedings of 30th Australian Legal Convention*. Melbourne, Australia: Anstat Legal Publishers.

Zhuge, H. (1998). Conflict group decision training: Model and system. *Knowledge-Based Systems, 11*(3-4), 191–196. doi:10.1016/S0950-7051(98)00045-8

Chapter 10

Conclusion:
Technological Support for Reasoning Communities

ABSTRACT

This chapter provides concluding comments on reasoning communities. Types of reasoning communities are identified and described. Technological tools appropriate for each type are discussed. Limitations of reasoning community ideas are described, and future developments are suggested.

INTRODUCTION

In this book, we have attempted to establish the notion of a reasoning community. Having embarked on the task of understanding what reasoning communities are, we have tried to understand the tasks that they need to perform so that we can better appreciate the requirements for supporting these tasks in a technological sense. We do not start by having as an aim the outcome that these groups reach consensus on an issue. The recognition and valuing of each individual's reasoning through the support of the reasoning community is the focus of a reasoning community. The central processes in this view are those of group coalescing of reasoning and individual coalescing of reasoning. The product of group coalescing is the co-operative

product as outlined. In general, this should take the form of an explicitly structured representation of the reasoning on an issue to which may be attached documents and other artefacts that provide evidence and support reasons. Additionally there may be critical comments and evaluation on the reasoning as it is currently manifested.

Figure 1 shows an overview of the main processes of a reasoning community and highlights the production of the collaborative reasoning product that is used by each individual to support their individual reasoning. At the core of Figure 1 is the collaborative product, typically the artefact document or coalesced representation of group reasoning that is generated as a result of the reasoning community's work. The figure shows that an individual's reasoning may occur with or

DOI: 10.4018/978-1-4666-1818-3.ch010

without the support of the collaborative product. An individual reasons to contribute to the product and may reason alone with or without using it. The coalesced group reasoning representation is constructed to support and assist individual coalescing and reasoning.

The key opportunities for providing technological support that are consistent with this relate to the process of group coalescing, the representation for the collaborative product of the coalescing and the use of the collaborative product in individual coalescing to individual judgment.

In the last two chapters, we have looked at what is being done to support reasoning in many areas and also what might be done with current tools in a pragmatic sense to support communities of reasoners. In this final chapter, we intend to envisage how technological support could work to better support reasoning communities given that we have discussed the key process elements,

the key requirements, the intermediate products as well as the role that natural language, narrative and knowledge representation play within these activities.

The technologies that may be used to achieve a more effective reasoning community will depend on the size and complexity of the community as we have seen. Accordingly, we proceed by considering technological support for different scales of reasoning community.

TYPES OF REASONING COMMUNITIES

We have examined a range of reasoning communities throughout the book and it is important to now provide an overview of these, particularly with regard to the differing levels of technological support that may be advantageous. Table 1 groups

Figure 1. An overview of a reasoning community

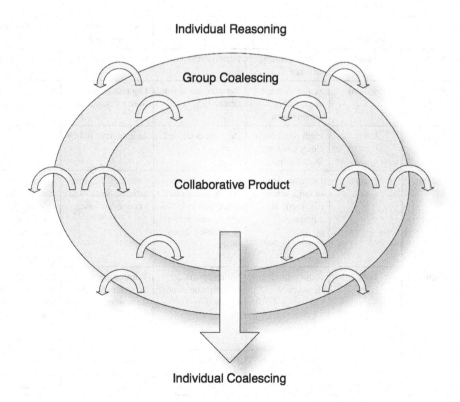

reasoning communities according to their size and the size of the intended audience. It also provides in summary form the type of group coalescing that occurs and the nature of the collaborative product.

SPECIFIC REASONING COMMUNITIES

In these, reasoning communities where the number of reasoners is small, reasoning is frequently expressed in narrative form and recorded as narrative text. Some examples that we have already mentioned are the cases below:

- Doctor and patient
- Refugee tribunal decision-maker and an applicant for refugee status
- Senior management team within an organization.

As discussed in Chapter 8, there is a trend within society for a large number of health consumers (patients) to move away from the paternalistic model where the doctor is expected to do the reasoning, towards a doctor-patient reasoning community where there is a joint reasoning process. In general, the doctor mobilises a greater knowledge of the coalesced medical reasoning on the issue and the patient a greater knowledge of the patient. The coalescing process can be considered as the iterative construction of a sequence of narratives until an agreed narrative that includes diagnosis, treatment and prognosis is established. This final narrative is the collaborative product although currently each individual probably keeps their own notes on this. The reasoning is very particular and targeted towards the treatment of the individual with little opportunity for reuse so there is little advantage in considering more formal representa-

Table 1. Types of reasoning communities

Scope	Size	Intended audience	Examples	Group coalescing	Collaborative product	Technology
Specific	Small	Small	Doctor-patient, Divorce	Iterative narrative	Common narrative	Narrative generation
Specific	Small	Medium	Senior management within organization	Iterative document drafts	Organizational policy document	CSCW for coalescing drafting, GoogleDocs
Broad	Small	Large	High court decisions, Cabinet, Dictatorship	Iterative document drafts	Judgment or policy	
Extensive	Medium	Medium	Large academic or large scientific/medical community	Process of systematising vocabulary, Process of publishing review articles. Cochrane Library process	Ontology. Review articles. Structured knowledge bases.	Ontology construction and management systems. Knowledge representation and management tools. Automatic summarization tools
Extensive	Medium	Large	Representative democracy	Green papers or consultation documents	White paper or government policy document	Automatic summarization tools. Tools for structuring and hyperlinking documents. Electronic meeting systems. Voting systems.
Universal	Large	Large	Participatory democracy	Blogs and Wikis, Argument mapping representations	Hyper-documents with knowledge bases	Large scale summarization and structured reasoning technologies.

tions of the reasoning or of technology to facilitate the coalescing process.

This small reasoning community is an example of one that is evolving with technological change. There are two parts to the reasoning, the medical reasoning and the patient information and reasoning. The most up-to-date medical reasoning is not available in any single compact form but there are resources on the Web that both doctor and patient can use to be informed about the most recent consolidation of evidence on particular medical issues -the Cochrane Collaboration for example. Of course, the doctor usually has a better knowledge of medical reasoning and is in a better position to interpret, understand and act on the most recent reasoning. These reasoning communities will benefit from the technological support provided by better coalesced medical knowledge and reasoning that is more accessible. A more automated Cochrane system that informs both doctor and patient will raise the level of reasoning within this community and improve outcomes. Furthermore, there are advantages in having patients with greater access to and understanding of the coalesced reasoning that is relevant to their issue. There are also advantages in providing the doctor with the patient's problem and symptoms prior to the consultation, for instance through an SMS or similar system to provide the doctor with a greater opportunity to individually reason.

In the case of the refugee decision-maker, the applicant for refugee status submits their case or story, the member (of the tribunal) considers this case in the context of the coalesced reasoning on refugee law and decision-making and may have a hearing with the applicant to clarify details of their submission. The decision-maker in this case benefits from having a product that represents the coalesced reasoning in this area. This is rarely available in a succinct, accessible, and useable form. Technologies for generating the coalesced knowledge in a form that is re-usable by these decision-makers would be very worthwhile. Furthermore, providing this to applicants may improve

the way in which they construct their case. Technology that assists in developing and formulating individual reasoning from the coalesced reasoning on refugee law would be advantageous. This technology has to be simple enough to use so that it unquestionably provides benefit to the human reasoner. The benefit may be in the formulation, communication and documentation of the reasoning so that it reflects individual reasoning steps that are in line with the law and current practice in a way that is transparent and understandable by the intended audience (in this case the applicant, other decision-makers and higher courts).

The refugee status decision-maker is an example of a small reasoning community that is dependent on the coalesced knowledge of a larger reasoning community involving the refugee decision-makers collectively and the high court that hears appeals of decisions and makes decisions that may change the law and practice regarding decision-making in this area. That is, the coalesced reasoning on refugee decision-making may be revised by the high court as well as collectively by the reasoning of decision-makers. It is therefore vital for the small reasoning community of a decision-maker and an applicant that the collaborative product of the larger community be well understood and readily utilised. The three areas for providing support with this small reasoning community are in the effective representation of the coalesced reasoning on refugee law that the participants in this community draw on, support for formulating reasoning from this and support for drafting documents that accurately present, document and communicate this reasoning. These are shown in Figure 2 as the three shaded regions.

In organizational management as in the case of a small senior management team, the coalesced reasoning is loosely represented by the policy, procedure, and strategy documents of the organization. In many organizations, these are usually stored on some form of intranet which may have a document management system in place. The representation of coalesced reasoning is therefore

Figure 2. Areas of technological support for the small refugee reasoning community

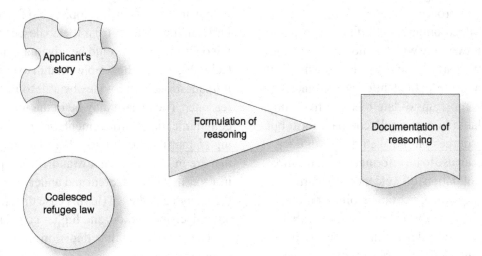

largely a repository of text documents and the reasoning is progressed through the development of draft documents that are requested from or put to the relevant groups within the organization. Reasoning is further progressed through discussion by the members of the senior management team and on the basis of these processes either new and revised policies are created and added to the repository or practical actions are taken based on and consistent with the reasoning in the repository.

The State Revenue Office for the State of Victoria example, that was discussed in Chapter 8 highlights an organization where senior management have seen a need to capture knowledge and reasoning within an organization in more than a simple repository. The coalesced reasoning is structured using a Wiki with a linked structure between the pages in the Wiki. The technological support required to achieve this is little more than the Wiki software and an understanding of ways in which knowledge might be organised. The gathering of organizational knowledge into this Wiki format is supposed to assist with retaining knowledge and reasoning capability within the organization. It provides staff and in particular new staff with a document resource that supports

their reasoning on issues to do with state revenue and the linking is designed to provide guidance and the capacity to drill down to obtain more detail on these issues. Group coalescing is done through senior staff vetting what is contributed to the Wiki and how it is linked. Reasoning by individual decision-makers is supported by searching the Wiki and following a trail of linked documents that satisfy the individual reasoners needs. The reasoning community comprises this group of senior staff who vet the Wiki material and structure. The intended audience is almost the whole staff of the organization that use the Wiki to assist in making their decisions. The effort put into structuring the Wiki is worthwhile because of the extent of reuse.

In summary for this group of reasoning communities that we call specific, technological support could be provided in the areas indicated in Table 2 and to the extent indicated. In the first two examples mentioned here, the reasoning community is dependent on the coalesced reasoning of a larger, external reasoning community. These small communities are best supported by having ready access to this coalesced reasoning in a useable form and having tools that assist the formulation of individual reasoning from this. In the last example, the coalesced reasoning is constructed within the community (organization) itself.

There have been many attempts at knowledge management systems for organizations and they vary in complexity but it seems reasonable to suggest that at least a structured document repository with hyperlinks whose structure is managed at an appropriate level within the organization would assist in organizational reasoning.

Broad Reasoning Communities

A broad reasoning community refers to one where the reasoning community itself is small but the intended audience is large. The typical examples would be a bench of High Court judges, a parliamentary cabinet, or indeed a dictatorship. In the case of high court judges, the coalesced reasoning is probably cognitively well assimilated for each judge but the relevant documents are usually referenced for the precise wording used. With this level of expertise and with only a few colleagues comprising the reasoning community there may not be much gain in a structured representation or in a computational representation. The judges' reasoning involves reading documents, listening to evidence and dialogue amongst themselves. However, a clear representation of the coalesced reasoning would be beneficial for the large intended audience.

The main technological support could be provided by developing a more highly structured representation of the coalesced reasoning relating to the particular aspect of law. This immediately benefits the intended audience because it assists in the communication of the decisions of the high court and in the situation and recording of the decision relative to existing reasoning and establishing new reasoning in the future. This will then support the high court judges in their reasoning in the future. Technology for drafting the necessary documents when the High Court hands down a decision would also be of assistance. As the judges coalesce, their reasoning through dialogue there is little technological assistance that can be provided in coalescing.

Extensive Reasoning Communities

In reasoning communities of a medium size such as many scientific, medical, and academic communities, the group coalescing process involves a process of standardising and systematising the vocabulary and a process of publishing scholarly review articles. In many academic areas this will involve the development of terminology but in areas of larger communities, ontologies and ontology tools provide support for this fundamental layer of reasoning and classification. The collaborative product, viewed as an overview of the total literature in an area can be very large as the literature in many specific areas is very large. We have suggested that the collaborative product in academic communities is the review articles that concisely situate the main reasoning in the area. Tools that are currently used in the construction of these review articles are document databases and search engines. The Cochrane Collaboration Library employs the systematic review process as a methodology for selecting papers that have carried

Table 2. Technological support for specific reasoning communities

RC Size	Intended audience	Group coalescing	Coalesced representation	Reasoning from CP	Document drafting
Small	Small	Tools may not be useful	Narrative or text	Tools may not be useful	Would be useful
Small	Medium	Tools useful with larger size	Structured and linked documents	Search and navigational tools	Yes

out randomized trial experiments and synthesizes a review that tries to capture the most recent evidence in reasoning on the particular topic. In addition to the specialised medical databases and search facilities, the tools that would assist this process are information extraction tools. More advanced text mining tools that work across the literature have the potential to assist in discovering new knowledge from the literature by throwing up possibilities for investigation as discussed in Chapter 9. In areas such as gene science or cancer research where there are ontologies developed it would seem reasonable to expect that the development of facilities for reasoning on top of the ontology would further assist reasoning across the groups of scientists working in these areas. The development of a network representation of the coalesced reasoning in many of these areas would mean that researchers could publish their peer-reviewed results but also make explicit the contribution and locate it in the correct place in a structured network computer representation. Tools for gathering papers as well as related papers that cite them already exist so it is easy to envisage an editable system that makes a first pass at locating newly published material relative to existing knowledge and reasoning. This approach could then underpin many possible views of the representation such as trees with document evidence attached to nodes.

Extensive reasoning communities where the reasoning community itself is of medium size (thousands) and the intended audience is large (millions) are exemplified by representative democracies. The way in which these work is very similar to the way in which management teams in organizations work but they are an order of magnitude larger. There is a broader range of issues and these are frequently dealt with through the drafting of green papers. These are broadly circulated within the larger intended audience of the community. These documents seek comment, ideas, proposals and input on the issue and the feedback is used to prepare a white paper. The white paper is an authoritative document that presents the government policy on an issue. The green paper forms part of the coalescing process and together with the input to the green paper and the white paper are one form of the collaborative product.

It is often difficult to review the path to the white paper, that is, to track the reasoning. A better representation of the coalesced reasoning would see more transparency and greater opportunity for reuse of information and reasoning gathered. The development of reusable structures like the generic argument structure for an issue is a way of representing the possible reasoning as well as actual reasoning within a structure. If the full model is used then different possible inferences can also be represented. There are two critical elements to such a structure. The first is that it has to have a level of abstraction so that different ways of reasoning can be represented within the structure. This has been discussed at length in Chapter 4. The second is that the construction of the structure is the responsibility of only a few individuals from the community that understand the representation. A GAS would be constructed by a few individuals from the reasoning community in the same way that a systematic review is constructed and critically reviewed by only a few representative participants of the reasoning community. The advantage comes in areas where there is likely to be good potential for reuse of reasoning.

Universal Reasoning Communities

These communities are large and involve everyone in the reasoning. There is an imperative for all participants to be informed and for the reasoning on an issue to be clearly represented and accessible. The group coalescing process has to be carried out in such a way that any participant can provide input. This requirement means that there is a need for an open consultative process. The means of achieving some coalesced collaborative product must still involve some initial draft green paper or 'first cut' at a reasoning structure on the issue, say a rough GAS. Chapter 5 provides a dialogue process for developing a GAS (see Table 3).

SPECIFIC REASONING COMMUNITY TASKS

Participant Selection

Subscribing to the notion of a reasoning community means that the membership of the community is taken seriously so there is a need for tools that support the identification of members or potential members that may meet certain requirements in terms of knowledge, expertise, or skills. In the same way that text mining tools could assist in drawing together the most recently published experimental evidence for the Cochrane Library and information extraction tools might assist in synthesizing a review, text retrieval, text mining and QA tools could assist with the task of identifying potential participants that meet certain requirements and criteria.

Communication Protocols

Communication protocols are shaped around the main activities that need to occur in our template of a reasoning community. Therefore, it is important for individuals to be able to communicate their individual reasoning to anyone in the community

or its intended audience in a form that is consistent with the structure of the coalesced reasoning.

It is important that any participant can have input to the coalesced reasoning (collaborative product) but the protocol here is that this be through the individuals that have control over the editing of this.

Robert's rules of order provides common rules and procedures for deliberation and debate within a community in the context of running a meeting in an orderly fashion. The conduct of all business is controlled by the general will of all participants. A reasoning community may reason about this approach and the right of the deliberate majority to decide. Robert's Rules have the intent of providing for constructive and democratic meetings. The rules respect the fundamental right of deliberative assemblies to have all questions thoroughly discussed before taking action. Each reasoning community may also want to control the communication technology and media that are used in communication of individual reasoning out of the community as well as into the collaborative product.

Decision-Making Protocols

If a reasoning community sees itself as having to make a decision on some issue then there needs to be agreement on decision-making protocols. A reasoning community can reason about the need to make a single community decision on an issue. In so doing it can then reason to decide on

Table 3. Technological support for extensive reasoning communities

RC size	Intended audience	Group coalescing	Coalesced representation	Reasoning from CP	Document drafting
Medium	Medium	Search engines, systematic review process	Review documents. Ontologies, Highly structured representation such as GAS	Ontology tools. Software agents	Would be useful
Medium	Large	Green paper process. Facilitator. Reasoning engineer	White paper. GAS	Navigational tools	Document drafting from structured representation

a communication and decision-making protocol for reaching a single consensual view on the matter. This already happens in some reasoning communities. For example, a jury is instructed on decision-making criteria both at an individual level and on the mechanism for coming to a decision. So, for example if the jury is instructed that they must be satisfied beyond reasonable doubt then there can still be doubt, but only to the extent that it would not affect a "reasonable person's" belief that the defendant is guilty. The precise meaning of words such as "reasonable" and "doubt" are usually defined within the jurisprudence of the jurisdiction and have to be explained to the jury members. For some trials, unanimity amongst the jury is required while for others it is not.

In many instances, there are also protocols for informal communication between participants of a reasoning community. An example of this is the *plea bargain* where the prosecution and the defense agree to settle the case against the defendant. The defendant agrees to plead guilty or no contest in exchange for some agreement from the prosecutor on the punishment.

For reasoning communities that are reasoning to their decision-making protocols it would be possible to develop knowledge-based systems that support the community in choosing a protocol that meets their needs. Currently, there are no such systems in existence of which we are aware.

There are also times when there are requirements for communication protocols between the reasoning community and the interested audience. In Australia, just after the attempted terrorist attack on the Glasgow Airport in 2007, an Indian doctor (Haneef) practising in Australia was charged under the newly established Australian terrorist laws.(The Guardian, 2010) The case had much publicity through the media as this was the first time that the Federal Police had used the laws to such an extent, to retain Haneef for questioning without a formal charge for an extended period. When Haneef's solicitor, out of frustration with the little information that was available to him,

leaked details of his client's case to the media, Peter Farris, QC made the point that this action compromised his client's chances of a fair trial. This is an example in which the boundaries between the reasoning community and the interested audience have been compromised.

Collaborative Product for Reasoning

The collaborative product of reasoning communities is a key resource for reasoning communities, both within the reasoning community and as we have seen earlier, by other related but often smaller reasoning communities. Recognition that reuse of this product is important for the effective functioning of these communities means that the representation of this collaborative reasoning product should be carefully considered so that it can best facilitate reuse.

The form of the product needs to be appropriate to the size and nature of the reasoning community and so we have seen a range of forms from a verbally agreed narrative, a structured and hyperlinked document database to ontologies and highly structured knowledge-bases. While Toulmin-and IBIS-based models of representation are useful and can capture a range of propositions they do not capture at sufficient level of generality a structure of reasoning that adequately allow the representation of a wide range of propositions in a form that is reusable by the community or other communities. A highly structured hyperlinked document repository can do this as can the GAAM framework for representing reasoning. These both require incrementally more effort in their construction but can also deliver a strong capacity to support reasoning through reuse. Our work with school students has indicated that when supplied with a pre-constructed generic argument structure on an issue there were indications of improvement in the communication of their reasoning on the issue. Using a pre-constructed GAS also produced a measured difference in learning and reasoning about action in educating nursing students about ventilated patients in a critical care setting. Therefore, there is some evidence that using a collaborative product can provide enhanced support for reasoning.

One of the major proposals made in this book is that an appropriate and structured product of coalesced reasoning should be used to better support individual reasoning and the development of the appropriate representation is a key element of providing technological support to reasoning communities. We have provided a number of examples of these representations.

Coalescing

Group coalescing of reasoning is often facilitated by one or more individuals (often called facilitators) as in the Delphi process. It is very common for the facilitators to act to bring the members of a reasoning group to a single view on an issue. This is not a requirement for a reasoning community as we have described it. It is important that the coalescing process capture and represent the breadth of reasoning in a form that is accessible for further use in formulating individual reasoning and judgment as well as possible use by related communities. It is important that breadth and diversity can be captured in the product and that the coalesced product is accepted by the community. The coalescing process in itself, does not entail the generation of consensus. Rather, consensus is regarded as one, of many, protocols for reaching decisions. The group coalescing process can provide some resilience in that coalesced reasoning can help in avoiding problems such as groupthink.

It needs to be recognised that the coalescing task will generally work by the reasoning community doing two main things:

1. Agreeing on a representation for the collaborative product
2. Identifying and agreeing on a small group of facilitators/reasoning engineers to construct the collaborative product by engagement with the wider community.

Agreeing on a representation for the collaborative product or coalesced reasoning requires an understanding of the nature of the representation and how each participant or member of the intended audience would use the coalesced reasoning. Currently this is a difficult exercise with participants in many reasoning communities acting in their own individual ways to gather information and reasoning from diverse sources without the resources of an up-to-date artefact of coalesced reasoning. Whilst many executive decision-makers may support their decisions through information gathering and research groups, for example the Gartner Group (Information Technology), few put thought into a coalesced reasoning product whose structure, at least, is reusable. The development of the use of coalesced reasoning products in reasoning communities has to be supported by developing technologies that can offer a range of representations for these communities to use. The current offerings for representations include hypertext structured document collections, Wiki structured resources, IBIS structures and generic argument structures.

Once agreement on a representation is reached then a small group of reasoning community participants take responsibility for the development of the structure of the coalesced reasoning and its population with the necessary content. Whilst the Delphi process is one that is commonly used, with facilitators having the responsibility for developing the reasoning towards consensus on an issue there are several limitations within this approach. It is directed towards achieving a consensus rather than generally supporting individual reasoning, it does not support reuse in general and it focuses on a process and an outcome rather than a product that participants can use. The engineers or facilitators are frequently participants of the reasoning community and so tools for the construction and maintenance of the coalesced reasoning need to be very easy to use. Some tools exist, such as gIBIS, Argument Developer, Argumed, and Wiki software but require further development.

Supporting Individual Reasoning

The aim of a reasoning community is to support the individual participant in their reasoning. A key component of this is the provision of the coalesced reasoning of the community. Although this may be constructed by a few individuals it is accepted by the whole community. The next main opportunity for providing technological support is through the individual use of this coalesced reasoning. The GAAM provides both a structure for coalesced reasoning and a template for individuals to develop their reasoning in. One such software tool for doing this is Argument Developer. Other approaches can use a hypertext or Wiki-based representation of the coalesced reasoning that allows an overview of the structure of the reasoning and access to the related documents. However, these rely on the individual to craft their reasoning into a new document.

Our experiences with Argument Developer suggest that whilst users find it excellent for novices and the training of individual reasoners within a community, it is not flexible enough to support expert reasoners. Stronger focus on more flexible tools is required to develop tools that are simpler and more readily adoptable by individuals, both novice and expert.

COMPLEX REASONING

Many practical reasoning situations involve complex reasoning and even in cases where we are reasoning to a single action, there are several separate criteria to be met. For example, when buying a car, we may want to satisfy several criteria that conflict. The end result is a decision to take a single action that solves the problem with understandable tradeoffs. In other situations, it may not be the case that a single action is the result of our reasoning. For example, in trying to provide customers with secure Internet banking services, banks have to take several actions and therefore each of these becomes an objective to be reasoned about separately. In these cases the reasoning community can be focused around all of the objectives simultaneously or restrict its attention to only some objectives.

Support tools for modelling these decisions are frequently very specific and many have been mentioned in Chapter 10. There is a need for tools to allow more reasoning in these complex cases that can involve understanding tradeoffs between the criteria. Underlying each objective, the reasoning tools that we have described in this book would be useful for each objective.

LIMITATIONS OF A REASONING COMMUNITY APPROACH

Effective collective reasoning is well known to be difficult to achieve. Reasons for this range enormously and include the psychoanalytic perspectives advanced by Bion (1968) who regards the endeavours of a group to be very easily sidetracked by the emotional needs of individuals. In software engineering, Dutoit et al. (2006) note that the difficulties groups have to reach and record design decisions collectively is so common that the phenomena has been called the Rationale Paradox. A plethora of argument visualisation schemes including many surveyed in earlier chapters of this text, have been developed specifically to help individuals reason in groups. However, somewhat ironically, in a survey of studies that evaluate their effectiveness, van der Braak et al. (2006), concludes that there is little conclusive evidence that argument visualisation schemes help improve decision-making, communication or deliberation in groups. Experiences of citizen juries in the deliberative democracy field reported by Niemeyer (2011) attest to the need for a highly skilled facilitator to guide a group toward any effective outcomes. The question naturally arises, why is reasoning in groups so difficult?

The reasoning community ideas presented here are advanced as a way to view the processes that occur when individuals reason collectively so that supportive technologies can better be designed. However, while we argue that making artefacts at each phase of a reasoning community explicit is desirable, a question that arises is, why do we see so little of this occurring now? For instance, in the engagement phase, making the rationale for selecting participants explicit, agreeing on a decision- making protocol and agreeing on the intended audience, is performed implicitly by most groups yet very rarely made explicit. If this is because groups are fundamentally battlefields that individuals enter to defend their claims as Mercier and Sperber (2011) claim, then making the artefacts in the engagement phase explicit serves no individual's interests. Dutoit et al. (2006) advocate that groups in intense software design dialogue do not take the time to interrupt the flow of creative consciousness to record rationales for the decisions they make, no matter how critical this is for project success. In this vein participants are unlikely to take the effort to make selection, decision-making protocols or intended audience assumptions explicit.

If coalescing of reasoning that involves the creation of a co-operative product using a representation such as the Generic Argument Structure (GAS) from the Generic Actual Argument Model advanced by Yearwood and Stranieri (2006), is so effective why do so few groups seek to do this? One reason is that the creation of a GAS is quite difficult to achieve. GASs have been developed in family law property distribution, refugee law, career counselling, water management, copyright law, taxation, copyright law, sentencing and intensive care. Each application has involved extensive effort on the part of a knowledge engineer who refined the structure with experts through many dialogues. This leads us to conclude that the GAAM is limited for coalescing of reasoning during an interactive meeting of reasoning community participants. However, the structure's utility

may lie more in its capacity to capture complex reasoning due to its two level model.

The reasoning community ideas have been advanced as a plausible view of group reasoning that can facilitate the identification of technologies to support participants in reasoning collectively. The approach is not advanced as a turnkey solution to challenges in supporting groups who must arrive at a decision. Clearly, the approach poses many questions. In the next section, we advance some issues for future development and offer some concluding remarks.

CONCLUDING REMARKS AND FUTURE DEVELOPMENT

The basis for the proposal of the notion of a reasoning community as presented here has its roots in three elements:

- The philosophical arguments for collective reasoning and decision making and what these mean
- Some small empirical studies that indicate some benefits in using structured reasoning approaches and representations—inconclusive at the moment
- Construction of a number of flexible decision-support and advisory systems that have been used.

There is a need to advance knowledge about the notion on a number of frontiers: through empirical studies, the development of software and systems to support the processes within reasoning communities and to step back and look at DSSs from the reasoning community framework to see how systems can be re-conceived and reconfigured in such a framework.

Empirical studies of groups reasoning to a decision need to be undertaken. These studies will compare how, the use of a reasoning community approach and structure affects the reasoning pro-

271

cess, with situations where traditional approaches are used. This research is itself complex because it is difficult to find the right measurable characteristics that highlight an improvement. In our work with schoolchildren, we focused on the extent to which they could communicate their reasoning to a conclusion. In work that we have just begun, we will consider whether the use of the reasoning community approach, in particular group coalescing with a highly structured collaborative product can improve deliberation over not taking this approach. There are now several situations in which groups deliberate in groups or teams to make decisions, which they expect to be better than decisions made by individuals within the team. Examples are multi-disciplinary medical teams and deliberative democracy fora in town planning and community decision-making. In many cases, these communities require effective processes to realize the hope of better reasoning and decisions.

Alongside the notion of a reasoning community is the question of tools to support the processes. As we have indicated in Chapter 9, there are considerable opportunities for the development of tools and software. Amongst these are representations and architectures for the collaborative product, tools to capture dialogue, tools to structure dialogue and contribute to the collaborative product as well as tools that enable the use of the collaborative product to support individual reasoning.

In particular, tools that can aid a coalescing process can act to increase the limits of bounded rationality. The collaborative product, itself does this to some extent, but tools that extract and present different perspectives from the collaborative product and can do the inverse task of integrating different perspectives are clearly required.

Chapter 9 presented a large range of decision support tools and GDSSs, yet the reality is that the uptake of these tools is less than hoped. We should consider, in detail, how the reasoning community framework might provide insight into configurations of tools and systems incorporating existing tools that are more effective in practice.

REFERENCES

Bion, W. R. (1968). *Experiences in groups: And other papers*. London, UK: Routledge.

Dutoit, A., & McCall, B. Mistrik, & Paech, B. (2006). Rationale management in software engineering: Concepts and techniques. In A. Dutoit, B. McCall, Mistrik, et al. (Eds.), *Rationale Management in Software Engineering*, (pp. 1-48). London, UK: Springer.

Mercier, H., & Sperber, D. (2011). Why do humans reason? Arguments for an argumentative theory philosophy, politics and economics program, University of Pennsylvania. *The Behavioral and Brain Sciences*, *34*, 57–111. doi:10.1017/S0140525X10000968

Niemeyer, S. J. (2011). Intersubjective reasoning and the formation of metaconsensus. In Yearwood, J., & Stranieri, A. (Eds.), *Technologies for Supporting Reasoning Communities and Collaborative Decision Making: Cooperative Approaches*. Hershey, PA: IGI Global. doi:10.4018/978-1-60960-091-4.ch002

The Guardian. (2010, December 23). Australia says sorry to doctor wrongly detained on terrorism charges. *The Guardian*. Retrieved 11 March 2012, from http://www.guardian.co.uk/world/2010/dec/23/australia-sorry-doctor-terrorism-charges.

Compilation of References

Ackermann, W. (1956). Begrndung einer strengen impli-cation. *Journal of Symbolic Logic, 21*, 113–128. doi:10.2307/2268750

Adlassnig, K., & Horak, W. (1995). Development and retrospective evaluation of hepaxpert-i: A routinely-used expert system for interpretive analysis of hepatitis a and b serologic findings. *Artificial Intelligence in Medicine, 7*(1), 1–24. doi:10.1016/0933-3657(94)00023-L

Adriaenssens, V., De Baets, B., Goethals, P., & De Pauw, N. (2004). Fuzzy rule-based models for decision support in ecosystem management. *The Science of the Total Envi-ronment, 319*, 1–12. doi:10.1016/S0048-9697(03)00433-9

Adrianto, L., Matsuda, Y., & Sakuma, Y. (2005). Assessing local sustainability of fisheries system: A multi-criteria participatory approach with the case of Yoron island, Kagoshima prefecture, Japan. *Marine Policy, 29*, 9–23. doi:10.1016/j.marpol.2004.01.004

Afshar, F., Yearwood, J., & Stranieri, A. (2002). Capturing consensus knowledge from multiple experts. In *Proceed-ings of ES 2002, the Twenty-Second SGAI International Conference on Knowledge Based Systems and Applied Artificial Intelligence*. Cambridge, UK: Springer.

Afshar, F., Yearwood, J., & Stranieri, A. (2006). A tool for assisting group decision-making for consensus outcomes in organizations. In Voges, K. E., & Pope, N. K. L. (Eds.), *Business Applications and Computational Intelligence* (pp. 316–343). Hershey, PA: IGI Global. doi:10.4018/978-1-59140-702-7.ch016

Alexander, R. (1992). Mediation, violence and the family. *Alternative Law Journal, 17*(6), 276–299.

Alexy, R. (1990). A theory of practical discourse. In Ben-habib, S., & Dallmayr, F. (Eds.), *The Communicative Ethics Controversy* (pp. 151–190). Cambridge, MA: MIT Press.

Ambler, S. (1996). A categorical approach to the semantics of argumentation. *Mathematical Structures in Computer Science, 6*, 167–188. doi:10.1017/S0960129500000931

Amgoud, L., Maudet, N., & Parsons, S. (2000). Model-ling dialogues using argumentation. In E. Durfee (Ed.), *Proceedings of the Fourth International Conference on Multi-Agent Systems (ICMAS-2000)*, (pp. 31-38). Boston, MA: IEEE Press.

Amgoud, L., Parsons, S., & Maudet, N. (2000). Argu-ments, dialogue and negotiation. In W. Horn (Ed.), *Proceedings of the Fourteenth European Conference on Artificial Intelligence (ECAI-2000)*, (pp. 338-342). Berlin, Germany: IOS Press.

Anderson, A. R., & Belnap, N. D. (1975). *Entailment -The logic of relevance and necessity*. Princeton, NJ: Princeton University Press.

Anderson, M., Meyer, B., & Olivier, P. (Eds.). (2001). *Diagrammatic representation and reasoning*. London, UK: Springer.

Antoniou, G. (1997). *Nonmonotonic reasoning with incomplete and changing information*. Cambridge, MA: MIT Press.

Antunes, P. C. C., & Dias, J. (2001). Applying genre analysis to ems design: The example of a small account-ing firm. In *Proceedings of the Seventh International Workshop on Groupware, CRIWG 2001*, (pp. 74-81). Darmstadt, Germany: IEEE CS Press. Retrieved from http://www.di.fc.ul.pt/paa/papers/criwg-01.pdf.

Antunes, P., & Costa, C. (2003). From genre analysis to the design of meetingware. In *Proceedings of the 2003 International ACM SIGGROUP Conference on Supporting Group Work*, (pp. 302-310). Sanibel Island, FL: ACM Press.

Antunes, P., Costa, C., & Pino, J. (2006). The use of genre analysis in the design of electronic meeting systems. *Information Research, 11*(3). Retrieved from http://www.di.fc.ul.pt/ paa/papers/ir-06.pdf.

Antunes, P., Ho, T., & Carrico, L. (1999). A GDSS agenda builder for inexperienced facilitators. In *Proceedings of the 10th EuroGDSS Workshop*, (pp. 1-15). Delft, The Netherlands: Delft University of Technology. Retrieved from http://www.di.fc.ul.pt/paa/papers/egdss-99.pdf.

Ardente, F., Beccali, G., & Cellura, M. (2003). Eco-sustainable energy and environmental strategies in design for recycling: The software endless. *Ecological Modelling, 163*(12), 101–118. doi:10.1016/S0304-3800(02)00418-0

Aristotle,. (1928). *The works of Aristotle. W. A. Pickard-Cambridge (Trans.)*. Oxford, UK: Oxford University Press.

Aristotle. (2006). *Prior and posterior analytics. A. J. Jenkinson & R. G. Mure (Trans.)*. Retrieved from http://www.digireads.com.

Arrow, K. J. (1963). *Social choice and individual values*. New York, NY: Wiley.

Avery, J., & Yearwood, J. (2002). A foundation for strange agent negotiation. In *Papers from the AAAI Workshop on Meaning Negotiation*, (pp. 72-77). Menlo Park, CA: AAAI Press.

Avery, J., Yearwood, J., & Stranieri, A. (2001). An argumentation based multi-agent system for etourism dialogue. In *Proceedings First International Workshop on Hybrid Intelligent Systems HIS 2001*, (pp. 497-512). Adelaide, Australia: ACM.

Ayoub, N., Martins, R., Wang, K., Seki, H., & Naka, Y. (2007). Two levels decision system for efficient planning and implementation of bioenergy production. *Energy Conversion and Management, 48*(3), 709–723. doi:10.1016/j.enconman.2006.09.012

Bailey, P. (1999). Searching for storiness: Story generation from a reader's perspective. In M. Mateas & P. Sengers (Eds.), *Narrative Intelligence: Papers from the AAAI Fall Symposium*. North Falmouth, MA: AAAI.

Ball, W. J. (1994). Using Virgil to analyse public policy arguments: A system based on Toulmin's informal logic. *Social Science Computer Review, 12*(1), 26–37. doi:10.1177/089443939401200102

Bannon, L. J., & Schmidt, K. (1989). CSCW: Four characters in search of a context. In *Proceedings of the First European Conference on Computer Supported Cooperative Work*, (pp. 358-372). London, UK: CSCW.

Bayles, M. D. (1990). *Procedural justice: Allocating to individuals*. Dordrecht, The Netherlands: Kluwer.

Bellucci, E., Lodder, A., & Zeleznikow, J. (2004). Integrating artificial intelligence, argumentation and game theory to develop an online dispute resolution environment. In *Proceeding of the 16th IEEE International Conference on Tools with Artificial Intelligence (ICTAI 2004)*, (pp. 7490754). Los Alamitos, CA: IEEE Computer Society.

Bellucci, E., & Zeleznikow, J. (2001). Representations for decision making support in negotiation. *Journal of Decision Support, 10*(3-4), 449–479. doi:10.3166/jds.10.449-479

Bellucci, E., & Zeleznikow, J. (2006). Developing negotiation decision support systems that support mediators: A case study of the family-winner system. *Artificial Intelligence and Law, 13*(2), 233–271. doi:10.1007/s10506-006-9013-1

Bench-Capon, T., & Sartor, G. (2001). Theory based explanation of case law domains. In *Proceedings of the Eighth International Conference on Artificial Intelligence and Law*, (pp. 12–21). ACM Press.

Bench-Capon, T. J. M., Lowes, D., & McEnery, A. M. (1991). Argument-based explanation of logic programs. *Knowledge-Based Systems, 4*(3), 177–183. doi:10.1016/0950-7051(91)90007-O

Bennett, H., & Broe, G. A. (2007). Judicial neurobiology, Markarian synthesis and emotion: How can the human brain make sentencing decisions? *Criminal Law Journal, 31*, 75.

Bennett, W., & Feldman, M. (1981). *Reconstructing reality in the courtroom: Justice and judgment in American culture*. Newark, NJ: Rutgers University Press.

Berman, D. H., & Hafner, C. D. (1995). Understanding precedents in a temporal context of evolving legal doctrine. In *Proceedings of the Fifth International Conference on Artificial Intelligence and Law*, (pp. 42-51). New York NY: ACM Press.

Bessette, J. (1994). *The mild voice of reason: Deliberative democracy & american national government*. Chicago, IL: University of Chicago Press.

Bion, W. R. (1968). *Experiences in groups: And other papers*. London, UK: Routledge.

Biswas, A. K. (2004). Integrated water resources management: A reassessment. *Water International, 29*(2), 248–256. doi:10.1080/02508060408691775

Black, J., & Bower, G. (1980). Story understanding and problem solving. *Poetics, 9*, 223–250. doi:10.1016/0304-422X(80)90021-2

Black, J., & Wilensky, R. (1979). An evaluation of story grammars. *Cognitive Science, 3*, 213–230. doi:10.1207/s15516709cog0303_2

Boley, H., Tabet, S., & Wagner, G. (2001). Design rationale of RuleML: A markup language for semantic web rules. In *Proceedings of the Semantic Web Working Symposium (SWWS 2001)*. Amsterdam, The Netherlands: IOS Press.

Bolger, F., Stranieri, A., Wright, G., & Yearwood, J. (1999). Does the delphi process lead to increased accuracy in group-based judgmental forecasts or does it simply induce Consensus Amongst Judgement Forecasters. *Technological Forecasting and Social Change, 78*(9), 1671–1680. doi:10.1016/j.techfore.2011.06.002

Bonjour, L. (1985). *The structure of empirical knowledge*. Boston, MA: Harvard University Press.

Branigan, E. (1992). Narrative comprehension and film. In Buscombe, E. (Ed.), *Sightlines*. New York, NY: Routledge.

Branting, K. (1994). A computational model of ratio decidendi. *Artificial Intelligence and Law: An International Journal, 2*, 1–31. doi:10.1007/BF00871744

Branting, L. (2000). *Reasoning with rules and precedents -A computational model of legal analysis*. Dordrecht, The Netherlands: Kluwer Academic Publishers.

Breuker, J., & Winkels, R. (2003). Use and reuse of legal ontologies in knowledge engineering and information management. In *Proceedings of the Workshop on Legal Ontologies and Web-Based Legal Information Management: Organised in Conjunction with the Ninth International Conference on Artificial Intelligence and Law*. New York, NY: Springer.

Breuker, J., Valente, A., & Winkels, R. (2005). Law and the semantic web. *Lecture Notes in Computer Science, 3369*, 36–64. doi:10.1007/978-3-540-32253-5_4

Brewka, G., Gordon, T., & Karacapilidis, N. (1995). Mediating systems for group decision making: The zeno system. In *Proceedings of the KI-95 Workshop 4 -Computational Dialectics: Models of Argumentation, Negotiation and Decision Making*. Retrieved from www.tfgordon.de/publications/Brewka1995a.pdf.

Brinker, M. (1993). Theme and interpretation. In Sollors, W. (Ed.), *The Return of Thematic Criticism* (pp. 21–37). Boston, MA: Harvard University Press.

Bromby, M., MacMillan, M., & McKellar, P. (2003). *Edu-KATE -A resource for learning the law of evidence*. Retrieved from http://www.caledonian.ac.uk/lss/global/contactmaps/staff/bromby/BILETA2003.pdf.

Brooks, R. (1991). Intelligence without representation. *Artificial Intelligence Journal, 47*, 139–159. doi:10.1016/0004-3702(91)90053-M

Brucher, H., & Baumberger, P. (2003). Using mobile technology to support edemocracy. In *Proceedings of the 36th Annual Hawaii International Conference on System Sciences*. Washington, DC: IEEE Computer Society.

Bruner, J. (1990). *Acts of meaning*. Boston, MA: Harvard University Press.

Buchanan, B., & Shortliffe, E. (Eds.). (1984). *Rule-based expert systems: The MYCIN experiments of the Stanford heuristic programming project*. Reading, MA: Addison Wesley Publishing Company.

Cabri, G., Ferrari, L., & Leonardi, L. (2005). A role-based mobile-agent approach to support e-democracy. *Applied Soft Computing*, *6*(1), 85–99. doi:10.1016/j.asoc.2004.12.001

Carbogim, D., Robertson, D., & Lee, J. (2000). Argument-based applications to knowledge engineering. *The Knowledge Engineering Review*, *15*(2), 119–149. doi:10.1017/S0269888900002058

Carvalho, A., Rocha, R., & Oliveira, M. A. (2004). SINUP: Using GIS to support e-democracy. *Lecture Notes in Computer Science*, *2739*, 341–344. doi:10.1007/10929179_61

Ceccaroni, L., Cortes, U., & Sanchez-Marre, M. (2004). Ontowedss: Augmenting environmental decision-support systems with ontologies. *Ontologies Environmental Modelling & Software*, *19*, 785–797. doi:10.1016/j.envsoft.2003.03.006

Ceri, S., Gottlob, G., & Tanca, L. (1990). *Logic programming and databases*. New York, NY: Springer-Verlag.

Chang, N.-B., Wei, Y., Tseng, C., & Kao, C.-Y. (1997). The design of a GIS-based decision support system for chemical emergency preparedness and response in an urban environment. *Computers, Environment and Urban Systems*, *21*(1), 67–94. doi:10.1016/S0198-9715(97)01009-0

Chatman, S. (1978). *Story and discourse: Narrative structure in fiction and film*. Ithaca, NY: Cornell University Press.

Cheng, J. (2001). Strong relevance as a logical validity criterion for scientific reasoning. In Proceedings of the 2001 International Conference on Artificial Intelligence, (pp. 916-923). Las Vegas, NV: ACM Press.

Cheng, J. (1996). The fundamental role of entailment in knowledge representation and reasoning. *Journal of Computing and Information*, *2*(1), 853–873.

Chisholm, R. M. (1963). Contrary-to-duty imperatives and deontic logic. *Analysis*, *24*, 33–36. Retrieved from http://www.citeseer.nj.nec.com/carlos00logical.html-doi:10.2307/3327064

Chklovski, T., Gil, Y., Ratnakar, V., & Lee, J. (2003b). Trellis: Supporting decision making via argumentation in the semantic web. In *Proceedings of 2nd International Semantic Web Conference ISWC 2003*. Berlin, Germany: Springer.

Choi, F. Y. Y. (2000). Advances in domain independent linear text segmentation. In *Proceedings of the 1st Meeting of the North American Chapter of the Association for Computational Linguistics (ANLP-NAACL-00)*, (pp. 26-33). San Francisco, CA: Morgan Kaufmann Publishers.

Christie, G. C. (1986). An essay on discretion. *Duke Law Journal*, *35*, 747–778. doi:10.2307/1372667

Chutimaskul, W., & Funilkul, S. (2004). The framework of e-democracy development. *Lecture Notes in Computer Science*, *3183*, 27–30. doi:10.1007/978-3-540-30078-6_5

Clark, P. (1991). *A model of argumentation and its application in a cooperative expert system*. PhD Thesis. Glasgow, UK: University of Strathclyde.

Clarke, C. L. A., & Cormak, G. V. (2000). Question answering by passage selection (multitext experiments for trec-9). In E. Voorhees & D. Harman (Eds.), *Ninth Text Retrieval Conference (TREC 9)*, (pp. 673-683). Gaithersburg, MD: National Institute of Standards and Technology (NIST). Retrieved from http://trec.nist.gov/pubs/trec9/papers/mt9.pdf.

Clement, A., & van den Besselaar, P. (1993). A retrospective look at pd projects. *Communications of the ACM*, *36*(6), 29–37. doi:10.1145/153571.163264

Cohen, P. (1985). *Heuristic reasoning about uncertainty: An artificial intelligence approach*. London, UK: Pitman.

Conklin, J., & Begeman, M. (1988). gIBIS: A hypertext tool for exploratory policy discussion. *ACM Transactions on Office Information Systems*, *6*(4), 303–331. doi:10.1145/58566.59297

Constantino-Gonzalez, M., & Suthers, D. (2003). Automated coaching of collaboration based on workspace analysis: Evaluation and implications for future learning environments. In *Proceedings of the 36th Hawaii International Conference on System Sciences HICSS-36*, (p. 32). Big Island, HI: IEEE Computer Society.

Correira, A. (1980). Computing story trees. *American Journal of Computational Linguistics*, *6*(3-4), 135–149.

Costa, C., & Antunes, P. (2001). Meetings as genre systems: Some consequences for EMS design. In *Proceedings of Group Decision & Negotiation 2001*, (pp. 261-263). La Rochelle, France: Group Design and Negotiation. Retrieved from http://www.di.fc.ul.pt/ paa/papers/gdn-01b.pdf.

Delanty, G. (2010). *Community* (2nd ed.). London, UK: Routledge.

Delgrande, J. (1988). An approach to default reasoning based on a first-order conditional logic: Revised report. *Artificial Intelligence, 36*(1), 63–90. doi:10.1016/0004-3702(88)90079-3

Denning, S. (2001). *The springboard: How storytelling ignites action in knowledge-era organizations*. Boston, MA: Butterworth Heinemann.

Dick, J. P. (1987). Conceptual retrieval and case law. In Proceedings of the First International Conference on Artificial Intelligence and Law, (pp. 106-115). New York, NY: ACM Press.

Dick, J. P. (1991). *A conceptual, case-relation representation of text for intelligent retrieval*. PhD Thesis. Ottawa, Canada: National Library of Canada.

Dickinson, H. (1998). Evidence-based decision making: An argumentative approach. *International Journal of Medical Informatics, 51*, 71–81. doi:10.1016/S1386-5056(98)00105-1

Doukas, H., Patlitzianas, K., & Psarras, J. (2006). Supporting sustainable electricity technologies in Greece using MCDM. *Resources Policy, 31*(2), 129–136. doi:10.1016/j.resourpol.2006.09.003

Doyle, J. (1979). A truth maintenance system. *Artificial Intelligence, 12*, 231–272. doi:10.1016/0004-3702(79)90008-0

Doyle, J. (1992). Rationality and its roles in reasoning. *Computational Intelligence, 8*(2), 376–409. doi:10.1111/j.1467-8640.1992.tb00371.x

Dreiseitl, S., & Binder, M. (2005). Do physicians value decision support? A look at the effect of decision support systems on physician opinion. *Artificial Intelligence in Medicine, 33*, 25–30. doi:10.1016/j.artmed.2004.07.007

Dryzek, J. (1990). *Discursive democracy: Politics, policy and political science*. Cambridge, UK: Cambridge University Press.

Dryzek, J. (2002). *Deliberative democracy and beyond: Liberals, critics, contestations*. Oxford, UK: Oxford University Press. doi:10.1093/019925043X.001.0001

Dryzek, J., & Niemeyer, S. (2006). Reconciling pluralism and consensus as political ideals. *American Journal of Political Science, 50*(3), 634–649. doi:10.1111/j.1540-5907.2006.00206.x

Dung, P. M. (1995). On the acceptability of arguments and its fundamental role in non-monotonic reasoning, logic programming and n-person games. *Artificial Intelligence, 77*(2), 321–357. doi:10.1016/0004-3702(94)00041-X

Dutoit, A., & McCall, B. Mistrik, & Paech, B. (2006). Rationale management in software engineering: Concepts and techniques. In A. Dutoit, B. McCall, Mistrik, et al. (Eds.), *Rationale Management in Software Engineering*, (pp. 1-48). London, UK: Springer.

Dyer, M. (1983). *In depth understanding: A computer model of integrated processing for narrative comprehension*. Cambridge, MA: MIT Press.

Eden, C. (1990). Strategic thinking with computers. *Long Range Planning, 23*(6), 35–43. doi:10.1016/0024-6301(90)90100-I

Elhadad, N., Kan, M.-Y., Klavans, J. L., & McKeown, K. (2005). Customization in a unified framework for summarizing medical literature. *Artificial Intelligence in Medicine, 33*(2), 179–198. doi:10.1016/j.artmed.2004.07.018

Emanuel, J., & Emanuel, L. (1992). Four models of the physician-patient relationship. *Journal of the American Medical Association, 267*(16), 2221–2226. doi:10.1001/jama.1992.03480160079038

Emery, M., & Purser, R. E. (1996). *The search conference: A powerful method for planning organisational change and community action*. San Francisco, CA: Jossey Bass.

Engisch, K. (1960). *Logische studien zur gesetzesanwendung* (2nd ed.). Heidelberg, Germany: Heidelberg Press.

European Union. (2004). *EU water initiative – Water for life*. Luxembourg, Luxembourg: Office for Official Publications of the European Communities.

Facione, P. (1990). *Critical thinking: A statement of expert consensus*. Millbrae, CA: California Academic Press.

Facione, P. (1992). *The California critical thinking skills test and manual*. Millbrae, CA: California Academic Press.

Fang, L., Hipel, W., Kilgour, D., & Peng, X. (2003b). A decision support system for interactive decision making, part 2: Analysis and output interpretation. *IEEE Transactions on Systems, Man and Cybernetics. Part C, 33*(1), 56–66.

Farley, A., & Freeman, K. (1995). Burden of proof in legal argumentation. In *Proceedings of Fifth International Conference on Artificial Intelligence and Law*, (pp. 156-164). ACM Press.

Felbaum, C. (1998). *Wordnet: An electronic lexical database for English*. Cambridge, MA: MIT Press.

Fes, J., Giupponi, C., & Rosato, P. (2004). Water management, public participation and decision support systems: The mulino approach. In C. P. Wostl, S. Schmidt, A. Rizzoli, & A. J. Jakeman (Eds.), *Complexity and Integrated Resources Management: Transactions of the 2nd Biennial Meeting of the International Environmental Modelling and Software Society*. Osnabruck, Germany: IEMSS. Retrieved from http://www.iemss.org/iemss2004/sessions/dss2.html.

Figueira, J., Greco, S., & Ehrgott, M. (2005). *Multiple criteria decision analysis: State of the art surveys*. New York, NY: Springer.

Fillmore, C. J., Johnson, C. R., & Petruck, M. R. (2003). Background to framenet. *International Journal of Lexicography, 16*(3), 235–250. doi:10.1093/ijl/16.3.235

Fishburn, P. C. (1970). *Utility theory for decision making*. New York, NY: Operations Research Society of America.

Fisher, R., Ury, W. L., & Patton, B. (1992). *Getting to yes: Negotiating agreement without giving in* (2nd ed.). Boston, MA: Houghton Mifflin.

Fisher, W. (1985). The narrative paradigm: An elaboration. *Communication Monographs, 52*, 347–367. doi:10.1080/03637758509376117

Fisher, W. (1994). Narrative rationality and the logic of scientific discourse. *Argumentation, 8*, 21–32. doi:10.1007/BF00710701

Fisher, W. (1995). *Narration, knowledge and the possibility of wisdom, rethinking knowledge: Reflections across the disciplines*. Albany, NY: State University of New York Press.

Fishkin, J. (1991). *Democracy and deliberation: New directions for democratic reform*. New Haven, CT: Yale University Press.

Fox, J. (1986). Knowledge, decision making and uncertainty. In Gale, W. A. (Ed.), *Artificial Intelligence and Statistics*. Reading, MA: Addison-Wesley.

Fox, J., & Das, S. (2000). *Safe and sound: Artificial intelligence in hazardous applications*. Menlo Park, CA: AAAI Press.

Fox, J., & Parsons, S. (1998). Arguing about beliefs and actions. In Hunter, A., & Parsons, S. (Eds.), *Applications of Uncertainty Formalisms* (pp. 266–302). Berlin, Germany: Springer. doi:10.1007/3-540-49426-X_13

Fox, S. M., & Gruninger, M. (1998). Enterprise modelling. *AI Magazine, 19*(3), 109–121.

Frege, G. (1884). *The foundations of arithmetic: A logico-mathematical enquiry into the concept of number* (Austin, J. L., Trans.). Evanston, IL: Northwestern University Press.

French, S., & Turoff, M. (2007). Decision support systems. *Communications of the ACM, 50*(3), 39–40. doi:10.1145/1226736.1226762

Frisby, D. (1978). Eine theorie des praktischen diskurses. In Oelmuller, W. (Ed.), *Normenbegrundung-Normen-durchsetzung. Berlin, Germany*. Paderborn.

Fürst, F., & Trichet, F. (2006). Reasoning on the semantic web needs to reason both on ontology-based assertions and on ontologies themselves. In *Proceedings of the World Wide Web Conference*. Edinburgh, UK: Aalborg University Press.

Geoffrey, N. (2005). Research in clinical reasoning: Past history and current trends. *Medical Education, 13*(4), 418–427.

Gershenson, C., & Heylighen, F. (2005). How can we think the complex? In Richardson, K. (Ed.), *Managing the Complex: Philosophy, Theory and Application* (Vol. 1, pp. 47–62). Charlotte, NC: Information Age Publishing.

Glymour, C., & Thomason, R. (1984). Default reasoning and the logic of theory perturbation. In *Proceedings of the AAAI Workshop on Nonmonotonic Reasoning*, (pp. 17–19). AAAI.

Goble, C., & Crowther, P. (1994). Schemas for telling stories in medical records, in M. Jarke, J. Bubenko, & K. Jeffery (Eds.), *Proceedings of the 4th International Conference on Extending Database Technology (EDBT)*. Cambridge, UK: Springer-Verlag.

Golder, C., & Coirier, P. (1996). The production and recognition of typological argumentative test markers. *Argumentation, 10*(2), 271–282. doi:10.1007/BF00180729

Goldman, A. (1999). *Knowledge in a social world*. Oxford, UK: Clarendon Press. doi:10.1093/0198238207.001.0001

Goldstein, J., Mittal, V., Carbonell, J., & Kantrowitz, M. (2000). Multi-document summarization by sentence extraction. In Proceedings of ANLP/NAACL 2000 Workshop on Automatic Summarization, (pp. 40-48). East Stroudsburg, PA: Association for Computational Linguistics.

Goodman, J. (2003). The pros and cons of online dispute resolution: An assessment of cyber-mediation websites. *Duke Law and Technology Review, 4*. Retrieved from http://www.law.duke.edu/journals/dltr/articles/2003dltr0004.html.

Gordon, T. (1995b). Zeno: A www system for geographical mediation. In M. Armstrong & K. Kemp (Eds.), *Collaborative Spatial Decision-Making, Scientific Report of the Initiative 17 Specialist Meeting, Technical Report*, (pp. 77-89). Santa Barbara, CA: Initiative 17.

Gordon, T. (2004). *Egovernance and its value for public administration: Knowledge-based services for the public sector*. Paper presented at the Symposium on Knowledge-Based Services for the Public Sector. Bonn, Germany.

Gordon, T. (2005). Information technology for good governance. In D. Bourcier (Ed.), *Proceedings of the French-German Symposium on Governance, Law and Technology*, (pp. 87-95). Paris, France: University of Paris.

Gordon, T. (2007). Constructing arguments with a computational model of an argumentation scheme for legal rules: Interpreting legal rules as reasoning policies. In R. Winkels (Ed.), *Proceedings of the Eleventh International Conference on Artificial Intelligence and Law*. New York, NY: ACM Press.

Gordon, T., & Karacapilidis, N. (1997). The zeno argumentation framework. In *Proceedings of the Sixth International Conference on Artificial Intelligence and Law*, (pp. 10-18). Melbourne, Australia: ACM Press.

Gordon, T., & Walton, D. (2006). The carneades argumentation framework: Using presumptions and exceptions to model critical questions. In *Proceedings of the First International Conference on Computational Models of Argument (COMMA 2006)*, (pp. 208-219). Liverpool, UK: IOS Press.

Gordon, T. (1995a). The pleadings game: An exercise in computational dialectics. *Artificial Intelligence and Law, 2*(4), 239–292. doi:10.1007/BF00871972

Gordon, T., & Marker, O. (2002). Mediation systems. In Marker, O., & Trenel, M. (Eds.), *Neue Medien in Der Konfliktvermittlung -Mit Beispielen Aus Politik Und Wirtschaft* (pp. 61–84). Berlin, Germany: Edition Sigma.

Gordon, T., & Richter, G. (2002). In Lenk, K., & Traunm¨uller, R. (Eds.). Lecture Notes in Computer Science: *Vol. 248–255. Discourse support systems for deliberative democracy*.

Gordon, T., Voss, A., Richter, G., & Marker, O. (2001). Zeno: Groupware for discourses on the internet. *K¨unstliche Intelligenz, 2*(1), 43–45.

Governatori, G., & Stranieri, A. (2001). Towards the application of association rules for defeasible rule discovery. In *Proceedings of the Fourteenth Annual International Conference on Legal Knowledge and Information Systems Jurix 2001*, (pp. 63-75). Amsterdam, The Netherlands: IOS Press.

Govier, T. (1987). *Problems in argument analysis and evaluation*. Dordrecht, The Netherlands: Kluwer.

Govier, T. (1992). *A practical study of argument* (3rd ed.). Belmont, CA: Wadsworth.

Graesser, A. (1981). *Prose comprehension beyond the word*. New York, NY: Springer Verlag. doi:10.1007/978-1-4612-5880-3

Grennan, W. (1997). *Informal logic: Issues and techniques*. Montreal, Canada: McGill-Queen's University Press.

Gross, T. (2000). Technological support for e-democracy: History and perspectives. In *Proceedings of 11th International Workshop on Database and Expert Systems Applications*, (pp. 391-395). London, UK: ACM.

Gruber, T. R. (1993). A translation approach to portable ontologies. *Knowledge Acquisition*, *5*(2), 199–220. doi:10.1006/knac.1993.1008

Guarino, N. (Ed.). (1998). Formal ontology in information systems. In *Proceedings of the First International Conference (FOIS 1998), Frontiers in Artificial Intelligence and Applications*. Amsterdam, The Netherlands: IOS Press.

Guarino, N., & Giaretta, P. (1995). *Towards very large knowledge bases: Knowledge building and knowledge sharing*. Amsterdam, The Netherlands: IOS Press.

Gürkan, A., Iandoli, L., Klein, M., & Zollo, G. (2010). Mediating debate through on-line large-scale argumentation: Evidence from the field. *Information Sciences*, *180*(19), 3686–3702. doi:10.1016/j.ins.2010.06.011

Habermas, J. (1984). *The theory of communicative action. Thomas McCarthy (Trans.)*. Cambridge, UK: Polity.

Hage, J. C. (1997). *Reasoning with rules: An essay on legal reasoning and its underlying logic. V Dordrecht*. The Netherlands: Kluwer.

Hall, M. J. J., Stranieri, A., & Zeleznikow, J. (2002). A strategy for evaluating web-based discretionary decision support systems. In *Proceedings of ADBIS2002 -Sixth East-European Conference on Advances in Databases and Information Systems*, (pp. 108-120). Bratislava, Slovak Republic: Slovak University of Technology.

Hall, M. J., Hall, R., & Zeleznikow, J. (2003). A process for evaluating legal knowledge-based systems based upon the context criteria contingency-guidelines framework. In Proceedings of the 9th International Conference on Artificial Intelligence and Law, (pp. 274-283). ACM Press.

Hall, M. J., Calabro, D., Sourdin, T., Stranieri, A., & Zeleznikow, J. (2005). Supporting discretionary decision making with information technology: A case study in the criminal sentencing jurisdiction. *University of Ottawa Law & Technology Journal*, *2*(1), 1–36.

Hamalainen, R. (2003). Decisionarium -Aiding decisions, negotiating and collecting opinions on the web. *Journal of Multi-Criteria Decision Analysis*, *12*, 101–110. doi:10.1002/mcda.350

Hamouda, L., Hipel, K., & Kilgour, D. (2004). Shellfish conflict in baynes sound: A strategic perspective. *Environmental Management*, *34*(4), 474–486. Retrieved from http://www.systems.uwaterloo.ca/Research/CAG/journals.htmldoi:10.1007/s00267-004-0227-2

Hamouda, L., Hipel, K., Kilgour, D., Noakes, D., Fang, L., & McDaniels, T. (2005). The salmon aquaculture conflict in British Columbia: A graph model analysis. *Ocean and Coastal Management*, *48*(7-8), 571–587. doi:10.1016/j.ocecoaman.2005.02.001

Hart, H. L. A. (1961). *The concept of law*. Oxford, UK: Clarendon Press.

Hart, H., & Honore, A. (1959). *Causation in the law*. Oxford, UK: Clarendon Press.

Hatcher, M. (1994). Voting and priorities in health care decision making, portrayed through a group decision support system, using analytic hierarchy process. *Journal of Medical Systems*, *18*(5), 267–288. doi:10.1007/BF00996606

Hathorn, L., & Ingram, A. (2002). Cooperation and collaboration using computer-mediated communication. *Journal of Educational Computing Research*, *26*(3), 325–347. doi:10.2190/7MKH-QVVN-G4CQ-XRDU

Hearst, M. A. (1997). Texttiling: Segmenting text into multi-paragraph subtopic passages. *Computational Linguistics*, *23*(1), 33–64.

Heckerman, D., Horvitz, E., & Nathwani, B. (1992). Toward normative expert systems: Part I: The pathfinder project. *Methods of Information in Medicine*, *31*(2), 90–105.

Hipel, K., Fang, L., & Kilgour, D. (2008). Decision support systems in water resources and environmental management. *Journal of Hydrologic Engineering, 13*(9), 287–300. doi:10.1061/(ASCE)1084-0699(2008)13:9(761)

Hitchcock, D. (1991). Some principles of rational mutual inquiry. In F. van Eemeren, R. Grootendorst, J. A. Blair, & C. A. Willard (Eds.), *Proceedings of the Second International Conference on Argumentation (AAAI 2000)*, (pp. 236-243). SICSAT.

Hitchcock, D., McBurney, P., & Parsons, S. (2001). A framework for deliberation dialogues, argumentation and its applications. In H. V. Hansen, C. W. Tindale, J. A. Blair, & R. H. Johnson (Eds.), *Proceedings of the Fourth Biennial Conference of the Ontario Society for the Study of Argumentation*. Windsor, Canada: University of Windsor.

Ho, T., & Antunes, P. (1999). Developing a tool to assist electronic facilitation of decision-making groups. In *Proceedings of the Fifth International Workshop on Groupware, CRIWG 1999*, (pp. 243-252). Cancun, Mexico: IEEE CS Press. Retrieved from http://www.di.fc.ul.pt/ paa/papers/criwg-99.pdf.

Horn, M. V. (1986). *Understanding expert systems*. Toronto, Canada: Bantam Books.

Howard, R. (1988). Panel remarks: CSCW: What does it mean? In *Proceedings of the Conference on Computer-Supported Cooperative Work*. New York, NY: ACM Press.

Hua, G., & Kimbrough, S. (1988). On hypermedia-based argumentation decision support systems. *Decision Support Systems, 22*, 259–275. doi:10.1016/S0167-9236(97)00062-6

Huizinga, J. (1972). *America: A Dutch historian's vision from afar and near*. New York, NY: Harper Torchbooks.

Hulstjin, J. (2000). *Dialogue models for inquiry and transaction*. PhD Thesis. Enschede, The Netherlands: University of Twente.

Hymes, C., & Olson, G. (1992). Unblocking brainstorming through the use of a simple group editor. In Proceedings of the Conference on Computer Supported Cooperative Work, (pp. 99-106). New York, NY: ACM Press.

Jackson, B. S. (1990). Narrative theories and legal discourse. In Nash, C. (Ed.), *Narrative in Culture: The Uses of Storytelling in the Sciences, Philosophy and Literature* (pp. 23–50). London, UK: Routledge.

Jaeger, P. (2004). The social impact of an accessible e-democracy: Disability rights laws in the development of the federal e-government. *Journal of Disability Policy Studies, 15*(1), 19–26. doi:10.1177/10442073040150010401

Jain, A. K., Murty, M. N., & Flynn, P. J. (1999). Data clustering: A review. *ACM Computing Surveys, 31*(3), 264–323. Retrieved from http://www.citeseer.ist.psu.edu/jain99data.htmldoi:10.1145/331499.331504

Janis, I. (1972). *Victims of groupthink: A psychological study of foreign-policy decisions and fiascoes* (2nd ed.). Boston, MA: Houghton Mifflin.

Janis, I. (1983). *Groupthink: Psychological studies of policy decisions and fiascos*. Boston, MA: Houghton Mifflin.

Jeffrey, P., & Gearey, M. (2006). Integrated water resources management: Lost on the road from ambition to realisation? *Water Science and Technology, 53*(1), 1–8. doi:10.2166/wst.2006.001

Jimenez, A., Mateos, A., & Ros-Insua, S. (2005). Monte Carlo simulation techniques in a decision support system for group decision making. *Group Decision and Negotiation, 14*(2), 109–130. doi:10.1007/s10726-005-2406-9

Joachims, T. (1998). Text categorization with support vector machines: Learning with many relevant features. In *Proceedings of the European Conference on Machine Learning*, (pp. 137-142). Berlin, Germany: Springer-Verlag.

Johnson, N. S., & Mandler, J. M. (1980). A tale of two structures: Underlying and surface forms in stories. *Poetics, 9*, 51–86. doi:10.1016/0304-422X(80)90012-1

Johnson, P., Zualkernan, I., & Tukey, D. (1993). Types of expertise: An invariant of problem solving. *International Journal of Man-Machine Studies, 39*, 641–652. doi:10.1006/imms.1993.1077

Johnson, R., & Blair, J. (1983). *Logical self-defense*. Toronto, Canada: McGraw-Hill.

Jones, A. (1990). Deontic logic and legal knowledge representation. *Ratio Juris, 3*(2), 237–244. doi:10.1111/j.1467-9337.1990.tb00060.x

Jones, A., & Sergot, M. (1992). Deontic logic in the representation of law: Towards a methodology. *Artificial Intelligence and Law, 1*(1), 45–64. doi:10.1007/BF00118478

Jong, G. D. (1982). Information extraction. In Lehnert, W., & Ringle, M. H. (Eds.), *Strategies for Natural Language Processing* (pp. 149–176). Mahwah, NJ: Lawrence Erlbaum.

Jorgensen, J. (1937). Imperatives and logic. *Erkenntnis, 7*, 288–296.

Kampen, J. K., & Snijkers, K. (2003). E-democracy. *Social Science Computer Review, 21*(4), 491–496. doi:10.1177/0894439303256095

Kaplan, B. (2001). Evaluating informatics applications -Clinical decision support systems literature review. *International Journal of Medical Informatics, 64*, 15–37. doi:10.1016/S1386-5056(01)00183-6

Kaszkiel, M., & Zobel, J. (1997). Passage retrieval revisited. In N. J. Belkin, A. D. Narasimhalu, & P. Willett (Eds.), *Proceedings of 20th Annual International ACM SIGIR Conference on Research and Development in Information Retrieval*, (pp. 178-185). Philadelphia, PA: ACM Press.

Kay, S., & Purvis, I. (1996). Medical records and other stories: A narratological framework. *Methods of Information in Medicine, 35*, 72–87.

Kazuaki, K. (2004). Techniques of document clustering: A review. *Library and Information Science, 49*, 33–75.

Kelsen, H. (1991). *General theory of norms*. Oxford, UK: Clartendon Press. doi:10.1093/acprof:oso/9780198252177.001.0001

Kersten, G., & Noronha, S. (1999). Negotiation via the world wide web: A cross-cultural study of decision making. *Group Decision and Negotiation, 8*(3), 251–279. Retrieved from http://www.iiasa.ac.at/Publications/Documents/IR-97-052.pdfdoi:10.1023/A:1008657921819

Kilgour, D. (2003). *Encyclopedia of life support systems*. Oxford, UK: EOLSS Publishers.

Kipper, K., Dang, H. T., & Palmer, M. (2000). Class-based construction of a verb lexicon. In *Proceedings of the AAAI-2000 Seventeenth National Conference on Artificial Intelligence*. AAAI.

Kling, R. (1991). Cooperation, coordination and control in computer-supported work. *Communications of the ACM, 34*(12), 83–88. doi:10.1145/125319.125396

Knight, K., & Luk, S. (1994). Building a large-scale knowledge base for machine translation. In *Proceedings of the 12th National Conference on Artificial Intelligence (AAAI 1994)*, (Vol 1), (pp. 773-778). Seattle, WA: AAAI.

Kock, N., & Antunes, P. (2007). Government funding of e-collaboration research in the European union: A comparison with the united states model. *Journal of e-Collaboration, 3*(2), 36–47. Retrieved from http://www.di.fc.ul.pt/ paa/papers/jec-07.pdf.

Krause, P., Ambler, S., Elvang-Goransson, M., & Fox, J. (1995). A logic of argumentation for reasoning under uncertainty. *Computational Intelligence, 11*(1), 113–131. doi:10.1111/j.1467-8640.1995.tb00025.x

Kulpa, Z. (1994). Diagrammatic representation and reasoning. *Machine Graphics and Vision, 3*(1/2), 77–103.

Kuziemsky, C., & Jahnke, J. (2005). Information systems and health care v -A multi-modal approach to health care decision support systems. *Communications of the Association for Information Systems, 16*, 407–420.

Lame, G. (2003). Using text analysis techniques to identify legal ontologys components. In *Proceedings of the ICAIL 2003 Workshop on Legal Ontologies & Web Based Legal Information Management*. New York, NY: ACM Press.

Larkin, J., & Simon, H. (1987). Why a diagram is (sometimes) worth ten thousand words. *Cognitive Science, 11*, 64–100. doi:10.1111/j.1551-6708.1987.tb00863.x

Laukkanen, S., Palander, T., Kangas, J., & Kangas, A. (2005). Evaluation of the multicriteria approval method for timber-harvesting group decision support. *Silva Fennica, 39*, 249–264.

Lave, J., & Wenger, E. (1991). *Situated learning: Legitimate peripheral participation*. Cambridge, UK: Cambridge University Press.

Lee, Y., & Koh, K.-K. (2002). Decision-making of nuclear energy policy: application of environmental management tool to nuclear fuel cycle. *Energy Policy, 30*(13), 1151–1161. doi:10.1016/S0301-4215(02)00004-6

Lehnert, W. G. (1982). Plot units: A narrative summarization strategy. In Lehnert, W. G., & Ringle, M. H. (Eds.), *Strategies for Natural Language Processing* (pp. 375–414). Hillsdale, NJ: Erlbaum.

Lenat, D., Prakash, M., & Shephard, M. (1986). Cyc: Using commone sense knowledge to overcome brittleness and knowledge acquisition bottlenecks. *AI Magazine, 6*(4), 65–85.

Leuski, A. (2001). Evaluating document clustering for interactive information retrieval. In *Proceedings of the ACM CIKM 2001 Tenth International Conference on Information and Knowledge Management*, (pp. 33-40). New York, NY: ACM Press.

Lichterman, P. (1996). *The search for political community: American activists reinventing commitment.* Cambridge, UK: Cambridge University Press. doi:10.1017/CBO9780511628146

Linstone, H. A., & Turoff, M. (1975). *The delphi method: Techniques and applications.* Reading, MA: Addison-Wesley.

Lipponen, L., Rahikainen, M., Hakkarainen, K., & Palonen, T. (2002). Effective participation and discourse through a computer network: Investigating elementary students computer supported interaction. *Journal of Educational Computing Research, 27*(4), 355–384. doi:10.2190/MGTW-QG1E-G66E-F3UD

List, C., & Pettit, P. (2002). Aggregating sets of judgments: Two impossibility results compared. *Economics and Philosophy, 18*, 89–110.

Littleboy, A., Boughen, N., Niemeyer, S., & Fisher, K. (2006). *Societal uptake of alternative energy futures: Final report. Technical report.* Newcastle, UK: CSIRO Energy Transformed Research Flagship.

Liu, X., & Wirtz, K. W. (2006). Decision making of oil spill contingency options with fuzzy comprehensive evaluation. *Water Resources Management, 21*(4), 663–676. doi:10.1007/s11269-006-9031-5

Llewellyn, K. N. (1962). *Jurisprudence: Realism in theory and practice.* Chicago, IL: The University of Chicago Press.

Lodder, A. (1998). *DiaLaw -On legal justification and dialog games.* PhD thesis.

Lodder, A., & Bol, S. (2006). *Towards an online negotiation environment: Legal principles, technical requirements and the need for close cooperation.* Retrieved from http://www.odr.info/papers.php.

Lodder, A., & Verheij, B. (1998). Opportunities of computer-mediated legal argument in education. In *Proceedings of the BILETA-Conference.* Dublin, Ireland: BILETA.

Lodder, A. (1999). *DiaLaw -On legal justification and dialogical models of argumentation.* Dordrecht, The Netherlands: Kluwer Academic Publishers.

Lodder, A. R., & Zeleznikow, J. (2005). Developing an online dispute resolution environment: Dialogue tools and negotiation systems in a three step model. *Harvard Negotiation Law Review, 10*, 287–337.

Loui, R., Norman, J., Altepeter, J., Pinkard, D., Craven, D., Lindsay, J., & Foltz, M. (1997). Progress in room 5: A testbed for public interactive semi-formal legal argumentation. In *Proceedings of the Sixth International Conference on Artificial Intelligence and Law*, (pp. 207-214). New York, NY: ACM Press.

Luce, R. D., & Raiffa, H. (1957). *Games and decisions.* New York, NY: John Wiley and Sons.

Luhn, H. P. (1958). The automatic creation of literature abstracts. *IBM Journal of Research and Development, 2*, 159–165. doi:10.1147/rd.22.0159

Luhrs, R., Malsch, T., & Voss, K. (2001). Internet, discourses and democracy. In T. Terano (Ed.), *New Frontiers in Artificial Intelligence: Joint JSAI 2001 Workshop Post-Proceedings.* London, UK: Springer.

MacCormick. (1978). *Legal reasoning and legal theory.* Oxford, UK: Oxford University Press.

Macintosh, A., Robson, E., Smith, E., & Whyte, A. (2002). Electronic democracy and young people. *Social Science Computer Review, 21*(1), 43–54. doi:10.1177/0894439302238970

Mackie, J. (1980). *The cement of the universe: A study of causation*. Oxford, UK: Clarendon Press.

Mahesh, K., & Nirenburg, S. (1995). A situated ontology for practical nlp. In *Proceedings of the IJCAI-95 Workshop on Basic Ontological Issues in Knowledge Sharing*. Ottawa, Canada: University of Ottawa.

Makau, J. M., & Marty, D. L. (2001). *Cooperative argumentation: A model for deliberative community*. Long Grove, IL: Waveland Press Inc.

Mandler, J. (1984). *Stories, scripts and scenes: Aspects of schema theory*. Hillsdale, NJ: Lawrence Erlbaum Associates.

Mandler, J., & Johnson, N. (1977). Remembrance of things parsed: Story structure and recall. *Cognitive Psychology*, *9*, 111–151. doi:10.1016/0010-0285(77)90006-8

Mango, L. (1994). Computer-assisted cervical cancer screening using neural networks. *Cancer Letters*, *77*(2/3), 155–162. doi:10.1016/0304-3835(94)90098-1

Mani, I. (2001). *Summarization evaluation: An overview*. Retrieved from http://citeseer.ist.psu.edu/mani01summarization.html.

Manville, B., & Ober, J. (2003). *A company of citizens: What the world's first democracy teaches leaders about creating great organizations*. Boston, MA: Harvard Business School Press.

Marashi, E., & Davis, J. P. (2006). An argumentation-based method for managing complex issues in design of infrastructural systems. *Reliability Engineering & System Safety*, *91*(12), 1535–1545. doi:10.1016/j.ress.2006.01.013

Marker, O., Hagedorn, H., Trenel, M., & Gordon, T. (2002). Internet-based citizen participation in the city of Esslingen: Relevance moderation –Software. In M. Schrenk (Ed.), *CORP 2002: Who plans Europe's future? Technical University International Symposium on Information Technology in Urban and Regional Planning and Impacts of ICT on Physical Space*. Vienna, Austria: Information Technology in Urban and Regional Planning.

Marshall, C. C. (1989). Representing the structure of legal argument. In *Proceedings of Second International Conference on Artificial Intelligence and Law*, (pp. 121-127). New York, NY: ACM Press.

Matthijssen, L. J. (1999). *Interfacing between lawyers and computers: An architecture for knowledge based interfaces to legal databases*. Dordrecht, The Netherlands: Kluwer Law International.

McBurney, P., Parsons, S., & Wooldridge, M. (2002). Desiderata for agent argumentation protocols. In *Proceedings of the First International Joint Conference on Autonomous Agents and Multiagent Systems: Part 1*, (pp. 402-409). New York, NY: ACM Press.

McBurney, P., & Parsons, S. (2001). Representing epistemic uncertainty by means of dialectical argumentation. *Annals of Mathematics and Artificial Intelligence*, *32*(14), 125–169. doi:10.1023/A:1016757315265

McBurney, P., van Eijk, R. M., Parsons, S., & Amgoud, L. (2003). A dialogue game protocol for agent purchase negotiations. *Journal of Autonomous Agents and Multi-Agent Systems*, *7*(3), 235–273. doi:10.1023/A:1024787301515

McCloskey, D. N. (1990). Storytelling in economics. In Nash, C. (Ed.), *Narrative in Culture: The Uses of Storytelling in the Sciences, Philosophy and Literature* (pp. 5–22). London, UK: Routledge.

McDermott, D., & Doyle, J. (1980). Non-monotonic logic. *Artificial Intelligence*, *13*, 41–72. doi:10.1016/0004-3702(80)90012-0

McGuinness, D. L. (1998). Ontological issues for knowledge enhanced search. In N. Guarino (Ed.), *Proceedings of the First International Conference on Formal Ontology in Information Systems*, (pp. 302-316). Trento, Italy: IOS Press.

McLauchlin, M. (1990). Explanatory discourse and causal attribution. *Text*, *10*, 63–68. doi:10.1515/text.1.1990.10.1-2.63

McMahon, C. (2001). *Collective rationality and collective reasoning*. Cambridge, UK: Cambridge University Press.

McNamara, P. (1996). Making room for going beyond the call. *Mind*, *105*(419), 415–450. doi:10.1093/mind/105.419.415

Melbourne Corporation. (2007). *Channel deepening project environment effects statement*. Technical report. Melbourne, Australia: Port of Melbourne Corporation.

Mercier, H., & Sperber, D. (2011). Why do humans reason? Arguments for an argumentative theory philosophy, politics and economics program, University of Pennsylvania. *The Behavioral and Brain Sciences*, *34*, 57–111. doi:10.1017/S0140525X10000968

Mochol, M. (2004). Discourse support design patterns. In A. Lodder (Ed.), *Essays on Legal and Technical Aspects of Online Dispute Resolution*, (pp. 61-74). Amsterdam, The Netherlands: CEDIRE: Centre for Electronic Dispute Resolution.

Morge, M., & Beaune, P. (2004). A negotiation support system based on a multi-agent system: Specificity and preference relations on arguments. In *Proceedings of the 2004 ACM Symposium on Applied Computing*, (pp. 474-478). New York, NY: ACM Press.

Morozow, O. (2006). *The heat is on: The future of energy in Australia. Technical report*. Melbourne, Australia: Commonwealth Scientific and Industrial Research Organisation.

Muecke, N., & Stranieri, A. (2008). An argument structure abstraction for Bayesian belief networks: Just outcomes in on-line dispute resolution. In *Proceedings of the Fourth Asia-Pacific Conference on Conceptual Modelling*, (Vol 67), (pp. 35-40). IEEE.

Nelson, E. J. (1933). On three logical principles in intension. *The Monist*, *43*(2), 268–284.

Ness, B., Urbel-Piirsalu, E., Anderberg, S., & Olsson, L. (2007). Categorising tools for sustainability assessment. *Ecological Economics*, *60*(3), 498–509. doi:10.1016/j.ecolecon.2006.07.023

Newell, A. (1982). The knowledge level. *Artificial Intelligence*, *18*(1), 87–127. doi:10.1016/0004-3702(82)90012-1

Newell, A., & Simon, H. (1976). Computer science as empirical inquiry: Symbols and search. *Communications of the ACM*, *19*(3), 113–126. doi:10.1145/360018.360022

Niemeyer, S. J. (2007). *Intersubjective rationality: Measuring deliberative quality*. Paper presented to Political Science Seminar, RSSS, ANU. Helsinki, Finland.

Niemeyer, S. J. (2011). Intersubjective reasoning and the formation of metaconsensus. In Yearwood, J., & Stranieri, A. (Eds.), *Technologies for Supporting Reasoning Communities and Collaborative Decision Making: Cooperative Approaches*. Hershey, PA: IGI Global. doi:10.4018/978-1-60960-091-4.ch002

Niemeyer, S., & Blamey, R. (2003). *The far north Queensland citizens' jury. Technical report*. Canberra, Australia: Land and Water Australia.

Noakes, D., Fang, L., Hipel, K., & Kilgour, D. (2005). The pacific salmon treaty: A century of debate and an uncertain future. *Group Decision and Negotiation*, *14*(6), 501–522. doi:10.1007/s10726-005-9005-7

Nute, D. (1988). Defeasible reasoning. In Fetzer, J. H. (Ed.), *Aspects of Artificial Intelligence* (pp. 251–288). Norwell, MA: Kluwer Academic Publishers. doi:10.1007/978-94-009-2699-8_9

Nute, D. (1994). Defeasible logic. In Gabbay, D., & Hogger, M. (Eds.), *Handbook of Logic in Artificial Intelligence and Logic Programming* (pp. 353–394). London, UK: Clarendon Press.

O'Brien, G. (2002). Participation as the key to successful change: A public sector case. *Leadership and Organization Development Journal*, *23*(8), 442–455. doi:10.1108/01437730210449339

O'Connor, M., Knublauch, H., Tu, S., Grosof, B., Dean, M., Grosso, W., & Musen, M. (2005). Supporting rule system interoperability on the semantic web with SWRL. In *Proceedings of the International Semantic Web Conference*, (pp. 974-986). Berlin, Germany: Springer-Verlag.

Ofoghi, B., Yearwood, J., & Ghosh, R. (2006). A hybrid question answering schema using encapsulated semantics in lexical resources. *Advances in Artificial Intelligence*, *4304*, 1276–1280.

Palmer, M., Kingsbury, P., & Gildea, D. (2006). The proposition bank: An annotated corpus of semantic roles. *Computational Linguistics*, *31*(1), 71–106. doi:10.1162/0891201053630264

Park, J., & Hunting, S. (2002). *XML topic maps: Creating and using topic maps for the web*. Boston, MA: Addison-Wesley.

Pennington, N., & Hastie, R. (1981). Juror decision-making models: The generalization gap. *Psychological Bulletin, 89*, 246–287. doi:10.1037/0033-2909.89.2.246

Pennington, N., & Hastie, R. (1986). Evidence evaluation in complex decision making. *Journal of Personality and Social Psychology, 51*, 242–258. doi:10.1037/0022-3514.51.2.242

Pennington, N., & Hastie, R. (1992). Explaining the evidence: Tests of the story model for juror decision making. *Journal of Personality and Social Psychology, 62*, 189–206. doi:10.1037/0022-3514.62.2.189

Pennington, N., & Hastie, R. (1993). Reasoning in explanation-based decision making. *Cognition, 49*, 123–163. doi:10.1016/0010-0277(93)90038-W

Perelman, C., & Olbrechts-Tyteca, L. (1971). *The new rhetoric: A treatise on argumentation* (Wilkinson, J., & Weaver, P., Trans.). London, UK: University of Notre Dame Press.

Pettit, P. (1993). *The common mind: An essay on psychology, society and politics*. Oxford, UK: Oxford University Press.

Phua, M.-H., & Minowa, M. (2005). A GIS-based multi-criteria decision making approach to forest conservation planning at a landscape scale: A case study. *Landscape and Urban Planning, 71*(2), 207–222. doi:10.1016/j.landurbplan.2004.03.004

Pinsonneault, A., Barki, H., Gallupe, R. B., & Hoppen, N. (1999). Electronic brainstorming: The illusion of productivity. *Information Systems Research, 10*(2), 110–133. doi:10.1287/isre.10.2.110

Polletta, F. (2006). *It was like a fever: Storytelling in protest and politics*. Chicago, IL: University Of Chicago Press.

Pollock, J. L. (1987). Defeasible reasoning. *Cognitive Science, 11*, 481–518. doi:10.1207/s15516709cog1104_4

Pollock, J. L. (1995). *Cognitive carpentry: A blueprint for how to build a person*. Cambridge, MA: MIT Press.

Prakken, H. (1991). A tool in modelling disagreement in law: Preferring the most specific argument. In *Proceedings of the 3rd International Conference on Artificial Intelligence and Law (ICAIL)*, (pp. 165–174). ICAIL.

Prakken, H. (1993a). A logical framework for modelling legal argument. In *Proceedings of the Fourth International Conference on Artificial Intelligence and Law*, (pp. 1-9). ACM Press.

Prakken, H. (1993b). *Logical tools for modelling legal argument*. PhD Thesis. Amsterdam, The Netherlands: Vrije University.

Prakken, H. (1996). Two approaches to the formalisation of defeasible deontic reasoning. *Studia Logica, 57*(1), 73–90. doi:10.1007/BF00370670

Prakken, H. (1997). *Logical tools for modelling legal argument*. Dordrecht, The Netherlands: Kluwer. doi:10.1007/978-94-011-5668-4

Prakken, H., & Sartor, G. (1996). A dialectical model of assessing conflicting arguments in legal reasoning. *Artificial Intelligence and Law, 4*(3-4), 331–368. doi:10.1007/BF00118496

Propp, V. (1968). *Morphology of the folktale*. Austin, TX: University of Texas Press.

Qin, X., Huang, G., Huang, Y., Zeng, G., Chakma, A., & Li, J. (2006). NRSRM: A decision support system and visualization software for the management of petroleum-contaminated sites. *Energy Sources, 28*, 199–220. doi:10.1080/009083190889951

Radev, D., Blair-Goldensohn, S., & Zhang, Z. (2001). Experiments in single and multidocument summarization using mead. In *Proceedings of the Document Understanding Conference*. New York, NY: ACM Press.

Raghu, T., Ramesh, R., Chang, A.-M., & Whinston, A. (2001). Collaborative decision making: A connectionist paradigms for dialectical support. *Information Systems Research, 12*(4), 363–383. doi:10.1287/isre.12.4.363.9705

Randolph, A., Haynes, R., Wyatt, J., Cook, D., & Guyatt, G. (1999). Users guides to the medical literature: How to use an article evaluating the clinical impact of a computer-based clinical decision support system. *Journal of the American Medical Association, 282*(1), 67–74. doi:10.1001/jama.282.1.67

Rawls, J. (1993). *Political liberalism*. New York, NY: Columbia University Press.

Raz, J. (1990). *Practical reason and norms* (2nd ed.). Oxford, UK: Oxford University Press.

Read, S. J. (1987). Constructing causal scenarios: A knowledge structure approach to causal reasoning. *Journal of Personality and Social Psychology, 52*(2), 288–302. doi:10.1037/0022-3514.52.2.288

Reategui, E., Campbell, J., & Leao, B. (1997). Combining a neural network with case-based reasoning in a diagnostic system. *Artificial Intelligence in Medicine, 9*(1), 5–27. doi:10.1016/S0933-3657(96)00359-4

Reay, T. (2000). *Making managerial health care decisions in complex high velocity environments.* Edmonton, Canada: Alberta Heritage Foundation for Medical Research.

Reed, C., & Rowe, G. (2004). Araucaria: Software for argument analysis, diagramming and representation. *International Journal of AI Tools, 14*(3-4), 961–980. doi:10.1142/S0218213004001922

Reidsema, C., & Szczerbicki, E. (2002). Review of intelligent software architectures for the development of an intelligent decision support system for design process planning in concurrent engineering. *Cybernetics and Systems, 33*, 629–658. doi:10.1080/01969720290040786

Reiter, R. (1980). A logic for default reasoning. *Artificial Intelligence, 13*, 81–132. doi:10.1016/0004-3702(80)90014-4

Rescher, N. (1976). *Plausible reasoning.* Amsterdam, The Netherlands: Van Gorcum.

Ridderikhoff, J., & van Herk, B. (1999). Who is afraid of the system? Doctors attitude towards diagnostic systems. *International Journal of Medical Informatics, 53*, 91–100. doi:10.1016/S1386-5056(98)00145-2

Rinner, C. (2001). Argumentation maps: GIS-based discussion support for on-line planning. *Environment and Planning. B, Planning & Design, 28*, 847–863. doi:10.1068/b2748t

Rittel, H. J., & Webber, M. M. (1973). Dilemmas in a general theory of planning. *Policy Sciences, 4*, 155–169. doi:10.1007/BF01405730

Rittel, H. J., & Webber, M. M. (1984). Planning problems are wicked problems. In Cross, N. (Ed.), *Developments in Design Methodology* (pp. 135–144). New York, NY: John Wiley and Sons.

Robert, C. (2001). *The Bayesian choice.* Berlin, Germany: Springer Verlag.

Robert, H. M. I. (2000). *Robert's rules of order* (10th ed.). Cambridge, MA: Perseus Publishing.

Rolf, B. (2003). Educating reason: From craft to technology. In *Proceedings 6th International Conference on Computer Based Learning.* Retrieved from http://www.athenasoft.org.

Rosenthal, S., & Finger, S. (2006). Design collaboration in a distributed environment. In *Proceedings 36th ASEE/IEEE Frontiers in Education Conference.* San Diego, CA: IEEE Press.

Ross, S., Fang, L., & Hipel, K. (2002). A case-based reasoning system for conflict resolution: Design and implementation. *Engineering Applications of Artificial Intelligence, 15*(3-4), 369–383. doi:10.1016/S0952-1976(02)00065-9

Rousseau, J. J. (1968). *The social contract.* Harmondsworth, UK: Penguin.

Rowe, G., Reed, C., & Katzav, J. (2003). *Araucaria: Marking up argument.* Paper presented at the European Conference on Computing and Philosophy. Glasgow, UK.

Rowe, G., Macagno, F., Reed, C., & Walton, D. (2006). Araucaria as a tool for diagramming arguments in teaching and studying philosophy. *Teaching Philosophy, 29*(2), 111–124.

Rowe, G., & Wright, G. (1999). The delphi technique as a forecasting tool: Issues and analysis. *International Journal of Forecasting, 15*, 353–375. doi:10.1016/S0169-2070(99)00018-7

Rumelhart, D. E. (1975). Notes on a schema for stories. In Bobrow, D. G., & Collins, A. (Eds.), *Representation and Understanding: Studies in Cognitive Science* (pp. 185–210). New York, NY: Academic Press.

Sadri, F., Toni, F., & Torroni, P. (2001). Logic agents, dialogues and negotiation: An abductive approach. In M. Schroeder & K. Stathis (Eds.), *Proceedings of the Symposium on Information Agents for E-Commerce, Artificial Intelligence and the Simulation of Behaviour Conference*. AISB.

Sager, J. C. (1994). Terminology: Custodian of knowledge and means of knowledge transfer. *Terminology, 1*(1), 7–16. doi:10.1075/term.1.1.03sag

Salton, G. (1971). *The SMART retrieval system: Experiments in automatic document processing*. Englewood Cliffs, NJ: Prentice-Hall.

Scaife, M., & Rogers, Y. (1996). External cognition: How do graphical representations work? *International Journal of Human-Computer Studies, 45*, 185–213. doi:10.1006/ijhc.1996.0048

Schank, R. (1986). *Explanation patterns: Understanding mechanically and creatively*. Hillsdale, NJ: Erlbaum.

Schank, R. C., & Abelson, R. P. (1977). *Scripts, plans, goals and understanding: An inquiry into human knowledge structures*. Hillsdale, NJ: Lawrence Erlbaum.

Schmandt-Besserat, D. (1996). *How writing came about*. Austin, TX: University of Texas Press.

Schmandt-Besserat, D. (1996). *How writing came about*. Austin, TX: University of Texas Press.

Schultz, T. (2003). An essay on the role of government for ODR: Theoretical considerations about the future of ODR. *ADR Online Monthly UMASS, 7*, 8.

Sebastiani, F. (2002). Machine learning in automated text categorization. *ACM Computing Surveys, 34*, 1–47. doi:10.1145/505282.505283

Sergot, M. J., Sadri, F., Kowalski, R. A., Kriwaczek, F., Hammond, P., & Cory, H. T. (1986). The British nationality act as a logic program. *Communications of the ACM, 29*(5), 370–386. doi:10.1145/5689.5920

Sgouros, N. (1999). Dynamic generation, management and resolution of interactive plots. *Artificial Intelligence, 107*, 29–62. doi:10.1016/S0004-3702(98)00106-4

Shih, H., Wang, C., & Lee, E. (2004). A multiattribute GDSS for aiding problem-solving. *Mathematical and Computer Modelling, 39*(11-12), 1397–1412. doi:10.1016/j.mcm.2004.06.014

Shoemaker, P. (1982). The expected utility model: Its variants, purposes, evidence and limitations. *Journal of Economic Literature, 20*, 529–563.

Shoham, Y. (1993). Agent-oriented programming. *Artificial Intelligence, 60*(1), 51–92. doi:10.1016/0004-3702(93)90034-9

Shortliffe, E. H. (1976). *Computer based medical consultations: MYCIN*. New York, NY: Elsevier.

Singh, M. P. (2000). A social semantics for agent communications languages. In F. Dignum, B. Chaib-Draa, & H. Weigand (Eds.), *Proceedings of the International Joint Conference on Artificial Intelligence (IJCAI 1999) Workshop on Agent Communication Languages*. Berlin, Germany: Springer.

Slob, W. H. (2002). How to distinguish good and bad arguments: Dialogico-rhetorical normativity. *Argumentation, 16*, 179–196. doi:10.1023/A:1015589400146

Slotte, S., & H¨am¨al¨ainen, R. (2003). *Decision structuring dialogue*. Technical Report E13. Helsinki, Finland: Systems Analysis Laboratory Research Reports. Retrieved from http://www.sal.hut.fi/Personnel/Homepages/RaimoH/publications.html.

Soulier, E., & Caussanel, J. (2002). Narrative tools to improve collaborative sense-making. In *Meaning Negotiation: Papers from the AAAI Workshop*, (pp. 5-9). Menlo Park, CA: AAAI Press.

Sowa, J. (1984). *Conceptual structures: Information processing in mind and machine*. Reading, MA: Addison-Wesley.

Sparck-Jones, K. (1998). Automatic summarising: Factors and directions. In I. Mani & M. Maybury (Eds.), *Automatic Text Summarization*, (pp. 1-12). Cambridge, MA: MIT Press. Retrieved from http://www.citeseer.ist.psu.edu/jones98automatic.html.

Stamper, R., Todd, B., & Macpherson, P. (1994). Case-based explanation for medical diagnostic programs, with an example from gynaecology. *Methods of Information in Medicine, 33*(2), 205–213.

Steenbergen, M., Bachtinger, A., Sporndliand, M., & Steiner, J. (2003). Measuring political deliberation: A discourse quality index. *Comparative European Politics, 1*(1), 21–48. doi:10.1057/palgrave.cep.6110002

Steiner, J., Bachtiger, A., Sporndli, M., & Steenbergen, M. (2004). *Deliberative politics in action: Analysing parliamentary discourse.* Cambridge, UK: Cambridge University Press.

Stein, N. L., & Glenn, C. G. (1979). An analysis of story comprehension in elementary school children. In Freedle, R. (Ed.), *New Directions in Discourse Processing* (pp. 53–120). Norwood, NJ: Ablex.

Stranieri, A. (1999). *Automating legal reasoning in discretionary domains.* PhD Thesis. Melbourne, Australia: La Trobe University.

Stranieri, A., & Zeleznikow, J. (2000b). Knowledge discovery for decision support in law. In S. Ang, H. Kremer, W. Orlikowski, P. Weill, & J. Degross (Eds.), *Proceedings of International Conference on Information Systems (ICIS 2000),* (pp. 635-639). Brisbane, Australia: ICIS.

Stranieri, A., & Zeleznikow, J. (2000c). Tools for intelligent decision support system development in the legal domain. In *Proceedings of the 12th IEEE International Conference on Tools with Artificial Intelligence (ICTAI 2000),* (pp. 186-189). Vancouver, Canada: IEEE Computer Society.

Stranieri, A., & Zeleznikow, J. (2001). Webshell: The development of web based expert system shells. In *Research and Development in Expert Systems XVIII: Proceedings of ES2001-The Twenty-First SGES International Conference on Knowledge Based Systems and Applied Artificial Intelligence,* (pp. 245-258). London, UK: Springer Verlag.

Stranieri, A., Yearwood, J., & Zeleznikow, J. (2001). Tools for placing legal decision support systems on the world wide web. In Proceedings of the 8th International Conference on Artificial Intelligence and Law (ICAIL), (pp. 206-214). St. Louis, MO: ACM Press.

Stranieri, A., Yearwood, J., Gervasoni, S., Garner, S., Deans, C., & Johnstone, A. (2004). Web-based decision support for structured reasoning in health. In *Proceedings of the Twelfth National Health Informatics Conference,* (p. 61). Brisbane, Australia: Health Informatics Society of Australia.

Stranieri, A., Yearwood, J., & Meikle, T. (2000). The dependency of discretion and consistency on knowledge representation. *International Review of Law Computers & Technology, 14*(3), 325–340. doi:10.1080/713673364

Stranieri, A., & Zeleznikow, J. (1998b). Split up: The use of an argument based knowledge representation to meet expectations of different users for discretionary decision making. In *Proceedings of Innovative Applications of Artificial Intelligence IAAI, 1998,* 1146–1152. Washington, DC: American Association of Artificial Intelligence.

Stranieri, A., & Zeleznikow, J. (2000a). Copyright regulation with argumentation agents. *Information & Communications Technology Law, 10*(1), 109–123. doi:10.1080/13600830124950

Stranieri, A., Zeleznikow, J., Gawler, M., & Lewis, B. (1999). A hybrid rule-neural approach for the automation of legal reasoning in the discretionary domain of family law in Australia. *Artificial Intelligence and Law, 7*(2-3), 153–183. doi:10.1023/A:1008325826599

Stromer-Galley, J. (2007). Measuring deliberations content: A coding scheme. *Journal of Public Deliberation, 3*(1), 1–37.

Surowiecki, J. (2004). *The wisdom of crowds: Why the many are smarter than the few and how collective wisdom shapes business, economies, societies and nations.* New York, NY: Doubleday.

Suthers, D. (1999). Effects of alternate representations of evidential relations on collaborative learning discourse. In C. M. Hoadley & J. Roschelle (Eds.), *Proceedings of the Third Conference on Computer Supported Collaborative Learning.* Mahwah, NJ: Lawrence Erlbaum Associates.

Suthers, D., & Hundhausen, C. (2002). The effects of representation on students' elaboration in collaborative learning. In Hoppe, H., Verdejo, F., & Kay, J. (Eds.), *Artificial Intelligence in Education.* Amsterdam, The Netherlands: IOS Press.

Swank, O. H., & Wrasai, P. (2002). *Deliberation, information aggregation and collective decision making.* Retrieved from http://papers.ssrn.com/sol3/papers.cfm?abstract_id=635285.

Swanson, D. R. (1987). Two medical literatures that are logically but not bibliographically connected. *Journal of the American Society for Information Science American Society for Information Science, 38*(4), 228–233. doi:10.1002/(SICI)1097-4571(198707)38:4<228::AID-ASI2>3.0.CO;2-G

Swanson, D. R., & Smalheiser, N. R. (1997). An interactive system for finding complementary literatures: A stimulus to scientific discovery. *Artificial Intelligence, 91*, 183–203. doi:10.1016/S0004-3702(97)00008-8

Swartout, B., Patil, R., Knuth, K., & Russ, T. (1996). Towards distributed use of large-scale ontologies. In B. Gaines & M. Musen (Eds.), *Proceedings of the 10th Workshop on Knowledge Acquisition for Knowledge-Based Systems*. Banff, Canada: ACM.

Szidarovszky, F., Gershon, M., & Duckstein, L. (1986). *Techniques for multiobjective decision making in systems management*. London, UK: Elsevier.

Tamura, H., Yamamoto, K., Tomiyama, S., & Hatono, I. (2000). Modeling and analysis of decision making problem for mitigating natural disaster risks. *European Journal of Operational Research, 122*(2), 461–468. doi:10.1016/S0377-2217(99)00247-7

Tata, C. (1997). Conceptions and representations of the sentencing decision process. *Journal of Law and Society, 24*, 395. doi:10.1111/j.1467-6478.1997.tb00004.x

Tavana, M. (2002). Euclid: Strategic alternative assessment matrix. *Journal of Multi-Criteria Decision Analysis, 11*(2), 75–96. doi:10.1002/mcda.318

Tavana, M., & Kennedy, D. (2006). N-site: A distributed consensus building and negotiation support system. *International Journal of Information Technology & Decision Making, 5*(1), 123–154. doi:10.1142/S021962200600185X

Tavana, M., Smither, J., & Anderson, R. (2007). D-side: A facility and workforce planning group multi-criteria decision support system for Johnson Space Center. *Computers & Operations Research, 34*(6), 1646–1673. doi:10.1016/j.cor.2005.06.020

Taylor, C. (1990). *Sources of the self*. Cambridge, MA: Harvard University Press.

The Guardian. (2010, December 23). Australia says sorry to doctor wrongly detained on terrorism charges. *The Guardian*. Retrieved 11 March 2012, from http://www.guardian.co.uk/world/2010/dec/23/australia-sorry-doctor-terrorism-charges.

Thorndyke, P. W. (1977). Cognitive structures in comprehension and memory of narrative discourse. *Cognitive Psychology, 9*, 77–110. doi:10.1016/0010-0285(77)90005-6

Toulmin, S. (1958). *The uses of argument*. Cambridge, UK: Cambridge University Press.

Trabasso, T., & Sperry, L. (1985). Causal relatedness and importance of story events. *Journal of Memory and Language, 24*, 595–611. doi:10.1016/0749-596X(85)90048-8

Trabasso, T., & van den Broek, P. (1985). Causal thinking and story comprehension. *Memory and Language, 24*, 612–630. doi:10.1016/0749-596X(85)90049-X

Trabasso, T., van den Broek, P., & Suh, S. Y. (1989). Logical necessity and transitivity of causal relations in stories. *Discourse Processes, 121*, 1–25. doi:10.1080/01638538909544717

Trufte, E. R. (1989). *Envisioning information*. Cheshire, CT: Graphics Press.

Twardy, C. (2004). Argument maps improve critical thinking. *Teaching Philosophy, 27*(2), 95–116.

Twining, W. (2002). *The great juristic bazaar: Jurists texts and lawyers stories*. London, UK: Ashgate.

US Senate Intelligence Committee. (2004). *Report of the select committee on intelligence on the US intelligence community's prewar intelligence assessments on Iraq*. Washington, DC: US Senate Intelligence Committee.

van de Ven, A. H., & Delbecq, A. L. (1971). Nominal versus interacting group processes for committee decision making effectiveness. *Academy of Management Journal, 14*, 203–212. doi:10.2307/255307

van de Ven, A. H., & Delbecq, A. L. (1974). The effectiveness of nominal delphi and interacting group decision making process. *Academy of Management Journal, 17*(4), 605–621. doi:10.2307/255641 van Dijk, T. A. (1989). Relevance in logic and grammar. In Norman, J., & Sylvan, R. (Eds.), *Directions in Relevance Logic* (pp. 25–57). Dordrecht, The Netherlands: Kluwer Academic Publishers. doi:10.1007/978-94-009-1005-8_2

van Gelder, T. (2001b). How to improve critical thinking using educational technology. In G. Kennedy, M. Keppell, C. McNaught, & T. Petrovic (Eds.), *Meeting at the Crossroads: Proceedings of the 18th Annual Conference of the Australasian Society for Computers*, (pp. 539-548). Melbourne, Australia: IEEE.

van Gelder, T., & Bulka, A. (2000). *Reason!able (version 1.1)*. Retrieved from http://www.goreason.com.

van Gelder, T. (2003). Enhancing deliberation through computer supported argument mapping. In Kirschner, P. A., Shum, S. J. B., & Carr, C. S. (Eds.), *Visualizing Argumentation: Software Tools for Collaborative and Educational Sense-Making*. London, UK: Springer Verlag.

van Heijst, G., Schreiber, A., & Wielinga, B. (1997). Using explicit ontologies in kbs development. *International Journal of Human-Computer Studies*, *46*(2/3), 183–292. doi:10.1006/ijhc.1996.0090

Vasconcelos, J., Kimble, C., Gouveia, F., & Kudenko, D. (2000). A group memory system for corporate knowledge management: An ontological approach. In *Proceedings of the First European Conference on Knowledge Management*, (pp. 91-99). Bled, Slovenia: Bled School of Management.

Verheij, B. (1996). *Rules, reasons, arguments: formal studies of argumentation and defeat*. Dissertation. Maastricht, The Netherlands: Universiteit Maastricht. Retrieved from http://www.metajur.unimaas.nl/ bart/proefschrift/.

Verheij, B. (1998). Argumed - A template-based argument mediation system for lawyers. In J. C. Hage, T. Bench-Capon, A. Koers, C. de Vey Mestdagh, & C. Grutters (Eds.), *JURIX: The Eleventh Conference on Legal Knowledge Based Systems*, (pp. 113-130). Nijmegen, The Netherlands: Gerard Noodt Instituut.

Verheij, B. (1999). Automated argument assistance for lawyers. In *Proceedings of the Seventh International Conference on Artificial Intelligence and Law, ICAIL 1999*, (pp. 43-52). ACM Press.

von Wright, G. H. (1951). Deontic logic. *Mind*, *60*, 1–15. doi:10.1093/mind/LX.237.1

Vreeswijk, G. (1993). Defeasible dialectics: A controversy-oriented approach towards defeasible argumentation. *The Journal of Logic and Computation*, *3*(3), 3–27.

Vreeswijk, G. (1997). Abstract argumentation systems. *Artificial Intelligence*, *90*, 225–279. doi:10.1016/S0004-3702(96)00041-0

Wagenaar, W. A., van Koppen, P. J., & Crombag, H. F. M. (1993). *Anchored narratives: The psychology of criminal evidence*. Hempstead, UK: Harvester Wheatsheaf.

Waismann, F. (1951). Verifiability. In Flew, A. (Ed.), *Logic and language*. Oxford, UK: Blackwell.

Walton, D. (1996b). *Argumentation schemes for presumptive reasoning*. Mahwah, NJ: Lawrence Erlbaum Associates.

Walton, D. (1997). *Appeal to expert opinion: Arguments from authority*. State College, PA: Penn State University Press.

Walton, D. N., & Krabbe, E. C. W. (1995). *Commitment in dialogue: Basic concepts of interpersonal reasoning*. Albany, NY: State University of New York Press.

Walton, D., & Godden, D. (2005). Persuasion dialogue in online dispute resolution. *Artificial Intelligence and Law*, *13*, 273–295. doi:10.1007/s10506-006-9014-0

Walton, D., & Krabbe, E. (1995). *Commitment in dialogue: Basic concepts of interpersonal reasoning*. Albany, NY: State University of New York Press.

Walton, D., & Krabbe, E. (1995). *Commitment in dialogue: Basic concepts of interpersonal reasoning*. Albany, NY: State University of New York Press.

Warren, W. H., Nicholas, D., & Trabasso, T. (1979). Event chain and inferences in understanding narratives. In Freedle, R. O. (Ed.), *New Directions in Discourse Processing*. Hillsdale, NJ: Erlbaum.

Weick, K. (1995). *Sensemaking in organizations*. Thousand Oaks, CA: Sage.

Welp, M. (2001). The use of decision support tools in participatory river basin management. *Physics and Chemistry of the Earth. Part B: Hydrology, Oceans and Atmosphere*, *26*(7), 535–539. doi:10.1016/S1464-1909(01)00046-6

Wenger, E. (1998). *Communities of practice: Learning, meaning and identity*. Cambridge, UK: Cambridge University Press.

Wheelen, S. A., Murphy, D., Tsumura, E., & Kline, S. F. (1998). Member perceptions of internal group dynamics and productivity. *Small Group Research*, *29*(3), 371–393. doi:10.1177/1046496498293005

White, H. (1981). The value of narrativity in the representation of reality. In Mitchell, W. (Ed.), *On Narrative* (pp. 1–4). Chicago, IL: The University of Chicago. doi:10.1086/448086

Whitehead, A. N., & Russell, B. (1913). *Principia mathematica*. Cambridge, UK: Cambridge University Press.

Wieringa, R., & Meyer, J. (1998). Applications of deontic logic in computer science: A concise overview. In *Proceedings of the ECAI-98 Workshop on Practical Reasoning and Rationality*. Brighton, UK: John Wiley and Sons.

Wigmore, J. H. (1937). *The science of judicial proof as given by logic, psychology and general experience*. New York, NY: Little, Brown and Company.

Wilensky, R. (1982). Points: A theory of the structure of stories in memory. In Lehnert, W. G., & Ringle, M. H. (Eds.), *Strategies for Natural Language Processing* (pp. 345–374). Hillsdale, NJ: Erlbaum.

Wilhelm, A. G. (2000). *Democracy in the digital age: Challenges to political life in the digital age*. New York, NY: Routledge.

Wohlrapp, H. (1998). A new light on non-deductive argumentation schemes. *Argumentation*, *12*, 341–350. doi:10.1023/A:1007791211241

Wooldridge, M. (2002). *An introduction to MultiAgent systems*. Hoboken, NJ: Wiley.

Wooldridge, M., & Jennings, N. (1995). Intelligent agents: Theory and practice. *The Knowledge Engineering Review*, *10*, 115–152. doi:10.1017/S0269888900008122

Woolf, S., Chan, E., Harris, R., Sheridan, S., Braddock, C., & Kaplan, R. (2005). Promoting informed choice: Transforming health care to dispense knowledge for decision making. *Annals of Internal Medicine*, *143*, 293–300.

World Legal Information Institute. (2007). *Website.* Retrieved from http://www.worldlii.org/.

Wright, S. (2006). Electrifying democracy? 10 years of policy and practice. *Parliamentary Affairs*, *59*(2), 236–249. doi:10.1093/pa/gsl002

Wyatt, J. (1997). Quantitative evaluation of clinical software, exemplified by decision support systems. *International Journal of Medical Informatics*, *47*, 165–173. doi:10.1016/S1386-5056(97)00100-7

Yearwood, J., & Meikle, T. (2000). Design and development of a decision support system to support discretion in refugee law. In *Proceedings of ES2000, the Twentieth SEGS International Conference on Knowledge Based Systems and Applied Artificial Intelligence*, (pp. 243–256). SEGS.

Yearwood, J., & Stranieri, A. (1999). The integration of retrieval, reasoning and drafting for refugee law: A third generation legal knowledge based system. In *Proceedings of the Seventh International Conference on Artificial Intelligence and Law. ICAIL 1999*, (pp. 117-137). ACM Press.

Yearwood, J., & Stranieri, A. (2000). An argumentation shell for knowledge based systems. In *Proceedings of IASTED International Conference on Law and Technology*, (pp. 105–111). IASTED.

Yearwood, J., & Stranieri, A. (2002). Generic arguments: A framework for supporting online deliberative discourse. In *Proceedings of the Thirteenth Australasian Conference on Information Systems (ACIS 2002)*, (pp. 337-346). Melbourne, Australia: ACIS.

Yearwood, J., & Stranieri, A. (2007). *A study of frameworks for structured reasoning on reasoning quality and knowledge*. Unpublished.

Yearwood, J., Avery, J., & Stranieri, A. (2006). *Interactive narrative by thematic connection of dramatic situations*. Paper presented at the Narrative and Interactive Learning Environments (NILE 2004). Edinburgh, UK.

Yearwood, J., Stranieri, A., & Avery, J. (2001). Negotiation and argumentation based agents to facilitate ecommerce. In *Proceedings of the International Conference on Advances in Infrastructure for Electronic Business, Science and Education on the Internet, SSGRR 2001*, (pp. 100–109). SSGRR.

Yearwood, J., & Stranieri, A. (2006). The generic actual argument model of practical reasoning. *Decision Support Systems, 41*(2), 358–379. doi:10.1016/j.dss.2004.07.004

Yong, J. S. (2005, July). *e-Government in Asia: Enabling public service innovation in the 21st century*. Times Media.

Yue, C. D., & Yang, G. (2007). Decision support system for exploiting local renewable energy sources: A case study of the Chigu area of Southwestern Taiwan. *Energy Policy, 35*(1), 383–394. doi:10.1016/j.enpol.2005.11.035

Zack, M. (1999). Managing organizational ignorance. *Knowledge Directions, 1*, 36–49.

Zeleznikow, J., & Bellucci, E. (2003). Family-winner: Integrating game theory and heuristics to provide negotiation support. In *Proceedings of Sixteenth International Conference on Legal Knowledge Based System*, (pp. 21-30). Amsterdam, The Netherlands: IOS Publications.

Zeleznikow, J., & Stranieri, A. (1995). The split up system: Integrating neural networks and rule based reasoning in the legal domain. In Proceedings of the Fifth International Conference on Artificial Intelligence and Law, ICAIL 1995, (pp. 185-194). New York, NY: ACM Press.

Zeleznikow, J., & Stranieri, A. (1997). Splitup: An intelligent decision support system which provides advice upon property division following divorce. In *Proceedings of 30th Australian Legal Convention*. Melbourne, Australia: Anstat Legal Publishers.

Zhuge, H. (1998). Conflict group decision training: Model and system. *Knowledge-Based Systems, 11*(3-4), 191–196. doi:10.1016/S0950-7051(98)00045-8

About the Authors

John Yearwood is Professor of Informatics and Dean of the School of Science, Information Technology, and Engineering at the University of Ballarat, Australia. His research spans areas of data mining, argumentation, reasoning, and decision support, and its many application in health and law. Professor Yearwood received a Queen Elizabeth II Fellowship from the Australian Research Council to work on argumentation and narrative. Professor Yearwood developed the Generic/Actual Argument Model (GAAM) for the representation of practical reasoning with co-author Andrew Stranieri. This model has been used in modelling decision making in discretionary domains such as family law, career advice, refugee law, intensive care, and research ethics. Professor Yearwood's research on learning algorithms, based on non-smooth global optimisation, have led to contributions in terms of the strategies for hybridisation. He has published over 150 peer reviewed journal and conference articles and books.

Andrew Stranieri Associate Professor, is the Director of the Centre for Informatics and Applied Optimisation in the School of Science, Information Technology, and Engineering at the University of Ballarat. He adapted his training in psychology and counselling experience to inform his research into cognitive models of argumentation and artificial intelligence. With co-author Professor John Yearwood, he developed the Generic/Actual Argument Model (GAAM). This research was instrumental in modelling decision making in refugee law, copyright law, eligibility for legal aid, sentencing, and research ethics developed by a spin-out company he managed. His research in health informatics spans data mining in health, complementary and alternative medicine informatics, telemedicine, and intelligent decision support systems. He is the author of over 100 peer reviewed journal and conference articles and books.

Index